# PARADOXES OF EUROPEAN LEGAL INTEGRATION

*In Memoriam*

*Henrik Zahle (1943–2006)*

# Paradoxes of European Legal Integration

*Edited by*

HANNE PETERSEN
ANNE LISE KJÆR
HELLE KRUNKE
MIKAEL RASK MADSEN
*University of Copenhagen, Denmark*

Routledge
Taylor & Francis Group
LONDON AND NEW YORK

First published 2008 by Ashgate Publishing

2 Park Square, Milton Park, Abingdon, Oxon OX14 4RN
711 Third Avenue, New York, NY 10017, USA

*Routledge is an imprint of the Taylor & Francis Group, an informa business*

First issued in paperback 2016



**British Library Cataloguing in Publication Data**
Paradoxes of European legal integration
1. European Union 2. Law - European Union countries - International unification 3. Legal polycentricity - Europe 4. European Union countries - Politics and government
I. Petersen, Hanne, 1951-
341.2'422

**Library of Congress Cataloging-in-Publication Data**
Paradoxes of European legal integration / edited by Hanne Petersen ... [et al.].
p. cm.
Includes bibliographical references and index.
ISBN 978-0-7546-7371-2
1. Law--European Union countries--International unification. 2. Legal polycentricity--European Union countries. 3. European Union countries--Economic integration. 4. Pluralism. I. Petersen, Hanne, 1951-

KJE960.P37 2008
341.242'2--dc22

2008017333

ISBN 13: 978-0-7546-7371-2 (hbk)
ISBN 13: 978-1-138-25417-6 (pbk)

# Contents

# Notes on Contributors

*Antonin Cohen* is Assistant Professor at the University of Picardie and researcher at the Centre Universitaire de Recherches sur l'Action Publique et le Politique at the Centre national de la recherche scientifique (CNRS), France.

*Yves Dezalay* is Directeur de recherches at the Centre national de la recherche scientifique (CNRS), Paris. His research focuses mainly on the emergence of international legal fields. Together with Bryant G. Garth he has written *Dealing in Virtue* (1996) and *The Internationalization of Palace Wars* (2002).

*Bryant G. Garth* is Professor of Law and Dean of Southwestern Law School, Los Angeles. From 1990 to 2004 he was Director of the American Bar Foundation, Chicago.

*Anne Lise Kjær* is Research Fellow at the Law Faculty, University of Copenhagen, and specializes in the field of law and language. Current research concerns cross-disciplinary studies of legal integration in Europe and combines theories of language, discourse, culture and law.

*Henning Koch* is Professor of Constitutional Law at the University of Copenhagen. He is the Director of the Centre for European Constitutionalization, a member of the Steering Committee for Centre for Advanced Security Theory and member of an Expert Committee on the Danish Security and Intelligence Service.

*Helle Krunke* is Associate Professor of European and Danish Constitutional Law at the Faculty of Law, University of Copenhagen. She was visiting fellow at the European University Institute, Florence and visiting academic at the University of Bristol, England.

*Pierre Legrand* is Professor of Law and Director of Postgraduate Comparative Legal Studies at the Sorbonne, Paris. He also acts as Visiting Professor, University of San Diego Law School, Senior Fellow, University of Melbourne Law School, and Visiting Professor, China University of Political Science and Law (CUPL), Beijing.

*Neil MacCormick* was Regius Professor of Public Law and the Law of Nature and Nations, University of Edinburgh, 1972–2008, and is now Emeritus. One of his major publications is *Institutions of Law* (2007).

*Mikael Rask Madsen* is Research Fellow in Sociology of Law at the Faculty of Law, University of Copenhagen, as well as an associate member of Centre de Sociologie Européenne, Paris. He is a member of the management team of the Centre for Studies in Legal Culture, University of Copenhagen.

*Heikki E.S. Mattila* is Professor of Legal Linguistics at the University of Lapland. His research interests are comparative law and legal languages, especially Latin and French. Recent publications include *Comparative Legal Linguistics* (2006).

*Kjell Å. Modéer* is Professor Emeritus of Legal History at Lund University, Sweden, and former holder of the Torsten and Ragnar Söderberg Foundation's Professorship in Memory of Samuel Pufendorf. His current publications are in the fields of comparative legal cultures and traditions, law and religion, and law and literature.

*David Nelken* is Distinguished Professor of Sociology and Legal Institutions and Social Change in the Faculty of Political Science of the University of Macerata, Italy. He is also a Visiting Professor of Law at Cardiff University and at the London School of Economics and at Utrecht University, the Netherlands.

*Hanne Petersen* is Professor of Law and a member of the management team of the Centre for Studies in Legal Culture at the University of Copenhagen. She was formerly Professor of Legal Science and Sociology of Law at Ilisimatusarfik, University of Greenland.

*Andreas Philippopoulos-Mihalopoulos* is Reader in Law, University of Westminster. His research includes critical theory, autopoiesis, law and literature, geography, philosophy, gender and art. He recently published *Absent Environments* (2007).

*Inger-Johanne Sand* is Professor of Public Law, University of Oslo and guest professor at Copenhagen Business School. She works within the areas of public law, European law, international constitutional law and contemporary legal theory.

*Ditlev Tamm* is Professor of Legal History and a member of the management team of the Centre for Studies in Legal Culture at the University of Copenhagen. He is the author of several books and studies within the field of Danish and European legal history, political history and cultural history.

*William Twining* is Quain Professor of Jurisprudence Emeritus, University College London. His books include *Globalisation and Legal Theory* (2000), *The Great Juristic Bazaar* (2002) and *General Jurisprudence* (forthcoming).

*Antoine Vauchez* is full-time researcher in Political Science at the Centre national de la recherche scientifique (CNRS), Paris. He is currently Marie Curie Fellow at the Robert Schuman Centre at the European University Institute, Florence.

*Edda Weigand* is Professor of Linguistics at the University of Münster, Germany, and President of the International Association for Dialogue Analysis (IADA), Bologna. Her theory of the 'mixed game' is based on a general notion of 'language as dialogue'.

# Acknowledgements

We would like to extend our gratitude to the many persons and institutions whose assistance and support have been indispensable for this project. We are grateful for having received financial support from the University of Copenhagen's research priority area, *Europe in Transition*. Without this support, neither the Skodsborg conference nor the present publication would have been possible. Thanks are also due to *Det Finneske Legat*, a trust administered by the Faculty of Law at the University of Copenhagen, for financial support of the Skodsborg conference. The interdisciplinary research project, *European Legal Understandings*, commenced on Henrik Zahle's initiative and resulting in this publication, was made possible by a generous research grant from the Danish Social Science Research Council. Last but not least, we would like to thank the participants at the conference for their invaluable contributions both in oral and written form, as well as acknowledging our indebtedness for invaluable help provided by our administrative staff: Birgit Jacobsen, Johanna Bach-Frommer and Inge Qviste.

# Chapter 1
# General Introduction: Paradoxes of European Legal Integration

Mikael Rask Madsen, Anne Lise Kjær, Helle Krunke and Hanne Petersen

There is little doubt that some of the most significant changes in Europe over the past 50 years have been linked to the efforts of integrating European economic, political and legal orders under the auspices of the EU and the Council of Europe. The new centrality of human rights, the creation of a common market structure, as well as the development of new inter-European understandings and communications, are all interconnected elements of a larger transformation of law in Europe. Whereas legal scholarship generally agrees on the importance of these processes, there is surprisingly little consensus on what is implied by the terminology *European legal integration*. A review of the relevant literature in both law and the social sciences suggests that the term covers a plurality of processes and subject-matters, ranging from basic analysis of the European institutions and their competences to the impact of supranational law-making on national ways of producing law, even national ways of life.[1] Moreover, it appears that European legal integration remains a highly political process where the distinction between the scientific analysis and the political agenda of European integration is not particularly clear-cut. Indeed, as can be observed across the considerable literature on the subject, European legal integration provides an enduring challenge to social scientists and lawyers, who have not yet been able to establish the integration processes as a coherent scientific object. This might indeed present the first 'paradox' of studying European legal integration.

This book is an attempt at understanding the broader processes of European legal integration. The basic claim is that the complexity of these processes can be comprehended neither by static concepts and descriptions nor by simply following the prescriptions offered by the legal categorizations of Europe issued from the ever-changing political agenda of European integration. We instead suggest rethinking European legal integration as a set of dynamic and even somewhat contradictory processes. Thus, the focus is on tensions or paradoxes of European legal integration. What we term *paradoxes* are in practice a set of relative oppositions which are important drivers in the continuous making of Europe. In this volume, we address four such paradoxes of contemporary European integration: *constitutionalization*

1 Cf. Gessner, V. and Nelken, D. (2007), *European Ways of Law: Towards a European Sociology of Law* (Oxford: Hart).

and *democratization*, *institution-building* and *market-making*, *language as a source of legal understanding and misunderstanding* and, finally, *exceptionalism* and *normalisation* in European legal integration. Although other relevant paradoxes could be identified, it is our assumption that this particular set of paradoxes, when presented in one collection, offers a framework for understanding some of the major interconnected processes making up the larger subject of European legal integration.[2] We are fully aware that by focusing on the tensions and paradoxes of the process we can only supply an unfinished picture of European legal integration. However, we invite the readers to draw the lines between the dots provided by this preliminary and impressionistic analysis.

## Legal Polycentricity and Legal Paradoxes

This book assembles a series of papers that were first presented at the conference *Towards a Common European Legal Thinking* in Skodsborg, Denmark, in the autumn of 2006. The original objective of the conference was to explore the many facets of European legal integration. To that end, a number of scholars from a variety of disciplines were invited to present their respective analysis of the subject. The Skodsborg conference was the outcome of a research project on *European Legal Understandings* initiated by Anne Lise Kjær, Helle Krunke and Mikael Rask Madsen and directed by the late Henrik Zahle. The overall aim of the project was to apply the insights deriving from a series of earlier works on legal polycentricity to the more specific question of European legal integration.[3] From the outset we were interested in finding multi-variable conclusions to issues that were typically categorized – organizationally and disciplinarily – in terms of a single structure and thus were assumed to have a single answer. Consequently, the intention was to use the notion of legal polycentricity in an analysis of one of the clearly most pluralistic legal constructions available: the European construction.

As many others have already acknowledged, to start thinking about Europe is to address a subject which has no single definition, substantially or formally.[4] Politically, but also legally and culturally, it is obvious that Europe functions as both a great 'uniter' and a divider – the vision of its actual impact and functions depends greatly on the place and position of the viewer. In the historical progression

2 In this respect we obviously draw on Boaventura de Sousa Santos' ideas of mapping law as well as holistic research notions such as Pierre Bourdieu's concept of a juridical field. See further in de Sousa Santos, B. (1987), 'Law: A Map of Misreading: Toward a Postmodern Conception of Law', *Journal of Law and Society* 14, 279–302, and Bourdieu, P. (1987), 'The Force of Law: Toward a Sociology of the Juridical Field', *Hastings Law Journal* 38:5, 805–53.

3 See Petersen, H. and Zahle, H. (eds) (1995), *Legal Polycentricity: Consequences of Pluralism in Law* (London: Dartmouth/Ashgate).

4 Cf. Arnaud, A-J. (1991), *Pour une pensée juridique européenne* (Paris: PUF).

of modern Europe, where the rise of a set of relatively well-defined nation-states was the defining moment, postwar European integration introduced a notion of community based on heterogeneity and difference – legally, linguistically and culturally. This not only challenged pre-existing ideas of national unity and homogeneity, but also eventually integrated national communities in a dynamic European community. Moreover, this dynamic Europe is not only the product of a limited process of Europeanization but also of globalization and Americanization. The outcome of these multiple and often competing processes is a social construct – and phenomenon – which defies a whole series of assumptions concerning the linkage between national law, culture, language and democracy. Politically, it is the cause of great transformations and, occasionally, social bewilderment; legally, it is the cause of new forms of legal polycentricity.[5]

With the sudden and tragic death of Henrik Zahle in the summer of 2006, the project on legal polycentricity in Europe was abruptly suspended. We decided to call on Hanne Petersen, co-author of the original polycentricity projects and the author of numerous publications on legal pluralism,[6] to help finalize both the project and the conference endeavour. It is, however, the participants of the Skodsborg conference who are to be thanked most for helping us to finally conceptualize some of the central dynamics of the polycentric legal, political and social field of European integration. Through the long and animated debates at the Skodsborg Hotel, it became clear that the mainstream notions and concepts describing European legal integration were mainly useful and persuasive within their respective research communities. Key notions such as constitutionalization were mainly applicable if viewed in isolation from other equally relevant and simultaneously working socio-legal processes such as democratization, supranationalization or regionalization, as well as market building and institutional transformations. This, however, also demonstrated the necessity of combining the mainly descriptive and static notion of legal polycentricity with a new dynamic approach in order to comprehend how conflicting policies and values are fundamental drivers of the larger processes of European legal integration.[7]

---

5 Somewhat similar observations have been made in political science. See for example Hooghe, L. and Marks, G. (2001), *Multi-Level Governance and European Integration* (New York: Rowman and Littlefield). See also Kaiser, W. and Starie, P. (eds) (forthcoming), *Transnational European Union: Towards a Common Political Space* (London: Routledge).

6 Petersen, H. (1996), *Home-knitted Law: Norms and Values in Gendered Rule-making* (London: Dartmouth/Ashgate) and Petersen, H. (2006), *Retspluralisme i praksis. Grønlandske inspirationer* [Legal Pluralism in Practice] (Copenhagen: DJØF).

7 Originally the polycentricity project also included a focus on the sustainability or 'ecologization' of law, that is, a combined focus upon the changing form and values underlying a pluralist understanding of law. In recent years, Henrik Zahle increasingly turned towards examining value issues in respect to legal forms and processes, especially in his essays on justice in legal practice based upon his experiences from 1999 to 2002 as a Supreme Court judge. See Zahle, H. (1994), 'Ecologization of Law. Introductory Remarks

This insight formed the background for our subsequent attempt at developing what might be described as a more holistic view of European legal integration which incorporated a series of interdependent socio-legal processes. The major challenge was to construct an interpretive framework which did not fall into the trap of reducing the complexity of a given social phenomenon to a self-limiting legal formula and description, as conventional legal analyses tends to do. The notion of paradoxes was introduced as a tool for connecting this plurality of partly conflicting processes of European legal integration which the contributions at the conference had pointed to. Therefore, due to the multitude of processes in question, the response could not be an explanation in terms of a 'European system', but rather an emphasis on how a set of concurrent – and often competing – processes makes up decisive dynamics of the on-going process of European legal integration. These paradoxes are not only related to the plurality of legal forms and norms, but also, and particularly, to the fact that no single process encapsulates the larger process. European legal integration is a framework notion for addressing how a multitude of processes correlate and compete. As a result, we do not apply the notion of paradoxes in a strictly logical sense, but rather as a tool for identifying the central dynamics of European legal integration, in particular the uncertain interplay of legal rules and norms, and a multitude of social, cultural and linguistic processes constituting law.[8] What makes these interdependent processes paradoxical is the fact that they are somewhat unpredictable and unfulfilled and thereby the essential cause of the dynamic nature of European law and integration.

## Four Paradoxes of European Integration

An analysis of the paradoxes of European legal integration clearly calls for an approach which combines insights, theories and methods from a variety of disciplines. The development of the very notion of paradoxes in this regard was in fact closely related to the experience at the Skodsborg conference where the participants came from disciplines which all had an interest in law, yet they rarely cooperated on understanding law: constitutional law, comparative law, sociology

to a New Perspective: Law and Ecology', *Retfærd* (special issue on *Law and Ecology*) and Zahle, H. (2003), *Omsorg for retfærdighed. Essays om juridisk praksis* [Care for Justice. Essays on Legal Practice] (Copenhagen: Gyldendal).

8 That this opposition is fundamental to social and legal analysis is hardly a surprise to lawyers who are accustomed to the fact that different interpretive strategies of the very same text produce fundamentally different outcomes. In the social sciences, however, the philosophy of paradoxes originally presented by Jacques Derrida in his famous deconstructions exhibiting how different interpretations of the same texts were possible through different rhetoric constructions was more ground-breaking. See further in Perez, O. and Teubner, G. (eds) (2006), *Paradoxes and Inconsistencies in Law* (Oxford: Hart). See also Derrida, J. (1976), *Of Grammatology* (Baltimore, MD and London: Johns Hopkins University Press).

of law, legal linguistics, legal philosophy and political science. Our original objective was not to advocate a trans-disciplinary research agenda, but rather to help cross-fertilize the various disciplines with insights from one another. Certainly the question of European legal integration presented itself from markedly different angles when we moved from one discipline to another. However, it is our basic claim that to start thinking of European legal integration in terms of paradoxical processes might provide the missing tools for linking these – at first glance – disjointed processes.

The chapters assembled in this book all examine European legal integration from a number of different academic and theoretical starting points. Reading them together and observing the correlations between issues as different as constitutionalization and the development of a common legal *lingua franca* might however be the first step towards comprehending the actual complexity – and the paradox – of European legal integration. The book is divided into four parts, each of which attempts to illustrate one of the four paradoxes identified above. Each of the parts is preceded by a introduction written by one of the co-editors.

The first part, 'European Law as a Process between Constitutionalization and Democratization', examines one of the most basic dilemmas of European legal integration: how the processes of constitutionalization and democratization have come to be viewed as contradictory. The on-going rationalization of European law is clearly a prerequisite for gaining greater transparency in the working of the EU legal order. Conversely, the much debated democratic deficit of the EU is seen by many as being only widened by instruments such as the European Constitution Treaty. This part seeks to rethink these two processes as interdependent with the goal of illustrating this central driving force of European law.

The second part, 'An Ever Closer Union – An Ever Larger Market', focuses on the ways in which the progress of the EU is in fact closely linked to the expansion of the EU inner market. The basic paradox – when seen from the point of view of European legal integration – is that these free-market dynamics are, on the one hand, institutionalized in the European treaty complex, and, on the other, only partly guarded by the supranational order provided by the European institutions. Adding the question of the ever-expanding European market to the already identified paradox of the interdependence of constitutionalization and democratization processes provides a further dimension to understanding European legal integration as the product of numerous interconnected processes.

The third part, 'Language as Barrier and Carrier of European Legal Integration', is centred on the communicative actions of the actors of European legal integration. The key players of European integration – jurists, judges and lawyers of the Member States – obviously belong to a plurality of legal cultures, speak a plenitude of different languages and bring into the European arena a series of divergent world views and practices of law. The paradox is that, on one hand, language and communication between the actors is the very prerequisite of integration, and, on the other hand, a basic source of misunderstandings that bar the success or even possibility of harmonizing and unifying the laws of the Member States. Addressing this fundamental issue in the light of the previous questions provides yet another element to developing a 'thick description' of European legal integration.

The fourth part, 'Exceptionalism' and 'Normalization', looks into the basic paradox of the co-existence of homogeneity and diversity in the European political and legal processes. It starts with the observation that (Scandinavian) lawyers and law have been important artisans of *nation-building* in countries where cultural homogeneity and value monism have been held in very high esteem through an 'iconization' of the Scandinavian welfare state. 'Small state status' has moreover coexisted with sentiments of 'moral superiority' during the golden age of the Scandinavian welfare state. These countries, which have valued homogeneity highly, were to become very reluctant members of the European community. To preserve local homogeneity they required European respect for diversity, which was seen, at that time, as being in contrast with dominant ideas of uniformity and equality in Europe's northern regions. This Scandinavian picture is contrasted with an analysis of Italy, where the ambition to become 'normal' and 'fully modern' has played a far more significant role. Despite this, the basic paradox – who gains and loses through the proposed introduction of common standards or through the upholding of diverse values and normative regimes – prevails and constitutes yet another central driver of European legal integration.

# PART 1
# EUROPEAN LAW AS A PROCESS BETWEEN CONSTITUTIONALIZATION AND DEMOCRATIZATION

## Chapter 2
# Introduction: European Law as a Process between Constitutionalization and Democratization

Helle Krunke

### The On-going Process of Constitutionalization

The Treaty on a Constitution for Europe might be seen as an attempt to constitutionalize European cooperation. The title could indicate such an assumption, at least to the ordinary EU-citizen. The lawyer notices the duality in the title – a duality which is a general characteristic throughout the treaty. Perhaps the important question is not whether the Treaty on a Constitution for Europe should be seen as a treaty, a constitution or maybe even both; maybe the treaty should just be seen as part of a process of constitutionalization, an ongoing process which started long before the convention on the treaty was even established and which will continue in the future.[1] It is difficult to tell exactly when the process started and when or whether it will end. This also implies that the Treaty on a Constitution for Europe, although not ratified by all the Member States and replaced by the Treaty of Lisbon, must still be seen as part of the European constitutionalization process.

The Treaty on a Constitution for Europe (and the Treaty of Lisbon) can and should not be separated from the rest of the constitutionalization process. First of all, it is important to state that the Constitutional Treaty has its roots in the former European treaties. New developments are introduced in the treaty but large parts are already part of the European legal order. Moreover, some of the new articles simply reflect case law from the European Court of Justice. This indicates that the articles simply transform something which was already part of the European legal

1 For a thorough discussion of the term 'constitutional momentum' and a division between a short-term constitutional momentum and a longer-term constitutional momentum, see for instance Walker, N. (2004), 'Europe's Constitutional Momentum and the Search for Polity', in Weiler, J. and Eisgruber, Chr. L. (eds), *Altneuland: The EU Constitution in a Contextual Perspective*, Jean Monnet Working Paper 5/04. See also Walker, N. (2004), 'After the Constitutional Moment', in Pernice, I. and Maduro, M.P. (eds), *A Constitution for the European Union: First Comments on the 2003-Draft of the European Convention* (Baden-Baden: Nomos), 23–43.

order from case law into written law. In other words, the treaty is part of the history of the European legal order.

On the other hand, the Treaty on a Constitution for Europe is also connected to future developments in the EU. In some recent cases from 2005, the European Court of Justice already seems to have used some of the new inventions of the Treaty on a Constitution for Europe as a source of interpretation even though the treaty had not entered into force.[2] One aim of the Constitutional Treaty was to eliminate the division of the European cooperation into three pillars.[3] This would, among other things, mean that the general principles would apply to all chapters of the Treaty on a Constitution for Europe, unless expressly excluded.[4] Today the EC's rules do not apply to pillars two or three (or *vice versa*) unless specified.[5] In the Pupino judgement from 2005 (Case 105/03), the European Court of Justice applied one of the general principles of the EC, the principle of loyalty, to pillar three. The principle of loyalty is stated in Article I-5 (2) of the Treaty on a Constitution for Europe. In the Pupino case, the Advocate General actually called upon the Treaty on a Constitution for Europe as a legal argument in the case, claiming that Article 34 (2) (b) EU must be interpreted in the same way as the third paragraph of Article 249 EC:[6]

> 33. The increasing degree of integration expressed in the phrase 'ever closer cooperation' is also shown by the development of the Treaty on European Union which, after its creation by the Treaty of Maastricht, was brought ever more closely into line with the structures of Community law by the Treaties of Amsterdam and Nice and is to be merged fully with Community law by *the Constitutional Treaty*. (italics added)

The European Court of Justice simply makes the following remark in its judgement:

> 33. It should be noted at the outset that the wording of Article 34(2)(b) EU is *very closely inspired* by that of the third paragraph of Article 249 EC. Article 34(2)(b) EU confers a binding character on framework decisions in the sense that they 'bind' the

2 See Krunke, H. (2007), 'The Indirect Effect of the Treaty on a Constitution for Europe', *Scandinavian Studies in Law*, 52, 187–202.

3 At the moment, European cooperation is divided into three pillars. Pillar one relates to supranational EC-cooperation. Pillar two concerns cooperation on Foreign and Security Policy. Pillar three relates to cooperation on Justice and Home Affairs. Cooperation under pillar two and pillar three is intergovernmental.

4 See Piris, J-C. (2006), *The Constitution for Europe: A Legal Analysis* (Cambridge: Cambridge University Press), 66.

5 See Articles 28 and 41 in the Treaty on a European Union, and Piris, *The Constitution for Europe*, 66.

6 See the Opinion of the Advocate General on C-105/03, 11 November 2004, paragraph 33.

Member States 'as to the result to be achieved but shall leave to the national authorities the choice of form and methods'. (italics added)

Doing this, the Court tones down the legal effect of the Treaty on a Constitution for Europe but still reaches a judgement consistent with the treaty.[7]

Another example of the European Court of Justice reaching a judgement consistent with the content of the Treaty on a Constitution for Europe is a judgement on environmental protection (Case 176/03), also from 2005. The question was whether some specific rules concerning environmental crime, including penalties, had to be adopted by way of a directive under pillar one (by the Council and the European Parliament), or as a framework decision under pillar three (by the Council). Criminal law is normally considered part of pillar three on Justice and Home Affairs, but the Court referred the power to require the Member States to impose criminal penalties in a number of environmental offences to the Community (pillar one). The result was consistent with Art. III-271 (2) of the Treaty on a Constitution for Europe which would make it possible to adopt a European framework law with content similar to the content of the framework decision discussed in the judgement.[8] [9]

Thus, the Treaty on a Constitution for Europe inspired the European Court of Justice *before* the treaty should have stepped into force and *after* the negative outcome of the referenda in France and the Netherlands,[10] and it might also in future inspire legal and political actors – whether consciously or unconsciously. Indeed, the treaty could become a source for interpreting existing treaties and European legislation, even though it has never come into force.[11] Because of the differences between the Constitutional Treaty and the Treaty of Lisbon such a development would be extremely interesting and significant. The changes of the Constitutional

7 On the Pupino case, see Fletcher, M. (2005), 'Extending "Indirect Effect" to the Third Pillar: The Significance of Pupino', *European Law Review*, 862–7, Spaventa, E. (2007), 'Opening Pandora's Box: Some Reflections on the Constitutional Effects of the Decision in Pupino', *European Constitutional Law Review*, 3, 5–24, and Krunke, 'The Indirect Effect of the Treaty on a Constitution for Europe'.

8 On the environmental protection case see White, S. (2006), 'Harmonisation of Criminal Law under the First Pillar', *European Law Review*, 81–92; Herlin-Karnell, E. (2007), 'Commission v. Council: Some Reflections on Criminal Law in the First Pillar', *European Public Law*, 13:1, 69–84; Krunke, 'The Indirect Effect of the Treaty on a Constitution for Europe'.

9 See also C-440/05 (Commission vs. Council) which also concerns the relationship between pillars one and three in the field of criminal justice.

10 Actually, the Court's decision in the Pupino-case (105/03) came only a few days after the referenda in France and the Netherlands. While the European Union was facing a political crisis and the future of the Treaty on a Constituion for Europe was uncertain, the European Court of Justice passed a verdict which was consistent with the Constitutional Treaty. This was repeated in case 176/03.

11 See Krunke, 'The Indirect Effect of the Treaty on a Constitution for Europe'.

Treaty were made as a response to the outcome of the referenda in France and the Netherlands. Thus, the European Court of Justice could – through a slow process – reach what was not possible to obtain by referenda among the European citizens. The recent judgements of the European Court of Justice mentioned above seem to support the thesis; hence they represent examples of the complex development of European law as a process between constitutionalization and democratization.

In addition to the Constitutional Treaty's role as a source of interpretation, the treaty has played an important part in the construction of the Treaty of Lisbon. As a result, large parts of the constitutional treaty have been copied to the Treaty of Lisbon.

The Treaty on a Constitution for Europe originates from and reflects a political/legal environment and culture which is still present after a suspension or even a definite rejection of the treaty.

As already indicated, the Treaty on a Constitution for Europe and the Treaty of Lisbon must be seen as elements in an ongoing process of constitutionalization in Europe. This is why it would not be correct to claim that European constitutionalization stopped when the Treaty on a Constitution for Europe was not adopted by all the Member States. It depends on what meaning one attaches to the concept of 'constitution'. In fact, the concept may be more culture specific and more contested than is usually presupposed. A European constitution may be said to arise not as an event, but as the outcome of a protracted process, by which constant and increasing contact and cooperation between European countries over a long period of time are being reflected in the national legal systems of Europe. Another possible way of understanding the notion of a 'European constitution' is to say that it is constructed discursively, through the invention of 'general legal principles' and 'common European values', applied as building blocks of law in the legal reasoning of international law courts in an attempt to compensate for the lack of shared understandings of law.

## The Paradoxes of European Constitutionalization and Democratization

It is (still) quite a common perception – at least in public debate – that European constitutionalization and democratization does not go hand in hand. In fact, it is often presumed that there exists a contradiction between the two processes. However, their relationship turns out to be much more complex and paradoxical. The discussion has many facets.

To illustrate the complexity, let us return to the Treaty on a Constitution for Europe and the Treaty of Lisbon. On one hand, one of the goals of the two treaties is to simplify the decision-making processes in the EU *inter alia* by replacing unanimous decisions by qualitative majority decisions in the Council of Ministers in a number of areas. This will of course weaken the national governments and thereby the national parliaments as they draw their influence from the national governments (mainly through their national European Policy Committees). On the other hand, the two treaties introduce an early warning system. This gives the national parliaments an opportunity to protest directly to the Commission, Council or European Parliament within eight weeks[12] if they find that a draft European legislative act does not comply with the Principle of Subsidiarity (see Article 6 of the Protocol on the Application of the Principles of Subsidiarity and Proportionality). The Commission, the Council and the European Parliament must take reasoned opinions into account (Article 7, part 1), though they are not legally bound by them. Each national parliament has two votes (in bicameral parliamentary systems each of the chambers has one vote). If a third of the votes or more expresses the view that the draft does not comply with the Principle of Subsidiarity, the draft must be reviewed. The EU legislator may maintain, amend or withdraw the draft. In any case, reasons must be given for the decision (Article 7, part 2). Furthermore, under the ordinary legislative procedure, a simple majority of the votes will entail a review of the proposal. The Commission may maintain, amend or withdraw the proposal. If the Commission maintains the proposal it must justify why it considers that the proposal complies with the Principle of Subsidiarity in a reasoned opinion. This opinion together with the opinions of the national parliaments is submitted to the EU legislator. Before concluding the first reading the EU legislator must consider whether the legislative proposal is compatible with the Principle of Subsidiarity taking particular account of the reasoned opinions of the majority of the parliaments and of the Commission. If, by a majority of 55% of the members of the Council or a majority of the votes cast in the European Parliament, the legislator is of the opinion that the proposal is not compatible with the Principle of Subsidiarity, the legislative proposal shall not be given further consideration (Article 7, part 3).[13]

Therefore, national parliaments loose influence in some aspects, yet at the same time they gain new ways to influence decisions. Furthermore, the citizens in the Member States are also given new ways to influence. According to article I-47, part 4, of the Constitutional Treaty and Article 1, part 12 (on Article 8 B, part 4), in the Treaty of Lisbon, one million citizens who are nationals of a significant number of Member States may take the initiative of inviting the Commission within the framework of its powers, to submit any appropriate proposal on matters where citizens consider that a legal act of the Union is required for the purpose of implementing the Constitution. By doing so, the national governments might

12 There are a few differences between the Treaty on a Constitution for Europe and the Treaty of Lisbon regarding the Protocol on the Application of the Principle of Subsidiarity and Proportionality. Thus in the Treaty on a Constitution for Europe the time limit is six weeks and in the Treaty of Lisbon it is eight weeks.

13 Article 7, part 3, regarding the ordinary legislative procedure was introduced in the Treaty of Lisbon. It was not part of The Treaty on a Constitution for Europe. The position of the national parliaments has been strengthened in the Treaty of Lisbon.

lose influence, but at the same time new forms of democratic influence, which cut across national borders and involve new parties, are included in the two treaties.[14]

Another example of the complex and paradoxical relationship between constitutionalization and democratization is the increased power that the Constitutional Treaty and the Treaty of Lisbon would transfer to the European Parliament. Members of the European Parliament are directly elected in their Member States, and large Member States are represented by more members than small Member States. Therefore, from the point of view of the European Union as a whole, more power to the European Parliament does seem to be a step in a more democratic direction. Viewed from a more national angle, however, at least when it comes to the smaller Member States, increased power to the European Parliament might not be seen as a democratic development. Precisely this democratic dilemma is discussed by Neil MacCormick in the chapter 'The Convention and its Constitution: All a Great Mistake?'. According to Neil MacCormick the state-by-state ratification process of the Treaty on a Constitution for Europe was not satisfactory from the point of view of democratic constitutionalism. The European voters should have been given the chance to view the treaty as Europeans and not just as members of the nation states. In that way, national issues would not have blocked the political debate and it would to a larger extend have been possible to discuss the content of the treaty and the future development of Europe seen as a whole.

From a democratic angle, it is always difficult to interpret the reasons for a negative outcome of a national referendum on European issues and to decide how to move on afterwards, and doing so raises many sensitive questions. This holds true not only for the recent Irish referendum on the Lisbon Treaty but also for the French and the Dutch referenda on the Constitutional Treaty. It was also the case as far as the Danish referendum on the Maastricht Treaty and the Irish referenda on the Nice Treaty were concerned.[15] In the chapter 'When "No" Means "Yes": A Constitution for Europe and the Limits of Ignorance', Andreas Philippopoulos-Mihalopoulos maintains that explaining the results of the referenda in France and the Netherlands by 'external' factors with no relevance for the content of the Treaty – for instance the Turkish membership, economy, immigration and

14 See Krunke, 'The Indirect Effect of the Treaty on a Constitution for Europe', 195–8, and Krunke, H. (2007), 'Developments in National Parliaments' Involvement in Ordinary Foreign Policy and European Policy', *European Public Law Journal*, 13:2, 335–48. On the early warning system see also Bausili, A.V. (2003), 'Rethinking the Methods of Dividing and Exercising Powers in the EU: Reforming Subsidiarity, National Parliaments and Legitimacy', in Shaw, J. et al. (2003), *The Convention on the Future of Europe: Working towards an EU Constitution* (Federal Trust), 113, and Piris, *The Constitution for Europe*, 116–17.

15 See the following articles in *European Constitutional Law Review*, 1:3 (2005): Krunke, H., 'From Maastricht to Edinburgh: The Danish Solution', 339–56; Costello, C., 'Ireland's Nice Referenda', 357–82; Wolf, S. and Mounier, G., 'France: The Come-Back of Political Parties', 383–92; 'Arjen Nijeboer, A. 'The Dutch Referendum', 393–405.

domestic issues – would not be correct, because it would mean separating the text from the context. According to Andreas Philippopoulos-Mihalopoulos (referring to Weiler) the fundamental paradox of constitutionalism is that a constituting *demos* is needed in order to produce a constitution that will in turn consolidate (if not create) the constituted *demos*. Whereas Neil MacCormick (together with many others) accentuates the referenda in France and the Netherlands as a set-back for the European integration and constitutionalization process, Andreas Philippopoulos-Mihalopoulos puts forward the thesis that the 'no's actually revitalize the democratic process in European constitutionalization. Therefore it is not a 'negative' result, but a positive one. This thesis reflects yet another paradox in the relationship between democratization and constitutionalization in European legal integration.

An additional paradox raised in the chapter by Neil MacCormick is that even though a referendum on the entire Treaty text would seem to be the most democratic solution, only a few voters would read the entire Treaty. Consequently, Neil MacCormick suggests that a more democratic solution would be to subject only parts of the treaty to a referendum. This might actually result in a more reasonable public debate.

Constitutionalization and democratization are closely connected with the concept of 'rule of law'. As Henning Koch shows in the chapter 'A Legal Mission: The Emergence of a European "Rationalized" Natural Law', the concept can be interpreted in different ways and the traditions might differ from country to country. Henning Koch examines the English, German and Danish understanding of the concept, with specific emphasis on the German tradition. He finds a very close connection between the German understanding of rule by law and the understanding of the concept in the European Community and Union context, not only as rule by written law but also as rule by unwritten principles. As Henning Koch points out concerning the European legal construction: 'This legal construction is produced through two in principle different mechanisms of "judicial activism". Firstly, by the inclusion of a revitalized source of law: law in the meaning of law and justice. Secondly, by the application of purposive (teleological) interpretation methods and so on in order to further the creation of a unified European value order.' Henning Koch prefers talking about a 'Constitutive European Law' instead of a European Constitutional Law thereby, as he states, 'removing any connotations of the necessity of a *demos* or *demoi* – but hopefully in the long run making a contribution to a true feeling of "a unity of diversity", which is more valid than just a motto in a Constitutional Treaty'.

The three contributors each provide us with a deeper understanding of the complexity of European law between constitutionalization and democratization. The subject is analysed from different legal perspectives: European Constitutional Law, Legal Philosophy and Comparative Constitutional Law. No final or easy solutions to the process of European constitutionalization are offered. Therefore, the three papers, when read in conjunction, reflect the paradoxes and complexity of the process.

# Chapter 3
# The Convention and its Constitution: All a Great Mistake?

Neil MacCormick

## Introduction: Observations about the 'European Convention'

While I was writing this text I was reminded of the robust constitution-scepticism of Jens-Peter Bonde, MEP, with whom I became very friendly during the period when I served in the European Parliament as one of the eight MEPs for Scotland from 1999 to 2004. His constant refrain was that the euro-elite, which he considered to be much over-represented in all the European Institutions, even the Parliament, had successfully insulated itself from genuine European public opinion.[1] He never tired of telling his opponents that if ever they put their ambitions for further European integration to the test of popular opinion in any Member State, they would lose. One cannot deny that he had a point. Yet there is a problem. The community institutions – Council, Parliament, Commission and Court – have presided over periods of historically unparalleled peace and prosperity among the states and peoples of Europe.

This prosperity of Europeans is not a zero sum game in which one becomes better off to the extent the neighbours become worse off. The European Community in its guise as a single market has shown that the prosperity of each part contributes to the prosperity of every other, though not always in the very short run. As a member of the European Parliament, I attended the ceremony in Strasbourg in May 2004 at which the ten new Member States were welcomed and their representatives took up seats in the Parliament. That was a remarkable and moving experience.

No less remarkable was the experience I had between 28 February 2002 and 17 July 2003, when I served as a substitute member of the European Parliament's delegation to the Convention on the Future of Europe (Jens-Peter Bonde was a full member). Representing the Scottish National Party, I was the substitute member of the two elected by the parliamentary group of the Greens and European Free Alliance. My colleague Johannes Voggenhuber, of the Austrian Green Party, ensured by well-timed partial absences that I had a full opportunity to participate in the Plenary Sessions, especially on 'regional' issues and those concerning the principle of subsidiarity. Substitutes had also a full part to play in Working

---

1 Bonde, Jens-Peter (2004), *Mamma mia: Om 25 års kamp for åbenhed i EU / Jens-Peter Bonde* (Denmark: Vindrose).

Groups and by way of written contributions to the proceedings and amendments to proposed constitutional texts. Against many expectations formed at the outset of the Convention's deliberations in February/March 2002, the Convention did succeed in producing the text of a draft European Constitution, which it delivered to the European Council in June/July 2003. No less surprising was the way in which the intergovernmental conference convened successively by the Italian and the Irish governments succeeded in obtaining the agreement of all the states, old and new members alike, to a lightly amended version of the Convention's text. This was agreed in June 2004 and finally, after all necessary linguistic refinement, signed by all states as a new Rome Treaty on 29 October 2004.

## Convention and Constitution

Whatever may be said about the quality of the draft constitution that the Convention produced, the process which produced it was remarkable for its openness and its discursive character. Debate was intense, and carried on in public. The Convention website and the associated Forum were open to public inspection, and still are. Members of the Convention consulted widely both in their home constituencies (mine was the whole of Scotland) and with sister parties in all corners of Europe. Admittedly, the openness of Convention proceedings was not fully mirrored in coverage in the press or other media in the Member States, at any rate not till the end, when the draft was almost complete – then they protested that all this had been cooked up more or less in secret in Brussels. Jens-Peter Bonde kept accusing us of working in a kind of hall of mirrors in which all we saw were the faces and all we heard were the voices of those who were already signed up to the integration project. The citizens of Europe in their great masses ignored what was going on, and we ignored them – not deliberately, but through a deep-seated problem of figuring out how to communicate with an audience which does not find institutional 'Europe' interesting.

The draft Constitution was, I think, just about as good as one could have contrived in all the circumstances of the years 2002–2004, if it were to be assumed that a constitution is what Europeans either need or want. The final form adopted in October 2004 at Rome modified the Convention's draft. It incorporated some further changes, some of them genuine improvements, to meet various sensitivities of particular Member States. In the real world, any constitutional developments have to be evolutionary, adjusting and improving the institutional package we have inherited. There is no room for revolutionary new beginnings. But there is room for real improvement.

In terms of increasing the democratic openness and controllability of the union's institutions, the constitution made excellent proposals. In relation to subsidiarity, the definition was improved and a process for increasing scrutiny was devised. In terms of trying to create conditions for an effective Commission and Council in a

Europe of 27 or more members, sensible compromises were achieved, as likewise in relation to the external representation of the Union.

Many people were exultant when the referendum first in France then in the Netherlands rejected ratification of the Treaty Establishing a Constitution for Europe. But, many were greatly disappointed. I am of the latter party. Let me repeat that the Treaty does a good job of restating in formal and explicit terms the existing functional but implicit constitution of the European Union that emerges from the Union and Community Treaties. This is a view for which I argued at length in my short book *Who's Afraid of a European Constitution?* of 2005. I shall not repeat the arguments on this occasion, nor shall I repeat the argument in my *Questioning Sovereignty* of 1999 concerning the importance of both democracy and subsidiarity in the Union. Let us for the moment simply suppose that in its substance there was quite a good case for ratifying and implementing the Constitution contained in the Treaty, as 15 Member States have so far decided. The assenters include Germany and Italy, and also Spain and Luxembourg, where referenda produced results opposite to those in France and the Netherlands.

Yet this is all to a degree irrelevant. Even if the case for the constitution was as good as I am inclined to claim it was, that constitution clearly cannot come into force in the current divided state of European opinion. Some kind of a 'Basic Treaty' may be rebuilt out of its ruins in the coming year and a half, and the forthcoming German presidency is rumoured to have ambitions in that direction. But the question for a Conventioneer must remain: What went wrong? Did we miss the moment, or was there no constitutional moment in the first place?

At the final meeting of the Constitutional Convention, on 12 June 2003, there were congratulatory speeches about the hard work its members had done and about their success in achieving a final text that secured consensus among the large majority of participants, whatever reservations on significant details individual members also had. The most amusing remark of the day was by French Conventioneer and former Minister for European Affairs Alain Lamassoure. He said that we had done quite well to achieve as much as we had in 18 months. Of course, it had taken us longer than the Americans took at Philadelphia. But then, he said, they had solved their British problem before their Convention started. With hindsight now, it turns out to have been a sad irony that another problem we had failed to solve was the then unperceived French one.

## Ratifying a Treaty and Adopting a Constitution

Even if there was a French problem, the real problem we all face lies deeper and implicates us all. The process of ratifying – or refusing to ratify – the Treaty Establishing a Constitution for Europe, signed in Rome on 29 October 2004, draws to our attention the paradox implicit in the hybrid entity that is a 'constitution-treaty'. In its nature as a treaty, it must be referred to each signatory state for ratification by whatever procedure is necessary to bring it lawfully into operation in respect of that state. Each state is entitled and even also obliged to weigh its merits as a treaty that will create obligations for the citizens and for the state. In its nature as a constitution, or at least a putative constitution, however, it is of interest to the citizens of the Union as such and to the Union as a whole. Implicitly, two questions are open:

- In each state, the question is: 'Shall we as Danes/French/Germans/Latvians/Maltese … agree to ratify this treaty in view of the balance of advantage and disadvantage we see for our own country in taking this step?'
- In the Union as a whole: 'Shall we as Europeans and citizens of the European Union adopt this constitution in view of the balance of advantage and disadvantage we see for our European Union in reshaping it as an entity so constituted?'

The ratification procedure that was mandated by the Treaty unfortunately failed to ensure that there was any way for the second question to be clearly articulated and answered. The process of state-by-state ratification involved a series of debates that focused firmly on the first question. They raised the second question only by implication, if indeed it is in some way implicit in the first. At least some of the citizens of all the Union's Member States could be presumed to think that a significant part of the good for their own country includes participating in and contributing to a well-constituted European Union. To that extent the question 'Is this constitution good for Europe?' is part of the question 'Is this treaty good for the UK [or for France or for whichever is your own Member State]?'

On 28 May 2005, in a lecture to the World Congress in Philosophy of Law at Granada, I put forward the argument that the state-by-state ratification process was quite adequate and not objectionable from the point of view of democratic constitutionalism. A similar point was previously advanced in *Questioning Sovereignty* (1999). I even suggested that the process of so adopting a constitution, if the constitution were indeed adopted, might be itself a vehicle for developing a sense of 'constitutional patriotism' in Europe. After the lecture, however, my friend and colleague Joachim Nergelius from Lund in Sweden took me aside and suggested I was mistaken. He said that the tone and content of the debate in France were not at all addressed to the European question – it was all about French politics and about the impact of a particular vision of Europe in France itself. The same, I must say, subsequently appeared to be true about the debate in the Netherlands.[2]

I was not able to be in France during the ratification debate, nor in the Netherlands, but the newspaper and television reports did bear out the substantial truth of this. In the UK, the ratification debate never really got into full swing,

2 Professor Nergelius made his point in the debate following my presentation of a lecture to the IVR World Congress in Philosophy of Law in Granada in May 2005. The lecture was published as 'The European Constitutional Process: A Theoretical View', *Anales de la Cátedra Francisco Suárez* 39 (2005), 299–319.

since the French referendum followed so closely on a British General Election in which the promised ratification referendum largely neutralized the constitution as an election issue. One can, however, say without fear of contradiction that the debate would have been almost entirely run along the lines of my first question, not my second one. A largely Euro-sceptical and deeply constitution-sceptical press had already set the scene for a debate of what I would consider a narrowly nationalistic, even little-Englander, kind. So I conclude that Nergelius was right and I was wrong about the character of the state-by-state ratification process.

However that may be, it is not for me as a retired politician (though still in full activity as a law professor and constitutional commentator) to decry the will of the people. Of course it is right that democratic states must decide questions of constitutional concern to themselves by some appropriate form of democratic constitutional decision-making. If a state's constitution requires or permits a referendum, then one cannot complain when the result goes against one, any more than the other side can if our side prevails. Nobody can and nobody should be able to force the people of France or of the Netherlands, or any other country, to sign up to a treaty that they believe to be on balance adverse to the best interests of their country.

In that case, however, what about the constitution? In what circumstances might we as Europeans get to decide about its quality as a constitution for our whole European confederation or commonwealth or whatever we shall call this entity of its own kind, this suigeneric Union? After all, 15 countries have already ratified, presumably on some mixed view about national interest and European common good. It seems a pity if the unexceptionable democratic right of each country to take its own view in its own time about ratifying the Treaty excludes the right of Europeans as Europeans to reflect on whether a constitution would be good to have, and in particular whether this constitution is worth having.

## An All-Europe Referendum?

From time to time during the Convention, the suggestion was raised that there might somehow be an all-Union referendum on a constitution – this one perhaps, or some other improved version. There are obvious legal and constitutional obstacles to achieving this. But in the aftermath of the French and Dutch referenda, a different possibility did occur to me. A Constitution Treaty could itself make a provision about an all-Europe referendum. The provision would be for a referendum to be held if all the states ratify the treaty. So the treaty itself would provisionally establish the constitution, but provide for its coming into force only if assented to by all the people and peoples of the Union through a single referendum.

At present, Article IV 447 provides that:

1. This Treaty shall be ratified by the High Contracting Parties in accordance with their respective constitutional requirements. The instruments of ratification shall be deposited with the Government of the Italian Republic.
2. This Treaty shall enter into force on 1 November 2006, provided that all the instruments of ratification have been deposited, or, failing that, on the first day of the second month following the deposit of the instrument of ratification by the last signatory State to take this step.

It would be possible to produce a different version of paragraph 2 as follows:

2. After all the instruments of ratification have been deposited, a referendum shall be held in each Member State during a single four day period starting on a date to be fixed by resolution of the European Parliament and the Council on a proposal by the Commission. The question to be posed is the following 'Shall the European Union adopt and put into effect the Constitution contained in the Treaty establishing a Constitution for Europe?', and the answer must be either 'Yes' or 'No'.

One could then add some essential further provisions.

a. This Treaty shall enter into force on the first day of the second month following the referendum provided that, taking account of the aggregate votes cast in the referendum, a majority of voters throughout the Union has voted 'Yes', and provided that in each of at least four fifths of all the Member States the majority has been for 'Yes'.
b. Special provision may be made for establishing a relationship between the Union and any state a majority of whose voters has registered a 'no' vote, if subsequent to that vote the state by its own constitutional process resolves to exercise the power of withdrawal from the Union under Article 1 (60) of this treaty. Such provisions shall be no less favourable than the relationship obtaining between that state and the other states of the Union under the Treaty on European Union and the European Community Treaty as these were in force on the day prior to entry into force of the present Treaty.

The idea is simple. Treaty ratification must still take place according to each state's constitutional process. But the incentive to include a referendum at this stage, unless such is a strict requirement of national law, would be greatly reduced from the present position. In ratification debates in national Parliaments, it would be clear that no Parliament was denying the citizens an independent say. For such a say would be expressly included in the Treaty being ratified.

## Towards a Real European Debate

Upon the suggested hypothesis, all Member States would be agreeing to a treaty that might come into force despite some single-country negative results. But notice the condition I suggest applying to this. The condition is that a state whose citizens found unacceptable the constitution thus adopted might then demand, and the state might in its own time decide in favour of, a withdrawal from full membership of the Union. This would seem to me to strike a fairer balance than at present between the pro-constitution citizens and states, and the anti-constitution ones. There is not, nor should there be, any guarantee that a procedure of this kind would produce either a majority for the constitution or a majority in a sufficient number of the states. The point is that there would be an opportunity for a real Europe-wide debate about what kind of Union, if any, the citizens want.

It would be a debate about whether it is right to give the EU a political constitution by the common will of citizens. The alternative is to muddle along with a 'constitutional charter' that has been spelled out of the treaties by the Court and carried on by the acquiescence of the states, sometimes a grumbling and reluctant acquiescence. An authentic constitutional patriotism in and for a European Union would require, surely, some such authentication as this, and might even emerge from the act of articulating it.

Of all the complaints about the European Union in its present form, the hardest to rebut is the objection that says the citizens never consented to more than a common market. But then they woke up to find themselves in an ever more expansive political union, now a political and monetary union for most of them. I used to think that only a certain kind of perhaps even rather paranoid British Euro-sceptic took this line. I never believed it myself, since at the time of the UK referendum of 1975 the political and constitutional implications of the EEC, as then established, were perfectly clear to me. But perhaps the perspective of a Professor of Public Law is indeed an unusual one in relation to matters of this sort. Again, it became clear during the French and Dutch referenda that more than a few citizens of these countries had the same opinion. I have also heard members of the UK's 'Yes' campaign of 1975 publicly acknowledge that the campaign instructions for members of the European Movement were clearly to stress the economic reasons for a 'Yes' vote while evading any joinder of issue about political implications. There has indeed been a democratic deficit in the process of authentication of the existing constitution of the Union.

## The Problem of Part III

If we really were looking to a Europe-wide constitutional referendum, there would be other things that might be done somewhat differently from the project of the 2002/3 Convention, carried on by the IGC up to the final meeting in Rome on 29 October 2004. The problem is Part III of the Constitution. This contains a great deal of matter which is not constitutional in any ordinary sense of the term. Part III deals with the policies and functioning of the Union, derived from the present Treaties but adapted to the new context. Its presence raised much adverse comment both in the UK in its preliminary skirmishes about the constitution and again, as it turned out, in France and the Netherlands. The real Constitution in the Giscardian draft was found in Part I – finally, 60 Articles in all, pretty straightforward and eminently readable. Add to that Europe's Charter of Rights – the Charter of Fundamental Rights of the European Union as elaborated by the Herzog Convention and adopted through the Treaty of Nice as a 'political declaration' only. As Part II of the Constitution this is also very clear and readable. The present Part IV amounts to 11 articles making essential 'general and final provisions', including provisions about adopting the Constitution and amending it in future. That again adds little to the bulk. A reasonable public debate could be held about a Constitution on that scale, which quite ordinary citizens could comfortably read on a Sunday afternoon.

The huge bulk of Part III on the other hand was rightly complained of in France. How can ordinary people come to any sensible decision about so huge a stack of complicated legal text? The answer is that they cannot. So a ratification referendum should focus on the more strictly constitutional elements in Parts I, II and IV.

This is not to repudiate Part III taken in its proper place. Properly understood, Part III is both essential and need not cause special concern. For all it does is adjust those existing basic rules of the Union and Community that are included in the two Treaties for the sake of conformity with the amended constitutional framework in Part I and to an extent Part II. From a Conventioneer's point of view, the adoption of Part III was never satisfactorily debated. The text came on to the Convention Agenda late in the day. It is really the result of a technical exercise, carried out with great skill by the legal experts of the three EU Institutions, to ensure that there would be no technical legal vacuum, and no needless legal uncertainty, if the new Constitution came into force. It would have been a disaster simply to adopt (or propose) a Constitution on the footing that all consequential amendments should be read into the *acquis communautaire*, simply as a matter of necessary implication. This would have caused huge but avoidable uncertainty about the rules that define EU policies with regard to the Single Market rules and related matters. On that ground, I have previously defended Part III as a reasonable effort to do a necessary job.

I now see that Conventioneers should have protested much more effectually at having Part III foisted on them and pushed into the Constitution. The job had to be done, but it did not have to be done in exactly that way. The Constitution as adopted should have been all and only what is now in Parts I, II and IV. Part III should have been an annexed Act subject to ratification on the basis of entering into force at the same time as the Constitution. Thus would have secured the necessary consequential amendments to carry forward the *acquis communautaire* into its new constitutional setting. If there were to be a Europe-wide referendum, it would not make sense to include 'Part III' in what we citizens are asked directly to ratify. It should be available for discussion as an indication that necessary adjustments can be, and will have been made, once the Constitution comes into force, if it ever does.

If it were done in this way, citizens could be voting on a reasonably compact and intelligible text, able to come to a reasonable understanding of what is at stake. That would surely be highly desirable.

## Conclusion: All a Great Mistake?

Is all this just a re-telling of the story of a great mistake? Was the idea of a constitution-treaty a bad one from start to finish, or did the Convention put its collective mind to seeking an answer to a question Europeans will have to answer in more decisive terms one day? Well, the European Council will certainly have to return some time soon – perhaps most effectively during the forthcoming German presidency – to the question how to make the Union's institutions reasonably workable in the context of yet further enlargement of the Union. This could not be a matter of simply resuscitating the 2004 Treaty-constitution. That would simply be an insult to the citizens of France and the Netherlands, asking them to re-think their opposition to that very constitution-treaty just as it stands.

But we might look again at two things: first, a slimmed down 'Basic Treaty' that captured what is currently in Parts I and IV of the 2004 Treaty, with appropriate reference also to the Charter of Rights; and second, a process of provisional ratification, to be followed by such a referendum as here proposed. In that case, no opponent of either constitution or indeed basic treaty would be deprived of the opportunity to take part in the final decision. No state would have to be forced into a union newly re-constituted under such new provisions, in the event that a sufficient European majority did bring this about. So at least it might be possible to offer this not just as a pipe dream, but also as one proposal for a way out of the present rather unsatisfactory impasse. Some mistakes were undoubtedly made in the Convention and after it. It cannot be dismissed, however, as 'all a great mistake'.

## Postscript

This Postscript was written in late August 2007, while a new IGC convened on 23 July was at work to produce, instead of the 'constitution', a new reformed version of the present Union and Community Treaties. The states' representatives were performing this task according to a mandate settled by the European Council in late June on the proposal of the German presidency. The mandate incorporated various 'red line' issues on which Member States like the UK and Poland absolutely insisted (the UK included: independence in Foreign Affairs, Justice and Home

Affairs issues; exemption from Court rulings on Charter of Rights; retention of commitment to 'undistorted competition'. The Polish government objected to the reduction of Poland's relative voting power in Council that would result from the switch to a double majority voting system there). That apart, what was proposed – as partly prophesied in the original version of this paper – was the drafting and adoption, not of a 'constitution' but of a 'Reform Treaty' that preserved the essence of the constitution while abandoning its form.

Although the word 'constitution' will be completely shunned, and some symbolism abandoned (flag, motto, national anthem), the Reform Treaty will indeed transcribe nearly all that was in the 2004 Constitution into two new Treaties that will result from implementing the Reform Treaty. The first, a reformed 'Treaty on European Union' will adopt much of the old Part I and Part IV. The second, a reformed version of what is now called the 'Treaty establishing the European Community' will have the name 'Treaty on the Functioning of the European Union', and will largely comprise the 'Part III' of 2004. The Union as such will acquire personality in law and the 'Community' and the whole 'pillar' structure will disappear as such. The Charter will not be replicated within the Treaties, but, in its amended form, will be acknowledged as having legal effect, subject to an arguable limitation of this in the case of the UK. Consistent with the adopted 'mandate', no room exists for new reforming moves, or attempts to place new limits on existing Union competences.

One might be forgiven for claiming that the new two-treaty solution broadly conforms to the suggestion above that Part III should never have been lumped together with the essentially constitutional elements that will now be the main meat of the Union Treaty. Although these elements do indeed remain essentially constitutional, the attempt to produce a formal as well as functional constitution is clearly abandoned, and with it, according to statesmen in many states, the need for resort to the referendum in any Member State whose own constitution does not affirmatively require this. The Treaties will also make clear that the Union can, by desisting from legislating on a given matter within its competence, return legislative competence on that matter to Member States. This will not normally require unanimity, since the Reform Treaty will apply co-decision between Council and Parliament much more extensively than at present, again in replication of the 2004 proposals. Law-making in Europe will thus become more transparent and democratic, while states, however, lose their power of veto in many areas in which they have retained it till now. Proponents of the belief that the states are the only true repositories of European democracy will therefore challenge the claim that the new treaties represent a gain for democracy.

It must also be said that my high-minded suggestion about the possibility of some kind of all-European popular endorsement of a constitutional reform has proved totally unrealistic in present circumstances. The process that was set in train with the establishment of the Convention, and the enthusiastic perception of a 'constitutional moment' in 2002/3 has led only to a re-run of the old method of intergovernmental treaty-reform, subject to whatever state-by-state ratification process each state's constitution requires. It does, however, remain to be seen whether or not in their substance the changes proposed by the Convention, now emerging in the two new Treaties, will prove to make the kind of improvement to the working of European Institutions that the Convention's majority foresaw.

# Chapter 4
# When 'No' Means 'Yes': A Constitution for Europe and the Limits of Ignorance[1]

Andreas Philippopoulos-Mihalopoulos

The Dutch and the French 'no' on the ratification of a Constitution for Europe is arguably one of the most significant 'constitutional moments' in the history of the European Union.[2] This is so, not only because they refer to a text for a proposed constitution for Europe, but also because they allow, if not oblige, us to rethink certain foundations of European constitutional theory. The 'no' has opened up a space of negation and questioning, which can no longer be ignored. It brings forth a fundamental shake up of the connection between the constitution and its *demos*, the text and its context, and the relation between law and politics. Whatever happens now, one thing is certain: Europe has irreversibly entered its 'constitutional moment' and is facing a space where the absence of certainty is embarrassingly obvious. The future of a European project, of a *finalit* and of integration has now been put into doubt. If European constitutionalism is to develop in a manner representative of the plural explosion of the European political sphere, it cannot afford to ignore this questioning.

A study of the 'no' requires a prior understanding of the concept of a constitution and its extant temporality as the text (the constitution itself) and its context (part of which is also the 'no'). In this sense, a constitution is the momentary revelation of difference between the constitutional text and its constituting/constituted context, and as such it can be described as a fracture, a Dostoevskyan laceration, self-

1 This is a reworked version of an earlier article 'Moment of Stasis: The Successful Failure of a Constitution for Europe', published in *European Law Journal* 14:6, 2008.

2 For an analysis of the 2005 referenda see Tridimas, G. and Tridimas, T. (2007), 'Electorates v Politicians: the 2005 French and Dutch Referendums on the EU Constitutional Treaty', in Albi, A. and Ziller, J. (eds), *The European Constitution and National Constitutions: Ratification and Beyond* (The Hague: Kluwer); Besselink, L. (2007), 'The Dutch Constitution, the European Constitution and the Referendum in the Netherlands', in Albi and Ziller, *The European Constitution and National Constitutions*; Ziller, J. (2007), 'French Reactions to the Treaty Establishing a Constitution for Europe: From Constitutional Welcome to Popular Rejection', in Albi and Ziller, *The European Constitution and National Constitutions*; Blockmans, S. and Prechal, S. (eds) (2007), *Reconciling the Deepening and Widening of the European Union* (The Hague: Asser Press).

imposed, self-executed, self-absorbed. At the same time, a constitution contains the mending of its very laceration, the disclosure of its normality, the continuity of its generation. Accordingly, the 'constitutional moment' is not, as Ackerman has described, the moment of discontinuity between what precedes and what follows the constitution,[3] but the moment at which the difference between a constitutional text and its context is simultaneously revealed and bridged. The 'moment' is not one of smooth generation or even eruptive revolution which nevertheless 'constitutes', but a continuity of events that include obvious and not so obvious constitutional acts.[4] Of course, this continuity can only be observed retrospectively, can be 'validated' only once the moment has passed.[5] And this includes the constitutional 'failure' in the form of 'no'. Speculations, analyses and strategic regroupings usually constitute the post-moment brouhaha of the failure.[6] The present contribution, however, is not performing any such necessary but essentially strained and lamenting operation. On the contrary, it revisits the moment of laceration and constitutes it in its full negativity. It deals with the failure of the text and in its context, and the constitution of a negative space of ignorance, hailed here as the only possible space in which a European constitutional moment can occur.[7]

I insist on the word 'failure', not from a eurosceptic or indeed a defeatist point of view, but because of its inherent negativity. This negativity presents me with ways to semiologize it as a space of questioning and revelation of the paradoxes peculiar to constitutionalism,[8] and as a resounding 'yes' to an implosive constitutional moment that distinguishes, ruptures, delimits and initiates more so because of its inclusive discordance. I show this while indulging my more general preoccupation with a theory of absence, and employing for this reason a deconstructed version of systems theory. Thus, I use systemic and deconstructionist tools in order to theorize

---

3 Ackerman, B. (1989), 'Constitutional Politics/Constitutional Law', *Yale Law Journal* 99, 453. For a contextual treatment of the moment see Walker, N. (2005), 'Europe's Constitutional Momentum and the Search for Polity Legitimacy', *International Journal of Constitutional Law* 3, 211–38.

4 Everson, M. (1998), 'Beyond the *Bundesverfassungsgericht*: On the Necessary Cunning of Constitutional Reasoning', *European Law Journal* 4, 389–410.

5 Castiglione, D. (2003), 'Reflections on Europe's Constitutional Moment' CIDEL Conference on 'Deliberative Constitutional Politics in the EU', Zaragoza, June.

6 See for example the entire volume of Albi and Ziller, *The European Constitution and National Constitutions*.

7 This is not simply the space of popular mobilization, which, as Walker, 'Europe's Constitutional Momentum and the Search for Polity Legitimacy' and Walker, N. (2005), 'Europe's Constitutional Engagement', *Ratio Juris* 18:3, 387–99, correctly states, is important but not adequate. As will become clearer later, it requires a conceptualization based on the circularity between text and *demos*.

8 See Maduro, M.P. (2003), 'Europe and the Constitution: What if this is As Good As It Gets?', in Weiler, J.H.H. and Wind, M. (eds), *European Constitutionalism beyond the State* (Cambridge: Cambridge University Press).

in a non-traditional, non-constitutional and non-liberal way the constitutional text of inclusive negation, the space of absence of a European *demos*, the locus of a non-integrated identity, and ultimately the moment of constitutional negation that, precisely because of their absent topography can be understood 'positively' and can be put in an operational counter-relation to traditional constitutional dogmatics.

## A Successful Failure

Several reasons have been offered for the ratification failure of the Treaty establishing a Constitution for Europe.[9] They can be summarized in four clusters:[10] first, that the failure cannot be attributed to the actual content of the text but to issues such as the Turkish membership, economy, immigration and so on; second, that it was domestic rather than European issues that were being judged; third, that there was a widespread public ignorance and lack of understanding of what the Constitution actually was about; and, fourth, the opposition was misdirected, since the text simply reiterated what the existing Treaties had already made a legal reality.[11] The above list can also be read as an incantation that deculpabilizes the text: the fault is not to be found in the text but in the *con*text; in fact, not even in its context, but in things unrelated to the text itself, side-issues, *quiproquos*, national failures, widespread vulgarity, that sort of stuff, that institute a further level of textual independence away from the context and deep into the wasteland of improbability. The text as such may not have been infallible, but it was not a *failure*. On the contrary, it *is* a success, patiently waiting to resurge somehow, in a new or similar form, when the context will be better equipped to accept it and the side issues sidelined.

Reading the bulk of the relevant post-referenda literature makes for an amusing exercise in autistic conceit. Democratic considerations aside, the problem can be located in the arbitrary delimitation of the constitutional text. To put it simply, what is the difference between a constitutional text and its context?[12] The recursivity between the text and the source, or in some respects the *pouvoir constitué* and the *pouvoir constituant*, can be variably put in terms of democracy, constitutionalism,

9 16 Dec 2004, OJ (C310) 1 (2004).

10 See de Burca, G. (2006), 'After the Referenda', *European Law Journal* 12:1, 6–8, who rightly dismisses that these reasons can be differentiated from the Constitution itself; also Sieberson, S. (2005), 'Worth Doing Well: The Improvable European Union Constitution', *Michigan Journal of International Law* 26, 586–617.

11 What Weiler, J.H.H. (2005), 'On the Power of the Word: Europe's Constitutional Iconography', in Curtin, D. et al. (eds), *The European Union Constitution: The Best Way Forward?* (The Hague: Asser Press), has called 'Nice-bis'.

12 Weiler, 'On the Power of the Word', has played with the textuality of the text by employing an implicitly theological/psychoanalytic notion of 'word' as the self-referential gesture that defines itself as a constitution. While this is not dissimilar to the present attempt, here I embrace text and context in their co-extensiveness.

legitimation, sovereignty and so on. Whatever its name, the text and the source remain tied together in an inextricable paradox of contemporaneity, in the sense that either of them is at the same time the condition and the result of the other. The source of the text is the power that the text consolidates and contains within its textuality. In its turn, the source of the text becomes itself textual and interdigitated at that particular moment and place with the text itself. Thus, context and text are coterminous in a process where the paradoxicality of recursivity is at its most evident.

On the paradoxical basis of co-extensiveness between text and context, any distinction between, on the one hand, the four groups of reasons given above for which the constitution was not ratified, and on the other the constitution itself, is arbitrary and indeed oblivious of the radically evident recursivity between the text and its context. Whether it is the loss of (the illusion of) national control, the oscillating boundary between state sovereignty and EU, the lack of social legitimation or the ignorance of something that should already be well known, their severance from the text itself is an attempt at bypassing the fundamental paradox of constitutionalism: that a constituting *demos* is needed in order to produce a constitution that will, in its turn, consolidate (if not create) the constituted *demos*.[13] In that sense, the possibility of a failed text (in its context) becomes remote, and the conditions take the blame.

But if things are seen from the perspective of the paradox itself, the message is positive and the experience of the constitutional 'no' becomes a trauma both anticipated and worth celebrating. A text that attempts to constitute both a past and a future, concreticize them and render them 'normal' and 'demotic' around its very presence (in the form of anticipated or well accepted presence), is also able to accommodate its very negation. The constitution includes its failure, and *this failure is precisely its success in constituting a demos*, for *demos* can no longer be understood solely as the body that receives and acquiesces, the moment that produces or the topology of assertion, but also the assertion of absence, the excess of apathy and the space where a visible negativity may be produced. Again, this is not said from an anti-constitutional point of view. On the contrary, it is said from a contextual point of view that describes a constitution as a thematizing operation that extends itself to the past as contextual anticipation and momentum, and to the future as an expectation-binding text. In that sense, the success of a constitution cannot only be judged by its ratification or lack of it, but, more importantly, by its total presence in the public arena.

It has to be emphasized that presence is not necessarily the visibilization of a positive occurrence. In this contextual mode of thinking about the text, presence is also the visibilization of an absence. Thus, through its failure, the text withdraws and leaves behind a trail of absence so potent that it results in the immediate

13 For a further description of such a circularity, which, however, stops short of including its failure, see Weiler, J.H. (2002), 'A Constitution for Europe: Some Hard Choices', *Journal of Common Market* 40:4, 563–80.

demythologization of the public space itself. There is nothing shared about this public space, no *one demos* to speak of, no constitutive collectivity, and this is precisely the success of the failure: that this absence has become visible and relevant. Several have repeatedly lamented the absence of such a space, Habermas arguably more vociferously than others: 'There is still no European public space, no transnational bundling of themes, no common discussion, each one of the votes takes place within the bounds of the individual country's public sphere.'[14] But Habermas's critique comes from a space of positive presence, and his rather strained distinction between the individual country's public sphere and that something else which may be taking place somewhere outside that (but where? and why?), allows the reader to perceive a nostalgia on behalf of the author for a space defined and positive. But any such distinction, even when performed in order to lament the occurrence of the distinction itself, is laboured and purposefully oblivious of the present multileveled space of plural geographical explosion witnessed in Europe. Talking about a distinction between national and transnational public spheres goes against the whole *absence of project* that is at the very (decentred) centre of Europe, and sides up simultaneously with both eurosceptics and europhiles that try to populate the void of Europe with something defined, positive, directional and finite.

And there is nothing wrong with the above epithets – except for when they are superimposed on a thing that resists them, suggested for an entity that is yet to be tied down, offered as *amuse-gueules* to someone who is simply satiated. More on the void follows later in this text. For the time being, it is important to clarify this: that the negativity of the ratification can be seen as a space of visible absence, not a space of a 'belonging-together' that produces majority decisions,[15] but an arena of question-marks where the paradox of constitutionalism in general and the European Constitution specifically is revealed and put into use, and the failure becomes, not a success, but a successful failure.

## Locating the Constitution

Classic constitutionalism thinks of the constitution as a legal text located atop the political. Thus, political powers are controlled and limited through their subjection to the rule of law.[16] This understanding of the relation between law and politics

14 Habermas, J., 'The Illusionary "Leftist No": Adopting the Constitution to Strengthen Europe's Power to Act', at <http://www.signandsight.com/features/163.html, 13/05/2005>, last accessed on 12/01/2007.

15 Grimm, D. (1995), 'Does Europe need a Constitution?', *European Law Journal* 1:3, 282–94.

16 See Closa, C. (2005), 'Deliberative Constitutional Politics and the Turn towards a Norms-Based Legitimacy of the EU Constitution', *European Law Journal* 11:4, 411–31, at 414.

on the basis of control is doubly misleading: first, it describes a causal connection of limitation and control between the legal and the political system (typically by inflating the legal ego to the point of omnipotence); and second, it ignores the fundamental paradox of the constitutional operation. An attempt to reflect the complexity of the issue comes from systems theory. Systems theory begins by differentiating between the various social systems, amongst them law and politics, on the basis of their function. Such differentiation leaves very little margin for zones of 'contact', mutual 'influence' or indeed control between systems. Thus, the attempt to place a constitution – by definition an amalgam of law and politics – anywhere within systems theory, poses at first instance a considerable challenge. This challenge has been met by Niklas Luhmann, the founder of systems theory, who considers a constitution an evolutionary development of the coupling between law and politics.[17] Epigrammatically, 'coupling' in systems theory is the production of a common systemic historicity that occurs through a process of reciprocal observation between systems, which, however, remain oblivious of the reciprocity of the process. A development of the Luhmannian position on the constitution has been offered by Michael Bommes[18] who suggests that a constitution emerges as the solution to the problematic level of advanced differentiation between law and politics.[19] It is interesting to note that, while the two positions obviously have the same root, they differ in that the latter is distinctly prescriptive, whereas the first is merely descriptive.

Treating a constitution as a solution means that there is a problem that can be observed across the two systems in a way that problematizes both equally. It is debatable whether this is possible within the ambits of systems theory. While an adequate exposé of the theory is clearly beyond the scope of this contribution,[20] it is arguably important to explain the reasons for which systems theory is a relevant theoretical option that can shed light on a paradox such as the constitutional failure. Systems theory's concept of functional differentiation stems from the foundational distinction between the system and its environment. Law and politics are distinct systems, floating in an environment of evolutionary opportunities. To such opportunities, systems are only cognitively open – that is, they learn

17 Luhmann, N. (1990), 'Verfassung als Evolutionäre Errungenschaft', *Rechtshistorisches Journal* 9, 176–220; see also King, M. and Thornhill, C. (2003), *Niklas Luhmann's Theory of Politics and Law* (London: Palgrave Macmillan).

18 Bommes, M. (1999), *Migration und nationaler Wohlfahrtsstaat: Ein differenzierungstheoretischer Entwurf* (Opladen: Westdeutscher Verlag).

19 Breda, V. (2006), 'A European Constitution in a Multinational Europe or a Multinational Constitution for Europe?', *European Law Journal* 12:3, 330–44; Albert, M. (2002), 'Governance and Democracy in European Systems: On Systems Theory and European Integration', *Review of International Studies* 28, 293–309, where systems theory is put together with contemporary European integration issues.

20 For a classic and concise introduction to Luhmann and the law, see King, M. and Schütz, A. (1994), 'The Ambitious Modesty of Niklas Luhmann', *Journal of Law and Society* 21:3, 261–87.

from environmental 'irritations' – but remain normatively closed – namely, they translate all irritations into their own systemic operations without having the capability of attributing them to the environment. This means that systems remain essentially closed and self-referring units that construct themselves, their irritations and their surrounding totality according to their own operations. Such an awkward and counter-intuitive starting kit seemingly does not promise much in terms of constitutional theory. Still, facilitated precisely by the concept of systemic closure, systems theory does away with the illusion of control and direct influence between law and politics – thus, the traditional constitutional description of political subjugation to the rule of law becomes a mere prescription and not an adequate description of a complex reality. Perhaps more important, systems theory can accommodate the fundamental constitutional paradox of the recursivity between the text and its source. It achieves this by delegating the constitution, not to politics or law exclusively, but simultaneously within and outside each of the two systems. Systems theory's most crucial notion, I argue, is neither the system itself, nor functional differentiation – possibly not even closure – but the systemic environment itself.[21] Although a correlative of the system, the systemic environment can never be observed and epistemologically assessed in itself, except as the definitional negative of the system; although it hosts the cognitive potentialities of the system, it remains inaccessible to all systems; and although it remains a common characteristic of every system, it cannot contain any collectivity or projected systemic overlap. The systemic environment is peculiar to each system, since all other systems constitute the environment as an amorphous, acephalous mass of systemic potentiality. The very location of the environment, outside yet potentially inside the system, internalized by the system's cognitive excursions but consistently different and deferred, alien and inalienable, alter and ego, is what makes the environment a universal depository of ignorance in a persistent relation of continuum and rupture with the system.

Michelle Everson is eloquently flirting with precisely this space of ignorance when she writes that constitutional acts are the limit between law and politics.[22] I take the limit to signify the line that distinguishes the system from its environment, the systemic boundary that separates the illusion of knowledge from the space of ignorance. Thus, I push the above definition a little further: *a constitution is the reciprocal limitation of ignorance of the limits between law and politics*. This definition is deliberately structured as a negative event. Even in their constitutional coupling, law and politics cannot perceive each other. They remain environment for each other. Their common boundary is that of the common ignorance of their limits: systems do not know their limits, indeed they do not know that they are limited. According to the system, systemic boundaries are coterminous with the

21 In the manner of an operational absence. See an elaboration of this in Philippopoulos-Mihalopoulos, A. (2007), *Absent Environments: Theorising Environmental Law and the City* (London: Routledge-Cavendish).

22 Everson, 'Beyond the *Bundesverfassungsgericht*'.

universe. Thus, whatever lies outside the limits of a system can only be observed as a non-system and only in absence of the system itself. But this basis of absence is, at least for the present rather deconstructed version of systems theory I put forth here, an adequate basis for the projection, not of a commonality between systems, but of the *absence* of commonality. Into the space of ignorance hosted by the systemic environment, a commonality of limitation can be proffered if suitably uttered in its soundless negativity. A constitution is the indication of such negativity, and a ratification failure an indisputable utterance of the impossibility of systemic omnipresence.

A constitution is seen here as a sonorous 'no' uttered by the ignorance of the limits of each system. Only afterwards does this become positive, in that each system's ignorance, despite itself, stands as the limitation of the other. It is the negativity of the trauma that renders visible the positive inner fold. But one necessarily starts with negation, the space of absolute sovereignty of each system, its exalted universality in terms of its own operations – for the system can see nothing but itself and its operations. What lies outside is nothing to the system – and that is where the constitution is to be found: excommunicated from both law and politics, beyond their sphere of control and exclusivity of operation, but still within the production/consumption of their cognitive domain which is the source of systemic evolution, learning and adaptation.[23] With the constitution, the 'other side' of the line is revealed in its absolute alterity as the thing that remains alien yet intricately woven with the system. A constitution remains an operation that perpetuates the systemic illusion of knowledge and control in both systems, while limiting both within their confines, thus converting their invisible limits into visible limitations.

In many respects, there is no difference between a constitution and its failure except as a matter of degree. A failure pronounces the systemic trauma in a possibly less disputable way. The constitutional moment is the locus of limitation, and whether this is because of a 'yes' or a 'no' is irrelevant. They both operate as the indication of systemic finality, of a purposeless *telos*, of a teleology that cannot stop talking. The *telos* is visible, except that this does not stop the system from becoming what its being dictates *in absentia* of the system. The constitution contains its failure, and all this is contained either side of the boundary separating law and politics in their reciprocal but blind miscomprehension and misattribution of their surrounding space of ignorance. The remarkable thing is that no system can reach beyond its boundary. Even so, there is one domain in which the 'no' makes a difference which goes beyond a difference of degree. This is the domain of legitimacy, that, depending on its exact location with regard to the system, affects the way the system understands this space of absence opened up by the constitutional operation.

23 Philippopoulos-Mihalopoulos, *Absent Environments*.

The classic distinction between normative and social legitimacy[24] can also be put in terms of internal and external legitimacy. Systemically speaking, the topology of the system is the space of knowledge where illusions of control are exerted. Thus, the legal system can only 'understand' the internal side of legitimation that corresponds to the normative check for consistency, while excluding the external side of legitimation that refers to political processes of the 'ambivalence of the social' as Christian Joerges puts it.[25] But, just as the text and its context are interdigitated, internal and external legitimacy collapse into each other and the distinction is quickly dissolved through their reciprocal limitation. Jiri Pribáñ points exactly to this transcendence without visibility when he writes: 'the social space of instability and constant confrontation is the space in which legitimation takes place ... Noise is not only contingent but also subversive.'[26] The distinction between on the one hand, the orderly illusion of systemic structure, and on the other, the whiteness of incomprehensibility as borne by the noisy horizon of probabilities, is a replication of the system/environment distinction, whose virginity however is retained only as a spectre in the self-description of the system. The environment is well within the system, an advance from the trenches of invisibility and into the sphere of systemic internalization. Each side of legitimacy internalizes the other side but without attributing it, without allowing it to become operable within. Thus, the social space of instability finds a place within the normative legitimation, and respectively, normative legitimation extends itself to the environment of society. However, their original location is not visible to the system. The maintenance of systemic closure requires the erasure of any external trace, and the system carries on its self-referential whirl by constructing the external as internal. The systemic universe is restored.

Things are different when negation lands on the terrain of legitimacy. The constitutional 'no' brings forth the other side of the limit, not as an operative terrain of colonization, neither as an internally attributable operation, but as an empty assertion: there is another side to it, to which, however, the system has no access. The 'no' is arguably the greatest test for the two systems' boundary perception, because it wedges itself in the system and questions the latter's boundary understanding of its jurisdiction: could it be the case that the law is

---

24 Or input and output legitimacy, as suggested by Scharpf, F., 'Interdependence and Democratic Legitimation', MPIfG Working Paper 98/2, 09/1998, <http://www.mpi-fg-koeln.mpg.de/pu/workpap/wp98-2/wp98-2.html>, last accessed on 13/01/2007; see also Gibbs, N. (2005), 'Examining the Aesthetic Dimensions of the Constitutional Treaty', *European Law Journal* 11:3, 326–42, for the role of the constitutional form (or aesthetic) in relation to normativity.

25 Joerges, C. (2006), 'On the Disregard for History in the Convention Process', *European Law Journal* 12:1, 2–5.

26 Pribáñ, J. (2001), 'Legitimation between the Noise of Politics and the Order of Law', in Pribáñ, J. and Nelken, D. (eds), *Law's New Boundaries* (Aldershot: Ashgate), 148.

not all there is? Could there exist anything communicable outside politics? The systems' doubting their extent is deeply unsettling – just like the constitutional 'no'. Of course, a system carries on internalizing its environment, and the 'no' immediately becomes part of the system. But there is an important difference from the previous distinction and its reciprocal internalization: here, the system can no longer ignore the *unheimlich* of the internalized. The space of negation floods into the system and remains there, a growth unfamiliar yet inalienable. With its simultaneous mirroring on both sides, the constitutional 'no' renders both the other side (internal or external) *and* the distinction itself transparently absent. This does not mean that the legal system dissolves, or indeed that politics or external legitimacy appear comprehensible to the legal system. It simply amounts to the revelation of a gaping hole within the system, an internalization of the other side of the limit as an aporetic wasteland crowned by a fumbling halo of closeness. And this is exactly the reason for welcoming the 'no': through this presence of absence, the limit becomes the limitation, the negative becomes positive, and the constitutional 'no' is transformed into a sonorous assertion of the limit. What the constitutional failure brings forth is the limit and its transcendence, its leaking universalism, a universalism without guarantees. A meek – even an informed – 'yes' would not constitute a passage to positivity. 'Yes' would signify business as usual, inertia, a non-constituted presence, a quietude that would be disquieting. Instead, the 'no' occupies the space of positivity, making its absence of commonality visible, rendering its extrasystemic transcendence a location of questioning and continuous redirection. In this case, 'no' is edifying, since it wraps the negative in a package of affirmation, of visibility of the invisible, thus rendering the limit a 'threshold', which, according to Agamben is not a limit but a point of contact with an exteriority that remains empty.[27]

Thus, the constitution is indeed between law and politics, but always on the other side of the limit, always in a niche of between, never to be explored by either law or politics. A constitutional act is a balancing act of veiled proximity, perpetually deferred and consistently different for both law and politics, free to roam in its own paradoxical utopia. Its visibility becomes blinding at moments of constitutional import – none more potent, indeed more 'constitutional', than a constitutional failure which drags along its collapse the two systems with their respective legitimating mechanisms, and renders them transparently alien and impregnable, yet contiguous and familiar to each other.

## The European Stasis

There are several interesting consequences of the constitutional 'no'. Except for the 'what now' type of consequences, exhaustively analysed in the literature,

27 Agamben, G. (1993), *The Coming Community*, trans. M. Hardt (Minneapolis, MN: Minnesota University Press), 66.

there are also the ones that can only be adumbrated once the space of absence is adequately comprehended (as precisely a *void* space) by the legal and the political system. At this period of 'reflection', the 'no' is still a colonizable space: shall we change the text to fit in with what we think that the people want? Shall we use referenda again? How long can we carry on reflecting for? Moving away from such valid but ultimately leading preoccupations, I want to explore perhaps a hope rather than an observation: that if adequately internalized in its full paradoxicality, the constitutional 'no' will question the habitual interpretation of the foundational Community concepts of European identity and the European *demos*. An adequate analysis of these is evidently beyond the scope of the present chapter; some brief comments, however, on their possible differentiated understanding are necessary in order to arrive at the final conceptualization of this argument, namely the constitutional moment.

The preoccupation with identity is particularly evident in a constantly redefined Europe that struggles, on the one hand with the burden of its historical role, and on the other with the impossibility of finding anything from which it could meaningfully distinguish itself.[28] Any opposition (currently a not indisputable opposition to the United States, and a fragmented reaction to global terrorism) is constructed on the line between a seemingly permeating belief in 'the European way',[29] and a certain syndrome-driven kick-reaction by a geopolitical presence all too conscious of its secondary position. On that basis, identity constructions tend towards the other side, across as it were, in a rather vainglorious attempt to embrace whatever is excluded. Thus Joseph Weiler: 'despite the boundaries which constitute the I and the Alien, one is commanded to reach over the boundary and accept him, in his alienship, as oneself.'[30] The quest for identity is once again constructed as a conscious move, which is enriched by a crossing in its turn conditioned by tolerance.[31] It is interesting once again to detect a nostalgia for an imagined period where boundaries were not only fixed but also wedged between different conceptions of egos: thus, I and Alter, or indeed alienship and oneselfness. But since Levinas's reconceptualization of the ethical relation between the self and other as the recursivity of invitation,[32] and the politicization of mainly geographical

28 Schlesinger, P. (2003), 'The Babel of Europe? An Essay on Networks and Communicative Spaces', CIDEL ARENA Working Paper 22/03, <http://www.arena.uio.no/cidel/publications.html>, last accessed 13/01/2007. Also Balibar, E. (2004), *We, The People of Europe?* (Princeton, NJ: Princeton University Press).

29 Rifkin, J. (2004), *The European Dream* (New York: Tarcher).

30 Weiler, J.H.H. (2003), 'Europe's Fateful Choice', in Weiler and Wind, *European Constitutionalism beyond the State*, 19.

31 See, for example, Weiler, 'A Constitution for Europe' and 'Europe's Fateful Choice', but also Menéndez, A.J. (2005), 'A Christian or a *Laïc* Europe? Christian Values and European Identity', *Ratio Juris* 18:2, 179–205, criticism of Weiler's *Un' Europa Cristiana*.

32 Indicatively, Lévinas, E. (1981), *Otherwise than Being or Beyond Essence*, trans. A. Lingis (The Hague: Martinus Nijhoff) and Derrida, J., *Adieu* (1999), trans. P. Brault and

fragmentation as the way into constructive difference,[33] it is really difficult to carry on talking about the need for identity on the basis of movement metaphors. Nothing can move across. What finds itself this or that side of the boundary – a boundary ever so fragile, mobile and mirroring that is hardly employable as a point of argument – are growths, excesses, shoots of the system itself in its frenzy for a consistent self-description. But we know – we ought to know – that. Identity, if at all relevant, can only be found in the spaces within Europe's self-description where the system is forced to renegotiate its boundaries in ways never before tested. At such *stases* of opposition, identity congregates and progressively disintegrates. There is nowhere to reach across to, nothing to welcome as alien or, worse, as oneself, for there is no-one to perform this movement.[34]

The constitution of a *demos* is also problematized by the lack of identity but, arguably, in a way more resonant of the void left behind. The constituting and constituted *demos* is at the same time the origin and recipient of the text. Further, *demos* is the context of the text, in that there is no reason to suggest a constitution if there is no simultaneous understanding of its co-extensiveness with the *demos* itself, the social space of prior legitimation. This means that *demos* is as textual as the constitution itself (and *vice versa*) –which redefines the idea of movement of the text from the sovereign (*demos*) to the people (*demos*) as a *stasis octroyée*.[35] Just as a constitution can only be if it has always already been there,[36] a constitution-creating gesture is a motionless mirroring between the two sides of a wildly fluctuating boundary. Resisting movement is more complex in the context of *demos* because it requires imagining the possibility of an *absent community*, namely a community whose core is precisely the absence of a commonality.[37] Cries in this direction (although not to the extent of absence) come from everywhere but perhaps more eloquently in Pribáň's counter-imagined Europe as the civic alternative to ethnic demology, which, especially when transposed to the collective

M. Naas (Stanford, CA: Stanford University Press).

33 Young, I.M. (1990), *Justice and the Politics of Difference* (Princeton, NJ: Princeton University Press).

34 An alternative to identity I have given elsewhere (Philippopoulos-Mihalopoulos, A. (2006), '*Before*: Identity, Gender, Human Rights', *Feminist Legal Studies* 14:3), is the concept of *ipseity*, as the self-referring absence of description. See also different conceptualizations of identity, mainly through the third term of immigration in Kostakopoulou, D. (2005), 'On the Move; Ideas, Norms and European Citizenship: Explaining Institutional Change', *Modern Law Review* 68:2, 233–67.

35 La Torre, M. (2005), 'Europe's Constitution in Times of Empire', *European Public Law* 11:1, 47–54, reminds us that a constitution is *octroyée*, namely 'given, granted, conferred'.

36 See following section.

37 This is a community based on negation (Blanchot, M. (1988), *The Unavowable Community*, trans. P. Joris (New York: Station Hill Press)) and the recognition of its inoperability (Agamben, *The Coming Community*). For an analysis see Philippopoulos-Mihalopoulos, *Absent Environments*.

arena, becomes a dangerous cradle of totalitarian demo(no)logy.[38] While the nationalistic vein is certainly not an accepted (although a probable) alternative, I wonder whether a reference to a civic European *demos* is not itself to a non-inconsiderable degree exclusive of the *horror vacui* that have been trammelling the European geography ever since Westphalia. I doubt whether the European *demos* can any longer be constructed as existing, possible or even desirable – even after the 'thick' language of law, as Přibáň suggests.[39] It is time that we replaced our desire for a European *demos* with the absence that occupies what used to be the centre of the debate between *Gemeinshscaft/Gesellschaft*. This is the opportunity for spaces of negation to become present and assert their absence in ways that will finally undermine centralist, all-thematizing and essentialist wet dreams. Europe is the locus of an absent community whose void is to be filled by the recognition of precisely such an absence, and the realization that this is the core of the European (non-)project – indeed, that this is the one, total space either side of the horizon, that can promise the non-locatedness of the European utopia. The absence which presents itself in the enclaves of negation is the tool that shifts the search for utopia, from the traditional Habermasian ideality of communication, to the positivization of the reality of miscommunication. Both of them are utopias, busy with projecting an ideal present into a potential future; but the former begins with an imposition (the *demos* needs to be constructed) whereas the latter with an exposition of its very own limits (the *demos* is *absent*). It is the very 'bitterness', added to the Preamble after the Polish intervention,[40] that like a *memento vanitas* dictates the remembrance of the limitations and the need for a reverberation of the historical process that has led Europe to describe itself the way it does.

The space opened up by the constitutional 'no' is the locus of reconceptualization of the foundational concepts that still attempt to shape Europe. The growth of negativity within organizes the European self-description, no longer according to its traditional aspirations, but to a consciousness of the limits, an awareness of a historicity of horror, and a utopia that defines itself in its absence rather than in its ideality. It requires a move away from movement and into a stasis of self-reference, where alterity can no longer be defined as other. The epistemological tools for such a move are not to be found in constitutional theory but, as Everson

38 Přibáň, J. (2005), 'European Union Constitution-Making, Political Identity and Central European Reflections', *European Law Journal* 11:2, 135–53. See also Breda, 'A European Constitution in a Multinational Europe or a Multinational Constitution for Europe?'.

39 Law's role, I find *contra* Přibáň, is precisely the positivization of this absence through the enablement of the space in which such an absence can be enacted.

40 '... reunited after bitter experiences ...', Preamble to the Draft Constitutional Treaty; see Joerges, 'On the Disregard for History in the Convention Process'.

points out,[41] in a 'return to legal-theoretical first principles' in whose relentless redefinition European theory has traditionally excelled.

## The Constitutional Moment

Can there be a constitutional moment in Europe?[42] How can such a moment fit in a constitutional continuity of events, a chain of already existing moments of constitutional import, a series of administrative acts that write the text imperceptibly yet indelibly, a thick collection of *acquis communautaire* that includes everything from constituting treaties to deconstituting opinions?[43] How can the period of 'signalling' for a constitutional consolidation be signalled out from an existing constitutional historicity?[44] What kind of discontinuity does the constitutional moment bring in the European things – for indeed, the discontinuity between the before and after is its fundamental trait.[45] What is more, it is particularly counter-intuitive to expect the apparition of a constitutional moment within the present discussion's parameters, where text and context are tautological, and where the textuality of the constituting operation is inclusive of its very failure.

Once again, a redefinition is in order, one that moves the discussion away from the historical uniqueness of the constitutional moment, and into a temporally-informed understanding of the process that will take into consideration not only the necessary 'already' nature of the moment, but also its 'always' consistent repeatability. To revisit briefly systems theory, systemic operations of any kind take place only at present, with systemic memory being a present construction of a past event (but always at present).[46] At the same time, nothing new can ever exist

41 Everson, M. (2007), 'Is it just me, or is there an Elephant in the Room?', *European Law Journal* 13:1, 136–45, at 137.

42 Ackerman, 'Constitutional Politics/Constitutional Law', for the concept of constitutional moment; also Walker, 'Europe's Constitutional Momentum and the Search for Polity Legitimacy', and Maduro, M.P. (2005), 'The Constitutional Treaty and the Nature of European Constitutionalism', in Curtin, *The European Union Constitution*.

43 Amongst others, Shaw, J. (2000), 'Process and Constitutional Discourse in the European Union', *Journal of Law and Society* 27:1, 4–37; Closa, 'Deliberative Constitutional Politics and the Turn towards a Norms-Based Legitimacy of the EU Constitution'; Besselink, 'The Dutch Constitution, the European Constitution and the Referendum in the Netherlands'; Everson, 'Is it just me, or is there an Elephant in the Room?'.

44 Fossum, J.E. and Menéndez, A.J. (2005), 'The Constitution's Gift: A Deliberative Democratic Analysis of Constitution Making in the European Union', *European Law Journal* 11:4, 380–410, 385.

45 Ackerman, 'Constitutional Politics/Constitutional Law'.

46 Luhmann, N. (1995), *Social Systems*, trans. J. Bednarz, Jr. (Stanford, CA: Stanford University Press) and (2004), *Law as a Social System*, trans. K Ziegert, ed. F. Kastner, R. Nobles, D. Schiff and R. Ziegert (Oxford: Oxford University Press); also, see my dealings with systemic memory in 2007.

within the system: normative closure dictates the superimposition of the same norms, like a DNA spiral, that through minor adaptations, deals with new situations through the same evolving tools. In the above sense, every event is both already in the system (otherwise it could have never been recognized by the system as being located within its boundaries) and always presenting itself as a new present mnemonic construction. An event appears 'every time once' with a relentless capacity of self-generation as an already past yet present event. This simultaneity of systemic structures provides the setting for the relativization of current thinking on direct influence and control amongst social systems, while explaining in a non-linear way the systemic becoming. The benefit of such thinking to constitutional theory is clear: if the constitutional moment is always already there, 'every time once' as a constructed mnemonic event whose moment has already passed, then one would have to look elsewhere in order to locate that moment: not at the moment of discontinuity but at the total moment before and after, signalling and consolidation, constituting and constitutive, text and context in their full co-extensiveness. It is in that fold that the discontinuity of the constitutional moment is to be sought, thus denuding the text from the heightened dogmatics of constitutional theory and landing it back in the mundane embrace of the context.

Indeed, the constitutional moment remains a moment of discontinuity, but only *after* the discontinued has been mended back to a continuity of contextualisation. The constitutional moment is the disclosure of difference: it brings the exposition of the rupture between text and context in a laceration that can never be observed as such but only as the precondition of its mending. It is the rupture that can only be observed once the continuum has been re-established. If the continuum between text and context is the minimum democratic guarantee, then it is indeed only through the standpoint of the present, where the continuum is regularly reasserted, that the rupture can be observed. The totality of rupture/continuum is a past event, always already in the system, constructed every time once by the continuous constitutionality of the quotidian. The constitutional moment is precisely this fragmented totality of rupture/continuum between text and context that can only be observed from the present once the moment has already elapsed.

The rupture between text and context is the defining moment of constitutionalism because it represents the only moment where the two values face each other in an uncompromising asymmetry. Text and context take a flight on either side of the mirror, separately but reflected by the other, idols of mutual constitution that need to gather their difference in order to throw themselves back into their synthesis. One has to remember though that their synthesis remains fragmented, on the antipodes of Hegelian *Sittlichkeit*, in a parallel co-extensiveness that can never be communicated, can never be shared by either the text or the context. The tautology between them exhausts itself in a reflective coupling, consistently limited by their reciprocal ignorance of the limits of each other.

Extant in time, systemic topology and memory, the constitutional moment cannot be isolated from other moments preceding and following, all more or less constitutional. Arguably a more apt name for the constitutional moment would be the Deleuzian *entre-moment*. Thus Gilles Deleuze: 'This indefinite life does not itself have moments, however close together they might be, but only meantimes (*des entre-temps*), between-moments. It neither takes place nor follows, but presents the immensity of the empty time where the event can be seen that is still to come and yet has already passed ....'[47] A constitutional *entre*-moment is one that includes rupture and continuum between the constituting and the constitutive because it extends itself to a continuity of overlapping absence of a temporal or spatial anchorage, and installs itself as the unique mundanity of the event that keeps on occurring without its ever being able to be observed in isolation.

So, what is the merit of a constitutional (*entre*-)moment in the manner defined above? Simply, it returns the constitution to its cradle, releasing it from its uniqueness and letting it play with the commonplace. It brings it closer to its space of legitimation, while reserving a side of the mirror for the necessary rupture of its creation – the moment where the stasis becomes *octroyée*. And it does not judge a constitutional act from its success or failure – at least not in the usual understanding of the terms. Rather, it conceives of the constitution as constitutive of its failure, in that, regardless of whether a constitution is accepted or not, in its rupture between text and context, it has created the space of absence and of questioning that is part of the constitutional process. In that sense, the constitutional moment of Europe is still with us, all around us, in a state of invisibility that facilitates cognitive fumbling in the dark. On account of the 'no', the constitutional moment can still not be observed – it is yet to come – but is more potent and more constitutive of its *demos* of absence, its borderless identity and its textuality. We are still in the process of 'mending' the rupture, and for that, we Europeans find ourselves floating in a constitutional *entre*-moment of a revolutionary withdrawal.

47 Deleuze, G. (1997), 'Immanence: A Life ...', *Theory, Culture and Society*, 14:2, 3–7, 5. Of course Deleuze refers to his conception of immanent life, which could be shown to have some parallels with the European constitutional process, but that would go beyond the scope of the contribution. See also Deleuze, G. and Guattari, F. (1994), *What is Philosophy?* (London: Verso), 158, where the *entre-temps* is described as 'no longer time that exists between two instants; it is the event that is a meanwhile ... it belongs to becoming'.

# Chapter 5

# A Legal Mission: The Emergence of a European 'Rationalized' Natural Law

Henning Koch

## Lost in Translation

Accuracy in the legal thinking on the European Union may be lost in translation.

In the latest Liber Amicorum to a lawyer – in honour of the Dane, Claus Gulmann – Peter Biering has written an essay in Danish titled in English: 'The Court and the Napoleon'.[1] Gulmann has recently retired from the position as a judge at the European Court of Justice (ECJ) serving from 1994 until 2006 – formerly functioning as Advocate General. Originally he held the chair as professor of international law at the University of Copenhagen. Biering is presently a partner at the private law firm engaged as the permanent Legal Advisor to the Danish Government. Before that he was a senior diplomat in the Ministry of Foreign Affairs, in which capacity he conducted a considerable number of cases before the ECJ and the Court of First Instance of the European Communities (CFI).

With an explicit reference to the Opinion from 1991 on the EEA (European Economic Area) agreement,[2] in which, as is well-known, the Court characterizes the Community treaties as a new legal order of a constitutional nature,[3] Biering writes: 'The court has described the EU as *"a community of law"*. ... The meaning

---

1 Biering, P. (2006), 'Domstolen og Napoleonskagen', in Fenger, N. et al., *Festskrift til Claus Gulmann* (Copenhagen: Thomson), 68–82. Napoleon in the English translation is the name of the pastry (not Danish!). In Denmark the closest equivalent is called a Napoleon *Cake*. The metaphor is applied to the Constitutional Treaty. The author is quoting (p. 68) the Danish Foreign Minister arguing that this document is a Treaty not a Constitution in as much as you eat the cake, not Napoleon!

2 Opinion 1/91 (Draft Opinion on the EEA) [1991] E.C.R. I-6079; cf. Douglas-Scott, S. (2002), *Constitutional Law of the European Union* (London: Pearson/Longman), 517.

3 The original sentences in para. 21 run: 'In contrast, the EEC Treaty, albeit concluded in the form of an international agreement, none the less constitutes the constitutional charter of a Community based on the rule of law. As the Court of Justice has consistently held, the Community treaties established a new legal order ...', 31 I.L.M. 442 (1992), 459 (net-access through Westlaw). See also Case 294/83, *Parti Écologiste 'Les Verts' v. European Parliament* [1986] E.C.R. 1339 (para. 23), where it states, 'the European Economic Community is a Community based on the rule of law, inasmuch as neither its Member States nor its Institutions can avoid a review of the question whether the measures adopted

is stated somewhat more precisely in English: *"a community based on the rule of law"*'[4] (my translation, italics in original).

Now, the reader must imagine, that the first quotation is originally written in Danish (that is, 'retsfællesskab'[5]) as is the rest of his article, whereas the second emphasis in Biering's own text is in English; identical to the official version of the case. His essay goes on: 'The rule of law simply denotes, that the EU is governed by law and justice – and not by force.' He continues by stating that all institutional decisions must be authorized in the Treaty or in secondary legal acts. He then writes that rule of law means 'to be administered legally', and finally he concludes that the enforcement of the rule of law is 'the mission of the Court'. This is the role of the Court from a Danish perspective.[6]

There are three significant – and astounding – points to be stressed when confronted with this particular characterization of the EU and EU-law.

Firstly, the total absence of a precise reference to the authority in the treaties with regard to the exercise of judicial power, that is, TEC art. 220 (formerly art. 164).

Secondly, the restriction to the clichéd European idea depicting a dichotomy between sheer international brute force and civilized international legal power as a sufficient explanation for the continuous development of the EU.

Thirdly, the fact that the legitimacy of the EU and the Court is sought to be proven by way of a British concept: the rule of law. From a linguistic angle the most palpable translation of 'retsfællesskab' in a Danish context is *not* 'rule of law'. And from a conceptual point of view the hereby created connotations are misleading.

The devil is in the translation.

## The English Perspective

Let us begin by looking at the English understanding of this concept. In a much-used comprehensive textbook on Constitutional Law in the United Kingdom the authors' exposition begins with the mammoth A.V. Dicey. In 1885 he introduces

---

by them are in conformity with the basic constitutional charter, the treaty.' The role of the ECJ is more apparent in the 1991 decision.

4 Biering, 'Domstolen og Napoleonskagen', 82.

5 Cf. p. 6102 of the Danish version. Full text is not available in this language or in English in the database of the ECJ <www.curia.europa.eu>.

6 Compare the description of the creation of the Court practice by Antonio Tizzano, Advocate General since 2000, in Fenger et al., *Festskrift til Claus Gulmann*, 474: 'Mais elle [the Court] l'a fait, et l'a fait à notre avis, d'une façon cohérente et équilibrée, vu le cadre global dans lequel elle a oeuvré et continue à oeuvrer, en recourant à la fois à une méthode d'interprétation "dynamique", "fonctionnelle", "téléologique", et en se référant aux "buts", aux "finalités", à "l'esprit" des Traités, etc.'. In this way *he* describes 'sa mission et son rôle'.

a couple of guiding principles of the British constitution, 'foremost among these being the rule of law'.[7] Dicey defines it by three characteristics:[8] 1) 'the absolute supremacy or predominance of regular law as opposed to the influence of arbitrary power' with reference to the prerogative of the legislative power; 2) 'equality before the law, or the equal subjection of all classes to the ordinary law of the land' with respect to the judicial power and 3) 'that with us the law of the constitution, the rules which in foreign countries naturally form part of a constitutional code, are not the source but the consequence of the rights of individuals, as defined and enforced by the courts', once again relating to the exercise of judicial power.

As is shown, the classic British ideology of the rule of law lends much power to the courts, but according to this textbook the core aspect in a modern sense of rule of law is still: government according to law which equates 'the principle of legality'. And by law is meant written law: 'The rule of law serves as a buttress for democracy, since new powers of government may be conferred only by Parliament.'[9] In stressing the sovereignty of Parliament (or the sovereignty of national parliaments in treaty building) there is seemingly a correspondence between the Danish and the British meaning of the concept.[10]

But Bradley and Ewing's textbook does not aspire only to trot in the footsteps of Dicey. The authors insist on a supplementary definition of 'rule of law'. They say: 'The requirement that government be conducted according to law (the principle of legality) is a necessary condition for the rule of law; but insistence on legality alone does not ensure that the state's powers are consistent with values such as liberty and due process. This emphasis is found in case-law of the European Court of Human Rights.'[11] The concept of the rule of law in this broader version therefore has a more substantive content, and while Bradley and Ewing admit that this is a contested view in legal philosophy: 'Many would conclude [including the authors] that the rule of law in a strong sense thrives only alongside values of human dignity, liberty and democracy.'[12]

A mere reference by a Danish author to the British concept of 'rule of law' is therefore superfluous and inadequate.

7 Bradley, A.W. and Ewing, K.D. (2003), *Constitutional and Administrative Law*, 13th edn (London: Pearson/Longman), 93.

8 Dicey, A.V. (1960), *Introduction to the Study of the Law of the Constitution* (with an introduction by E.C.S. Wade), 10th edn (London: Macmillan), 202–3.

9 Bradley and Ewing, *Constitutional and Administrative Law*, 96–7.

10 Michel Rosenfeld (I) (2004) analyses the US concept of the rule of law in 'Constitutional Adjudication in Europe and the United States: Paradoxes and Contrast', *International Journal of Constitutional Law*, 2:4, 643–50.

11 Bradley and Ewing, *Constitutional and Administrative Law*, 96. This quoted piece of text did not form part of the 11th edition from 1993, thus antecedent to the Human Rights Act of 1998.

12 Bradley and Ewing, *Constitutional and Administrative Law*, 99. This conclusion is only found in the latest edition, too.

## The German Perspective

Now let us turn to a German textbook on European Law by Thomas Oppermann.[13] Oppermann, who served as an expert on EEC-law from 1960 to 1967 in the German Federal Ministry of Economy and was later appointed professor in Tübingen, uses the phraseology: 'Rule of Law im materiellen Sinne' as the trait of the EU.[14] Thus the discussed concept is twofold: we may speak of 'the rule of law' or the 'rule of law in a substantive meaning'.[15] What is the latter?

The rule of law today signifies a particular legal system governed by written as well as unwritten principles, so called 'general principles of law'.[16] The principles regard the separation of powers, judicial, including constitutional, review by courts, justiciable human rights, public authority only through law, effective complaint procedures, proportionality between means and ends, state responsibility (that is, liability without contract) and so on.

These elements constitute 'the community of law'. This is a literal translation of a German word: 'Rechtsgemeinschaft'.[17] As bluntly stated by Ingolf Pernice: 'Der Begriff der Rechtsgemeinschaft gründet sich auf den des Rechtsstaats, wie er sich in Deutschland herausgebildet hat.'[18]

This is the terminology of Walter Hallstein. Hallstein, born 1901, was one of the founding fathers of the EEC. In 1941 he was appointed Direktor des Instituts für Rechtsvergleichung und des Instituts für Wirtschaftsrecht at the University of Frankfurt, a university that he rebuilt in the democratic era after the war as its Rector for three years. He was permanent secretary of the Federal Chancellor's Ministry (1950) and the Ministry of Foreign Affairs (1951), both positions under Konrad Adenauer, and he was the first president of the European Commission (1958–67), winning the fundamental cases *Van Gend en Loos* (1963) and *Costa v. Enel* (1964) about direct effect and the supremacy of EEC law. He – a protestant – was elected as a member of the Bundestag representing the CDU (Christian Democratic Union) from 1969 to 1972.[19]

---

13 Oppermann, Th. (2005), *Europarecht*, 3rd edn (München: Beck).

14 Oppermann, *Europarecht*, 81.

15 Peczenik, A. (1995), *Vad är rätt? – Om demokrati, rättssäkerhet, etik och juridisk argumentation* (Stockholm: Norstedts Juridik), 60–61, 66–7, 196–9.

16 Critical to the notion of a substantive democracy is Hartley, T.C. (2003), *The Foundations of European Community Law*, 5th edn (Oxford: Oxford University Press), 133–5.

17 This term is used in the first sentence of the quotation from the German version of Opinion 1/91 in supra note 3.

18 Pernice, I. (2003), 'Begründung und Konsolidierung der Europäischen Gemeinschaft als Rechtsgemeinschaft', in Zuleeg, M. (ed.), *Der Beitrag Walter Hallsteins zur Zukunft Europas* (Baden-Baden: Nomos), 57. Zuleeg was a judge at the ECJ 1988–94.

19 Loth, W. (2003), 'Europäische Politik mit Walter Hallstein', in Zuleeg, *Der Beitrag Walter Hallsteins zur Zukunft Europas*, 28–37.

During the difficult deliberations over the Schuman Plan, Hallstein put through the demand – originally opposed by the French, including Jean Monnet – that a strong European Court of Justice was necessary for a new European order. He was of the firm conviction that the community had to be a community of law, and as such a court was mandatory.[20]

In his own comparative research on private law his theoretical stance was an anti-positivist attitude turned against the monopoly of law stemming from the nation state, since: 'Alle nationale Rechtsordnungen sind Zweige am Baum der abendländischen Kultur, also Erzeugnisse eines "einheitlichen Kulturkreises".' Hallstein's standpoint was inspired by Joseph Kohler's idea of law as 'Kulturerscheinung'.[21] In Kohler's later works he was chasing the identification of human universals.[22]

This, then, explains why Hallstein in his article 'Zu den Grundlagen und Verfassungsprinzipien der Europäischen Gemeinschaften'[23] often stressed, as the former President of the European Court of Justice (1994–2003), Gil Carlos Rodriguez Iglesias, has written:

> ... dass die Gemeinschaftsorgane verplichtet sind, die allgeimen Rechtsgrundsätze zu beachten, die sich aus dem Recht der Mitgliedstaaten ergeben und die als allgemeines ungeschriebenes Gemeinschaftsrecht das geschriebene Vertragsrecht ergänzen.

And Iglesias continues:

> Es sollte nicht übersehen werden, dass dem Grundrechtsschutz aufgrund von Gemeinschaftsrecht mittlerweile ein eigenes Gewicht zukommt. Das heist zum einen, dass Grundrechte auf Gemeinschaftsebene nicht auf dem kleinsten gemeinsamen Nenner beruhen, und zum anderen, dass dem Bürger aus dieser Entwicklung autonome Rechte erwachsen, die unter bestimmten Voraussetzungen auch von den nationalen Gerichten zu schützen ist.[24]

---

20 Steinberg, R. (2003), 'Grusswort anlässlich des Festaktes im Rahmen des Walter-Hallstein-Symposiums', in Zuleeg, *Der Beitrag Walter Hallsteins zur Zukunft Europas*, 107.

21 Rehbinder, E. (2003), 'Die Grundlegung einer europäischen Ordnungspolitik an der Universität Frankfurt am Main', in Zuleeg, *Der Beitrag Walter Hallsteins zur Zukunft Europas*, 22.

22 Whitman, J.Q. (2003) 'The Neo-Romantic Turn', in Legrand, P. and Munday, R. (eds), *Comparative Legal Studies: Traditions and Transitions* (Cambridge: Cambridge University Press), 321.

23 Hallstein, W. (1965), 'Zu den Grundlagen und Verfassungsprinzipien der Europäischen Gemeinschaften', in Hallstein, W. and Schlochauer, H.-J. (eds), *Zur Integration Europas: Festschrift für Carl Friedrich Ophüls* (Karlruhe: Müller), 1–18.

24 Iglesias, G.C.R. (2003), 'Begründung und Konsolidierung der Europäischen Gemeinschaft als Rechtsgemeinschaft', in Zuleeg, *Der Beitrag Walter Hallsteins zur Zukunft Europas*, 95.

What was the fundamental idea behind the European Economic Community in Hallstein's own words? In three ways it was intended to be a phenomenon of law: 'Sie ist Schöpfung des Rechts, sie ist Rechtsquelle und sie ist Rechtsordnung.'[25] Or in English: it is a system that creates law, that serves as a source of law and that constitutes a legal order.[26]

The creation of law was the imperative point: 'Das ist das entscheidend Neue, was sie gegenüber früheren Versuchen auszeichnet, Europa zu einigen. Nicht Gewalt, nicht Unterwerfung ist als Mittel eingesetz, sondern *eine geistige, eine kulturelle Kraft, das Recht.* Die Majestät des Rechts soll schaffen, was Blut und Eisen in Jahrhunderten nicht vermochten' (my italics).[27]

If you follow the Danish justification of the idea behind the EEC/EU and the ECJ compared to this outspoken ideology – you are far from half way to an understanding. In particular the mere reference to 'the principle of legality' is unsatisfactory. The Danish specialist in EU law explains the renunciation of war and conquest as also mentioned in my quotation of Hallstein, but he refrains from elaborating on what law then is in a European context.[28]

Hallstein regarded the development of the European integration as the result of an ongoing battle of law: a conglomerate of connections and conflicts of substantive interests and immaterial forces. He was therefore a lawyer in the true tradition of Rudolph von Ihering (1818–92) ('Kampf ums Recht', 1872) and especially his later developed 'Interessenjurisprudenz'.[29]

---

25 Hallstein, W. (1969), *Der unvollendete Bundesstaat. Europäische Erfahrungen und Erkenntnisse* (Düsseldorf and Wien: Econ), 33.

26 Later he added 'Rechtspolitik' (legal policy) in Hallstein, W. (1979), *Die Europäische Gemeinschaft*, 5th edn (Düsseldorf and Wien: Econ), 51.

27 Hallstein, *Der unvollendete Bundesstaat*, 33–4.

28 The Danish professor of European Law at the University of Copenhagen, Hjalte Rasmussen, seems to argue vehemently against the creation of law primarily from a pragmatic and strategic point of departure. He states that the rationale behind the legal literature critical to judicial activism, including his own famous *Habilitationsschrift* ((1986) *On Law and Policy in the European Court of Justice: A Comparative Study in Judicial Policymaking* (Dordrecht: Martinus Nijhoff)) 'always was that if the Court went too far too often, the member states one day would discover that the Court swallowed up their sovereignty. What the counter reaction then would be, one can only surmise'. Thus my translation from p. 698 of his textbook: Rasmussen, H. (2003), *EU-ret i kontekst*, 5th edn (Copenhagen: Thomson). At the same time he concludes p. 694 and p. 708 that the active role of the Court cannot be understood from a Danish legal philosophy point view maintaining the importance of predictability and objectivity, which indeed is true, but he does not replace this deficit with an analysis of the German influence or legacy – or gives any other plausible and coherent *legal* explanation for that matter. He only refers to fantasy in the minds of the judges and/or their propensity to policy making in the name of integration, p. 461.

29 Michael Kilian, M. (2001), 'Der Visionär – Persönliche Erinnerungen an Walter Hallstein', in Classen, C.D. et al. (eds), *In einem vereinten Europa dem Frieden der Welt zu dienen …*, Liber amicorum Thomas Oppermann (Berlin: Duncker and Humblot), 135.

Serving 'The Majesty of Law' – in Hallstein's perspective – is the mission of the court. A prime example of the canonization of 'das Recht' is article 6, paragraph 1, of the Treaty of the European Union (Amsterdam): 'The Union is founded on the principles of liberty, democracy, respect for human rights and fundamental freedoms, and the rule of law …' – already stated in the preamble of the Maastricht Treaty.[30]

## European Jurisprudence

In my interpretation this is exactly why the former president of the ECJ for almost ten years, Gil Iglesias, in his laudatory article to commemorate Walter Hallstein, expresses the view that there is no contradiction between the Court's role of being a 'motor of integration' and its role as 'the guardian of the Community Constitution'. It is much more about the former position being part of the latter: 'Mit anderen Worten: Die Wahrung des Rechts bedeutet auch die Wahrung und das "Ernstnehmen" der bei jeder Vertragsänderung wiederholt proklamierten Vertragsziele.'[31] In yet other words: there is a close link between the conservation of law and the creation of law[32] leached through the explicitly written purposes of the EC/EU regulation.[33]

But Iglesias' predecessor, the Danish judge Ole Due, presiding over the Court from 1988 to 1994, chooses another road. He wrote in Danish an article in 2001 on 'The interpretation methods of the ECJ and the Vienna Convention on the Law of Treaties'. Due stresses that the point of departure for the Court is most often 'the ordinary meaning to be given to the terms of the treaty', thereby quoting the first element of interpretation in article 31, paragraph 1, of the Convention. He then

30 Zuleeg, M. (2003), 'Der unvollendete Bundesstaat: Vision oder Realität?', in Zuleeg *Der Beitrag Walter Hallsteins zur Zukunft Europas*, 99–100.

31 Iglesias, 'Begründung und Konsolidierung der Europäischen Gemeinschaft als Rechtsgemeinschaft', 95. Former judge Pierre Pescatore writes in his article (1994) 'Jusqu'où le juge peut-il aller trop loin?' in the *Festskrift til Ole Due* (Copenhagen: Gad) (at 305): 'Tout au long des vicissitudes de la vie communautaire, et souvent à contrecourant, la Cour a pris l'attitude spontanément optimiste du juge, qui est de "prendre le droit au sérieux". Or, c'est précisément cet effect, de pure optique, qui a valu à la Cour d'apparaître comme "moteur du progress", alors qu'en réalité il s'agissait d'éviter l'enlisement progressif du processus.' This judge, who was a member of the Luxembourg delegation negotiating the original EEC treaty and a member of the Court for 18 years (1967–85), refers to Ihering and 'Kampf ums Recht' as well, see footnote 6 on p. 332.

32 The German version of the second sentence in the Opinion 1/91 para. 21 (compare supra note 3) runs: 'Nach ständiger Rechtsprechung des Gerichtshofes haben die Gemeinschaftsverträge eine neue Rechtsordnung geschaffen, …'. In French: 'Selon une jurisprudence constante de la Cour de justice, les traités communautaires ont instauré un nouvel ordre juridique …'. Both quoted from the database <www.curia.europa.eu>.

33 Cf. below.

continues: '... the formulations of EC rules more often than is the case with regard to national rules give rise to doubts. The EC Treaty makes use of broad, imprecise concepts, that are seldom defined in the text.'[34] He briefly mentions teleological interpretation, emphasizes the principle of '*effet utile*' and points to the increasing use of autonomously created 'general principles of law'.[35]

What is remarkable about president Due's theoretical contribution is that on the one side he discusses in great detail the principles of the Vienna Convention, although it did not enter into force until 1980, which is much later than many of the ground-breaking decisions by the ECJ as Due readily admits, and on the other side he makes no reference whatsoever to the fundamental authority of the ECJ, article 220.

The Danish president of the CFI, Bo Vesterdorf, in an article in the *International Journal of Constitutional Law* makes a clear connection between the acceptance of constitutional norms in the jurisprudence and article 220, continuing: 'From a more academic point of view, it is also widely accepted that the ECJ frequently resorts to interpretative techniques and trade-offs that are quite typical of constitutional adjudication.'[36]

## Law and Law

Now what is so interesting about this apparently 'invisible' first article in the Treaty's section on the Court of Justice?

It simply states, in the original English version, that the Court of Justice: 'shall ensure that in the interpretation and application of this Treaty *the law is observed*' (my italics). And in the original German: 'sichern ... *die Wahrung des Rechts* bei der Auslegung und Anwendung dieses Vertrags' (my italics).[37] By a simple word-

34 Due, O. (2001), 'EF-domstolens fortolkningsmetoder og Wienerkonventionen om Traktatretten', in *Festskrift til Ulf Bernitz* (Europarättslig Tidskrift), 73.

35 Due, 'EF-domstolens fortolkningsmetoder og Wienerkonventionen om Traktatretten', 74–5 and 79.

36 Vesterdorf, B. (2006), 'A Constitutional Court for the EU?', *International Journal of Constitutional Law* 4:4, 609–10. In his following article editor-in-chief Michel Rosenfeld (618–51) is not using article 220 as an authority. He writes: 'If one compares the ECJ and the Supreme Court, on the one hand, with the German Constitutional Court, on the other, one notices that neither of the former is explicitly empowered to engage in authoritative constitutional review whereas the latter is' (p. 620). Nor does he make any references to article 6, paras 1 and 2, of the Treaty of European Union (Amsterdam) when writing about the Court's protection of human rights. It is absolutely correct, though, that there is no specific EC/EU-constitutional text with specifically coined rights of a legally binding nature, as he states at p. 623.

37 The phraseology of the Treaty establishing a Constitution for Europe article I-29 uses the same words both in English and in German. In French it is: 'le respect du droit'.

for-word comparison 'the law' and 'Recht' are equivalent. Can we be sure? How does it sound in translation, not 'origination'?

An indirect way to sort this out would be to look at the German Basic Law. In article 20, subsection 3, it is written: '... the judiciary [shall be bound] by law and justice.' Or rather is translated into, because in German it states: '... die Rechtsprechung sind an Gesetz und Recht gebunden.' Now, would there be a conceptual difference in the German wordings between their Basic Law and their version of the EC Treaty?

Law is not the law. Or law may mean two things. It may stand for statutory law or it may connote statutory as well as non-statutory law (or, simplified, written/unwritten law). 'Recht' in German can also be 'gesetztes' or 'ungesetztes Recht' ('geschriebenes/ungeschriebenes Recht'). It is obvious that the German Basic Law refers to 'Recht' in the last meaning, since 'Gesetz' is mentioned specifically as the first concept. 'Recht' in this context therefore signifies a *thin* concept. As already mentioned, the 'unofficial'[38] German translation makes the following out of 'Gesetz und Recht': 'law and justice'. In this respect the whole phrase might be equivalent to the Roman law coupling of *lex* and *jus*.

What has all this to do with the European legal level?

Under the heading of 'Non-national law' former judge of the ECJ (1979–90), Thijmen Koopmans, has frankly stated:

> The impact of Community law on legal evolution is generally considered as illustrative of a new legal climate in which the course of legal evolution is not exclusively determined by the State and its institutions. It does not square with traditional legal theory based upon the sovereign State or a sovereign Parliament ... Representatives of Member States participate in Community legislation – often, not always. Law, however, is more than legislation, in Community matters as much as elsewhere, or even more. The distinction between '*ius*' and '*lex*' ... represents a general feature of the search for law. It is recognized by the EEC-treaty itself, as article 164 [now article 220] submits Community legislation to the requirements of legality.[39]

'Recht' in article 220 therefore covers a *thick* version of the concept, that is, 'gesetztes' plus 'ungesetztes Recht', as in the original English text: the law represents the total meaning of law and justice.[40] This nexus between the German

---

38 That is, a national legal text only has one official version: the national language.

39 Koopmans, T. (1994), 'Sources of Law: The New Pluralism', in *Festskrift til Ole Due*, 194.

40 Sceptical and critical of this interpretation, see Hartley, *The Foundations of European Community Law*, 133–5, cf. 79–83, and Rasmussen, *EU-ret i kontekst*, 167 and 461. See also O'Neill, A. (1994), *Decisions of the European Court of Justice and their National Implications* (London: Butterworths).

Basic Law and the Treaty on the European Community is very clear, explicit and decisive at least from a German point of view.[41]

Returning to Peter Biering's article, legality (or more correctly quoted 'legally administered') or in his preferred words 'the rule of law' (in the classical sense of legislation) is subsequently not an adequate description of the authority of the Court of Justice.[42] Though Biering actually uses the Danish version of the pair of concepts – 'lov og ret', albeit without a specific reference to article 220 – he does not offer the Koopmans explanation, that is, the understanding of 'community of law' as a 'Rechtsgemeinschaft'.[43]

The latter theoretical understanding explains the authority for 'the judicial activism' or 'Rechtsfortbildung' of the ECJ. According to the jurisprudence of the Court a host of 'general principles of (community) law' has been deduced from – or from time to time rather induced into[44] – the concept of 'Recht' or 'law' through the Zweigertsche concept of 'wertenden Rechtsvergleichung'[45] (value-oriented comparison of law), that is, the process of scanning for the best common solution in the traditions of the Member States. This development depicts Hallstein's idea of a 'sachlogische Metode', an autonomous creation of law through Community recourse to the common general principles of law of the Member States, a reference notably – and nobly – to the very unwritten principles of basic and human rights.[46]

## The German Stance

Clearly this production of law by the ECJ has been inspired by the exemplary detailed regulation of the German Basic Law and by the enormous and richly facetted precedence from the German Federal Constitutional Court.[47] And the

---

41 Pernice, I. (2004), 'Europäisches und Nationales Verfassungsrecht', *Walter Hallstein Institut-paper* 13/01, Humboldt Universität zu Berlin, 25 and 29–30. See also Häberle, P. (2005), *Europäische Verfassungslehre*, 3rd edn (Baden-Baden: Nomos), 152–3 and 400–404.

42 In article 230 (formerly article 173) it reads: 'The Court of Justice shall review the legality of acts …', and in German: 'Der Gerichtshof überwacht die Rechtmässigkeit der … Handlungen …'.

43 Häberle, *Europäische Verfassungslehre*, at 397 expresses it thus: 'die Spannung von "Gesetz und Recht" … steht zwischen Positivität und Wertung', and at 399: 'Ursprung dieser verschiedenen verfassungsrechtlichen Gewährleistungen ist der Gedanke des Vertrauensschutzes, ja letzlich die "Idee der Gerechtigkeit".' See also Oppermann, *Europarecht*, 140.

44 Koopmans, 'Sources of Law', 198.

45 Oppermann, *Europarecht*, 144.

46 Oppermann, *Europarecht*, 143 and 145–52.

47 Discreetly, Tizzano, in Fenger et al., *Festskrift til Claus Gulmann*, 472: 'Il faut cependant rappeler, en passant, que la protection de ces droits est entrée dans le système

political inevitability for the other Member States to follow suit has been supported by the fact that an ever-rising level of legal protection on the basis of human dignity has been and still is a precondition for continuous German membership of the European Union.

It must be well remembered that in the foundational phase of the European Economic Community, it was regarded by the allied powers out of security policy necessity that all Member States had to offer a 'sacrifice of sovereignty'[48] to the common good of Europe in order to prevent a perception by West Germany – itself now an occupied and divided nation – of falling sole victim to foreign powers, thereby nourishing a dangerous nationalistic return which could suck uncontrollably on a replay of the old stab-in-the-back legend.[49] Such a historic view demands a continuous solidarity on the part of the other members of the European Union to act accordingly.[50]

In order to be able to adopt the accession law to ratify the Maastricht Treaty on the European Union, Germany had to amend its own Constitution. The new article 23, subsection 1, in my translation runs: 'The German Republic participates in a realization of a united Europe through the development of a European Union, which is committed to democratic, rule-of-law [*rechtsstaatlichen*], social and federal principles as well as to the principle of subsidiarity, and which guarantees a protection of basic rights in all essentials comparable to the protection of this Basic Law.'[51]

Before this explicit constitutional amendment, two decisions from the Constitutional Court (Solange I and II) had unmistakably issued a reservation of sovereignty – or a 'warning' if you wish – with regard to the consequences for the validity of EC-regulation on German soil: firstly, until the human rights protection was substantially improved;[52] and secondly, only if it is no longer upheld at the

communautaire grace à la Cour (et également, pour render homage à la vérité, grace à l'impulsion de certaines Cours constitutionnelles) et a été ensuite insérée dans les texts …'.

48 Cf. Neuss, B. (2000), *Geburtshelfer Europas? Die Rolle der Vereinigten Staaten im europäischen Integrationsprozess 1945–1958* (Baden-Baden: Nomos), 276–7.

49 Cf. Lundestad, G. (1998), *'Empire' by Integration: The United States and European Integration 1945–1997* (Oxford: Oxford University Press), 23 and 27.

50 Cf. Koch, H. (2002), 'Det Europæiske Statsfællesskab – et trojansk næbdyr', in Pedersen, Th. (ed.), *Europa for Folket? – EU og det danske demokrati* (Magtudredningen) (Aarhus Universitetsforlag), 68–82.

51 Cf. Hirsch, G. (1999), 'Eine Grundrechtscharta für Europa?' (Vortrag am Walter Hallstein-Institut für Europäisches Verfassungsrecht der Humboldt-Universität zu Berlin am 5. Juli 1999), FCE 5/99, 4–5: 'Die konstituierenden Strukturen der deutschen Verfassungsordnung sind immun gegen Eingriffe der Gemeinschaftsorgane. Zu diesen Essentialia gehören die Rechtsprinzipien, die dem Grundrechtsteil des Grundgesetztes zugrundeliegen. Der Wesensgehalt der deutschen Grundrechte darf somit auch nicht durch Gemeinschaftsakte verletzt werden.' Hirsch was judge at the ECJ from 1994 to 2000.

52 Entscheidungen des Bundesverfassungsgerichts (BVerfGE) 37, 271 (Solange I) from 1974, cf. BVerfGE 89, 155 (Maastricht, nicknamed by some German legal

now achieved level[53] in the whole of the EU.[54] With the recent 'European Arrest Warrant Act Case' of 2005 the German Constitutional Court (temporarily) nullified the concrete legislation implementing the Framework Decision on the European Arrest Warrant and the Surrender Procedure between the Member States of the European Union, because the national act violates the provision in the German Basic Law on extradition of German citizens (article 16, subsection 2) in not meeting the legal requirements of proportionality. Only one dissenting judge found a direct violation of article 23, especially the principle of subsidiarity.[55] A new piece of legislation can therefore be expected to establish the necessary coherence between the two norm systems.

## The Purposes of the EC/EU

The creative interpretation by the ECJ is to a large extent due to – and legitimized by – the loose descriptions of the many *explicit purposes* of the EC/EU. It should be noted that these purposes formally are *intra* – not *extra* – *vires*, that is, forming a direct part of the legal source; in contrast to the mere preambular goals.

As Oppermann rightly puts it: 'Teleologische Auslegung und richterliche Rechtsfortbildung gehen öfters ineinander über.'[56] The purposive interpretation[57] signifies a judicial approach whereby the written text in its systematic context is 'opened up' in order to pursue the true meaning and spirit of the particular superior community norm.[58]

Michel Rosenfeld emphasizes that the French style ('the court "speaks" the law or the Constitution in the name of the republic as an indivisible whole') is more a formality covering the reality of the jurisprudence. He says: 'Viewed in the light of its constitutional jurisprudence, however, the ECJ – like, for that

---

commentators as 'Solange III') from 1993 stressing the concept of the Member States being 'Herren der Verträge'.

53 BVerfGE 73, 387 (Solange II) from 1986 and BVerfGE 102, 147 (Bananenmarkt) from 2000.

54 Oppermann, *Europarecht*, 153 and Douglas-Scott, *Constitutional Law of the European Union*, 440–41.

55 BVerfG, 2 BvR 2236/04 of 07/18/2005. Dommer Bross' dissenting opinion is found in paras 132–53.

56 Oppermann, *Europarecht*, 209.

57 Peczenik, *Vad är rätt?*, 362–77 and Zahle, H. (2005), *Praktisk retsfiloso* (Copenhagen: Chr. Ejlers), 71–2 and 272.

58 Lasser points out that the ECJ has adopted a *meta*teleological approach referring to: 'the purposes, values, or policies underlying not so much the *particular* piece of legislation at issue, but those underlying the EU's legal structure *as a whole*' ('meta' purposes) at 208, in Lasser, M.de S.-O.L'E. (2004), *Judicial Deliberations: A Comparative Analysis of Judicial Transparency and Legitimacy* (Oxford: Oxford University Press). I can lend my support to this conceptualization.

matter, Member State constitutional courts such as Germany's – is increasingly functioning more like a common law court. This is due, in part, to the generality of constitutional norms, and, in part, to the open-ended meaning of constitutional values, such as dignity, or constitutional principles, such as non-discrimination.'[59] And he continues: 'Finally, ECJ judgments have not remained static, since their length and content have evolved, if not their form. This evolution has been from a style and rhetoric that were thoroughly French to something somewhat closer to the U.S. model',[60] which he describes in few words: 'judges "make" or infer or construct the law.'[61]

Opponents from a civil law tradition might scornfully talk of 'free law'. Instead I find it more appropriate to talk about 'white letter law' supplementing the more concise, literal black letter interpretation. Needless to say there are still limitations. Obviously the particular interpretation is framed by the text of the provision in question, by its textual connection with the surrounding provisions, and by the total context. The letters on the lines cannot be ignored, but there are relevant elements 'in between and around' these lines to be considered as well, thus creating an interpretational conglomerate.

Rosenfeld makes an important observation:

> Although the nature of the arguments to which the Supreme Court and the ECJ resort overlap significantly, the purposes to which these arguments are put by each court differ widely. The Supreme Court uses different arguments *plurally* to ward off or defuse internal threats to its authority and to the prevailing constitutional balance. The ECJ, on the other hand, combines these arguments to bolster its metateleological approach, which it deploys as its main weapon against external threats. … For its part, the external threat to the ECJ, … is that posed by the member states and their constitutional courts, in particular. Moreover, that external threat extends not only to the ECJ but also to the EU itself.[62]

## The Danish Reception

How has this legal development been received in Denmark as a representative of Scandinavian realism?

---

59 Rosenfeld. M. (II) (2006), 'Comparing Constitutional Review by the European Court of Justice and the U.S. Supreme Court', *International Journal of Constitutional* Law, 4:4, 629–30, cf. 635.

60 Rosenfeld (II), 'Comparing Constitutional Review by the European Court of Justice and the U.S. Supreme Court', 640.

61 Rosenfeld (II), 'Comparing Constitutional Review by the European Court of Justice and the U.S. Supreme Court', 636.

62 Rosenfeld (II), 'Comparing Constitutional Review by the European Court of Justice and the U.S. Supreme Court', 645.

As its point of departure the Danish Supreme Court in our Maastricht case of 6 April 1998[63] rightly refers to article 164 (now article 220), ruling on a great number of age-long contested questions: on the ambiguity of the EC/EU powers, on the ECJ monopoly of interpretation, on contextual and teleological methodology and on the Court's creative enterprises. The Supreme Court states, as part of its *ratio decidendi*:[64]

> In pursuance of Article 164 of the Treaty, the European Court of Justice shall ensure that in the interpretation and application of the Treaty the law is observed, and under Article 173 of the Treaty the Court of Justice shall review the legality of acts of the institutions of the Community. ...
>
> The fact that the detailed determination of the powers vested in the institutions of the Community may give rise to doubts, and that the jurisdiction to give rulings concerning the interpretation of such questions is transferred to the EC Court of Justice cannot in itself be regarded as incompatible with the requirement for specification in sect. 20 of the Constitution.[65]

---

63 UfR (*Ugeskrift for Retsvæsen*) 1998.800 H (in the first footnote there is an explicit reference to the German Maastricht Case of 1993). For commentaries, see Spierman, O. (1998), 'Hvad kommer efter tyve? En analyse af Højesteretsdommen i "Grundlovssagen"', UfR (*Ugeskrift for Retsvæsen*), 325–35; Koch, H. (1999), 'Dansk forfatningsret i transnational belysning', *Juristen*, 213–28; Due, O. (1999), 'The Danish Ratification of the Maastricht Treaty before the Danish Supreme Court', in *Mélanges en homage à Michel Waelbroeck* (Bruxelles: Bruylant), 313–31; Harck, S. and Palmer Olsen, H. (1999), 'Decision concerning the Maastricht Treaty', *The American Journal of International Law*, 93:1, 209–14; and Rasmussen, H. (2000), 'Confrontation or Peaceful Co-existence? On the Danish Supreme Court's Maastricht Ratification Judgment', in O'Keefe, D. (ed.), *Liber Amicorum in Honour of Lord Slynn of Hadley: Judicial Review in the European Union Law* (The Hague: Kluwer Law International), 377–90.

64 According to the unofficial translation delivered by the Supreme Court.

65 Sect. 20, subsection 1, is framed as follows according to this particular translation: 'Powers vested in the authorities of the Realm under this Constitutional Act may, to an extent specified by statute, be delegated to international authorities set up by mutual agreement with other states for the promotion of international rules of law and co-operation.' In the Supreme Court's Judgment of 12 August 1996 on the admissibility (*locus standi*) of the case (UfR (*Ugeskrift for Retsvæsen*) 1996.1300H) the phrase 'to an extent specified by statute' was translated as 'to a more specified extent'. In the translation by the Ministry of Foreign Affairs the wording is: 'to such extent as shall be provided by statute'; cf. The Constitutional Act of Denmark, published by the Parliament in 1999, <www.folketinget.dk/pdf/constitution.pdf>. A historic description and an analysis of the use of sect. 20 (and sect. 42, subsection 6) is given in Koch, H. (2001), 'The Danish Constitutional Order', in Kellermann, A.E. et al. (eds) *EU-enlargement: The Constitutional Impact at EU and National Level* (The Hague: T.M.C. Asser Press), 109–16.

> The fact that the EC Court of Justice in its interpretation of the Treaty also attaches importance to factors of interpretation other than the wording of the provisions, including the objectives of the Treaty, is not in violation of the assumptions on which the Act of Accession was based, nor is it in itself incompatible with the demand for specification in sect. 20 (1) of the Constitution. The same applies to the law-making activities of the EC Court of Justice within the scope of the Treaty.

As can be seen, this is a very candid and far-reaching, actually somewhat overlooked, part of the Court's very long decision. It encompasses basically the whole judicial development of – and the applied methodology in – the ECJ. It also contains a reservation, though, with regard to the future.

The Supreme Court acknowledges the authority and monopoly of the ECJ, but maintains the Danish reserve sovereignty – if only in extraordinary cases:

> By adopting the Act of Accession it has been recognised that the power to test the validity and legality of EC acts of law lies with the EC Court of Justice. This implies that Danish courts of law cannot hold that an EC act is inapplicable in Denmark without the question of its compatibility with the Treaty having been tried by the EC Court of Justice, and that Danish courts of law can generally base their decision on decisions by the Court of Justice on such questions being within the limits of the surrender of sovereignty. However, the Supreme Court finds that it follows from the demand for specification in sect. 20 (1) of the Constitution, held against the Danish courts' access to test the constitutionality of acts, that the courts of law cannot be deprived of their right to try questions as to whether an EC act of law exceeds the limits for the surrender of sovereignty made by the Act of Accession. Therefore, Danish courts must rule that an EC act is inapplicable in Denmark if the extraordinary situation should arise that with the required certainty it can be established that an EC act which has been upheld by the EC Court of Justice is based on an application of the Treaty which lies beyond the surrender of sovereignty according to the Act of Accession. Similar interpretations apply with regard to community-law rules and legal principles which are based on the practice of the EC Court of Justice.

With regard to the last sentence one comment seems pressing, when testing the replacement of the words 'the EC act' by the words 'legal principles' in the last but one sentence: it shall be extremely difficult to establish any 'required' level of (higher) 'certainty' about a discrepancy in the interpretation of a legal principle created by the ECJ on the basis of an assumption of the existence of 'constitutional traditions common to the Member States' (art. 6, paragraph 2 of the Treaty of The European Union) compared to a national Danish interpretation of its own tradition, given that the very surrender of sovereignty is attached to evasive purposes.

This then is the Danish position at the present time. How does this understanding correspond to Danish theory on constitutional law?

The relevant rules on judicial power are found in article 3 and article 64 of the Constitutional Act of Denmark. The third sentence of article 3 states, 'Judicial authority shall be vested in the courts of justice', and the first sentence of article

64, reads, 'In the performance of their duties the judges shall be governed solely by the law.'[66]

In one of his classical studies which formed the basis of his contemporary textbook on Danish constitutional law, the preeminent, internationally renowned, legal scholar, Alf Ross took up an intransigent attitude with respect to the role of courts. He regarded the function 'to judge' as an executive role, in many ways similar to that of the administration's, in the sense that both branches of state only possessed the authority to issue legal acts and decisions: 'according to the law, bound by the law and in completion of the intentions of the law'.[67] Law in this connection being equivalent to formal, original (as Act of Parliament) or delegated legislation.[68]

Henrik Palmer Olsen in his doctoral dissertation (Habilitationsschrift) characterizes this standpoint as 'an almost caricatured law positivism'[69] – a position Ross, in his general theory of law, totally abstained from, which Olsen elegantly reveals.[70]

Ross's opportunistic interpretation must be understood as his postwar contribution to the social engineering of a social democratic welfare state centred on and fully controlled by the representative body in the heydays of Danish parliamentarism – and as his corresponding rejection of a more sophisticated model of state powers in neutral equilibrium. In the same study he described the doctrine of the separation of powers as 'a programme for the liberal state'.[71]

66 The Constitutional Act of Denmark of 5 June 1953, <www.folketinget.dk/pdf/constitution.pdf>.

67 Ross, A. (1959), *Statsretlige Studier* (Copenhagen: Nyt Nordisk / Arnold Busck), 68, cf. 53–4 and 64. Of course Ross also stressed the differences between the judicial and the executive power. The former is in possession of the residual competence between the two and is guaranteed total independence from the legislator, the ministers and the administration in a personal as well as organizational meaning (but as indicated not in the material sense!).

68 This was not an isolated, idiosyncratic position. Russell Hardin refers to the fact, that the German lawyer and social scientist Hermann Heller in 1933 defined constitutionalism as government entirely by the legislature. He quotes Heller's definition from the Encyclopaedia of Social Sciences: 'Thus in the constitutional state the legislative and governmental agencies enjoy a virtual monopoly of political power to the exclusion of the administrative and the judicial' (Heller, H. (1993), 'Power, Political', in Seligman, E.R.A. and Johnson, A. (eds), *Encyclopaedia of the Social Sciences* (New York: Macmillan), XII, 300–305, at 301), see Hardin (1999), *Liberalism, Constitutionalism and Democracy* (Oxford: Oxford University Press), 'Preface' at ix.

69 Olsen, H.P. (2005), *Magtfordeling. En analyse af magtfordelingslæren med særligt henblik på den lovgivende magt* (Copenhagen; Jurist- og Økonomforbundet), 296 ['Separation of Powers – An analysis of the theory of the separation of powers with a special attention to the legislative power]. The book includes a 30-page summary in English.

70 See Ross, A. (1974), *On Law and Justice* (London: Stevens & Sons), 29–107, and cf. Olsen, *Magtfordeling*, 276–82 and 291–7.

71 Ross, *On Law and Justice*, 25.

His enormous influence over the minds of Danish lawyers, politicians and civil servants from the 1960s until recently[72] did not reflect a majority position from a legal historical perspective. His clinical definition of the role of judges in a constitutional context has very few – if any – predecessors or successors.

Knud Berlin, who taught constitutional law at the University of Copenhagen from 1910 to 1934 in the labile incipiency of parliamentarism, writes in his textbook:

> And even if judges must be governed by the law as laid down by the legislative power, the statutory interpretation to be applied by the judiciary does not consist in slavish submission to the letter of the law, and where the words of the law are uncertain, the law can only be definitely established through case law. Thus, the courts in fact create law, and even more so where no specific statutory authority exists, and where the courts must therefore themselves act as legislators in order to be able to decide a given legal issue, by finding and formulating the rule of law on the basis of fundamental statutory principles or legal and cultural tradition.[73]

Poul Andersen, who is normally regarded as the father of Danish Administrative Law, was responsible for teaching constitutional law at the same university before and during the Second World War. In his comprehensive and delayed textbook, published after the latest revision of the Danish Constitution in 1953, he states:

> In the provision of the Constitution (Article 64, first sentence) stating that the courts must be governed by the law, 'law' means 'valid law', that is to say, not merely rules of law as laid down by statutes in the formal sense, but also orders and regulations; not merely general statutes, but also provisional statutes and the Constitution; not merely written law, but also unwritten law.[74]

Max Sørensen from the University of Aarhus, former president of the European Human Rights Commission (1968–72) and former judge at the ECJ (1972–75), was the legal expert who originally drafted the new provision, Article 20 of the Danish Constitution providing the legal authority for the Government and the Parliament in the future to access the EEC without a formal amendment according to the traditional procedure of article 88. In his textbook on constitutional law he writes:

---

72 He held the chair in Constitutional Law 1958–69, but his textbook from the first (1959) until the posthumous edition in collaboration with Ole Espersen (1980) was part of the mandatory curriculum until 1986, when the present textbook by Henrik Zahle was published.

73 Translation by Helle Pals Frandsen from Berlin, K. (1939), *Den danske Statsforfatningsret* (Copenhagen: Nyt Nordisk / Arnold Busck), Part 2, p. 308.

74 Translation by Helle Pals Frandsen from Andersen, P. (1954), *Dansk Statsforfatningsret* (Copenhagen: Gyldendal), 576–7.

On the other hand, the fact that a judge in his judicial capacity solely has to be governed by the law does not imply that he only has to apply the rules laid down by formal statutes. In this context, the word 'the law' must be taken to mean 'valid law'. This term comprises not just formal statutes, but also orders and regulations, customary law and unwritten legal doctrines as expressed in case law, and generally the factors normally included in the legal and judicial method which is generally accepted by society.[75]

My predecessor as professor of constitutional law at the University of Copenhagen, Henrik Zahle, who so suddenly and so sadly passed away in July 2006, is the author of the textbook of today, that has now been used over a 20-year period and has appeared in four editions including a preliminary. As part of his constitutional legacy, he states:

Undoubtedly, this rule [Sect. 64, subsection 1] does *not* imply that judges are only to comply with statutory law as adopted by the Danish Parliament and affirmed by the Government. ... Judges are bound by statutory law. Statutory law is a part of the legal framework to be applied in deciding an individual case. We have other sources of law than statutory law, i.e. legal custom, case law, legal literature, legal and cultural tradition.[76]

Of law in 'a technical sense' – it is not the issue, he maintained. And he referred specifically to 'law and justice of the land'[77] *and* in the same breath to the first principal figure of Danish constitutional theory, Henning Matzen. Matzen lived from 1840 to 1910 and produced a constitutional textbook in three volumes in the period 1881–88 in the most turbulent years of Danish constitutional strife between King and Parliament. His book appeared in four editions, the last after the turn of the century. Matzen's interpretation of the much-mentioned word 'law' from article 64 was simply: 'So, like lex terrae in our older law, this expression equals law and justice of the land'.[78]

Denmark, too, as part of a new European order is at the beginning of a post-parliamentarian age.

75 Translation by Helle Pals Frandsen from Sørensen, M. (1973), *Statsforfatningsret* (Copenhagen: Jurist- og Økonomforbundet), 157–8.

76 Translation by Helle Pals Frandsen from Zahle, H. (2001), *Dansk forfatningsret II – Regering, forvaltning og dom*, 3rd edn (Copenhagen: Chr. Ejlers), first part of quotation p. 104 and second part p. 106.

77 Zahle, *Dansk forfatningsret II*, 104.

78 Translation by Helle Pals Frandsen from Matzen, H. (1899), *Den danske Statsforfatningsret* (Copenhagen: Universitetsforlaget (J.H. Schultz)), Part 3, 3rd edn, 295.

## Conclusion

As I have tried to describe, inaccuracy – partly due to poor 'cultural translation' in the handling of foreign basic concepts of a legal philosophical kind relevant to European constitutional law – as well as a lack of knowledge of the German intellectual positions and political influence has overshadowed the understanding of the legal mission of the ECJ, which is safeguarding the autonomous emergence of a 'rationalized' European natural law.

The rationality indicates a moral choice. A choice based on the conviction that the Member States are able to choose and construct the common good for European citizens as part of the 'Vergangenheitsbewältigung' of the common European heritage in order to strive to avoid a repetition of the disasters of the twentieth century. In this endeavour there is a melancholic element of atonement which is facing backwards and a steadfast element of prevention which is pointing forward. This intellectual politico-legal enterprise forms part of what I would prefer to call 'constitutive European Law', instead of European constitutional law, thereby removing any connotations of the necessity of a *demos* or *demoi* – but hopefully in the long run making a contribution to a true feeling of 'a unity of diversity', which is more valid than just a motto in a Constitutional Treaty.

The law and justice of the EU is governed by a *telos*, or rather multiple *teloi*, as prescribed in the relevant treaties. The constitutive European Law serves as a corrective binding element to the Member States' parliamentarian, administrative and judicial decisions.

This legal construction is produced through two, in principle different, mechanisms of 'judicial activism'. Firstly, by the inclusion of a revitalized source of law: law in the meaning of law and justice. Secondly, by the application of purposive (teleological) interpretation methods and so on in order to further the creation of a unified European value order.[79]

In the Danish legal literature there has been a good deal of focus on the latter aspect, whereas the former – and most fundamental – issue has been heavily underexposed; or at maximum revealed in minor articles primarily in French or English scattered in numerous *Festschrifts*!

79 Koch, H. (2007), 'The Right of Resistance', *Scandinavian Studies in Law*, 52, 155–86. Rosenfeld rightly stresses an important ideological difference here between Europe, especially Germany, and the United States. He says: 'In the American context, values and policies cannot be directly linked to the Constitution but, rather, emerge in the broader context of the Constitution as law embedded in the American rule-of-law tradition', cf. Rosenfeld (I), 'Constitutional Adjudication in Europe and the United States', at 651. This is due to the Lockean philosophy of 'human autonomy'. See also 650 and 661–2. In the Treaty establishing a Constitution for Europe (Official Journal of the European Union C 310 of 16 December 2004), it says in article I-19 para. 1: 'The Union shall have an institutional framework which shall aim to: promote its values, advance its objectives ….' One of these institutions is The European Court of Justice.

# PART 2
# AN EVER CLOSER UNION – AN EVER LARGER MARKET: LAWYERS AND THE TRANSNATIONAL CONSTRUCTION OF EUROPEAN INSTITUTIONS AND MARKETS

# Chapter 6

# Introduction: An Ever Closer Union – An Ever Larger Market: Lawyers and the Transnational Construction of European Institutions and Markets

Mikael Rask Madsen

It has become commonplace in law and political science to analyse European legal integration starting with the ever-changing institutional order of Brussels. Long dominant, this 'institutionalist approach', however, tends to construe European construction mainly in analytical terms deriving – implicitly or explicitly – from the national construction of the state. The state has become a more or less clear *Leitmotiv*, even an implicit ideal type, in the effort to explain a whole series of European transformations: from processes of constitutionalization (*in lieu* of a constitution), to claims concerning the rise of European civil society (*in lieu* of actual participatory democracy participation). There is no doubt, of course, that the issues of constitutionalization and democratization of Europe, as we saw in the first part of this book, are both central and important, yet, European legal integration as a broader phenomenon can be captured neither by an analysis of *only* these processes, nor by other approaches that derive mainly from pre-constructions stemming from the nation-state.[1] Generally, this part suggests that it might be beneficial to examine these issues in the context of how a set of increasingly powerful free-market dynamics have come to influence European legal integration. The paradox is that these free-market dynamics are on the one hand institutionalized in the European treaty complex, and on the other hand only partly guarded by the supranational order provided by the European institutions. Hence European legal integration is neither just an institutional progression increasingly resembling the state, nor simply an entirely market-driven enterprise,

1 One of the recurring dilemmas as to understanding European legal integration is the fact that the dominant institutionalist view of Europe tends to construct a limited object of study which is only vaguely differentiated from the on-going political quarrels of European politics. See further in Kauppi, N. and Madsen, M.R. (2007), 'European Integration: Scientific Object or Political Agenda?', *Praktiske grunde - Tidsskrift for kultur- og samfundsvidenskab*, 1, 28–31. See also Rumford, C. and Delanty, G. (2005), *Rethinking Europe: Social Theory and the Implications of Europeanization* (London: Routledge).

yet the tension between the two appears central for understanding the broader social construct of European Law.

It is the basic claim of this part of the book that if European legal integration has to be analysed more comprehensively, it has to be reconsidered with respect to at least two processes of varying historical impact: an institution-building process and a market-making process. Thinking of Europe – and more specifically European law – in terms of intertwined processes of institution-building and market-making suggests that the main dynamics might be found elsewhere, or at least on different levels, than what is often assumed in both law and political science. In this respect, all chapters assembled in this section agree on the point that the only way to carry out such an analysis is to break with the tradition of thinking of the European level as a residual to the national level, that is, to reframe the object of study in a more transnational fashion. In her chapter, Inger-Johanne Sand particularly underscores that the objective is not simply to give up on institutions in this regard but to resituate them within a more transnational framework, which is both more dynamic and uncertain than what is normally assumed in European studies. The remaining chapters by Yves Dezalay and Bryant Garth, Antoine Vauchez and Antonin Cohen moreover claim that legal actors might provide the 'missing link' between these processes. What at first glance might appear as separate social spheres – institutions and markets – might in fact be linked if one examines the role of legal actors as intermediaries. These chapters in each of their own ways view European lawyers as brokers, having multiple roles as, among others, *institution builders* and *market makers*, as well as *constitution builders* and *democracy makers*.[2] It is the overriding claim of this part that such approaches allow for a more holistic view of the broader processes of European legal integration.[3] Thus, the objective is to rethink these processes as interdependent and co-related producers of a broader European legal space made up by both markets and institutions, as well as processes of democratization and constitutionalization.

## Institutions and Markets

Historically, the blending of the market and the fabrication of an institutional structure has been an issue practically from day one of the process commonly referred to as European integration. The European institutions and the common market were not successive developments but integrated processes from the

2 The notion of 'Democracy Makers' draws on Guilhot, N. (2005), *The Democracy Makers: Human Rights and the Politics of Global Order* (New York: Columbia University Press).

3 See further in Madsen, M.R. (2006), 'Transnational Fields: Elements of a Reflexive Sociology of the Internationalisation of Law', *Retfærd*, 3:114, 23–41. See also the theoretical part of Kauppi, N. (2005), *Democracy, Social Resources and Political Power in the European Union* (Manchester: Manchester University Press).

outset. The original European construction of the Cold War period was obviously very focused on institutional solutions and marked by a strong ideology of saving Europe from both its own destructive forces and the expansion of Soviet-style Communism.[4] Another response to these multiple challenges was to mobilize the market – both as a constraint and as an opportunity – in the process of integrating a Europe which had fallen victim to its own devastating rivalries;[5] that is, to move the European 'contests' to a new semi-regulated playing field in the form of a common market. The very first step towards European integration, the European Coal and Steel Community (ECSC), had the precise purpose of developing a common market which at one and the same time would help deter future military conflicts in Europe. The ECSC also saw the invention of European law as the tool for achieving these ends. Yet as Antoine Vauchez points out in his chapter, early European law and institutions were very different from what is often now assumed. It was a fragmented legal order concerned with legal issues of a very limited scope, and operating only on an occasional basis.[6] Furthermore, it was a legal order where the agendas of European legal integration and European political integration were anything but separated. This, however, served a purpose in itself, namely to build up the legitimacy of law as the means for political transformations.[7] Moreover, this original construction of European law was to become part of its legacy in the sense that one of the most striking dynamics of this legal field was to remain its meddling with the political integration agenda.

These interplays of market logics and institutional and legal dynamics were to be taken to a whole new level with the Rome Treaty signed in 1957. With the agreement on a Customs Union, a process of further market-making was made possible. This not only triggered the rise of larger European markets but eventually also transnational competitions within formerly closed – even monopolized – professional milieus. Focusing on the world of legal professionals, Yves Dezalay and Bryant Garth's chapter takes this analysis to new grounds by suggesting that US law firms in fact played a pivotal role in the construction of a European *legal market*. From the beginning, the opening of European markets in fact implied international and transnational processes. Yet, it is equally clear from recent research that these transformations were far from separate from the ideals

4 See Cohen, A., Dezalay, D., and Marchetti, D. (2007), 'Esprits d'État, entrepreneurs d'Europe', *Actes de la recherche en sciences sociales*, 166/167, 4–13.

5 This process of mutual destruction is masterfully captured in Charle, C. (2001), *La crise des sociétés impériales: Allemagne, France, Grande-Bretagne 1900–1940* (Paris: Seuil).

6 Although it is often ignored, it is important to note that the rise of European law was also influenced by the processes taking place under the auspices of the Council of Europe, in particular the development of the European human rights institutions.

7 This is explored in Madsen, M. (2007), 'From Cold War Instrument to Supreme European Court: The European Court at the Crossroads of International and National Law and Politics', *Law and Social Enquiry* 32: 1, 137–159.

of federalizing Europe and, thus, the constitutionalization and democratization debate addressed in the previous part.[8] The federalist question and its associated institutional issues were always very present, not only during the negotiations of the founding treaties but also in the first major decisions of the European Court of Justice on 'direct effect' and 'supremacy'.[9] When read in the context of Antoine Vauchez's analysis, the famous notion of the 'ever closer Union' might in fact be better understood if it is seen as part of this twin-process of institutions and markets and not only in respect to questions of civil participation and institutional engineering.

These interplays also confirm the overriding thesis that the rise of European law as such is linked to this grand scheme of both institution-building and market-making. In the process of achieving this by all means uncertain objective, European law and associated legal institutions eventually – and somewhat by surprise – became very central engines for securing these goals. It is well-known that the ECJ in this regard came to play the role as an engine of integration.[10] On the political and institutional level, this continuous development was further fuelled by the initiatives of the Delors administration of the mid-1980s and especially the Single European Act (1986). In her chapter, Inger-Johanne Sand focuses on the construction of the boundaries of this new and ever-expanding market. She particularly examines the complex ways in which procedures and practices were progressively constructed in interplays between institutions taking unintended trajectories. There is not much doubt that the way in which European law was to help construct an 'ever larger market' was not only partly foreseen. This development was also largely due to the way in which the regulation of the free movement of goods, services, capital and persons was interpreted in close symbiosis by the ECJ and the Commission; these institutions were at one and the same time both seeking to enhance institutional powers and expand the market. Yet Inger-Johanne Sand suggests that this was to a large extent an unexpected development and in many ways more a discontinuity than continuity of the original plans. Her conclusion is that such hypermodern legal constructs cannot be understood as simple legal transplants but have to be re-conceptualized in terms of transnational processes;

---

8 See, for example, Cohen, A. (2007), 'Constitutionalism without Constitution: Transnational Elites between Political Mobilization and Legal Expertise in the Making of a Constitution for Europe (1940s–1960s)', *Law & Social Inquiry* 32:1, 109–35.

9 Recent attempts at revisiting the historiography of European legal integration make this very clear. See particularly Boerger, A. (2007), 'The Background of the Institutional Set Up of the European Court of Justice: Revisiting the Negotiations on the ECSC and the EC', and Rasmussen, M. (2007), 'How to Revolutionise European Law? A History of the European Court of Justice from 1958 to 1964', both papers presented at the conference, 'The Historical Roots of European Legal Integration', University of Copenhagen, 26 October 2007.

10 See, for example, Rasmussen, H. (1986), *On Law and Policy in the European Court of Justice* (Dordrecht: Nijhoff).

that is, the object of study can be neither limited to specific institutional designs nor demarcated within the traditional dichotomy of national/European.[11]

## Law, Lawyers and Transnational Legal Processes

Building on these findings, Inger-Johanne Sand makes a case for then exploring these processes in terms of communication following Niklas Luhmann. Another equally relevant suggestion is found in the remaining chapters by Antonin Cohen, Yves Dezalay and Bryant Garth, and Antoine Vauchez. They use the sociology of Pierre Bourdieu to point out the fact that the 'missing link' might very well be the very operators of these processes: the jurists. However, they do not claim that the solution is simply to bring the social actors back in, but that the relative autonomization of European law is closely linked to the rise of a set of European legal actors differentiating the practice of European law. From the point of view of both law and legal sociology, this can hardly be considered a radical suggestion, yet it reveals the fact that knowledge on European legal professionals is close to non-existent.[12] To some extent this is due to the way in which the leading studies of European legal integration have almost entirely focused on institutional aspects. Authors such as Alec Stone Sweet, Wayne Sandholtz and Neil Fligstein have mainly used a combined governance and institutionalist perspective in the analysis of European integration through law.[13] In the related neo-functionalist research agenda, other leading US scholars such as Joseph Weiler, Anne-Marie Slaughter and Karen Alter have equally contributed to securing the ECJ a central place in the analysis of what is European integration.[14] Although these studies do not themselves analyse legal actors *per se*, they do not claim that the rise of legal professional practices on a European level are unimportant. The jurists have

11 See in this respect the chapter by David Nelken included in the fourth part of this book.

12 For a long time the only source was a single article: Schepel, H. and Wesseling, R. (1997), 'The Legal Community: Judges, Lawyers, Officials and Clerks in the Writing of Europe', *European Law Journal* 2, 165–88.

13 The titles of their works are in themselves telling of this academic enterprise: Stone Sweet, A. (2004), *The Judicial Construction of Europe* (Oxford: Oxford University Press); Sandholtz, W. and Stone Sweet, A. (1998), *European Integration and Supranational Governance* (Oxford: Oxford University Press); Stone Sweet, A., Sandholtz, W. and Fligstein, N. (2001), *The Institutionalization of Europe* (Oxford: Oxford University Press).

14 Mattli, W. and Slaughter, A-M. (1998), 'Role of National Courts in European Integration', in Slaughter, A-M., Stone Sweet, A. and Weiler, J. (eds), *The European Court and National Courts: Doctrine and Jurisprudence* (Oxford: Oxford University Press); Weiler, J. (1994), 'A Quiet Revolution: The European Court of Justice and its Interlocutors', *Comparative Political Studies* 26:4; Alter, K. (2001), *Establishing the Supremacy of European Law: The Making of an International Rule of Law in Europe* (Oxford: Oxford University Press).

just remained '*terra incognita*' in the analysis of European legal integration, as Antoine Vauchez bluntly puts it.

In his chapter, Antonin Cohen provides a detailed view of the way in which legal actors were mobilized during the major institutional make-over which the drafting of the European Constitution implied. Cohen's analysis concerns both the structural level and the level of agency. He specifically seeks to establish a structure of relations between a transnational European political space and an international academic field. The point is that the treaty reform process was the product of a circulation of legal categories and ideas that finally made it into the European Convention and ultimately European Constitution. Such an analysis is in fact closely linked to the studies presented in the chapters by Antoine Vauchez as well as Yves Dezalay and Bryant Garth. All authors claim that legal actors have been attracted to the European construction since the late 1940s. Yet, rather than accepting the idealistic idea of the self-fulfilling prophecy of law – that law on a European level is simply the natural progress towards an eventually normalized European 'rule of law' – they seek a very different explanation. They argue that law and legal expertise from the outset of European integration became a powerful resource in the more general competitions taking place at the emerging field of power in Brussels. Investments in institutions and new markets not only went hand in hand, they were part of broader international transformations concerning defining the proper legal model for international and transnational exchanges.

Inger-Johanne Sand's chapter provides an alternative analytical path for understanding the same processes, with the suggestion of looking into forms of communication. It is however the common view of all these chapters that European legal integration necessarily has to be understood as a transnational process rather than what is generally the norm. One way of operationalizing such an approach is to include the interplay of the European institutions and market in this analysis. Moreover, such an approach helps break with the implicit assumption in studies of European integration that some more or less hidden rationale drives processes of European legal integration. More concretely, this approach breaks with the assumption that European legal integration follows a sort of rationalization process as for example prescribed in Max Weber's sociology of law. Inger-Johanne Sand relies on Niklas Luhmann to explain how the interplay of political, economic and legal logics produced what were by all accounts by all means surprising legal and institutional developments. The Bourdieuian approach used in the chapters of Antonin Cohen, Yves Dezalay and Bryant Garth, and Antoine Vauchez in fact point to a similar phenomenon by challenging the implicit connection between the rise of a European rule of law and a more general normalization of European legal and political affairs. What is implied by such structural sociological approaches is not only related to the outcome of specific interplays of law and markets, but is also highly revealing in respect to the processes of constitutionalization and democratization addressed in the previous part. Basically, European law is not simply produced within a specially fabricated framework – be it the Convention drafting the European Constitution Treaty, the ECJ or the rules of the inner market

– but is the dynamic output of a series of transnational processes which since the beginning of the European adventure have tended to take surprising turns. Comprehending these 'turns' and thus making them somewhat less surprising can in fact only be achieved if one is ready to view the paradox of the interplay of markets and institutions as a fundamental dynamic – and driver – of European legal integration, rather than analysing these processes separately.

# Chapter 7

# Re-Structuring States by Exporting Law: American Law Firms and the Genesis of a European Legal Market

Yves Dezalay and Bryant Garth

The majority of the analyses of the role of law in the construction of Europe are either implicitly or explicitly built on an idealistic vision according to which advances in the role of law in Europe are part of a more general phenomenon of the growth – even a return[1] – of law in the sense of giving judges a major role as arbiters of the political game.[2] The consolidation of a Europe of law would then belong to an encompassing general 'rights revolution',[3] brought by legal professionals who are assuming their proper role as defenders of public liberty against arbitrary or unreasonable exercises of state power.[4]

Instead of this teleological perspective of the universal progress of law (and through the law), we have elected to examine the transformations in legal practice in Europe as one of the means – and effects – of a competition among different expertises and different fractions of elites in national fields of state power. This internal competition reappears as part of an international competition about the imposition of a dominant legal model – the so-called 'rule of law'. The large corporate law firms of Wall Street – and their imitators from the City of London – constructed international as well as European markets in business law. Later, the major transnational NGOs emerged to adopt the same combination of lobbying and legal activism inspired by US practices.

---

1 Cohen-Tannugi, L. (1989), *Le droit sans l'Etat. Sur la démocratie en France et en Amérique* (Paris: Puf); (1985), *La métamorphose de la démocratie* (Paris: Odile Jacob).

2 Shapiro, M. and Stone Sweet, A. (2002), *On Law, Politics and Judicialization* (Oxford: Oxford University Press); Hirschl, R. (2004), *Towards Juristocracy: The Origins and Consequences of New Constitutionalism* (Cambridge, MA: Harvard University Press); Guarnieri, C. and Pederzoli, P. (2002), *The Power of Judges: A Comparative Study of Courts and Democracy* (Oxford: Oxford University Press); Tate, N. and Vallinder, T. (1997), *The Global Expansion of Judicial Power* (New York: New York University Press).

3 Epp, C.R. (1998), *The Rights Revolution: Lawyers, Activists and Supreme Courts in Comparative Perspective* (Chicago, IL: University of Chicago Press).

4 Halliday, T.C. and Karpik, L. (1997), *Lawyers and the Rise of Western Political Liberalism* (Oxford: Clarendon).

The Cold War and fights over global hegemony have helped nourish the competition between elite professionals, and in that global competition the value of resources of symbolic capital strongly depends on positions occupied in national spaces. Advances or losses in the value of different varieties of national legal capital must therefore be examined in the light of their own political histories. This analysis must be undertaken not only for the merchants of law but also for the legal activists located in NGOs. Their authority and credibility must be refurbished constantly through investments in national fields of state power. That investment is necessary to avoid the risk of obsolescence or devaluation of legal capital, which is always threatened by other forms of state expertise.

The genesis of the legal construction of Europe, therefore, which is inscribed within Cold War strategies, exemplifies the interconnection of professional strategies and hegemonic struggles. George Ball, the legal advisor to Jean Monnet, and numerous lawyers tied to major Wall Street law firms and the networks associated with the so-called Foreign Policy Establishment, were strongly implicated in the projects promoting the political reconstruction of Europe after the Second World War.[5] Later, when the leaders of the European Roundtable of Industrialists pushed the Delors Commission to accelerate the development of the internal European market, the large US law firms were the first to invest in Brussels in order to claim the position of privileged operators in the new space of economic activity. Their expertise in business law produced the models for the new regulations taking the place of national models. This precocious investment in the economic and also political construction of Europe permitted the major Wall Street law firms, and later their imitators from the City, to dominate the European market in business law – structured to conform to their interests and those of their multinational clientele.

In this way, the key actors of the Europe of law became organized according to political and economic stakes determined for the most part outside European borders. In order to understand this process, therefore, it is necessary to sketch, even if only in summary form, the hegemonic struggles that overturned the international hierarchy of national legal fields, placed their autonomy in question, and built an international legal market.[6] Before examining the first stages of the

5 Cohen, A. (2005), 'La constitution européenne. Ordre politique, utopie juridique et guerre froide', *Critique Internationale* 26, 119–31.

6 This global history of the restructuring of national fields of power is certainly also written simultaneously within competition between the protagonists of global cities (Sassen), those located at the periphery of the new hegemonic order. The transatlantic competition is evident also through putting into question issues about state expertises exported overseas by European "imperial societies" (Charle). See Sassen, S. (2001), *The Global City: New York, London, Tokyo* (Princeton, NJ: Princeton University Press) and Charle, C. (2001), *La crise des sociétés impériales: Allemagne, France, Grande Bretagne 1900–1940* (Paris: Seuil). Nevertheless, for reasons of space, we leave the examination of these issues to other works. See for example Dezalay, Y. and Garth, B. (2008), 'Law, Class, and Imperialism', SSRN: <http://ssrn.com/abstract=1092161>.

implantation of the US law firms in Europe, notably through the development of a market in international commercial arbitration, it is necessary to begin with a brief recap of the social history that structured the different national professional fields, since that history explains the institutional and political resources that legal professionals could mobilize in strategies of international expansion.[7]

## Hegemonic Logics, Professional Structures and International Competition in Law

The global promotion of the rule of law has for more than two decades been one of the essential components of a hegemonic strategy to remake national fields of state power to conform to the logic of the US model, making states more open to US influence and interests.[8] This legal imperialism, while the subject of generous programmes to promote democracy and economic development, owes much of its success to its ability to generate strong local support. The particular attraction comes from the fact that the new markets offer a new political legitimacy to legal elites who had lost their privileged positions within nation states originally constructed by and for a 'republic of lawyers'.[9] A lawyers' golden age allowed them to be at the centre of a political game organized around the law and the state. The political game was diffused by imperial societies into imported states constructed along the same model by lawyer-compradors educated in the European schools and then converted into founding fathers of new nation states.[10]

### *The Legal Field as Agency and Stakes of the Cold War*

Despite the promising beginnings of legal notables as founding fathers of new states, their political capital declined during the period of the Cold War through political and social struggles. The elite lawyer-politicians appeared too linked to

7 Elements of this chapter draw on a previously published article: Dezalay, D. (2007), 'Vendre du droit en (ré-)inventant de l'Etat. Stratégies constitutionnelles et promotion de l'expertise juridique dans le champ du pouvoir de l'Etat', in Cohen, A. and Vauchez, A. (eds), *La Constitution européenne. Elites, mobilisations, votes* (Brussels: Editions de l'Université de Bruxelles), 271–90.

8 Dezalay, Y. and Garth B.G. (2002), *The Internationalization of Palace Wars: Lawyers, Economists, and the Contest to Transform Latin American States* (Chicago, IL: University of Chicago Press).

9 See for example Abel-Smith, B. and Stevens, R. (1967), *Lawyers and the Courts* (London: Heinemann); Dezalay, Y. (1992), *Marchands de droit* (Paris: Fayard); and Karady, V. (1991), 'Une nation de juristes. Des usages sociaux de la formation juridique dans la Hongrie d'Ancien Régime', *Actes de la recherche en sciences sociales*, 86/87, 106–24.

10 On these issues, see respectively Charle, *La crise des sociétés impériales*; Badie, B (1992), *l'Etat importé. L'occidentalisation de l'ordre politique* (Paris: Fayard); and Dezalay and Garth, *The Internationalization of Palace Wars*.

the large landowning classes and too ready to defend those class interests in the guise of protecting political liberties. In the most fragile or exposed states, in fact, elite lawyer-politicians were rapidly eliminated by military or civil dictatorships and replaced by technocrats in the field of economic development seen to be more useful and more accommodating.[11] Elsewhere, and notably in Europe, the hostility of elite lawyer-politicians to the social state and to state economic interventionism led to their marginalization from the ruling bureaucracies that presided over economic reconstruction after the Second World War.

The United States was the only major exception to the more or less dramatic devaluation of the political capital of lawyers in the period before and after the Second World War. US lawyers played a central role in the reorganization of the structures of the US federal state through complementary reform strategies, one in national politics and the other on the international scene. Putting themselves in the service of the Roosevelt administration in order to defend New Deal policies from attacks by leaders of the bar, a meritocratic group of young Jewish lawyers in particular succeeded, in the words of Auerbach , in turning the New Deal in effect into a 'lawyers' deal'.[12]

At the other extreme, relying on the Cold War strategy that they helped to inspire, the patricians of US law became the managers of a hegemonic politics orchestrated by the so-called Foreign Policy Establishment. For nearly half a century, this club of 'wise men' and elder statesmen functioned as the 'left hand of the state' or more precisely as a state authority that transcended partisan politics.

Therefore, the exacerbation of domestic struggles by international competition provoked contrasting effects on the political capital of lawyers in different national settings. The contrast was a result of the different positions occupied in the new global order. In Wall Street and Washington, DC, the professionals behind the rule of law were able to profit fully from investments in new state structures. In contrast, in peripheral outposts of the Cold War, the political capital accumulated by the first generation of legal notables – once revered as founding fathers of the nations – declined precipitously. In the European countries, the situation was not so dramatic, but most legal commentators nevertheless lamented a 'decline of law', a diminished role of judges, and more generally a devaluation of the role of law and lawyers in the field of state power.[13]

---

11 Dezalay, Y. and Garth, B.G. (2006), 'Les usages nationaux d'une science "globale". La diffusion de nouveaux paradigmes économiques comme stratégie hégémonique et enjeu domestique dans les champs nationaux de reproduction des élites d'Etat', *Sociologie du travail* 48:308.

12 Auerbarch, J.S. (1976), *Unequal Justice: Lawyers and Social Change in Modern America* (Oxford: Oxford University Press). See also Irons, P.H. (1982), *The New Deal Lawyers* (Princeton, NJ: Princeton University Press), and Shamir, R. (1995), *Managing Legal Uncertainty: Elite Lawyers in the New Deal* (Durham, NC: Duke University Press).

13 Abel-Smith and Stevens, *Lawyers and the Courts*.

### *Political Strategies and the Division of Labour of the Legal Field*

The dramatically contrasting evolutions in the different legal fields resulted in part from a geo-political logic, but they also developed from different national histories that shaped the relationship between law and politics. In particular, different national histories produced particular hierarchical structures that defined the legal and political division of labour – and therefore the strategies for the accumulation of legal capital through investments in the political field. In this respect, the contrast between the different sides of the Atlantic is again quite marked.

The US legal field is characterized by a pronounced social and professional diversity, with multiple lines of recruitment ranging from highly selective legal academies and occupations to relatively open educations and careers. Further, the lines between legal careers are also relatively open in the United States, allowing a circulation among different positions in the legal field. This mobility permits the most entrepreneurial of lawyers to accumulate quite varied combinations of legal capital and social resources.

The internal competition among legal agents in the United States is also played out on the political field. The relatively open competition leads to quite diverse yet complementary political strategies that join together to support the extension and renovation of markets for the production of the rule of law, including strategies through legal clinics or public interest law.[14]

In contrast, the long political history of the European legal fields has led to a codification of a quite hierarchical division of labour linked to pronounced stratification in legal markets.[15] Each of the segments of the market is protected by barriers to entry that are all the more rigid since built on a professional hierarchical elite privileging high priests of the law and deprecating so-called legal merchants – especially those linked to a 'vulgar' clientele. The various categories of practice in a stratified market increase the cost and risk of potential conversions of political capital into legal capital – a situation hardly likely to lead legal elites, for example, to invest in radical or militant politics. Further, the enduring restrictions on entry have long favoured a strong family role in the accumulation and reproduction of legal capital – increasing also the social homogeneity of the relatively closed circle that makes up the professional elite.

These Malthusian strategies go with a political divide between conservatives and more progressive reformers corresponding to two fractions of the property-holding classes. The high cost of legal services has made law a privileged instrument for the defence of large family estates and dominant commercial positions. Elite lawyers can serve the well-to-do at the same time they invest in politics, but the investments are highly circumscribed. In particular, elite legal practice is not inconsistent with public engagement on behalf of high-minded

14 Scheingold, S. (1974), *The Politics of Rights: Lawyers, Public Policy and Political Change* (New Haven, CT: Yale University Press).

15 Dezalay, *Marchands de droit*.

causes such as political liberalism or nationalism, since building an appropriate national prominence leads also to prosperous clients. In contrast, however, the social and professional structure of the elite group tends to preclude work on behalf of activists in social movements for which group members and their clients have very little affinity.

While somewhat schematic and oversimplified, this comparison of the structures of the legal field explains to a great extent the political investments of legal agents and the political uses of law.

### *From Profitable Political Investments in International Markets to Business and Corporate Law*

By establishing themselves at the forefront of the Cold War, the leaders of the major Wall Street law firms accumulated important political capital that they could monetize. They could arrogate to themselves the most profitable legal business from the market in corporate law that they had helped develop and globalize. But this imperial strategy did not triumph without some collateral damage – in the dominated legal fields found in the outposts of the Cold War as well as in Europe. The debacle experienced by the imported legal regimes was further exacerbated by the loss of market position by the Europeans.

The decline in international influence of European legal approaches was accelerated by the weakness of domestic positions modelled after Europe – with the same Cold War logic at work in each instance. In fact, throughout Europe, legal professionals lost a great part of their capital because of their efforts to privilege the protection of the interests of the most affluent classes, neglecting the issues raised by debates focused on 'social questions'. Further, the majority of the legal elites had taken part openly in challenges to the reformist strategies connected to the social state. They were therefore poorly placed to compete on markets of exportation of legal expertise involving new technologies of law and development created to be effective 'antidotes to communism'.

The European legal fields were thus doubly affected by the logic of the Cold War. The weakening of their position within the fields of European state power undermined them in the old imperial societies and in peripheral states as leaders sought to reinforce their networks of influence in the new international competition for legal universalism.

## The Emergence of the European Legal Field as an Off-shore Market for Exporting the 'American Way' of Law

US lawyers were very present in Europe after the Second World War, contributing to build the basis of a transatlantic partnership quite active in the construction of

Europe.[16] The influence of the US legal field also benefited substantially from strategies of reconversion among the most cosmopolitan of European legal elites.

Within the academic world, drawing on the diaspora of legal academics who fled from Nazi regimes and the prominent US postwar position, most prestigious law schools in the United States began to attract a number of cosmopolitan law graduates from Europe. In particular, they attracted those anxious to cross the Atlantic in order to gain a legal education and credentials that would help make up for the declining value of their local credentials on the market of elites. The declining value resulted both from the shrinking of legal markets in relation to new kinds of expertise – economics, political science and management in particular – but also through an increase in supply through the proliferation of faculties of law, drawing middle-class students aiming to accumulate the capital traditionally associated with degrees in law. As we pointed out for some Latin-American States like Argentina,[17] the United States had less need to invest in imperial politics when there were local professional elites ready and able to pay the high costs of this strategy of reconversion made necessary by their exclusion or marginalization from the field of state power – once considered their exclusive domain. The existence of strong motivations among the importers thus reduces significantly the costs of exportation associated with a politics of symbolic imperialism.

At the same time, the interests of the importers contributed to orient the operation and content of the exported products. Instead of seeking the reform of legal or judicial institutions, in particular, they began to build a kind of parallel legal market at the margin or more specifically across the frontier of national legal boundaries. The exportation of US legal practices toward Europe, built on strategies of reconversion by a small minority of professional elites with familial and cosmopolitan resources, clashed with French institutional barriers built over a long period of time and hardened by close links between the political capital of legal notables and the authority of the state. Legal markets were traditionally protected by monopolies guaranteed by public authority to different categories of legal practitioners, such as notaries, *huissiers* or barristers and solicitors. As with respect to the faculties of law (and likewise the Inns of Court in Great Britain), it was not only a matter of a hierarchically structured mode of production of law, but also lines of reproduction of elites and the content of the expertise that benefited from this state protection. The legal order generally was sheltered by the national public order.

This protected and closed system, instead of weakening from the fact of the loss of influence by the lawyer politicians, grew stronger – at least initially. In fact, the shrinking of political opportunities led to the reinforcement of the protectionist barriers to entry. The context characterized by a threatened and embattled legal elite served to limit the implantation of the US legal model within national legal spaces. Not surprisingly, US philanthropic foundations seeking to reform Europe along US

16 Cohen, 'La constitution européenne'.

17 Dezalay and Garth *The Internationalization of Palace Wars*.

lines invested not in the faculties of law but rather in new competing expertises, in particular economics and management.[18] The same strategy, essentially investing on the margins or outside of the national legal field, was found in the actions of the small cosmopolitan elite that had the resources to obtain a second legal diploma in the United States.

Despite the high costs of US legal education, there were great rewards in Europe attached to a strategy of double legal credentialing. It allowed those with dual expertise and connections to serve as local scouts and courtiers for Wall Street law firms. The firms needed insider help as they sought to build branches in Europe to follow and serve multinational clientele seeking to take advantage of the opportunities offered by the postwar European reconstruction.

The protectionist strategies of the professional hierarchies that controlled the main European legal institutions were therefore double-edged. On one hand, they certainly provided a form of refuge from the US legal approaches rapidly moving from across the Atlantic. On the other hand, they discouraged most European professionals from investing in the transnational markets that were expanding rapidly around them. Leading Wall Street law firms gained a strong position in Europe in part because of their deep ties to US companies going abroad, but they also thrived because they were well introduced into the familial and professional network of legal elites who had already become familiar with US businesses and the US production of law. Ironically, therefore, Europeans who often were the descendants of the old '*noblesse de robe*' helped facilitate the implantation in European capitals of a new mode of legal production. The new model brought an industrial logic and a division of labour that posed a dangerous threat to the traditional mode associated with the *noblesse de robe*. The US mode of legal production brought together a formidable concentration of human resources and forms of symbolic capital mobilized to conquer the new legal markets.

The converted renegades from the old legal elite also played the role of liaison when the growth of the markets made it necessary to gain at least tacit recognition by local legal authorities. This liaison role expanded as these de-territorialized enclaves began to handle transnational disputes involving high stakes politically and financially, such as the great petroleum arbitrations or the disputes connected to the huge infrastructure projects financed by the petro-dollars of the 1970s.[19] The new US-style law firms needed at least *ad hoc* institutional protection from local legal jurisdictions in order to build their positions and credibility. They obtained that protection through the cooperation of the local correspondents drawing on local legal capital – which came from academic reputations or positions of leadership in the bar within the leading jurisdictions of the host countries.

---

18 Gemelli, G. (2006), 'Networks as Drivers of European Scientific Integration: The Role of the Ford Foundation in the Sixties', paper presented at ESSE, 23–24 June 2006.

19 Dezalay, Y. and Garth B.G. (1996), *Dealing in Virtue: International Commercial Arbitration and the Construction of a Transnational Legal Order* (Chicago, IL: University of Chicago Press).

The growth of the European market of business and commercial law was therefore the product of multiple converging interests including hegemonic politics, an industrial logic, and the reconversion and revalorization of national elites. The circumstances of this genesis help to explain the very particular structure of this new field of legal practice – situated both at the crossroads and the margins, but also located above national legal fields. The polycentric structure of this professional space, a structure found also at the beginning of the development of the European Court of Justice,[20] provides both the strength and the limits of this European business and commercial law practice.

The strength is that the agents who invested in this area could accumulate diversified combinations of legitimate legal capital that allowed these new forms of legal expertise and practice to gain a universal stature that transcended the differences of the national legal systems. On the other side, however, the ambiguity of the institutional status of this transnational market made the legal capital accumulated within it difficult to convert in national legal fields, where business lawyers had for a long time struggled for recognition of the value of their expertise and practices. The practices of the new transnational market, in addition, remained tainted by other factors. The expertise, in particular, rested on an external mode of production, and the practice focused on transnational arenas that did not easily succumb to control by local legal and professional jurisdictions designed under the auspices of a nation state. Despite their undeniable success, therefore, the hybrid lawyers were treated as expatriates of law, always suspected of having broken their ties with the national traditions and cultures through which the European legal fields had built their credibility and permanence.

These strategic ambiguities are found in the institutions around which the new corporate legal markets took shape. Instead of being constructed on a European base, the transnational markets presented themselves as the juxtaposition of competing national initiatives. This characterization was especially clear in the market for international commercial arbitration, where the major US law firms were the principle beneficiaries of a competition that they had themselves helped produce among national centres seeking the local profits of off-shore justice.[21] Paris, London, Geneva, Vienna and Stockholm, seen as the principle 'sites of arbitration' in Europe, competed not only by asserting the quality and discretion of their local arbitrators and arbitration lawyers, but also the autonomy that the arbitrations would have from local legal authorities and rules.

The genesis of the investment in extraterritoriality in the world of international commercial arbitration is indicative of the strategies evident in the construction of a Europe of law. While their implantation in London met with some resistance by the practitioners of corporate law among a small group of practitioners seeking to defend their monopoly and experiment in the new transnational markets, the Wall Street law firms were able to gain from a relative disinterest among the elite of the

20 See further in the chapter by Antoine Vauchez included in this volume.

21 Dezalay and Garth, *Dealing in Virtue*.

Paris bar. They could develop a market in Paris for what remained a marginally legitimated practice, and they succeeded in helping establish the hybrid and relatively poorly protected status of '*conseil juridique*'.[22] Paris did not offer the same facilities as London from the point of view of language and legal culture, and it lacked the array of businesses and institutions created to serve the multinational corporations with the growth of the market in Eurodollars in the 1960s. But the absence of a corporate bar integrated into the Parisian legal bar made it so that Paris placed relatively few obstacles in the way of the development of a new legal practice – serving the growing transnational markets with a kind of common law practice based in a civil law country.

The type of extra-territorial legal practice found in Paris was hardly unprecedented in colonial histories. The imperial countries often built enclaves to provide some minimum of legal security within peripheral *entrepôts*. The international market for business and commercial law in Europe therefore benefited in essence from the existence of a 'duty free zone' that permitted the practitioners to gain some distance from the rules of national jurisdictions. As in the colonial enclaves, the operators could use their privileged position to handle disputes with a kind of *ad hoc* justice. The International Chamber of Commerce in Paris, which served as the institutional site for the International Court of Arbitration, was centrally involved in the great petroleum disputes of the 1970s – and was even more central to the disputes that grew out of the huge projects built with petrodollars.

These successes increased the visibility of this market as professionals from different places competed to participate in activities that were both profitable and prestigious, and which granted great freedom to the parties in the choice of rules and the choice of counsel. Any strategy of attacking national legal monopolies directly in order to draw local bars into this market was abandoned. The extra-territorial corporate law firms were simply better equipped than European nationally-based lawyers to handle the large transnational disputes, and they could also take advantage of the opportunities available from the competition among competing legal capitals.

After an initial start-up phase of heavy investment in deregulation and competition for the market of international commercial arbitration, the leaders of this transnational business justice began naturally to curb a perceived over-competition that might threaten the credibility of the entire enterprise. The tacit gentlemen's agreement still characteristic of the field of international commercial arbitration was even more effective since it was built on the strength of interpersonal connections linking this small network of learned international practitioners – a network denounced by critics as an 'arbitration mafia'. One therefore finds a mixture of competition and tacit cooperation among those in Europe who dominated the field of international commercial arbitration.

22 Boigeol, A. and Dezalay, Y. (1997), 'Des agents d'affaires au barreau: la construction d'un espace professionnel', *Genèses* 27.

The protagonists of international commercial arbitration helped to construct a distinct field of practice. The pioneers were linked to the Wall Street law firms set up in European capitals to serve their multinational corporate clients. They had their local supporters and collaborators educated in the United States. And there were groups of US lawyers who became temporary European expatriates. The extension of this market more generally was accompanied by a Europeanization both among the clients and the legal practitioners.

Lacking the power to move up the hierarchy in the rather closed world of the Wall Street law firms, the European professionals educated in the United States also found themselves taking steps to overcome the local resistance of professional hierarchies to the new kinds of practice. They began to open up local spaces for more entrepreneurial initiatives where they could build their positions and practices. They used the increasing international competition to argue for a new model of practice that would break the traditions that had restrained competition among 'brothers at the bar'.

For example, the British reformers behind the 'Big Bang' of reform in legal services – keeping in line with the deregulation in financial markets – said it was necessary to deregulate in order to keep the City of London at the core of the European market in business and commercial law. The industrial strategy of the new entrepreneurs in Britain was inspired by the success of the accounting firms in their relatively quick and initially quite successful move from international auditing to advising. The strategy involved internationalization and rapid growth accelerated by mergers and alliances with local firms abroad – in Europe, but also in the former colonies. But this quick and relatively successful 'catch-up' strategy also had limits. Despite or because of the scope of their geographical diversification, the 'magic circle' firms of solicitors based in London became neither as profitable nor as influential as their US counterparts – who could also draw on their close connections with the Wall Street financial world.

As with respect to international commercial arbitration, the growth of the European market of business law was inscribed within a logic of transatlantic relations that exacerbated the competition between national elites to gain positions at the top of the second tier. These national divisions were found even in the core of certain British solicitors firms that developed two-headed structures – one British and one German – to manage tensions associated with different legal cultures.[23] Therefore, even in the firms that appeared to be the relative winners in the market of European business and commercial law, the reality was hardly a homogeneous or even autonomous European legal model.

Even if seeking to emulate the model of the US corporate law firms, the European variant differed in one key respect. In the United States, the corporate law firms had developed mechanisms for the permanent reconstruction of their

23 Morgan, G. and Quack, S. (2006), 'The Internationalisation of Professional Service Firms: Global Convergence, National Path-dependency or Cross-border Hybridization?', *Research in the Sociology of Organizations* 24, 415–44.

legitimacy through investments in the political field, both through lobbying and representing clients, but also in non-governmental organizations (NGOs) that make-up an opposing and complementary pole of US legal practice. In fact, as seen in the transformations of the politics of environmental protection in Europe, the leading London firms, in contrast to those across the Atlantic, assiduously keep their distance from the NGOs of environmental protection.[24]

For a dramatic example, on one side the elite firm of Skadden Arps in New York City, known for its entrepreneurial and legal aggressiveness, overtly supports CIEL (the Center for International Environmental Law) both professionally and financially. CIEL, which is active in the environmental movement and in the anti-globalization arena, takes pride in the legal notables from corporate law firms who serve on its board. The graduates of top US law schools fight to gain positions as young lawyers or as law clerks spending their law school summers at CIEL, and they use the value of the CIEL credential to obtain jobs at leading law firms, including Skadden Arps.

This situation is unimaginable on the other side of the Atlantic. There young lawyers risk their entire professional careers if they become identified with FIELD, CIEL's counterpart, even for a brief time, despite the fact that both organizations came from the same initiative funded by the Ford Foundation before separating into two organizations. This marked difference is true even though one of the leaders of a major London firm, in charge of the firm's environmental department, has long served as Chair of the Board of FIELD. One could easily multiply such examples to illustrate the almost complete break between these two poles within the universe of legal professional practice in Europe – even between the liberal and reformist fraction of the world of business law on one side and the most moderate and academic side of the activist world on the other side.

The same contrast is found in the networks of power more generally. It is true that there are increasing numbers of top functionaries and politicians from the European Community or particular countries drawing on their political capital to join corporate law firms. But this relatively recent phenomenon occurs much less frequently than in the United States and is still not considered a matter of routine.[25] More importantly, this mobility is still one-way, more according to the traditional model of '*pantouflag* ' at the end of a governmental career. Most of the leaders of the law firms do not encourage, and many actively discourage, lawyers from seeking to move into government or politics. Here, too, there is a reflexive desire to keep a distance from the political world. The enduring nature of this attitude is

24 Dezalay, Y. (2007), 'From a Symbolic Boom to a Marketing Bust: Genesis and Reconstruction of a Field of Legal and Political Expertise at the Crossroads of a Europe Opening to the Atlantic', *Law & Social Inquiry* 32:1, 161–81.

25 Indeed, according to one of its members, the Council of the Paris Bar has debated for several years whether a French-qualified lawyer could rejoin the bar after a career as a minister in the European Community.

a testimony to the fact that it is deeply anchored in the *habitus* that characterizes European legal elites.

The reticence of European legal practitioners of corporate law with respect to politics is manifested not only on the national but also at the European level. Certainly the firms do recruit young lawyers who have some experience with the European bureaucratic machinery – acquired from apprenticeships (stages) or short stints with one or another of the institutions of Brussels or Luxembourg. But these connections are accumulated in order to facilitate lobbying with the correct entities and individuals in the European bureaucracy. They are pragmatic and fragmented investments for the particular needs of clients. The leading European corporate law firms have prospered behind the scenes in the construction of Europe. They have no interest in the institutional structures to which they shape their practices.

One can hypothesize more generally that, in contrast to the generation of pioneers surrounding Jean Monnet and George Ball, the entrepreneurs of business and commercial law in Europe have not invested in the construction of Europe as a political project. According to this hypothesis, they have largely been content to take advantage of the opportunities that the new markets and institutions have presented. If this hypothesis proves to be true, which is not yet clear, there are important implications that follow. The legal entrepreneurs, after all, have contributed greatly to define the stakes of and to enhance a European politics and the role of law in that politics. The hypothesis helps explain why one finds a general fragmentation in the emergence of numerous domains of European politics – including the environment,[26] human rights[27] and immigration policy.[28] Further, since the lines of cleavage for a particular issue or the temporary alliances formed for particular opportunities do not coincide with specific domains, the diversity of the field of European politics is even greater.

Under these conditions, it is difficult to find a place from which to examine and see progress toward the 'construction of Europe' as a legal achievement. This prescriptive construct has an ambiguity tied to the multiplicity of stakes and strategies that it covers. There is a case, as we have tried to show, for the construction of a 'Europe of law', with a symbolic presence inscribed in international hierarchical struggles that go along with a redefinition of the internal rules that contribute to legitimate the division of labour in the legal field. The efforts to constitutionalize a state of European law, however, cannot escape the professional struggles that determine the stakes behind European law – and that also are the product of those stakes.

26 Dezalay, 'From a Symbolic Boom to a Marketing Bust'.

27 Madsen, M.R. (2005), *L'Emergence d'un champ des droits de l'homme dans les pays européens: enjeux professionnels et stratégies d'Etat au carrefour du droit et de la politique (France, Grande-Bretagne et pays scandinaves, 1945–2000)*. Doctoral Thesis, l'École des hautes études en sciences sociales, Paris.

28 Buchet de Neuilly, Y. (2001), *L'Europe de la politique étrangère* (Paris: Economica).

When promoters of a Europe of law use the concept, it serves as a tactical argument to legitimate their political and professional interests. Not surprisingly, given the account of the sources for the various investments that are working to transform European legal practices and hierarchies, the promotion of a Europe of law only increases the opposition of European social groups. As Bourdieu noted, in order to produce the effects of belief, it is necessary that the legal clerics themselves believe sufficiently to sacrifice, even if only partially, their own personal interests.

# Chapter 8

# (Re)Constructing the Boundaries of the Market: EU Law and Institutions Analysed through the Lens of Discontinuity

Inger-Johanne Sand

## Introduction: Continuity and Discontinuity in Political and Legal Organizations

The last fifty and particularly the last twenty years have seen remarkable, unexpected and significant changes in the political and legal institutions in the developed countries in general and in Europe in particular. More or less stabilized democratic, executive and judicial institutions in the nation-states have been supplemented and changed by the emergence of regional, supra- and international institutions with more comprehensive and effective political and legal power than previously. The new international and regional organizations increasingly have supra- and international competences overlapping and even competing with nation-states' own material competences, with direct or indirect effect for their territories and citizens.[1] Their core legal competences have been on the regulation of free movement, trade and competition law rather than on social and protective regulation.

The EU is probably the most prominent, most developed and most ambitious example of these.[2] The institutional changes created by the EU, as an exemplary, but also unique, case, include many different dimensions. First of all, some form of multi-level governance system has been created, with active, comprehensive and partly overlapping legislative, executive and judicial institutions which both cooperate and compete with nation-state institutions, but it still has many unclear and unfinished relations.[3] The concept and the practices of sovereignty have been significantly changed. Different conceptions of society and citizenship, and different types of loyalty, are implied in these changes.[4]

---

1 Sand, I-J. (1998), 'Understanding the New Forms of Governance: Mutually Interdependent, Reflexive, Destabilized and Competing Institutions', *European Law Journal*, 3: 4, 271–293.

2 Weiler, J. (1990), 'The Transformation of Europe', *Yale Law Journal* 100: 1, 1, and (1999), *The Constitution of Europe* (Cambridge: Cambridge University Press), chs 8 and 9.

3 Weiler, 'The Transformation of Europe'; and *The Constitution of Europe*, chs 8 and 9.

4 Weiler, *The Constitution of Europe*, ch. 10.

Secondly, new combinations and forms of division of powers between the different branches of government (executive, legislative and judicial) have been created with unavoidable consequences for the forms of democracy.

Thirdly, the EU has a comprehensive, but not all-encompassing or general set of substantive competences where trade and competition regulation have been the initial and the dominant substantive competences such that they also influence the configuration of other substantive competences. The substantive competences of the EU are thus asymmetric compared to the universal model of legislative powers.

Fourthly, the configuration of and the relations between the political and the legal systems on the level of the EU, or the region, are different than on the level of nation-states which have been socially and culturally stabilized over longer periods of time. The political and legal systems of the Member States have had much longer to develop structural couplings with their social, economic and cultural environments than the EU has had. Furthermore, the political and legal communications on the level of the EU are developed in a different and more abstract context, isolated from vital parts of social life.

In the following I will argue that these four dimensions of the changes of politico-legal institutions of the EU (in particular) have contributed to more significant and deeper changes in the government and governance of the Member States and of the community/union than many of the current theories of EU governance will admit to. I will also argue that some of the changes have been unexpected in their scope and depth, and that we are still lacking in theories, understanding and description of how some of these changes occurred. I will argue that the dynamics between the Commission, Council and the Court, as well as the Member States, in establishing the legal scope of the supranationality and its consequences has not been fully understood. Part of the reason may be that the two levels of governing have been seen too much as entities, and that the differentiation and interactive dynamics of law, expertise and politics and the gaps of meaning between these have not been sufficiently emphasized.

The literature on the EU, its institutions and its legal system is rich and diverse. By being in many respects the most successful and most remarkable of the 'new' international organizations and treaties of the post-Second-World-War era, the EU and its emergence have been the objects of intense and inter-disciplinary academic, theoretical and political analysis: What is it? How did it become what it is? What are the relations between the organization and its members? and so on. The analysis has oscillated between comparisons with nation-states and with other international organizations. Existing political and legal theories have been applied. Of particular interest has been the exploration of the EU as partly a supranational organization. The close and many-dimensional combinations of supra-, inter-, trans-national and national levels and competences have been another focus. There have been intergovernmentalists, neo-functionalists, institutionalists, constitutionalists and so on.[5] Many, however, have also emphasized and concluded by seeing the EU as *sui generis*, as a new type of organization exceeding existing political and constitutional theories.[6] I will argue, however, that the *sui-generis* line of argumentation has not been sufficiently exploited, and that there are several aspects of the EU, its organization and treaties which have not been recognized or sufficiently emphasized. In the following I will also argue that vital aspects of its emergence were not anticipated: not the scope of its competences, not the political success, not the efficiency of the market, not the legislative activities and not the strong position of law.

The question then is: how do such paradigmatic and comprehensive and also unexpected and unpredicted institutional changes in the politico-legal landscape occur? In the following I will suggest that some of these changes may be better understood by applying theories of functional and communicative differentiation, of the dynamics of complexity and contingency and of continuity/discontinuity. Partly I will propose a perspective of change and discontinuity as an alternative to one of incremental institutional change. Rather than seeing the new EU and other international politico-legal institutions as continuances of previous institutions, I propose a combination of continuity in terms of certain general politico-legal ideas and normative patterns, and of discontinuity in terms of to some extent quite radical changes of specific institutions and their mutual interactions.[7] Partly I will propose applying the theories of functional and communicative differentiation in order to analyse how the new institutions and their procedures and competences emerge as a result of highly complex interactions between the different communicative rationalities at work.[8] The theories of communicative differentiation see the institutions not only as entities, but also as communicatively differentiated and fragmented. Law, politics and markets have their specific trajectories, but are also closely interrelated and inter-dependent. Understanding the specific dynamics

5 See among many others. Weiler, 'The Transformation of Europe'; and *The Constitution of Europe*, chs 8 and 9; Scharpf, Fritz (1996), 'Negative and Positive Integration in the Political Economy of the European Union', in Marks, G., *Governance in the European Union* (London: Sage); Kohler-Koch, G. (1996), 'Catching up with Change: The Transformation of Governance in the European Union', *European Public Policy*, 3:3; Joerges, C. (1999), 'Bureaucratic Nightmare, Technocratic Regime and the Dream of Good Transnational Governance', and Joerges, C. (1999), 'Good Governance Through Comitology', in Joerges, C. and Vos, E. (eds), *EU Committees: Social Regulation, Law and Politics* (Oxford: Hart); Joerges, C. (2006), 'Constitutionalism in Postnational Constellations: Contrasting Social Regulation in the EU and in the WTO', in Joerges, C. and Petersmann, E-U. (eds), *Constitutionalism, Multi-Level Trade, Governance and Social Regulation* (Oxford: Hart).

6 Sand, 'Understanding the New Forms of Governance'.

7 Foucault, M. (1991), 'Politics and the Study of Discourse', in Burchell, G., Gordon, C. and Miller, P. (eds), *The Foucault Effect* (London: Harvester Wheatsheaf).

8 Luhmann, N. (1981), *The Differentiation of Society* (New York: Harvester Wheatsheaf); and (1984), *Soziale Systeme* (Frankfurt: Suhrkamp), chs 1 and 2.

and changes between these communicative codes may be quite important for understanding the changes in the configuration of what democracy is. Law has clearly played a different and more prominent role in the evolution of the EU institutions than in the Member States pre-EU, and the interactions between law and politics may also have developed new trajectories and normative patterns.

Two types of application of these analytics which I want to mention here are first, Saskia Sassen's development of a new set of concepts and vocabulary for the transnational field (with analytic borderlands as an example), and second, Gunther Teubner's similar attempt to develop a set of concepts for law in complex and global societies (reflexive law and hybrids could serve as examples).[9] Sassen describes the new trajectories and institutions resulting from the new relations between the national and the inter- and transnational, but in doing so attempts to describe these as they are, or may be, in a qualitatively new way or as situations in process, by, for example, focusing on *analytic borderlands* and *frontier zones* and on new or exchanged functions for both the national and the international institutions.

New spatio-temporal orders have been created between various international, regional and national institutions which cannot be described in terms of hierarchy or formal rules, but contain a variety of relations between the different levels.[10] Complex apparatus of actually functioning, layer-upon-layer, multi-level governance have been created in at times incremental and at times more abrupt ways, and in at times well planned and at other times more unforeseen ways.[11] Instead of distinct legislative, executive and judicial organizations, the new supra- and international institutions may rather be described as new variations of or different combinations of such competences. They operate in new institutional landscapes, and they stand in different relations to the citizenry and the relevant civil societies compared to nation-state institutions.

In the following I will discuss the EU as exemplary of one of the new, and in a certain sense successful, international and regional political and legal institutions created by the nation-states, but which has been given competences not only to govern internationally, but also to intervene actively in the internal operations of the nation-states in far more comprehensive and effective ways than previously.[12]

---

9 Saskia Sassen (2006), *Territories, Authorities, Rights* (Princeton, NJ: Princeton University Press), ch. 8; Gunther Teubner (1982), 'Reflexives Recht', *Archiv für Recht- und Sozialphilosophie*, LXVIII; (1997), 'The King's Many Bodies', *Law and Society Review*, 31: 4, 763ff; (2003) 'Coincidentia Oppositorum: Hybrid Networks Beyond Contract and Organization', *Storr's Lectures* October 8, 2003 (Yale Law School).

10 Sassen, *Territories, Authorities, Rights*, ch. 8, 'Assembling mixed spatial and temporal orders'.

11 Kohler-Koch, 'Catching up with Change'.

12 Weiler, J. (1999), 'The Constitution of the Common Market Place: Text and Context in the Evolution of the Free Movement of Goods', in Craig, P. and de Burca, G. (eds), *The Evolution of EU Law* (Oxford: Oxford University Press).

## The EU as a Case of Organizational Construction – and Supra-nationality as a New Mode of Governance

The EC/EU has had a remarkable trajectory as an international organization. It has developed unprecedented comprehensive supranational competences and significant effectiveness in terms of implementation for an international organization.

EU law has become an effective, working legal system in a relatively short time. The main material competences have been the functioning of a liberal internal market and effective competition law regulation. The Court has developed into a full-fledged judicial court. Implementation in the Member States has functioned relatively well, partly due to the referral of questions to the ECJ by the national courts, while the internal market has functioned beyond expectations. The European economic systems have been changed radically from mixed economies to market-driven liberal regimes: functioning markets being the main dynamics. The Commission and the Court quickly developed into effective, functioning institutions. Politically the EU has developed into a vital international organization – unprecedented for such a body – with deep and comprehensive political cooperation among Member States. Together this has changed vital aspects of the European economic system, the European legal system and its institutional and political architecture.[13]

However, as they transpired, the more exact ambitions – in the evolution and emergence of the European Community and the Union – were not anticipated by anyone – not the scope of its competences, the political success, the efficiency of the market, the legislative activities or the strong position of law. My proposition here is that the accumulated changes have gone beyond the intentions and the texts of the common decisions. The legal system has become more effective and autonomous. The economic regime has become more market-driven and more effective. The different institutions and competences have evolved in at times unexpected and unplanned ways. Some of these changes will be mentioned here shortly and then developed further in the following paragraphs. I will attempt to apply the theories presented above in order to produce some new nuances on the trajectory of the EU and its institutions.

The EU has developed more comprehensive and effective supranational powers than any other international organization has previously. This has occurred, not as one planned process, but in various steps and in differing ways. Some of the steps have been the result of unprecedented combinations of law, markets and politics. One such step was the inclusion in the preamble of the Rome Treaty of 'the peoples', and not only the states, of Europe. It marks the treaty as possibly something more

13 de Burca, G. (1999), 'The Institutional Development of the EU: A Constitutional Analysis', in Craig and de Burca, *The Evolution of EU Law*; Weiler, J. (1999), 'The Autonomy of the Community Legal Order: Through the Looking Glass', in Weiler, *The Constitution of Europe*.

or different than most international treaties. By referring to 'the peoples' the treaty contains an element of constitutionality. It was also a vital element in the argumentation of the Court in its first decisions on direct effect and supremacy.[14] In these cases the Court could have concluded differently. As the decisions were made they had a vital impact on the ensuing practice of both the Commission and the Court, and became a critical part of the *acquis communautaire*. The decisions made by the Court may be seen in the context of the new and particular European political situation and the emphasis in the treaty on the creation of a functioning internal market. Politics and markets may have influenced the decision more than usual for a judicial court decision.

The EC/EU have from the start developed comprehensive and relatively well-functioning organizations, considering that it operates on a regional/international level and without clear precedents for such organizations: a strong executive in the Commission, comprehensive legislative powers and practices in the Council and the Parliament, and an effectively-functioning judicial Court have emerged. The Commission and the Court have both been vital in the stabilization and the remarkable expansion of powers. They are both defined as European institutions in the treaties, meaning that their only legal and political basis is the treaties. They have also been given autonomous competences, independent of the Member States, by the treaty texts. Significant contribution to legislation initiative and authoritative interpretation and implementation is performed by the Commission and the Court.

Since its beginnings, the powers of the EU have been expanded in several ways, through an active and ambitious Commission, a dynamic Court and new legislative competences. One of the vital and more remarkable modes of expansion has been the Commission's and the Court's interpretation and practice of EC art. 28 (30) and the rules of free movement. By emphasizing effectively-functioning and trans-boundary markets over regulatory and social protection goals, when the latter may be discriminatory or function as obstacles to trade, the Court has contributed to an expansive interpretation of the freedom of movement over social regulation. In order to avoid any possibly protectionist measures, any Member State arguing in favour of regulations which might result in the above-mentioned consequences had in fact to carry the burden of proof for such measures being compliant with art. 30 (36) or otherwise societally vital.[15]

The dynamic and expansive approach of the ECJ (and of the Commission) towards articles 28 and 30 has been a critical part of the more general expansion of the competences and the practices of the EU institutions. Starting with the Statistical Levy case, 24/68, what this has illustrated is that the distinction between

14 Case ECJ 26/62 van Gend en Loos, and 6/64 Costa vs. ENEL. Weiler, 'The Transformation of Europe'.

15 Weiler, 'The Transformation of Europe'; Joerges, C. (2005), 'Free Trade: The Erosion of National and the Birth of Transnational Governance', *European Review*, 13, 93–117.

*negative and positive integration* by the EU was impossible to hold up, and thus also the equivalent distinction in status of legitimacy.[16] When the decision is made actively to protect a functioning liberal market against any protectionist measures, it follows that there will be complex and ultimately political decisions to make in the drawing of the boundaries between a non-protectionist market on the one hand and social, environmental and health regulations on the other. The consequence of this is that it has become impossible to restrict the EC/EU from functioning as a more technical-administrative institution whose legitimacy may be limited to just that. When the boundary is passed from negative to positive integration, the door is inevitably opened to more complex decisions and relations between the EC/EU and its Member States.

A crucial part of this expansion was driven by the Court on a case-by-case basis (see below), even though the trajectory of this practice does seem to be somewhat contingent on whatever cases are brought up by political authorities, or by the private parties themselves. The legislators accepted the success of the expansive practice and developed the mechanism of harmonizing directives in order to attempt a better balance between regulatory goals. Later, more explicit regulatory goals beyond the internal market were included. The expansion of competences in the EU therefore seems to be the result of a variety of interactions between different EU and national organizations and also private parties. It also appears that this has been a quite uneven, unplanned and unpredicted path, and not the result of grand plans. It may also be described as a scheme of complex possibilities and the contingent selections that have been made.

My proposition here is that the accumulated changes of the EU as a politico-legal organization have gone beyond the intentions and the texts of the common decisions. To reiterate: the legal system has become more effective and autonomous. The economic regime has become more market-driven and more effective. Some of the changes have been accumulative, step-by-step and/or as the result of at times intransparent changes in the practices of institutions rather than of explicit formal decisions. Some vital changes have to some extent been created beyond the boundaries of democratic decision-making. My next proposition is that these are changes which cannot be explained only by reference to the political will or rationality of the different actors, or to the formal relations between them. More diverse theories on political and legal communication and on organizations may be necessary.

16 Weiler, 'The Transformation of Europe'; Scharpf 'Negative and Positive Integration in the Political Economy of the European Union'.

## New Types of Organizations: Breaking the Boundaries of the National/International

Firstly, I propose that the EC/EU institutions and treaties are new constructions changing the boundaries between the nation-states and the international organization and the distinctions of the national, the regional and the international in law and politics. Secondly, I propose that the EC/EU is an attempt to combine the different levels of government in new and unprecedented ways, in contrast to keeping them separate. Thirdly, the EC/EU structure represents a new pattern of legislative, executive and judicial institutions with a new form of division of power and with possible consequences for the relationship between law, politics and the executive. Fourthly, the treaties give preference to some material political goals over others, for example the functioning of a common or internal market for the participating countries. Fifthly, the institutions, treaties and the ensuing decision-making creating political, legal and economic communications have emerged with more openness and contingency than in the equivalent nation-state-based institutions because the EU evolves in a more open and heterogeneous context. The EU does not have one people, one notion of territory, one notion of a common history and culture, one common language and so on. The context is more heterogeneous and less historically framed than in a nation-state. The emergence of institutions will then probably be more open and contingent. All these aspects have, I propose, affected the relations between law and politics and between law and politics and the areas they regulate.

The EU may, then, be seen as an entity which has evolved by the interaction between the political, the legal and the economic communications systems, over time also including scientific communication and mass-media. I will propose that these systems have proved to be partly autonomous in their emergence and partly influenced by their interaction with each other. The interaction does not, however, seem to be part of any path-dependent or patterned institutional development. There have been unexpected and surprising outcomes in the emergence of the communicative functions and in how they interact. For the legal system I do not see any patterned or tradition-carrying European legal thinking behind its emergence. Nor do I see the emerging EU legal system as a harmonized or internally rational regime. It seems rather to be the result partly of complex processes and partly of certain aspects of its actualized and historic context. Both the legislation and the adjudication by the Commission and the Court can be described as uneven processes, where some principles or standards weigh in heavily and give it some direction, but where there is still a great deal of unpredictability.

## The Asymmetry of the Legal System

The most focal dynamic of the evolution of EU law has been the legal construction of the market by way of the articles on the free movement of goods, services, capital and persons, arts 28 (30), 49 and so on and the chapter on competition law. The Commission and the Court have over time engaged in a dynamic and expansive interpretation of these articles in the direction of creating an increasingly liberal market with a clear focus on the free movement of goods (and later also of persons, services and capital), and on a strict implementation of the ban on state subsidies. The general tendency of the Commission and the Court has been to have a high ambition towards the creation of an effective and functioning internal market by using the means provided by the treaties. The EC/EU treaties and their constructions of law are characterized by the combination of creating a relatively ambitious and vertically integrated legal system and having delimited material competences with a focus on market and competition law.

The Commission and the Court have been given the procedural competences to create a close to wholly vertically integrated legal system with an autonomous court and with the use of legal and economic sanctions. It is important to remark here that the Court has been constructed as a traditional court with the competences to solve the cases on a fully autonomous and judicial basis. The Court and the Commission have also been given the political context to be ambitious and effective within the framework of the treaties. Part of the political context has also been to emphasize the creation of an internal and effective market in order to increase the competitiveness of Europe in relation to the United States and Japan. The economic discourse of the EU institutions, as for other similar institutions, has also increasingly been a liberal and neo-liberal discourse with an emphasis on a well-functioning market without external interventions. At the same time the EC/EU institutions have been implementing and practising a delimited treaty in terms of material competences. The material competences are enumerated in the treaty and are confined, at least initially, primarily to market and competition law. Social rights, environmental and health protection and other collective rights have been dealt with primarily as part of or as consequences of the definition and delimitations of the market, free movement and competition.

The well-functioning and effective market judged on the basis of a neo-liberal market definition has been the main and dominating substantive goal in EU law. The ECJ's definition of free movement and a functioning market has changed over the years, moving steadily towards an increasingly comprehensive and neo-liberal definition where the focus has been on the market, and with a disregard for the effects on other areas. The result of the combination of a highly qualified and effective court and asymmetrical and delimited material competences has been that the regulated and adjudicated area has become paradigmatically expansive – whereas or because other legal areas have been non-existent or underrepresented. Market and competition law, however, is relatively simply defined in the treaties, a clear example of the reduced complexity which law generally is. Legally speaking there have been many ways of interpreting the critical articles. The question is why the direction has been towards the neo-liberal and autonomous market.

The answers offered here lie in the application of the theories of communicative differentiation and specifically in how the interaction between law, politics, economics and science has been played out in the interaction between the EU institutions and the Member States.

As mentioned above, the legal system of the EU is asymmetrical in several ways compared to the comprehensive legal systems of the nation-states. The procedural and judicial elements of the EU legal system are relatively well developed whereas the material elements are enumerated and delimited. The material focus is on market and competition law. When these areas are effectively implemented and interpreted, they tend to become increasingly expansive in relation to the bordering areas because the latter do not have any autonomous legal representation in themselves in the treaties. They are mainly represented and dealt with indirectly as boundaries or side-effects. In the later years this situation is somewhat changed, but it is still market and competition law which provide the primary dynamics of law in EU law. Other considerations are dealt with indirectly. In market law it is the free movement which is the primary distinction and the point of observation from where other aspects are surveyed. The various cases will then oscillate in relation to the distinction of free movement and probably move in the direction of how 'free movement' and liberal markets are defined in economic theory or in political discourse as well as legally. Other considerations are not dealt with in themselves, but as obstacles to or contexts for 'free movement' and thus always seen in relation to the primary distinction.

## The Legal Construction of the Internal Market and of Free Movement

It is an underlying thesis of my argument here that the legal construction of an open internal market in the EC/EU and its relatively effective functioning have been the vital and decisive basis for the success of the organization. Though there may have been many elements enabling or explaining this construction and how it has functioned, in this very short and unavoidably simplified argument, I will focus on the role of the interpretation and application of art. 28 (30) by the Commission and the Court in the construction of the internal market and the notion of free movement. While there have been other elements, the interpretation and application of this article has been crucial. The argument also rests upon the presumption that the construction and functioning of a common and an internal market has been the vital basis for the success of the EU as a political, economic and legal construction and also the precondition for the later more political and re-regulatory strategies. I will also argue that the construction and functioning of the internal market has not been a straightforward and predictable result of political and legal decision-making, but rather a result of complex combinations of political, legal and economic communication.

Already in the original Rome Treaty there were crucial articles on the prohibition of customs duties (tariffs) and of quantitative restrictions to trade across Member State boundaries. Explicit hindrances to import and export were clearly forbidden. The relevant articles also included the term 'mechanisms having an equivalent effect'. However, the scope of this was not specified in either political or legal communications. The Rome Treaty and the later treaties are, then, political and semi-constitutional texts rendering the further application to the legal system. Thus the political version of the definition of the common market had a rather indeterminate scope. The preamble of the treaty and other political communications did, however, include positive and expansive formulations on the emergence of a common and functioning market. A common market and the free movement of goods were from the start intended as the critical mechanisms of a closer integration between the Member States and of the Rome Treaty as an ambitious form of cooperation. The more exact application was handed over to the legal system.

In the Member States, market and competition law and other regulatory purposes were dealt with on the basis of political decision-making and discretion. No regulatory goals were prioritized apart from those with constitutional protection. Because there had been traditions of trade restrictions across state boundaries, with tariffs and quotas, the prohibitions of these meant that a new balance, without existing precedence, must be struck between economic and other regulatory considerations.

In the Statistical Levy case (24/68, *Commission v. Italy*) it was decided that a charge levied on both imports and exports, with the purpose of collecting statistics on Italy's trade, must be seen as having an effect equivalent to customs duties, EC articles 9, 12, 13 and 16. This was the start of a dynamic and expansive interpretation of the term 'mechanisms having an equivalent effect'. It meant an opening of the creation of a trade discourse which also included other trade articles of the treaty, not only concerning the prohibition of discrimination imports/exports, but also any unjustified obstacles to trade. The argumentation in Statistical Levy is quite expansive on what may be seen as having an equivalent effect. In a following case, Dassonville (8/74, *Procureur du Roi v. Dassonville*), the interpretation of art. 30 (now 28) was actualized. Here the discourse on 'any rules ... hindering, directly or indirectly, actually or potentially, intra-Community trade ...' was continued.[17] The formulations and the decisions of both cases led to the creation of not only a regime of 'fair trade', but a regime which was more expansive and which was constructed to eliminate all forms of discrimination and all unjustified obstacles to trade.[18] The way the Dassonville decision is formulated, it expands further the Statistical Levy argumentation by including not only those measures governing access to the market, but also potentially all regulations concerning the market itself. The Court here makes a decision to interpret the potentially open formulations of art. 28 (30) of 'mechanisms having an equivalent effect' and of 'quantitative restrictions' in the most open and expansive manner. These two decisions are, in the words of Weiler, 'canonical' of the economic constitution of Europe.[19] The decisions are

17 ECJ case 8/74 *Procureur du Roi v. Dassonville.*

18 Weiler, *The Constitution of Europe*, 352 ff.

19 Weiler, *The Constitution of Europe*, 353.

part text interpretation and part teleological interpretation. The choice is made to interpret 'equivalent effects' in a broad and expansive manner; a choice which could have been different.[20] The implication is that if the common market is to function effectively, not only explicit but also disguised protectionism should be included in the discourse of what may be considered discriminatory or obstacles to trade. When the door has been opened to an interpretation of art. 28 (30) that emphasizes the effective functioning of the market to the effect of also including disguised obstacles within the discourse of possible obstacles in the market, then it is also opened to widely discretionary and complex decisions. In effect, the Court will be asked to render political decisions. The implication is also that the Court has signalled the inclusion in the possible reach of art. 28 (30) both rules barring access to the market and other regulations of the market affecting sales. This is another extension of the interpretation of the article. The market-oriented and expansive interpretation of art. 28 (30) partly has the implication of creating a preference for the functioning of free markets over social regulations and partly has the implication that the Court is given the competence to draw the lines. There is, then, both a *substantial* question and a *procedural* question at stake here. The Dassonville case did not decide the direction of all similar later cases, but it contributed significantly to the legal construction of an emphasis on an effectively-functioning market and a scrutiny of any regulations hindering the market. By interpreting 'equivalent effects' in a wide manner, the Court opens up for a discretionary competence of reviewing regulations of the market in relation to art. 28 (30).

This line of reasoning was confirmed in the Cassis-de-Dijon case where a decision by German authorities on not to import French black-berry liquor was struck down as unjustified.

In a later case, Keck (case C-267 and 268/91 Criminal Proceedings against Keck and Mithouard), the extent of art. 28 (30) was again tried. The case concerned regulations on Sunday trading. Here the court decided to delimit the scope of art. 28 (30) and what should be seen as unjustified obstacles to trade. Regulations on Sunday trading were seen as general regulations and not as hindrances to cross-border trade.

Article 28 (30) has always been limited in its scope by the *exceptions* clause in art. 30 (36). The protection of human health and the environment may be a legitimate reason for market regulations. The practice on art. 30 (36), however, shows that the exception clause is not accepted as an open invitation to discretionary review. The possible exceptions are scrutinized in terms of whether they are necessary and proportionate. Scientific evidence is applied as demanded documentation for the former. In the Cassis case (case 120/78, *Rewe-Zentrale AG v. Bundesmonopolverwaltung für Branntwein*) the exception clause is extended to include other non-economic policies when these are deemed to be more important than the protection of a free market. This was probably a response to art. 30 (36)

20 Weiler, *The Constitution of Europe*, 360.

obviously being too narrow when the discretion of art. 28 (30) was opened up as it was.

As a point of departure, all measures which have similar consequences as 'quantitative restrictions' are included and then subjected to certain conditions and exceptions. Exceptions must be reasonable and seen as necessary in order to protect accepted interests or vital purposes, or they must be covered by the specified exceptions in art. 30; here also regarded as necessary in order to protect the interests in question. The exceptions are tried by the Commission and the Court, and the Court reviews any national policies and regulations which are brought before it in relation to the articles on free movement and competition. Member States must show or document that the exceptions are reasonable and/or necessary in relation to the interests they are presumed to protect. 'Reasonable' and 'necessary' have been interpreted objectively and strictly so that the main goal of free movement can be achieved without a speculative and uncertain web of exceptions. Allowed restrictions to trade under art. 36/30, due to the protection of the environment and human health, must be deemed necessary, and there must be documentation of scientific proof that the protective measures are necessary and do work. The exceptions must also be deemed proportional in relation to what they are presumed to achieve. Protectionist measures must not go further than necessary in order to achieve the goals.

## The Construction of Law and the Interaction between Law, Politics and Markets

The question now is how the terms of 'free movement', markets, competition, state subsidies and so on have been defined in the legal discourse. They have not been sufficiently clearly defined in the treaty or directive texts seen in relation to how they have been applied. While this is not necessarily a departure from other legal texts and other interpretive situations, two aspects of EU law make the condition more acute. Partly, EU market and competition law has been interpreted in a relatively dynamic way, and partly EU law has been developed in a more elite and expert-like environment and with less interest from a surrounding civil society or polity.[21] There are thus fewer chances for a public debate on EU legislation or court cases compared to the situation in Member States. Input to the interpretive processes of law is therefore more elitist and less generally contextual than in many other situations. When the question is asked within a purely legal context and rationality, I would propose the answer lies partly in the general internal systemic nature of law, and partly in the asymmetrical nature of the treaties.

Vital aspects of the evolution of the EU may, I propose, be described or explained by applying the theories of modern societies as functionally and communicatively

21 Joerges, 'Bureaucratic Nightmare, Technocratic Regime and the Dream of Good Transnational Governance', and 'Good Governance Through Comitology'.

differentiated, as developed by the German lawyer and sociologist Niklas Luhmann.[22] According to these theories, modern societies consist of political, legal, economic, scientific, mass-medial and other forms of communication. These forms of communication evolve around a specific code – legal/non-legal, power/not power and so on – autonomously and become increasingly specialized. The EC/EU treaties and institutions have been ambitious, but also, to some extent, open and unclear. They have represented a new sort of international organization, so it has obviously been difficult to tell exactly how they would evolve. There was no precedent, no pattern. My proposal is that the political, legal and economic communications of the EU have developed autonomously and in parallel, but they have also been coupled and have influenced each other and been mutually interdependent, albeit without any one steering centre or dynamic. Further, they have thus combined and influenced each other in contingent and unexpected ways. The different functions and their interactions are characterized by complexity – internally and between them – and by contingency.[23]

Law in general evolves on the basis of the distinction law/non-law.[24] Within law there are also different sub-systems regulating the different areas of law. Here, different standards will be the distinctions of these areas. 'Free movement' is one such standard. Such distinctions will evolve self-referentially but also dynamically, dependent on the input they receive from their context. In the national legal systems, the sub-systems of law have developed within and as part of a comprehensive legal system, and have therefore been exposed to input also from all the other legal subsystems and thus to a wide range of considerations. The EU legal system is, however, delimited and asymmetrical. EU market and competition law has therefore been developed relatively autonomously and with substantial distance from other legal areas and other social considerations. They are not part of fully comprehensive legal systems such as the legal sub-systems of national legal systems. The distinctions such as 'free movement' and competition will thus probably evolve more autonomously and expansively, in their self-referential way, than if they were part of more comprehensive legal systems. Even if the EU legal system has become more diverse, including more forms of social and environmental regulation, the regulations on free movement and competition law still form the core of the legal system. Their expansive interpretation in relation to other considerations and other areas of law is still functioning.

Initially the political system voiced its ambitions of a more effective and common market functioning across state borders with the dual purpose of creating a basis for a more stable political cooperation over time and of economic growth, but without the exact models for how this was to be organized. This was backed by economic theory; first of creating a larger market without the obstacles of borders

---

22 Luhmann, *Soziale Systeme*, chs 1 and 2.

23 Sand, 'Understanding the New Forms of Governance'.

24 Luhmann, N. (1992), 'Operational Closure and Structural Coupling', *Cardozo Law Review*, 13, 1418.

and import tariffs and later by theories of more effective markets without regulatory differences and obstacles. By the creation of treaties and directives, the political system hands vital parts of the more precise construction and implementation of the internal market and its regulation over to the legal system. The *political* context of the legal system has been the overall regulations in the treaties, namely that it has been politically decided to create a full-fledged and autonomous court with all the judicial qualities, but without considering the consequences of this, because this is not really possible for the legal system. At the same time the political signals were the creation of an effectively-functioning market within the EU, and that all protectionist measures among the Member States must be abolished. The political message has also above all been to emphasize the need to improve the economic competitiveness of the EU in relation to the United States and Japan.

The *economic* system and how it functions have changed since 1960. The goal of the EU, however, has throughout this period been an effectively-functioning and liberal market. From the economic system to the legal system, the message has been that the definition of a functioning market has been the abolishment of all unnecessary and protectionist restrictions to the market. From the start the message has been an effective internal market. Particularly from the 1980s the competitiveness in relation to the United States and Japan was emphasized. This moves the attention from the internal market to its relative competitiveness as a whole in relation to other regions or states. The general economic ideologies move throughout the period towards being not only liberal, but neo-liberal. Neo-liberalism is connected to the idea that the market is the basic organizing factor of society. The most effective market is best for all – the consequence is to include also the financial criteria of the market. This creates a general standard for what to use capital for. The most financially efficient use of capital is always preferred.

The *legal* operations, however, also have their relative autonomy. I have above described the institutional framework of EU law, with an emphasis on its combined attempts to be effective and have full-fledged judicial courts and having delimited and asymmetric material competences. From this I have concluded that the regulations on free movement and competition law have become so expansive because they have been the main material competences of EU law.[25] They have expanded self-referentially because they have not been part of a more comprehensive legal system and have thus to a lesser degree been seen in relation to other social considerations.

The emphasis on having as few restrictions to trade as possible has led to a certain pattern of interpretation of the various terms which are applied in such cases. The formulation 'quantitative restrictions and all equivalent measures' could have been interpreted and applied in several different ways. The Court decided to interpret it step by step by defining both 'restrictions' and 'all equivalent measures' openly and expansively. Exceptions were thus strictly reviewed. The terms 'necessary', 'reasonable', 'objective' and so on were applied in order to review and to delimit

25 Joerges, 'Free Trade' and 'Constitutionalism in Postnational Constellations'.

the exceptions and their scope. The argumentation has thus developed a pattern over time which is applied in all such cases. The variation of cases has contributed to more and more nuances in the pattern, but the liberal market-orientation has been retained. The variations have contributed to an increasingly consequent market-orientation rather than the opposite.

Communicative differentiation in its radical version of Niklas Luhmann's systems theory means seeing 'the social' as consisting of communications and of communicative systems, such as the functional systems of law, politics, the economy and so on. Communication in society and in organizations is then differentiated into a variety of systems which are linked and dependent on each other, but which also do not communicate directly in terms of meaning. Communication is then doomed to conditions of complexity and contingency.[26] Organizations communicating in the codes of politics, law, markets and so on may communicate both very precisely when referring to well-known links between the systems, but also in extremely complex, open and contingent ways leading to unexpected interactions and results.[27] The consequence of this is that when constructing and running multi-coded and complex organizations there will be the inevitable risk of gaps and lack of communication between the communicative systems and codes involved.

## Competition Law – Ban on State Subsidies

In EC art. 81, in the chapter on rules on competition, there is a general ban on prevention, restriction and distortion of competition. In art. 82 there is a prohibition on abuse of dominant position. In art. 87 there is a prohibition on any state aid distorting or threatening to distort competition by favouring certain undertakings or productions. These are general rules on competition law which are not very different from the previous competition law regimes of the Member States. Also, in this field of economic law, the regulations have been interpreted and applied within a discursive pattern of economics, favouring the ideals of a free and liberal market with as little state intervention as possible.

Previously, European state aid had been allowed for several social and industrial purposes, almost on a discretionary basis. State aid had been used after the Second World War to establish and run many types of industries in Europe. Infrastructures and state services have also been established and run generally by public authorities or as state companies.

26 Luhmann, *Soziale Systeme*, chs 3 and 11.

27 Luhmann, N. (1992), 'Demands on Politics', in Luhmann, N., *Risk: A Sociological Theory* (Berlin: de Gruyter), 145ff; Nassehi, A. (2005), 'Organizations as Decision Machines: Niklas Luhmann's Theory of Organized Social Systems', in Jones, C. and Munro, R. (eds), *Contemporary Organization Theory* (Oxford: Blackwell).

Under art. 87 it has been presumed that *all services* which could be said to be of an economic character were included under the ban of state aid. The vital difference compared to previous competition law regimes is, however, that under EC law 'services of an economic character' is interpreted to mean all services which can potentially be distributed by the market. This not only means those services which actually and currently are market organized, but all those which potentially could be organized that way. Today this includes most services. The economic regime has shifted from regulatory and mixed-economy, social democratic regimes to a predominance of, albeit regulated, liberal markets where partly the presumption is that most activities can be produced and organized on a market basis, and partly that the economy is and should be basically market-driven, as a legal presumption.[28]

The legal presumption of a liberal, market-based economy is new. It has not previously existed in Europe to that degree. Within the Member States competition law may have been market-oriented, but it has also been balanced in relation to other social and national policies. It has been part of a mixed economy system. It has also been part of a comprehensive legal system where other considerations and legal fields have been part of its legal context.

EU competition law and trade law thus have a different legal context. They are the primary legal fields and dynamics of EU law. Their codes and dynamics can thus evolve more self-referentially without being part of a broader legal context. The liberal economic distinctions are the primary positively-given distinctions of the legal system. They are applied and will evolve without the resistance and context of other legal fields of the national legal systems. When they are related to the various possible social exceptions in EU law, these exceptions do not have sufficient positive self-representation in the legal system. They are exceptions.

The economic ideology of the EC has been the creation of an internal and undisturbed market, with free movement, competition and increased competitiveness in relation to other actors. This has been backed up institutionally with administrative and judicial controls and review mechanisms. This has been done simultaneously with the creation of a new and more liberal economic ideology where global competition has been the primary goal and standard.

To achieve this, a general standard of the marketplace has been deemed necessary. This has meant the ideal of a purification of the market as such, with as little state intervention as possible, apart from the regulations to create and stabilize the market, and a conscious change from the mixed economies with state-owned corporations and public services. Saskia Sassen has written that financial norms have become the criteria for economic policies and the core dynamic of the

28 Green Paper on Services of General Economic Interest, COM (2003) 270; White Paper on Services of General Economic Interest, COM (2004) 374; Hancher, L. (1999), 'Community, State and Market', in Craig and de Burca, *The Evolution of EU Law*.

economic system.[29] Increasingly all capital is being subsumed under one type of standards for financial markets.

In the mixed-economy state several general services were presumed to be public and to be paid for or subsidized by public authorities. The economic administration of those services was decided on a discretionary basis by political authorities. Under EU law services which potentially can be organized on the market, cannot receive state subsidies. The economic presumption on services is thus changed.

Also services of general economic interest are included in the ban on state subsidies, unless this rule obstructs the performance of the services, in law or in fact. Only services which cannot function on a market basis if they are to perform their tasks, can be included in the exception.

First the competition law authorities and then the Court may review the practices of the Member States in this area, under EC law. It is thus no longer up to the discretion of the national political authorities to apply these rules. The review mechanisms include the rights to decide on: whether or not a certain service can potentially be organized on a market basis; whether or not it is a service of general economic interest; whether or not it is a service of general economic interest which needs to be excepted from the state subsidy rules; whether or not the state subsidy in question has effects on intra-Community trade.

When services of general economic interest have been reviewed by the ECJ in relation to the rules on state subsidies, how the services *are* organized and how they *could* be organized is thoroughly examined. In relation to health services, it has been accepted that the Member States are free to organize these as they choose. There is a large degree of discretion here because it is accepted that health services are very expensive and at the same time a crucial welfare service which it may be vital for all citizens to have access to. It is thus accepted that the Member States may decide that all citizens should have equal access to these services and at the same quality. Such services are also seen as both an individual and a collective asset. Various forms of direct public financing or insurance arrangements are then accepted under the principle of solidarity. If, however, the factual arrangements are more market-oriented, some kind of consequence may be demanded.

## Complexity and Discontinuity: How Do We Identify Institutional Change?

There have been dramatic and radical changes in the procedures, the institutions and the institutional patterns of political and legal decision-making throughout the last 50 years and in particular the last 20 years in the EU and its Member States. The more distinct boundaries between the national, regional and international have been broken down. The institutions on these levels now form and continuously develop complex, non-hierarchical conglomerates and multi-level interactions

29 Sassen, *Territories, Authorities, Rights*, 249ff.

where they overlap, coordinate actions and compete in new and still partly changing and unstable organizational and normative patterns.[30] The relations are continuously changing politically and in practice; furthermore the relations are not always distinct formally and legally, leaving it at times unclear how power is dispersed.[31]

My proposition is that EU institutions and their relations to the Member States constitute qualitatively new relations between the inter- and supranational and the national levels by way of the particular type of interdependencies that have been created.[32] They should, then, not only be seen as a continuation of previous international organizations, but also as a discontinuation and as qualitatively new types of politico-legal institutions. The EU seems to emerge as an accumulated result of the interactions between these decisions and of unexpected or unpredictable trajectories of and between the competences of the Commission, the Council, the Parliament and the Court (as a full-fledged judicial autonomous court). The combination of a different division of powers between the branches of government of European as opposed to national-historical contexts and of the asymmetric substantive competences of the EU, I argue, have contributed to the emergence of several changes in the configuration of and the relations between political and legal communication and thus also to changes in how power emerges and is distributed. The status of the Commission and the Court as fully European, treaty-based and autonomous institutions and as producers of interpretation of the treaties and of legal communication may be decisive elements in the explanation of the emergence and the configuration of the EU as it is today and in some of the radical changes in the relations of institutions and in the emergence of a more market-driven regulatory system.

The Council of Ministers is in effect a coupling between the treaty-based EU and the Member States. It allows a double loyalty. The Commission and the Court, however, are treaty-based and have the competences to be fully autonomous on that basis. They develop politics and law on a European basis, and they have been given relatively vital decision-making power which they also have used. Consequently there are some significant differences between the EU institutions and the comparable politico-legal and constitutional-based institutions of the Member States regarding the configurations of political and legal competences and decision-making. Some EU institutions are distinctly European and autonomous, others have a more mixed basis and frame of reference. The Commission and the Court have vital responsibilities for the legal decision-making of the EU, and they are at the same time more autonomous in relation to the Member States than the

30 Sand, 'Understanding the New Forms of Governance'.

31 Teubner, G. (2004), 'Societal Constitutionalism: Alternatives to State-Centred Constitutional Theory?', and Inger-Johanne Sand, 'Polycontextuality as an Alternative to Constitutionalism', both in Joerges, C., Sand, I-J. and Teubner, G. (2004), *Transnational Governance and Constitutionalism* (Oxford: Hart).

32 Weiler, 'The Autonomy of the Community Legal Order'.

Council and the Parliament. This might provide a basis for a relative strengthening of the legal part of the dynamics compared to the political part.

The *political* communication in the EU institutions will tend to combine references to the European and the local, national levels. Strong Member State interests may hinder new legislation. If the relevant question is to be *legally* decided, the competences and the frames of reference are more clearly European and cannot be stopped by national arguments or interests. I argue that the division between legal and political decision-making is stronger in the EU than within the Member States also because the *legal* and the *political* communication have different frames of reference and different contexts. This may strengthen the autonomy of the legal communication in the EU in relation to politics more than between comparable communications on the national level. Even if law and legal decision-making also have considerable autonomy on the national level, there is a common frame of reference and also many more arenas or organizations which function as structural couplings between law and politics. The nationally-based legal communication will therefore to a larger degree, or more systematically, receive a variety of political and other social information on a range of common arenas or contexts. The autonomous law will thus on the national levels be corrected or 'kept up to date' by their social and political many-layered contexts in a different way than is possible on the European and supranational levels. The consequences of this might be furthered by the asymmetric composition of substantial competences on the supranational level.

One could generally say that nation-state institutions and their legal and political regimes are comprehensively embedded in social, cultural, historical and political contexts, and thus have developed a variety of structural couplings to other organizations or social systems. The legal and political communications consequently share vital aspects of their social contexts or frames of reference. On the regional, supra- and international levels, legal and political communication and institutions will to a lesser degree have such developed structural couplings to other organizational systems. Their structural couplings are more to other functions' systems and to their generalized and more abstract forms of communication as they will often lack the references to local social and political contexts. The preconditions and the contexts for legal and political communication on these levels are thus quite different in terms of sensitivity to their contexts.

From the start there has also been a relatively developed legal system in the EU, with the treaties, the legislative process and the fully autonomous court. The directions taken by the Court early on have enabled continuous judicial review of directives and regulations in relation to the treaties, thus also establishing a vertical integration of the legal system. The preliminary rulings by the Court on the request of the national courts, art. 234 (177), have been a vital element in establishing a more active authority of the Court in the Member States too. The legal system of the EU has therefore in many ways been more developed than the political-democratic part of it. The institutional and procedural development of the legal system have, however, not been matched by the material competences of the Court. The material competences have been asymmetric, primarily based in the economic area, on the regulation of the market and the freedom of movement. The result is that while parts of the legislative area of the Member States are also covered by EU legislation and by the Court's jurisdiction, other parts are not. An asymmetry then arises within the regulatory field due to the more intensive judicial review of the areas covered by EU law compared to other areas. It is unclear whether the relative strength of the legal system has been an intended part of the EU architecture. It seems relatively clear, however, that the position of the legal system has been established by decisions which are not necessarily coupled. Parts of the responsibility certainly rest with the Court and its decisions establishing an effective judicial review. Another crucial factor has been art. 234 (177), the effects of which, in practice, were probably not foreseen. Different and interacting decisions have since then coincided to create the legal system of the EU as it is.

It was a clear and intended goal of the EC/EU from the Rome Treaty onwards to use a common or internal market and economic cooperation as means to develop integration and peace among the Member States. I propose, however, that the relative effectiveness of the functioning of the market in relation to other regulatory goals was not foreseen, but emerged as a result of a combination of political, economic and legal dynamics and particularly as a result of certain decisions by the Court. It was probably presumed that integration via a common or internal market could function as 'a negative integration',[33] that is, without vital repercussions for other regulatory areas. In effect and by the decisions of the Court, some of which are mentioned above, the regulations of the market and of competition law in the EC treaty have been interpreted and implemented so effectively that they have turned into a 'positive' market regulation. Art. 28 (30) has not been interpreted in a minimalist fashion, but in an affirmative, extensive and positive fashion. As a result, other regulatory goals have also been included and compared to the market standards. A 'positive integration' of the EC treaty into national regulatory law was over time constructed, but on the premises of the standards of the market and of free or fair competition. Regulation of the market and of competition has been the preferred regulatory goal of the EU. Other regulatory goals have been included in so far as they have been consistent with the market standards. Hence an asymmetric regulatory system emerged with an effective implementation of market and competition law goals, and only more indirect and ineffective implementation of other goals. The asymmetry is to a significant degree a result of decisions by the Commission and the Court and by the regulatory pattern thus emerging. The 'market' as part of the legal and regulatory system of the EU may then be seen as a construction resulting from various – and not necessarily coordinated – decisions by different institutions. It can be seen more as a result of a play of complexity

---

33 Scharpf, 'Negative and Positive Integration in the Political Economy of the European Union'.

and contingency in a complex field of regulation and of different rationalities of regulation than as a result of transparent and intended decision-making.

## Hybrids and Analytic Borderlands: New Institutional Relations

In previous phases of internationalization the emphasis was on clear distinctions between national and international institutions and their competences. In the current era of multi-level governance the focus is more on the varieties of relations between institutions on the different levels. The institutions cooperate, coordinate, compete and overlap. They are not ordered hierarchically, but heterarchically. The most distinct element is, however, that the combined efforts of institutions on different levels are often necessary in order to operate vital political and legal procedures and to make decisions. New, intensive and complex forms of interdependence have been created where it may be difficult to say what the most decisive elements are.

Saskia Sassen has emphasized the relations and the interactions between these institutions as vital sites of action and thus also of analysis today. She has proposed applying the concepts of analytic borderlands and frontier zones on these relations and interactions[34] and also emphasized how globalization relies upon the new and interactive relations and interdependencies between the institutions. The relations between supranational and national institutions are primary examples of this. The relations between the ECJ and the national courts are good examples. Results are achieved only by complex relations between several institutions. The EU Commission has been a vital factor in the power of the EU *vis-à-vis* the Member States, but it has also relied on the Member States and their participation for its final legitimacy.

Many of the new inter-, supra- and transnational institutions have developed far beyond the expectations of the initiators. This may be a consequence of the unpredicted practices and trajectories of each institution and of unpredicted interactions between several institutions. Factual regionalization and globalization may be factors behind the unexpected institutional trajectories. International trade has developed beyond expectations and has produced new practices and new trajectories which again have led to new institutions.

The perspectives of *complexity/contingency* and *continuity/discontinuity* as analytical approaches to the new trajectories of international institutions and between national and international institutions may be critical in understanding the comprehensiveness, the radicality and the paradigmatic break of some of the recent institutional changes. If we do not see the new qualities and the paradigmatic breaks, we may not be able to see or to understand the consequences of these changes.

---

34 Sassen, *Territories, Authorities, Rights*, ch. 8, 379ff.

# Chapter 9
# Transnational Statecraft: Legal Entrepreneurs, the European Field of Power and the Genesis of the European Constitution

Antonin Cohen

What is wishfully thought as the construction of Europe could be more accurately depicted as a series of heterogeneous and competing enterprises – political, bureaucratic, legal, academic, economic, but also military and police – partly coordinated and in tune with one another, partly autonomous and out of tune with each other. At regular intervals, a treaty is intended to give the appearance of a 'construction' to this 'configuration', in particular by merging institutions or at least streamlining the division of labour between institutions resulting from these various enterprises. This constantly renewed political and juridical order tends to record the endogenous practices of these different institutions, now formalized by a series of competences, rules and procedures, legalizing this division of labour. The treaty establishing a Constitution for Europe does not escape this logic. Except that, for the first time in the history of European integration, under the impact of the enlargement of the European Union (EU) to the countries of eastern Europe and the implementation of a common security and defence policy that tend to accentuate the interdependences and/or to blur the boundaries between the Council of Europe, the North Atlantic Treaty Organization, the Western European Union and the EU, the drafters had to proceed to a global reconfiguration of the division of labour that imposed itself after the Second World War.[1]

Each treaty reform, coordinating mobilizations that occur in parallel in different social universes and different institutional arenas, is an opportunity for a specific category of agents to promote their specific 'expertise' and shape the institutions and rules that make the complex architecture of the EU. Whatever their official (and most of the time changing) positions – academic, bureaucratic, political or even judicial – these agents, half legal professionals, half political entrepreneurs (and *vice versa*), institution-building engineers

---

1 Cohen, A. (2006), 'De congrès en assemblées: La structuration de l'espace politique transnational européen au lendemain de la guerre', *Politique européenne* 18, 119–31.

specializing in European issues, find in the multiplicity of European venues and issues and in the multiplication of European norms and forms the terrain (not to say the jungle) best suited to their 'claim of jurisdiction',[2] either to formalize their content, or to reform the containers. Such an investment in 'institutional reform' is an important condition of the perpetuation of their power on the 'construction' of Europe and the reproduction of their specific capital in the European 'configuration'.

## Competition between Elites and Legal Expertise

European integration history in many ways illustrates the part played by politico-legal entrepreneurs in interpreting the treaties, inside and outside legal institutions such as the European Court of Justice (ECJ) or the European Court of Human Rights (ECHR), or even drafting constitutional treaties in favourable political contexts.[3] This chapter argues that these agents played a central part in the genesis of the constitutional treaty, both in the early working groups and committees that paved the way to a European Constitution and in the Convention finally entrusted with drafting such a Constitution. By focusing on the social construction of the transnational public debate on the 'form' of the EU, this chapter aims at highlighting the structure of relations between the European transnational political space and the international academic field in the genesis of this treaty reform. The circulation of legal categories in and out the Convention, as well as the empire of law over the internal structures and debates of the Convention, have to be understood in the light of the social characteristics of this constitution-making elite.

The European Constitution can, in fact, be analysed as the product of the structural relations between different kinds of elites, embedded in a series of long-term transformations now resulting in the formation of a European field

2 Abbott, A. (1988), *The System of Professions: An Essay on the Division of Expert Labor* (Chicago, IL: University of Chicago Press).

3 On the role of jurists in the construction of a European political order, see Cohen, A. and Vauchez, A. (2007), 'Law, Lawyers, and Transnational Politics in the Production of Europe', *Law & Social Inquiry* 32:1, 75–199; Cohen, A. and Vauchez, A. (2005), 'Les juristes et l'ordre politique européen', *Critique internationale* 26, 97–158; Vauchez, A. (2007), 'Une élite d'intermédiaires: Genèse d'un capital juridique européen (1950–1970), *Actes de la recherche en sciences sociales* 166/167, 54–65.

of power.[4] In this configuration of 'interdependent elite groups',[5] some agents in particular are in a position to contribute, simultaneously, to the political structuring of this power configuration and to the social construction of the legitimate categories in which it is commonly thought. These legal/institutional experts who make a profession out of producing 'universal' symbolic forms and norms (that is, institutions and constitutions) are able, not only to circulate these categories in different social circles (including when formally disagreeing on the forms themselves),[6] but also to continuously change positions in the European field of power so as to make these categories efficient. Most of our *representations* of Europe as a 'construction' have actually been forged by this particular type of agents. This is the reason why the analysis of such a configuration should not be limited to the formal characteristics of the institutional positions these actors hold individually, which tend to depict these actors as mainly *representatives* of national governments and parliaments or European institutions. When analysed as groups of trajectories, these interdependent elite groups appear to be much more than that. The total social space in which the members of the Convention evolve, for instance, does not have the clearly defined institutional boundaries (between the European and the international, the supranational and the national, the public and the private) that dominant academic representations of European integration tend to acknowledge. The European field of power does not stop at the *edge* of the EU, but reaches beyond into a transnational space that includes academic institutions such as the European University Institute (EUI) in Florence, political organizations such as the European Movement International (EMI) and its national equivalents, non-EU European institutions such as the parliamentary assemblies of the Organization for Security and Cooperation in Europe (OSCE) and the North Atlantic Treaty Organization (NATO), international organizations such as the World Trade Organization (WTO) or the International Monetary Fund (IMF), as well as think tanks, law firms, corporations and so on.

Of course, the complex question of the structural relations between the national fields of power – of which the formation of a European field of power would be both the cause and the effect – cannot be reduced to the somewhat limited interactions that have brought about this constitutional project. However, these

4 On the notion of field of power: Bourdieu, P. (1989), *La Noblesse d'Etat: Grandes écoles et esprit de corps* (Paris: Editions de Minuit). On the reconfiguration of national fields of power under the impact of internationalization processes: Dezalay, Y. (2004), 'Les courtiers de l'international. Héritiers cosmopolites, mercenaires de l'impérialisme et missionnaires de l'universel', *Actes de la recherche en sciences sociales* 151/152, 5–35; and Dezalay, Y. and Garth, B.G. (2002), *The Internationalization of Palace Wars: Lawyers, Economists, and the Contest to Transform Latin American States* (Chicago, IL: University of Chicago Press).

5 Elias, N. (1985), *La Société de cour* (Paris: Flammarion), 310.

6 Shared representations of law and politics are much stronger than apparent disagreements in all the controversies on the point of knowing if the draft is a 'treaty', a 'constitution' or a 'constitutional treaty'.

structural relations form the background of this chapter. The interdependences and competitions that unite and oppose the different kinds of dominant elites in Europe – economic, political, bureaucratic, academic or otherwise – in a series of confrontations and negotiations to impose 'the principle of dominant domination' and, thus, the 'legitimate principle of legitimization'[7] are now framed in a European transnational field of power where the stake remains the distribution of power over the State, albeit through transnational institutions. The first 'market' opened to international competition as a result of the institutionalization of a European transnational space after the Second World War, well before the Treaties of Rome were even signed, is the market of the specific capitals possessed by these interdependent and concurrent elite groups in their respective social fields and national fields of power: economic, political, bureaucratic or academic capitals, which 'exchange rate' is also being established, since then, in a transnational space that co-determines their relative value in the various national fields of power.

More than others, the national legal fields have been affected by this general process under the influence of both the formation of a European economic market and the production of a European legal corpus resulting in the expansion of new legal markets and new bodies of specialized knowledge. In other words, they have been affected not only by the empowerment of a supranational Court of Justice vested with the power of arbitrating and regulating in last instance conflicts arising from this economic market, which, indeed, has had a *direct effect* on the national legal systems;[8] but also because of the drastic changes within traditional national academic hierarchies and legal markets that resulted from this new deal, with the emergence of European Community (EC) law redefining the different branches of legal knowledge and practices. In many ways, the Treaty establishing a Constitution for Europe can be read as the latest attempt on the part of legal/institutional professionals, be they academic experts in close connection to the political field or political entrepreneurs coming from the academic field, to convert a specific kind of capital (law) into a principle of determination of the value of all other kinds of capitals within the European field of power; and even more specifically, as the indirect product of the creation of transnational communities or national bodies of professionals specializing on European law and institutions and the simultaneous transformation of related legal and political disciplines.[9] A group

---

7 Bourdieu, *La Noblesse d'Etat*, 376.

8 Stone Sweet, A. (2004), *The Judicial Construction of Europe* (Oxford: Oxford University Press); and Alter, K. (2001), *Establishing the Supremacy of European Law: The Making of an International Rule of Law in Europe* (Oxford: Oxford University Press).

9 On the production of a body of specialized legal knowledge and its effects on the political game, see François, B. (1993), 'Justice constitutionnelle et "démocratie constitutionnelle": Critique du discours constitutionnaliste européen', *Droit et Politique* (Paris: Puf), and François, B. (1990), 'Une revendication de juridiction: Compétence et justice dans le droit constitutionnel de la Ve République', *Politix* 10/11, 92–109. On the formation of transnational communities of specialized lawyers and their boomerang effect

of professionals whose presence at both ends of the production of this reform has been one of the conditions of its success.

In what follows, I will, first, analyse how expert knowledge has been mobilized by various academic and political committees that paved the way to the European Convention, and then, explore the social profiles of the members of the Convention in order to measure the weight of academic and legal capitals in this process of treaty reform.

## Experts and Entrepreneurs in the Genesis of the European Constitution

Despite the fact that, in 1986, the ECJ reframed the founding treaties as the 'constitutional charter' of the EU, and that, in 1984 and 1994, the European Parliament (EP) drafted a European Constitution, it was not really until the end of the 1990s that these different strategies to constitutionalize the EU converged on the political agenda.[10] If this collective action primarily arose on a point of legal order (the reorganization of the treaties), within the expert committees created under the umbrella of the EUI, it quickly became a political issue (the need for a constitution), under the impulse of the committee on institutional affairs of the EP. Whatever the venues, however, this question mainly remained the 'monopoly' of a transnational community of legal/institutional professionals, using different modes and channels of expression. Indeed, if the Amato Report (1999) was issued by experts mainly coming from the academic field strangers to the political field, the Duhamel Report (2000) gave voice to transnational entrepreneurs also coming from academia, but much more directly engaged in politics.

---

(according to Madsen's expression), not only on the national legal fields, but on the European field of power itself, see Schepel, H. and Wesseling, R. (1997), 'The Legal Community: Judges, Lawyers, Officials and Clerks in the Writing of Europe', *European Law Journal* 3:2, 165–88 (regarding EC law) and Madsen, M.R. (2005), *L'émergence d'un champ des droits de l'homme dans les pays européens: enjeux professionnels et stratégies d'État au carrefour du droit et de la politique (France, Grande-Bretagne et pays scandinaves, 1945–2000)*. Sociology PhD thesis (Paris: EHESS) (regarding Human Rights Law).

10 One must keep in mind that the legal discourse on the constitutional 'nature' of the European treaties was born in the early 1950s in the context of political mobilization that resulted in the early drafting of a Constitution for Europe. Cohen, A. (2007), 'Constitutionalism without Constitution: Transnational Elites between Political Mobilization and Legal Expertise in the Making of a Constitution for Europe (1940s–1960s)', *Law & Social Inquiry* 32:1, 109–35, and Stein, E. (1981), 'Lawyers, Judges and the Making of a Transnational Constitution', *American Journal of International Law* 75:1, 1–27; Stone Sweet, *The Judicial Construction of Europe* and Stone Sweet, A. and. Brunelli, T. (1998), 'Constructing a Supranational Constitution: Dispute Resolution and Governance in the European Community', *American Political Science Review* 92:1, 63–81.

These two reports, precisely separated by the political turn of the debate on the highly expected institutional reform (that is, German Minister of Foreign Affairs Joschka Fischer's speech in May 2000), illustrate the range of arguments, the 'technical' and the 'political', used to justify the 'necessity' of, not only reforming the institutions for an enlarged Europe, but also 're-forming' the whole architecture of the treaties. A range of arguments that would go on to structure, via the Laeken Declaration which turned them into joint 'objectives', the work of the Convention itself, as well as the repertoire of justification and internal architecture of the treaty: to reform the institutions (part 1), to reorganize the treaties (part 2, later part 3 after inclusion of the Charter of Fundamental Rights), and to constitutionalize the whole thing. The first report, commissioned in 1998 by the committee on institutional affairs of the EP (1994–99) and drafted by a group of experts headed by Giuliano Amato, appears as an exposé of three distinct strategies (complete with options and variants) to 'reinforce the constitutional nature of the treaties'.[11] This was rapidly followed by a second report, on a fairly identical question, the 'reorganization of the treaties', even if presented in a more technical manner. Drawn up by a group of experts under the coordination of Claus-Dieter Ehlermann and Yves Mény, it was this time requested by the European Commission.[12] The Duhamel Report, meanwhile, issued by the committee on constitutional affairs of the EP (1999–2004), underlined that the 'form' of the texts governing the EU ('an accumulation of long and complicated treaties') was 'difficult to use both for experts and for the general public', and thus proposed that a 'single "framework Treaty" which is clear and concise' be drafted, containing only 'fundamental constitutional provisions', in other words, a true 'European Constitution'.[13]

The first expert committee that began meeting in 1998 under the chairmanship of Giuliano Amato was made up of high profile professors in political science and law, such as Stefano Bartolini, Renaud Dehousse, Bruno De Witte, Luis Diez-

11 Interestingly enough, the abridged English version of this report is much more explicit than the original extended French: whereas the English report bluntly asks 'What form of Constitution for the European Union', the French report more elusively asks 'What Constitutional Charter for the European Union' (in the term preferred by the ECJ in 1986). Likewise, it is assumed that there is a constitutional 'nature' more than a constitutional 'character' of the treaties: European Parliament (1999), *Quelle Charte constitutionnelle pour l'Union Européenne? Stratégies et options pour renforcer le caractère constitutionnel des Traités* (*What form of Constitution for the European Union? Strategies and options to reinforce the constitutional nature of the Treaties*) Political Series 105 and 105A EN.

12 Robert Schuman Centre for Advanced Studies (2001), *A Basic Treaty for the European Union: A Study of the Reorganisation of the Treaties* (Florence: EUI); followed a few weeks later by a second volume on the 'treaties' amendment procedures': Robert Schuman Centre for Advanced Studies (2000), *Reforming the Treaties' Amendment Procedures: Second Report on the Reorganisation of the European Union Treaties* (Florence: EUI).

13 European Parliament (2000), *Report on the Constitutionalisation of the Treaties*, A5-0289/2000, 2000, 7.

Picazo, Yves Mény, Philippe Schmitter, Armin Von Bogdandy and Joseph Weiler, as well as members of the Brussels administration, like Hervé Bribosia and Claus-Dieter Ehlermann. The majority of them (Bribosia, Dehousse, De Witte, Diez-Picazo, Ehlermann, Mény, Von Bogdandy) were also part of the committee that met the following year to draw up a second report, joined by the likes of Grainne de Burca, Allan Dashwood, Jean-Victor Louis, Francis Snyder, Antonio Tizzano, Jacques Ziller and Philippe de Schoutheete (special advisor to and representative of Commissioner Michel Barnier, responsible for institutional reform). It should be emphasized how much the composition of this quite 'select' group of people owes to the formation of a transnational community of specialists in EC law and institutions at the crossroads of international academia (law and political science) and supranational bureaucracy (legal and administrative), whose geographical and social point of intersection is located at the EUI in Florence – a community that this group tends to subtly 'incorporate'. Giuliano Amato himself, future vice-president of the Convention, being a perfect example of a constitutional politico-legal entrepreneur: holding a law degree from the University of Pisa (1960) and a Master in comparative constitutional law from Columbia Law School in New York (1962), Amato was a professor at the University of Rome before being elected as Member of Parliament (1983) and holding various ministerial portfolios, Minister of Constitutional reform from 1998 to 1999, Minister of Finance from 1999 to 2000, and Prime Minister from 2000 to 2001.

With the exception of Hervé Bribosia (holding a degree in European and international law from the Catholic University of Louvain, Bribosia was a member of the permanent representation of Belgium during the intergovernmental conference that led to the Treaty of Amsterdam before becoming a member of the group of political advisors to the European Commission later detached to the permanent secretariat of the European Convention), or Claus-Dieter Ehlermann (holding a PhD in law from the University of Heidelberg, Ehlermann was Director General of the Legal Service of the European Commission from 1980 to 1990, then Director General for Competition from 1990 to 1995, before entering the WTO's Appellate Body from 1995 to 2002, and becoming a member of the law firm Wilmer, Cutler & Pickering in 2002), the intersecting trajectories of the various academic members of this expert group, which all go through or end at the EUI, cover a large fraction of the international academic field in political science and law: the Universities of Florence, Trieste, and Geneva (Stefano Bartolini), Sciences Po Paris (Renaud Dehousse), the Universities of Brussels (Jean-Victor Louis), Maastricht (Bruno De Witte) and Malaga (Luis Diez-Picazo), the Max Planck Institute for Comparative Public Law and International Law in Heidelberg, the Free University of Berlin and the Goethe University of Frankfurt (Armin Von Bogdandy), La Sapienza in Rome (Antonio Tizzano, Advocate General at the ECJ since 2000), the College of Europe in Bruges (Jacques Ziller), University College

London and the London School of Economics (Francis Snyder), as well as New York University (Joseph Weiler).[14]

If any of this academic expertise has had any effect on the course of the political mobilization in favour of a European Constitution, this was not so much because of the intrinsic strength of the intellectual arguments made in these various reports, as a result of the successful importation of academic categories and logics into the political arena, a *transfer* that was largely favoured by a series of 'double agents'. Quite telling in this regard is the composition of the committee on constitutional affairs of the EP that drafted the Duhamel Report, mainly comprising lawyers including well-known university law professors,[15] and of the delegation of 16 members of the EP at the Convention, largely coming from the ranks of this committee. Half of the representatives of the EP at the European Convention were full members of the committee on constitutional affairs (1999–2004) – three quarters if we include the alternate members – including the chairman of the delegation Iñigo Mendez de Vigo. This proportion rises to more than four fifths if we take into account other positions occupied, either in the former committee on institutional affairs (1994–99) and in the intergroup 'European Constitution' of the EP (1999–2004),[16] or in the Convention which drafted the Charter of Fundamental Rights (1999–2000). Regarding diploma and occupation, half of them hold a law degree (at the undergraduate or postgraduate level) – plus one alumni of the ENA and two graduates in political science – and half of them had worked in higher education as a first occupation, including well known law professors. In fact, a small set of people in this group did cumulate various

14 The case of Joseph Weiler, who holds a PhD from the EUI (1982), now a Professor at NYU's Law School and Jean Monnet Chair, is a good example of the international channels of circulation of the notion of 'constitutionalization' (and 'constitution') from the practice of legal actors involved in European legal integration to the scholarly description (and prescription) by scientific actors apparently external to this process, and *vice versa*. See for example, Weiler, J. (1999), *The Constitution of Europe: 'Do the New Clothes Have an Emperor?' and other Essays on European Integration* (Cambridge: Cambridge University Press) and Weiler, J. (2002), 'A Constitution for Europe? Some Hard Choices', *Journal of Common Market Studies* 40:4, 563–80.

15 For more details on this committee: Cohen, A. and Weisbein, J. (2005), 'Laboratoires du constitutionnalisme européen. Expertises académiques et mobilisations politiques dans la promotion d'une Constitution européenne', *Droit & Société* 60, 353–71; Guillaume, M. (2006), 'Les constituants au Parlement européen: Profils, trajectoires et capital juridique des eurodéputés impliqués dans l'activité constitutionnelle sous la 5ᵉ législature (1999–2004)'. Paper presented at the conference *Capitales et capitaux juridiques en Europe*, Sorbonne, Paris.

16 The intergroup for a European Constitution was created in 1999 by Jo Leinen, member of the Party of European Socialists and then Chairman of the European Union of Federalists, and the secretariat of the intergroup was outsourced to the EUF. See Dutoit, L. (2003), 'L'influence au sein du Parlement européen: les intergroupes', *Politique européenne* 9, 123–42.

positions during the constitutional process, like Olivier Duhamel, a public law and political science professor at Sciences Po in Paris, who was a member of the two successive committees and the intergroup, Andrew Duff, the director of the Federal Trust, who was a member of the first Convention, of the constitutional committee and of the intergroup, or Iñigo Mendez de Vigo, who belonged to all of them.

It would be difficult, actually, to find a more perfect example of the relationship between legal knowledge and political mobilization than that of Iñigo Mendez de Vigo, whose entire trajectory is situated at the crossroads of politics and law. Legal advisor to the Spanish Parliament from 1981, appointed chief of inter-parliamentary affairs in 1982, then special advisor to the Secretary General of the Council of Europe between 1994 and 1999 (Marcelino Oreja, European Commissioner from 1994 to 1999), Mendez de Vigo was simultaneously a professor of constitutional law at the Law Faculty of the Complutense University of Madrid between 1981 and 1984 and professor of EC law at San Pablo Catholic University of Madrid between 1986 and 1991 (he was also a visiting professor at the International Institute of Human Rights in Strasbourg between 1986 and 1989), later holder of the Jean Monnet chair of the Complutense Law Faculty from 1999 to 2003, chairman of the board of the Institute of European Studies at San Pablo, while also working as a barrister in Madrid, partner in several law firms including, eventually, his own. When Spain joined the EC, and Mendez de Vigo the Partido Popular, he became a Member of the EP, in 1989, and was re-elected in 1994 and in 1999. A member of both committees on institutional (1994–99) and constitutional affairs (1999–2004) (vice-chairman of the former), he was elected as chairman of the delegation of the EP to the first Convention (of which he was the vice-president), and then as chairman of the delegation of the EP at the second Convention, member of the Praesidium, after he had represented the EP at intergovernmental conferences, in 1997 for the Treaty of Amsterdam, and in 2001 for the Treaty of Nice.

Iñigo Mendez de Vigo, through his many institutional, national and international, positions and occupations, as well as his pan-European professionalization – which perfectly illustrates the channels of international circulation of legal capital and the total transnational institutional space in which it can be valued – is the ideal-typical incarnation of these political entrepreneurs coming from academia that eased the transfer of academic discourse and categories about EU institutions and law into the repertoire of collective action concerning the political form of the EU.[17] And, it is a series of similar

17 As Carlos Closa Montero points out, in Spain, only academics specializing in 'European Affairs', particularly lawyers, were really mobilized for the European Constitution. In this politico-academic repertoire once again, Iñigo Mendez de Vigo was omnipresent, a member of the Consejo para el debate sobre el futuro de la Union Europea, created in the building of the Ministry of Foreign Affairs for the Secretary General of the Government Presidency, and of the Real Instituto Elcano de Estudios Internacionales y

characteristics and trajectories that tend to collectively personify the members of the European Convention.

## The European Convention and the European Field of Power

While the idea of a Convention was an original step in the treaty negotiation process, it was not entirely new if we recall that, in the early 1950s, the draft of a European Constitution had been drawn up by an *ad hoc* assembly in many ways comparable to the Convention. Of course, this (relative) politicization did not entirely expropriate the usual groups of actors specialized in treaty negotiation among EU bureaucratic and diplomatic, as well as legal personnel.[18] The Convention, however, was obviously the realm of high profile politicians, comprising an important proportion of former presidents, including Valéry Giscard d'Estaing himself, prime ministers, ministers and members of parliaments. Important as it was, nevertheless, this political capital was not the only feature shared by the members of the Convention, also enjoying a significant and specialized academic capital, including a large number of members trained in and/or practising law. As well, the total social surface this institutional group covered was far from limited to the political positions held at national (government/parliament) or European Union (Parliament/Commission/Council) level, but stretched over a very large portion of the European transnational field of power.[19]

---

Estrategicos, a think tank created in this perspective in 2002. See Closa Montero, C. (2004), 'The Spanish Intellectual Debate on the Future of the EU: Who Was Mobilized and with What Effects?', *South European Society and Politics* 9:1, 82–96.

18 Buchet de Neuilly, Y. (2007), 'Des bâtisseurs de traités. Continuités et discontinuités du processus conférentiel', in Cohen, A and Vauchez, A. (eds.), *La Constitution européenne. Elites, mobilisations, votes* (Bruxelles: Editions de l'Université de Bruxelles).

19 The following development is based on the analysis of the characteristics and trajectories of the members of the European Convention (level and type of degree, professional trajectory, and institutional positions). The data covers the 105 members of the Convention at the time when the draft treaty was completed (out of a total 246 listed), i.e. the representatives of heads of State and governments, of national parliaments, of the European Parliament and Commission, both from EU Member States (66) and candidate Member States (39), including of course the presidency of the Convention, but not alternates or observers. This list does not take into account either the many replacements within the Convention between 2002 and 2003, equalling to 22 per cent of the total (23 out of the 105 seats were actually traded). For the sake of simplification, the Member States are designated as 'EU 15', and the candidate countries as 'EU 10+3'. The number of members of the Convention included in the various breakdowns, varying according to available data, is always specified (n = x). For further methodological elements and empirical details, see Cohen, A. (2007), 'Constitutionnalistes en quête de Constitution. La Convention dans le champ du pouvoir européen', in Cohen, A. and Vauchez, A. (eds), *La Constitution européenne. Elites, mobilisations, votes* (Bruxelles: Editions de l'Université de Bruxelles).

Regarding, first, the type of degree held by academic discipline, a majority of the members of the Convention had a degree in either law, economics, political science or related disciplines: 35 per cent in law, 18 per cent in economics, 11 per cent in political science – to which one should add the unclassifiable French ENA alumni. These figures vary, however, when distinguishing the western and the eastern parts of Europe. Among the members of the Convention EU 15 with third-level degrees (61 out of 66), 43 per cent held a law degree (n = 57).[20] Adding economics and political science (15 per cent each), as well as ENA alumni, this amounts to a total of 80 per cent for this conglomerate, which, while certainly made up of disparate bodies of knowledge, should be compared to the equally disparate conglomerates of all other social and human sciences (including literature, philosophy, psychology, sociology and education), representing 12 per cent, or of 'hard' sciences (from medicine to neurology to chemistry), representing 5 per cent. Although law, economics and political science remain dominant among the members of the Convention EU 10+3 with third-level degrees (39 out of 39), 23 per cent holding degrees in law, the same in economics, and 5 per cent in political science, amounting to a total of 51 per cent, there is still more room here for the hard sciences (12 per cent) and medicine (7 per cent). The changing proportion of law and economics degrees among the members of the Convention EU 15 and EU 10+3 is all the more apparent at the level of PhD. Amongst the 21 per cent of members of the Convention EU 15 holding a PhD, more than 40 per cent held a PhD in law, while among the very high proportion of 46 per cent of members of the Convention EU 10+3 holding a PhD, 44 per cent held a PhD in economics (half of which were earned in the United States).

These general figures alone, however, do not fully reflect the very real effects of this academic capital on the internal division of labour at the Convention. Some of the working groups created within the Convention were for the most part composed of lawyers, like in the case of the working groups on the legal personality of the EU chaired by Giuliano Amato, or on Freedom, Security and Justice, chaired by John Bruton. These scholarly characteristics were also quite apparent in the composition of the Praesidium of the Convention, comprising 12 members (14 if we take into account the replacements) plus one 'invitee' representing the candidate countries,

---

20 Even when compared to the total number of members of the Convention EU 15, including those with no qualifications (n = 62), this figure remains very high, around 40 per cent. This is significantly higher than in most EU countries' parliamentary assemblies at the end of the 1990s, for example France, Netherlands or Germany, where they represent about a quarter and a fifth of all members of parliament, much higher than in Denmark (one tenth), about equivalent to the Italian level. This, however, is slightly less than at the European Commission (45 to 50 per cent). On these two points of comparison, see Best, H. and Cotta, M. (eds) (2000), *Parliamentary Representatives in Europe 1848–2000: Legislative Recruitment and Careers* in *Eleven European Countries* (Oxford: Oxford University Press); MacMullen, A. (1997), 'European Commissioners 1952–1995: National Routes to a European Elite', in Nugent, N. (ed.), *At the Heart of the Union: Studies of the European Commission* (London: Macmillan).

**Table 9.1 Education of the Members of the Praesidium of the European Convention**

| *Name* | *Degree* | *University* | *Discipline* |
|---|---|---|---|
| Amato | Master | University of Pisa / Columbia University Law School | Law |
| Barnier | ESCP | Ecole Supérieure de Commerce de Paris | Economics |
| Bruton | Licence / Inn | University College Dublin / Kings Inns | Law |
| Christophersen | Master | University of Copenhagen | Economics |
| Dastis | Licence / Diploma | Diplomatic School | Law / International Relations |
| Dehaene | Licence / Doctorate *Honoris Causa* | University of Namur / University of Louvain | Law / Economics |
| Giscard d'Estaing | *Polytechnique* / ENA | *Polytechnique* / Ecole Nationale d'Administration | – |
| Hänsch | Master / Doctorate | Universities of Cologne, Paris and Berlin | Political Science / Philosophy |
| Katiforis | Master | University of Athens / LSE | Law / Economics |
| Mendez de Vigo | Licence | Complutense University of Madrid | Law |
| Palacio | Licence | *** | Law / Political Science / Sociology |
| Papandreou | Master | Amherst College / LSE | Sociology |
| Peterle | Licence | University of Ljubljana | History / Economics |
| Stuart | Master | Manchester Polytechnic / University of London | Economics / Law |
| Vitorino | Master | University of Lisbon | Law / Political Science |

*Note*: Giorgos Papandreou took over from Giorgos Katiforis in the Praesidium in February 2003 and Alfonso Dastis from Ana Palacio in March 2003. Alojz Peterle was 'invitee' at the Praesidium as 'the' representative of the candidate countries. All undergraduate degrees (three years after A levels) are indicated as 'Licence' (particularly for Bachelors of Arts), and postgraduate degrees (four or five years after A levels) marked as Master (in particular the '*maîtrises*'). For the '*écoles*' and '*grandes écoles*' the name or acronym of the institution has been noted instead of the name of the degree. Two degrees are mentioned when one is from a university and the other from a professional institution (such as Kings Inns), or when the discipline is not the same.

of which nine held law degrees (three coupled with economics and three with political science), excluding the rather unique case of Valéry Giscard d'Estaing (see Table 9.1).

As the Table 9.1 let us glimpse, a significant number of the members of the Convention studied in a country other than their country of nationality. Besides Giuliano Amato, this is notably the case for the Greek members of the Praesidium, Giorgos Katiforis and Giorgos Papandreou, who both earned their Master at the London School of Economics, before Katiforis became Prime Minister Papandreou's economic advisor. Outside the Praesidium, this is also the case for Jose Borrell and Lamberto Dini, who did part of their studies in the United States, at Stanford University in the case of Borrell, at the University of Michigan in the case of Dini; but also for those, more numerous, who did part of their studies in Europe, at the Free University of Brussels, where Andrew Duff and Linda McAvan both got their Master, at the EUI in Florence, where Gijs de Vries did his postgraduate studies, or at Sciences Po Paris, where the three delegates from Luxembourg, Ben Fayot, Paul Helminger and Jacques Santer, earned the diploma (Helminger also holding a Master in political science from Stanford University; and Santer a PhD in law from the University of Strasbourg).

More generally speaking, out of the 105 members of the Convention (n = 100), over 35 per cent completed part of their studies in a country other than their own, among whom about 15 per cent studied in the United States. But these general figures once again mask important discrepancies between the 'Old' and the 'New' Europe: if fewer than one tenth of the members of the Convention EU 15 obtained a university degree (undergraduate or postgraduate) in the United States, almost one quarter of the members of the Convention EU 10+3 did; and while a quarter of the EU 15 members studied abroad, more than half of the EU 10+3 members did, mostly in the United States (Princeton, Georgetown, Washington or Harvard), the UK (LSE, King's College or Oxford), or, less frequently, in France (Sciences Po, IAAP-ENA) – and, for the older ones, in the Soviet Union.

If we now consider the type of occupation held by sector of activity, we find that among the EU 15 members (n = 61), a high proportion (30 to 40 per cent) had worked in higher education, as professors or researchers, before entering politics In comparison, the next largest sectors – justice (barristers and magistrates), on the one hand, and the press, publishing and the media (most of them being journalists, and ... Italians), on the other hand – only represented around 10 per cent each, followed by administration and diplomacy, business and banking, or even medicine. If academia was the dominant sector at the Convention, this was even accentuated among EU 10+3 members (n = 37), since 40 to 50 per cent had worked in higher education – administration and diplomacy, here leading justice and the press.[21] While Giuliano Amato had had a long career

21 These numbers are purposely vague given the difficulties of categorizing by profession such a population of 'professional politicians'. If the number of members of the

in academia (1964) before taking up responsibilities at the higher level of the Italian Socialist Party (1978), others entered their academic and political careers almost simultaneously: Gijs de Vries, for instance, born in 1956, taught political science at the University of Leiden (1981–84), while also being a city councillor (1982–84), before he became Member of the EP in 1984 and topped the list of the People's Party for Freedom and Democracy in the European elections in 1989.

More than a specific professional profile, however, what most certainly characterizes the trajectory of most of the members of the Convention is the multiplicity of professional activities and institutional positions. Just like Iñigo Mendez de Vigo, the members of the Convention cumulate activities and positions in the most varied sectors, at the national and international, local and European levels. The Portuguese representative of the Commission, Antonio Vitorino, born in 1957, was successively Member of Parliament in 1980 and Secretary of State in 1984, in Portugal, before becoming Secretary of State in 1986, this time in Macao, then returning to Portugal as a judge at the Constitutional Court in 1989, changing national and European responsibilities like a beat of a metronome, Member of the EP (1994), Minister of Defence and Vice Prime Minister of Portugal (1995), European Commissioner (1999), all while pursuing a university career in Lisbon, as assistant professor (1982) and professor (1986). In much the same vein – although in a decidedly French manner – Hubert Haenel, representative of the French Parliament, born in 1942, was a magistrate in the central administration of the ministry of Justice, secretary general of the Conseil Supérieur de la Magistrature, then technical advisor to the President of the Republic on legal and judicial matters (1975–77), associate professor at the University of Aix-Marseille III (1976), member of the Conseil d'Etat (1977), continually alternating or accumulating local, national and even European positions, such as mayor (1977), senator (1986), vice president of the Alsace Regional Council (1992), president of the Senate's delegation for European Union (1999), and member of the first Convention (2000).

---

Convention never having had any other career 'before' their entry into politics (whether their political career originated with local government, party politics or ministerial staff) is quite low, the biographical information available is not specific enough to conclude whether the professions indicated were actually practised – this being particularly the case with 'barristers' (the example of John Bruton, who publicly states in his curriculum that he has never practised law, being very rare) – nor if they were practised 'before' the 'political career'. The proportion of members of the Convention coming from academia being so high when compared with other institutions, national or European, then it must be clearly stated that, as far as we can tell, the profession considered has been practised between graduation and initial political responsibilities (or another profession) and is not just a secondary occupation, as is often the case with all sorts of professionals hawking their 'expertise' on the academic market. Whatever criteria one chooses, however, this was the largest group at the Convention.

The analysis of their trajectory prior to entry at the Convention also highlights the total social surface covered by its members – a surface subtly stretching from the IMF (of which Lamberto Dini is the former executive director) to the College of Europe in Bruges (of which Jean-Luc Dehaene is chairman of the board), including the Council of Bars and Law Societies of Europe (of which Ana Palacio was vice-president), consultancies such as KREAB (of which Henning Christophersen is a senior partner), think tanks like the Federal Trust (of which Andrew Duff is the former director), public and private companies (of which several members of the Convention had been or were administrators or managers) – and particularly the total transnational political space in which these trajectories are embedded. This space extends to transnational parties, evidently, but also includes the European Movement, as much in its international organization, the EMI, of which Valéry Giscard d'Estaing was chairman from 1989 to 1997 and then honorary chairman, as its national ones: the EM France, of which Hubert Haenel, Alain Lamassoure, Pierre Lequiller and Pierre Moscovici (a short time member of the Convention) had been or were chairman or vice-chairman, the EM Finland (Vilen), Ireland (Roche), Germany (Brok, who was both vice-chairman of the EM and chairman of Europa-Union) and so on. This space also includes, of course, the Convention that drafted the Charter of Fundamental Rights, of which a large proportion of the members of the Convention EU 15 were also members (25 per cent), and the various parliamentary assemblies which, while situated 'outside' the EU, participate in the system of international division of institutional labour that has been institutionalized as such in the early 1950s: the parliamentary assemblies of the Council of Europe, WEU, NATO and OSCE.

Actually, along with the delegations for the EU accession negotiations and, to a lesser extent, missions (to the EU or NATO) and observer positions (at the Commission), these assemblies have been the primary locus of socialization with European politics for the representatives of the candidate countries, considering the fact that at least one quarter of the EU 10+3 members are or were members of the parliamentary assembly of the Council of Europe, the Slovakian representative Irena Belohorska having represented her country at all three parliamentary assemblies of the Council of Europe, the WEU and NATO.

## Conclusion

The much-commented consensus method at the Convention may have had, as an unspoken prerequisite, a coalition of pre-existing social dispositions most appropriate in this institutional space, that went far beyond the partisan differences (denied, anyway, by the alphabetical seating of the members);[22] a set of dispositions

22 President Valéry Giscard d'Estaing imposed on the members of the Convention to be seated in *alphabetical order* in order to blur the frontiers between delegations, nations and parties, while for instance the socialist members of the EP were asking that the members of the Convention be seated by political party. See Magnette, P. (2004), 'La Convention

that was not limited to their prior socialization in the transnational institutions where they could have held positions, but was much more profoundly rooted in pre-accorded academic, or even professional backgrounds. Only when analysing the social characteristics and trajectories of the members of the Convention can one understand the apparently spontaneous adjustments of these dispositions, as much to one another, as to both the institutional proceeding (deliberation) and decision-making procedure (consensus) which structured the internal work of the Convention – some kind of 'academic' 'conference' with written contributions, speech-timing, working and discussion groups, an atmosphere in which 'voting' and 'politics' could well have been unwelcome.

Paul Magnette has pointed out that the final draft that came out of the Convention owed a lot to the 'ways of reasoning' that men such as Olivier Duhamel and Giuliano Amato managed to impose at the Convention, mostly in the name of 'simplification'.[23] Beyond the Convention itself, it must be emphasized that the strength of the juridical categories that continuously framed this constitutional mobilization is less a 'natural' result of the 'logical' construction in which the arguments were moulded, than of the influence – from one end of the process to the other – of a particular type of social actors for whom the 'logic' of law and institutions is the specific capital, that is, legal/institutional professionals. In the competitions that constantly opposed the different kinds of state nobilities (economic, bureaucratic, political and legal) since the very beginnings of European integration to impose a legitimizing principle on which to build this transnational order (the market, technical competence, parliamentary representation, law), the treaty establishing a Constitution for Europe could well have been a window of opportunity to formalize a new power settlement in which legal professionals could have found a new source of power over the State, in its national and transnational forms. The EU constitutional moment has often been described in terms of (indistinctly) political and academic oppositions, such as federalism and sovereignism, the supranational and the intergovernmental, globalization and Europeanization, neo-liberalism and neo-populism, etc. While structuring the public debate on the issue, these are mainly 'labels' or 'stigmas', around which different kinds of elites struggle in a both national and transnational configuration. However, the (re)emergence of the European Constitution as an issue of collective action, both at the national and transnational levels, owes as much to a set of political strategies that are manifest in the use of such labels, as to, less manifestly perhaps, the long-term transformations that affected the structural relations between dominant elites in Europe. To the intrinsic transformations of the European field of power and their repercussions at the national level (on the supply side) corresponds a series of morphological transformations more specific

européenne: argumenter et négocier dans une assemblée constituante multinationale', *Revue française de science politique* 54: 1, 5–42.

23 Magnette, P. (2005), 'In the Name of Simplification: Coping With Constitutional Conflict in the Convention on the Future of Europe', *European Law Journal* 11:4, 432–51.

to these elites and particularly to legal elites (on the demand side). That is: on the supply side, both the increasing number of elective positions that resulted from the direct election of the EP and the diversification of European political elites that followed each enlargement of the EU (particularly to countries like Spain or Portugal where political elites are traditionally and principally juridical, and where bridges between fields of professional activity are much more important), on the one hand, and the great many opportunities for legal expertise offered as much by European institutions as by pro-European movements or think tanks, on the other hand; on the demand side, the formation of a community of lawyers specializing in EC law and institutions resulting from the activities of the ECJ and the creation of a European legal market (with new university courses and major changes with regards to the traditional hierarchies between the different branches of law), on the one hand, and the transformations of juridical activities on a more international scale, which allowed the 'pure jurists' to make their legal expertise (almost) as valuable as 'legal merchants' on different markets, national and international, political and economic.

From this specific point of view, the European Constitution can be understood as a form of social reaction that the pure jurists (and part of the academic and political world with them) tried to oppose to the transformations of the national and international legal order, that the legal merchants managed to impose upon them. Faced with the 'constitutionalization of the market', of which the ECJ was a willing agent, the final step in *a reversal of the order of legal things*, in which the market drives a supranational law now superior to national laws, the promotion of a 'true' Constitution, one that will put things back *in order*, might not be anything but a response internal, albeit international, to the legal world.

# Chapter 10

# How to Become a Transnational Elite: Lawyers' Politics at the Genesis of the European Communities (1950–1970)

Antoine Vauchez

Euro-lawyers can appear as an enigma to anyone studying the EU polity. While European studies have given law a critical role not only as the engine of the integration process but also as the principal source of legitimacy of the EU itself, we actually know very little about the people whose task it is to control and develop European law. The invitation issued more than twenty years ago by prominent scholars from the field of European studies to analyse the 'community of EC lawyers'[1] (that is, those who 'create' everyday law, such as the judges at the Court of Justice, law professors, business lawyers, barristers or the legal advisors to the EC institutions, and so on) has hardly been accepted.[2] In comparison with other professionals whose role in the European construction is widely known (such as national and EU civil servants, journalists, lobbyists or unionists[3]), Euro-lawyers remain a sort of *terra incognita*.[4] While jurists appear in some respects to be omnipresent in the European construction – their contributions are noticeable

1 Shapiro, M. (1980), 'Comparative Law and Comparative Politics', *Southern California Law Review* 53, 537–42, and Stein, E. (1981), 'Lawyers, Judges and the Making of a Transnational Constitution', *American Journal of International Law* 75:1, 1–25.

2 This is actually one of the ambitions of the Polilexes (Politics of International Legal Expertise in European Societies) research group. A bibliography can be found at <http://www.u-picardie.fr/labo/curapp/ATIP_AVpolilexes/ATIPav_Biblio.html>. A sample of this work is presented in a symposium recently published in *Law and Social Inquiry*. See particularly the introduction: Cohen, A. and Vauchez, A. (2007), 'Law, Lawyers and Transnational Politics in the Production of the European State', *Law and Social Inquiry* 32:1, 75–82.

3 See for example the analysis of the emergence of EU professionals in Georgakakis, D. (2002) (ed.), *Les métiers de l'Europe politique. Acteurs et professionnalisations de la construction européenne* (Strasbourg: Presses Universitaires de Strasbourg).

4 This is without any doubt one of the most striking dead angles of the neo-functionalist literature on the legal processes of the European construction. This literature has shown no interest in legal players as such and their parts in definition of the EU, its institutions, and of the principles of legitimization on which it is founded. Cf. Vauchez, A. (2007), 'Embedded Law: Political Sociology of a European Community of Law', *EUI Working Paper* RSCAS 23.

everywhere – they are at the same time almost invisible, as the 'social ensemble' they constitute fails to exist as an organized and unified group or profession. Decades of mobilizations in building a dense network of transnational legal associations like the Fédération internationale pour le droit européen (FIDE), professional bodies such as the Conseil consultative des barreaux de l'Europe, and specialized law journals or research institutes such as the Académie de droit européen de Trèves have not succeeded in building a common understanding of what a Euro-lawyer is – or should be.[5]

As Euro-lawyers are absent as a scientific object and hardly present as a professional group, they remain in many ways the black hole of the EU polity. It is likely that this relative invisibility relates to the striking *juridisme* of European studies. Paradoxically, jurists frequently appear in this literature as purely legal animals. By considering them only from the angle of the purely legal objectives which lawyers themselves attach to their practice, research has so far failed in examining them as social players able to constitute – by their specific expertise, but also by the multiple positions they occupy in EU polity – one of the core elites of the European construction. Sociologically, however, the fact that lawyers at one and the same time are both omnipresent and invisible may actually be related to the very position lawyers have managed to secure themselves within the European construction. This chapter is precisely arguing that these central characteristics have deeper roots as they in many ways are the outcome of how a transnational elite of lawyers established itself in the early years of the EC construction: as an elite 1) positioned *in-between* the variegated set of Euro-implicated groups and institutions (omnipresence); 2) whose permanence at the core of EU polity depends on its collective ability to maintain the general view that they have no specific interest or stakes in the European integration process (invisibility).

This chapter, concerned with the early years of the EC (1950–1970), analyses the formation of such a transnational elite.[6] Just as there is no 'Immaculate Conception' of European law, there is, this chapter argues, no *ex nihilo* creation of a transnational European legal elite detached from national linkages and exclusively devoted to the promotion of a supranational European justice. As I will show in the first part of the analysis, the first lawyers involved in EC affairs constituted a composite set of actors pursuing a multitude of contradicting interests. Thereby, they hardly formed an easily recognizable 'epistemic community' converted to the idea of a federal legal order, as a retrospective look at the 'founding fathers' of EC law might suggest at first glance. These lawyers were instead assigned very different social mandates and, in many ways, reproduced the sectorial and national divisions that characterize the first phase

5 See Vauchez, A. (2008), 'The Force of a Weak Field: Law and Lawyers in the Government of Europe', *International Political Sociology*, 2: 2, 113–117.

6 Elements of this chapter draw on a previously published article: Vauchez, A. (2007), 'Une élite d'intermédiaires: Genèse d'un capital juridique européen (1950–1970)', *Actes de la recherche en sciences sociales*, 166/167, 54–65.

of the European polity. The emergence of a 'transnational legal authority', that is, a European-wide body of experts able to persuasively interpret EC treaties, is thus highly puzzling: how did specific individuals managed to be recognized *internationally* as authoritative experts of EC law while there seemed to be no possible common ground for the different Euro-lawyers? The chapter provides a tentative answer in the second part. In such a fragmented European legal field, I argue, the possession of a set of specific resources enabling lawyers to bypass and circumvent the many dividing lines that ordinarily structured lawyers' viewpoints (nationality of origin, type of clients, and so on) was crucial. In other words, I argue that Euro-lawyers established themselves not so much as an elite of an emerging European power (as their national counterparts), but more so as an elite of *brokers* interceding between different European and national elites (political, administrative, economic and intellectual, and so on) making up the nascent Europe.[7]

## The Emerging European Legal Field as a Segmented Space

In this first part, I will outline the nascent European legal field (hereafter ELF) with the objective of examining its segmentation along national and sectorial lines. Here is not the place to discuss at length the notion of field. Suffice it to say that its usefulness lies in its capacity to seize what brings and keeps together European legal actors, namely, the contest for control over the specific symbolic resources of Euro-law and the capacity to speak persuasively in the name of that specific body of law[8]. Basically, Euro-lawyers should not be considered as free-floating actors making up EC law independently of one another and the other social fields, but as an emerging structure.

7 Talcott Parsons was among the first sociologists to suggest the role of lawyers was 'an interstitial one' and consider this as 'the most important fact' as it allowed lawyers to 'penetrate[e] the boundary between public and private capacities and responsibilities'. Still, this functionalist perspective failed to account for the historical variations in the roles lawyers have managed (or failed) to secure themselves in different social and political settings. Cf. Parsons, T. (1964), *Essays in Sociological Theory* (New York: The Free Press), 375. Research on lawyers as brokers also includes Charle, C. (1989), 'Pour une histoire sociale des professions juridiques à l'époque contemporaine. Note pour une recherche', *Actes de la recherche en sciences sociales* 76/77, 117–19 ; and, concerning international fields, Dezalay, Y. (2004), 'Les courtiers de l'international', *Actes de la recherche en sciences sociales* 151/152, 5–35.

8 Bourdieu, P. (1987), 'The Force of Law: Toward a Sociology of the Juridical Field', *Hastings Law Review* 38, 805–53.

*Euro-Lawyers and their Multiple Mandates in the EC Polity*

Due to the diversity of the social groups that are somehow involved in this Common Market process, it comes as no surprise that European integration is followed by an equally unprecedented diversification of international legal practices. This is particularly striking when compared to the rather limited opportunities and venues lawyers had in traditional international politics. The classic ideal of the lawyer-politician involved in international affairs, embodied by prominent jurists such as Fernand Dehousse, Walter Hallstein, Jean Rey, Paul-Henri Spaak or Pierre-Henri Teitgen, remained, however, very much the norm. Yet, the EC polity offered new avenues for these jurists interested in both legal engineering and political action. Correspondingly, one also finds, in the first phase of the construction of the European community, a number of specialists of international legal affairs: on the one hand, a range of 'state lawyers' (*jurisconsultes*) whose task was to participate in the negotiation of treaties in the domain of European diplomacy,[9] and on the other hand, public international law professors involved in the building of an EC academic space by investing in a number of journals and research institutions specialized in Euro-law during the 1960s.[10] But far from being solely a law 'to be', as was the case a few years earlier when lawyers from different pan-European political movements and associations were called upon to imagine future institutional schemes for a European government,[11] European law has already at this point become more of a law 'in the being'. This, crucially, opens up the space for more enduring professional *specialization* in European legal affairs for these jurists.

The activity of the ECJ was certainly very limited at the time with an average of about ten judgements a year between 1952 and 1963. Generally, this prevented the emergence of specialized judicial milieus.[12] However, because of the range of

9 Through the various working groups, mandated by the six founding Member States, these legal experts were closely involved in the writing of the treaties of Paris and Rome. See Pescatore, P. (1981), 'Les travaux du "groupe juridique" dans les négociations des Traités de Rome', *Studia diplomatica* XXXIV, 159–78.

10 Especially in the universities of Brussels (1961), Cologne, Hamburg, Leiden, Liege (1964), Nancy, Padua, Paris (1963) who followed the early creation of similar departments at the universities of Sarre (1954) and Turin (1951).

11 See Cohen, A. and Madsen, M.R. (2007), 'Cold War Law: Legal Entrepreneurs and the Genesis of a European Legal Field (1945–1965)', in Gessner, V. and Nelken, D. (2007), *European Ways of Law: Towards a European Sociology of Law* (Oxford: Hart Publishing) and Madsen, M.R. and Vauchez, A. (2005), 'European Constitutionalism at the Cradle: Law and Lawyers in the Construction of a European Political Order (1920–1960)', in Jettinghoff, A. and Schepel, H. (eds), *In Lawyers' Circles: Lawyers and European Legal Integration* (The Hague: Elsevir), 15–34.

12 The 'Euro-litigation data set' which we are currently developing within the Polilexes group suggests that the EC law did not undergo any real specialization before the 1980s. See Marchand, C. and Vauchez, A. (2007), 'Counting Lawyers that Count: A

social domains affected by the rise of the European Community – coal and steel, agriculture, social areas, customs, taxation, trade, patents and so on – a market for European legal counselling did emerge. The development of the sectorial negotiations within the Committee of Permanent Representatives (Coreper) stimulated a range of specialized government departments (foreign affairs, foreign trade, economics, finance, agriculture and so on) to engage legal experts. This, they felt, was necessary for them to maintain their position in the national debates over the definition of their country's 'European position'.[13] Beginning in the early 1960s, the proliferation of working groups and committees working under the auspices of the European Commission, responsible for the objective of establishing a set of standards for a common market, also attracted an increasing number of jurists to Brussels. These jurists, as well as a growing number of civil servants, were charged with representing their respective governments in the different areas now touched by EC policies. Likewise, the creation of a genuine EU bureaucracy during the 1960s also implied the creation of an in-house legal department employing some thirty lawyers. These lawyers were charged with establishing legal measures for the work of the European Commission and representing the Commission before the Court of Justice. Besides these developments, European legal work was generated by the coal and other industrial companies (Charbonnage de France, Messerschmidt, Thyssen, etc. ), as well as by a growing number of multinational corporations (banks, Philips, Shell, Unilever, etc.) and lobbying associations such as the American Chamber of Commerce in Brussels where a group of lawyers had specialized very early on in the EC law-making process. Last but not least, national legal professions developed an interest in Euro-law in so far as the Rome Treaty was stipulating the freedoms which would affect directly the legal professions themselves. Within the well-established Union internationale des avocats an Advisory Commission of Bars was created in 1961 (later renamed the Council of Bars and Law Societies of Europe), which was immediately granted advisory status by the European Commission.

This sketchy mapping of the various legal venues opened by the European Communities suggests that these first Euro-lawyers were far from constituting a transnational and unified group that would spontaneously agree with the idea of European legal federalism. Firstly, the different segments of this emerging legal market were rarely secant. Strikingly, the lawyers pleading before the ECJ, the lawyers engaged in defending the legal professions in Brussels before the Commission, or even those who promoted the case of EC law through the

Sociology of the Lawyers Pleading to the European Court of Justice (1952–1977)', paper presented at the Law and Society Conference in Berlin, July 2007.

13 A general survey of the different national administrative configurations is presented in Spierenburg, D. and Poidevin R. (1993), *Histoire de la Haute autorité de la CECA. Une expérience supranationale* (Brussels: Bruylant).

Fédération internationale pour le droit européen (FIDE)[14] were rarely the same.[15] But the absence of a unified group was foremost due to the fact that lawyers were linked to the construction of Europe through many different and often contradicting interests (diplomatic, bureaucratic, economical and professional, whether they be national, transnational or European). As a consequence, their views mirrored the divisions that had characterized this first phase of the European polity. Whereas the Member States' legal advisers were displaying their disagreement with the idea of the 'supremacy' of this new body of law over national law, their fellow countrymen (and often former colleagues) affiliated with the legal service of the European Commission would fiercely defend the opposite view.[16]

### *Closed Linguistic Markets*

The absence of any European legal common sense was even more striking if one examines the linguistic segmentation of this emerging field of practice. The different spaces where this first European Community law was applied were characterized by a so-called 'dictatorship of flags'. The equal or, at least, the fair representation of each of the Member States was unanimously deemed *the* essential condition for EC institutions to produce *authentically* European policy outcomes. This particular attention to the balancing of the different 'national legal traditions' resulted in a segmentation of the European legal market in as many markets as there were if not nations, then at least linguistic communities and with relatively little exchange between them.

A number of studies have demonstrated that this political claim for geographic balance between the six Member States was one of the best established logics of the EC political-administrative space. From the very beginning, the High Authority (ECSC Treaty) and later the European Commission had organized themselves by separating the 'big countries' (Germany, France and Italy) which received two seats within the Collège des commissaries, and the 'small countries' (Belgium,

14 FIDE is a pan-European association of jurists which was first created in 1952 and then re-launched with the help of the European Commission in the early 1960s. Cf. Alter, K. (2007), 'Jurist Social Movements in Europe: The Role of Euro-Law Associations in European Integration (1953–1975)', *EUSA Review* 6–12.

15 Among the 115 repeat-players of the European Court of Justice identified in the above-mentioned 'Euro-litigation data set' during the 1952–77 period only 15 actually belonged to the pan-European association of jurists (the Fédération internationale pour le droit européen) and very few of them were members of the Commission consultative des barreaux des six pays du marché commun.

16 The president of the Court of Justice (1962–65), André Donner states: 'while practically every legal counsel of the community institutions has adhered to the confederate or prefederal school, legal counsel of the ministries of foreign affairs have sided, with few exceptions, as unreservedly with the international organization school.' Donner, A. (1968), *The Role of the Lawyer in the European Communities* (Chicago, IL: Northwestern University Press), 6.

Holland and Luxemburg) which received one seat.[17] In a context where there was no alternative principle of legitimacy within EC institutions, these divisions would then be reproduced basically at all levels of the Brussels administration (general secretariat, general directorates, etc.).[18] As a matter of fact, neither the legal service of the Commission nor the ECJ itself were able to avoid this requirement of a 'fair' geographical representation. 'The necessity of having lawyers of different nationalities'[19] – a statement that had been repeated on several occasions by the members of the Commission, particularly concerning the legal service – had its counterpart in the European Court for which a 'just "diplomatic balance" had been reached' during the negotiations of the Treaty of Rome between 'the egalitarian principle between the countries (only one judge from each country, the second Dutch judge was appointed as representative of the union), and the fundamental but unwritten principle of French–German parity'.[20] This subtle political equilibrium was seen as an essential condition for the viability of such a supranational Court, as Pierre Pescatore, then a high–ranking diplomat from Luxemburg, has noted:

> It would be impossible in the long run within the European Community to maintain the bonds so closely as the Treaties proscribe, (...) if the Member States are not convinced that in each case, the Court of Justice understands in detail each Member State, and that it has a direct knowledge of the national law and the situation of its national interests.[21]

But what is even more striking is that this traditional diplomatic pattern also spread outside the EC institutions themselves and actually structured the surrounding *transnational* legal spaces, including the academic networks and the European professional organizations. Certainly, the imperative was not the same, as these academic or professional circles favoured the liberal ideal of an international legal community based on equal importance of its members and their free scientific discussion (instead of the rules dictated by power politics). However, it was, at the end of the day, the presence of the *different* national representatives that gave validity and legitimacy to what was being accomplished in these fora. This can be seen in, for example, the fact that the debates of the FIDE congresses were essentially structured by the reports made by the various *national* sections. Any under-representation of a particular national chapter was actually considered

17 See Georgakakis, D. and de Lassale, M. (2007), 'Genèse et structure d'un capital institutionnel européen', *Actes de la recherche en sciences sociales* 166/167, 38–52.

18 Condorelli-Braun, N. (1972), *Commissaires et juges dans les communautés européennes* (Paris: LGDJ).

19 Spierenburg and Poidevin, *Histoire de la Haute autorité de la CECA*, 249.

20 Lagrange, M. (1979), 'La CJCE du Plan Schuman à l'UE', in *Mélanges Fernand Dehousse*, Vol. 2 (la construction européenne), 127–37, 129.

21 Pescatore, P. (1965), 'Zehn Jahre Rechtsprechung des Gerichtshofs der Europäischen Gemeinschaften', Institut für das Recht der Europäischen Gemeinschaften, Cologne.

as a potential threat to these organizations' ability to construct an authentically European legal opinion. The intrusion of this diplomatic logic within the legal arenas did not mean that each of the national representatives was supposed simply to *represent* national political interests. Yet, the distance to the interests of the respective home countries was relative considering that lawyers, as other experts of state matters, had traditionally been expected to act as spokespersons for their governments on the international scene.[22] But, it is telling of the fact that in legal affairs, as elsewhere in the emerging EC polity, each person obtained a great deal of his legitimacy by the very fact that he embodied a 'national tradition'.

This omnipresence of this *geopolitical* concern within the legal realm itself[23] had further consequences. It contributed – at least partially – to splitting up the emerging European legal spaces into as many national sub-spaces. There is probably no better example of this than the functioning of the ECJ itself. As the Member States had refused to chose *one* language only for its proceedings, the Court adopted instantly a plurilinguistic language policy, which was – in the eyes of the first judges – the only real option in order to deliver decisions considered as legitimate by the legal elites of the different Member States. As a matter of fact, with 'the procedural language [being] the national language of the defence', emphasis had been put on the necessity of equal access to the Court of lawyers for the different Member States. Due to this, it soon became custom that the different participants in a case (litigants, legal counsellors from the European Community institutions, government jurisconsults and even *juges-rapporteurs*) would be of the same nationality. The only exceptions would be a handful of cosmopolitan lawyers or lawyers from bilingual states (Belgium and Luxembourg).

A good example of these issues as well as the kind of disputes the Court had to adjudicate during its first years of existence was a litigation between some steel companies and the High Authority concerning the setting of common prizes: the case of Barbara Erzbergbau AG and other companies versus the High Authority which was settled by the Court in its judgement of 10 May 1960. The complaining German steel companies were represented by six German lawyers and law professors. Moreover, the Länder which had joined the complaint had themselves hired four lawyers and professors. In its defence, the High Authority had called upon one of its German legal advisors who himself was associated with two exterior legal consultants, also German. It was also the German General Advocate of the Court of Justice, Karl Roemer, who presented conclusions on the case. In total, this ECJ dispute had engaged no less than fourteen lawyers in a competing process of interpreting the treaties on behalf of clients as different as

22 Concerning this issue, see Sacriste, G. and Vauchez, A. (2007), 'The Force of International Law: Lawyers' Diplomacy on the International Scene in the 1920s', *Law and Social Inquiry* 32:1, 83–107.

23 The way Euro-law was produced mirrored this concern, which can be seen in the preference amongst the judges of the Court and professors of law for comparativism as the most legitimate way to build ECJ legal principles.

those of companies, of the Länder and of the EC institutions. Yet, the conflict was only fought by *German* lawyers – one legal advisor, one General Advocate of the Court, six lawyers and six law professors.

The system basically implied that each of the national groups took part *in turn* and *in its own language* in the construction of ECJ jurisprudence. Everything happened as if, in order to be fully legitimate, this judicial confrontation over the interpretation of this transnational body of law had to be performed on an exclusively national basis. It was simply as though European legal disputes had to be dealt with through some sort of national delegation that would resolve the matter among fellow countrymen. This national, or at least linguistic, division of the European legal practice that can be observed in almost similar terms in the administrative, jurisdictional or academic arenas was one important driving force behind the segmentation of this emerging legal field.

## How to Become a 'Founding Father': Roads towards European Legal Authority

The sectorial and national fragmentation of this early ELF in many ways contradicts the common assumption that Euro-lawyers from the very beginning formed a transnational *community* organized around a common belief in a federal legal order. Indeed it is a sociological puzzle how, in such a social and political setting, a form of European legal capital actually emerged – that is, the formation of a specific authority in interpreting and unveiling the meaning of the EC treaties, recognized *across* the national and political divisions. Instead of hypothesizing on the pre-existence of such a European legal capital, what I will do here is analyse the accumulation of resources (social, legal, scholastic, political and so on), as well as the social conditions for this accumulation, which were the background to the rise of a number of authoritative legal positions. The following basically argues that to become a 'founding father' of the European legal system, praised and recognized Europe-wide, one had to be able to transgress the sectorial and national boundaries that configured this emerging legal field at its early stage. In other words, being recognized as an authoritative Euro-lawyer meant first and foremost that one had to surpass the ordinary divisions that structured the European legal practice.

### *The Limited Weight of Legal Cosmopolitanism*

The above-mentioned national segmentation of the ELF should however not lead to downplaying the development of transnational legal networks. In this respect, the FIDE was one of the most important organizations for Euro-lawyers. With its 1961 congress held in Brussels and its tight association with the European Commission, this little club gained a whole new importance. Every two years, between two and three hundred jurists (judges, business lawyers, European civil servants, professors of law and so on),[24] coming from the six Member States met at congresses: Brussels in 1961, The Hague in 1963 and Paris in 1965. Besides the FIDE meetings, a whole range of university symposiums were taking place with a growing frequency throughout the 1960s as new university departments specialized in EC law developed. These different fora of European legal mobilization certainly constituted a critical space for defining the areas and urgent matters of European Community law.[25] Moreover, they contributed to establishing what was to be seen as the professional excellence of this self-proclaimed 'advancing army of Euro-lawyers'.[26] Among others, they would help define the contours of a truly 'European way of reasoning that could break up frontiers … and be liberated from the strictly national claims',[27] and of a truly *European* lawyer interested in other legal cultures and therefore capable of rising above national traditions in order to pursue adequate European legal solutions.

The ability to integrate fully in this 'Community atmosphere' and to excel within it was clearly dependent on the possession of certain fundamental skills which eased the comprehension of the 'legal languages' of the other Member States. Certainly, linguistic competence was one of the key resources in this respect, particularly for those speaking 'secondary' languages (Italians, Flemish and Dutch) whose intervention in European legal arenas depended largely on their capacity to master one of the dominant languages (German and even more so French). Generally speaking, plurilinguistic skills were crucial for accessing new audiences and clientele, as was the case with lawyers originating from bilingual countries (Belgium and Luxemburg). These lawyers capable of pleading, and arguing in several languages could access a more variegated set of national legal sub-fields of EC law. This was, for example the case for Jossé Mertens de Wilmars (1912–2002). President of the Belgian Council for the European Movement and MP (1951–61) for the Christian-Social Party, he had been simultaneously a lawyer capable of defending Belgian as well as French and Dutch companies before the

24 Among the 70 members of the French section of the FIDE (also named Association Française des Juristes Européens) one finds in 1963, apart from the general lawyer of the Court of Justice, Maurice Lagrange, and the secretary of the European Commission of Human Rights, 34 lawyers, 11 magistrates, five members of the Council of State, eight professors of law, the president of the Seine Bankruptcy Court (Tribunal de Commerce de la Seine), two *agrées*, one solicitor [*avoué*], one public notary [*notaire*], the president of the Company of legal experts, the president of the European Commercial Federation Council, one director of the administration of the Ministry of Public Enterprise and two former cabinet ministers (Maurice Faure, Mayer who was the former president of the CECA). See *Bulletin de l'Association française pour le droit européen* 11/12 (1963), 5.

25 Vauchez, A. (2008), 'At the Origin of EU Legal Commonsense: From Van Gend en Loos and Costa v. ENEL to the Europeanization-through-case-law narrative', *EUI Working Paper*, RSCAS.

26 de Vreese, A. (1965), in *Cahiers de Bruges*, Dossier spécial '*Droit communautaire et droit national*', 14, 399–400.

27 Arithmos (1965), 'Propos européens', *Cahiers du droit européen* 1, 95.

ECJ. This helped him establish a solid reputation in the domain of EC law which would be an essential element in his nomination in 1967 as judge at the ECJ, and then as president (1980–84). But, being multilingual was not in itself decisive if it was not supported by a mastery of the different 'legal languages', that is, the terms, the categories, the institutions of the 'legal traditions' of the six Member States. The ability to compare the six national legal cultures and to draw learnedly on the various categories and theories each of them offered was a crucial competence in these early transnational legal arenas.

In this respect, studies at foreign law faculties and, more importantly, continuous contact with foreign legal cultures was a primary asset. The Luxembourgian Pierre Pescatore (b. 1919), who was to be appointed at the Court for 18 years, portrays this type of cosmopolitan legal excellence: this multilingual diplomat (capable of speaking French, English, German, Spanish and Dutch with equal mastery), educated at foreign universities (in Tübingen, Germany and Louvain, Belgium), professor at the universities of Liege and Nancy, as well as the Academy of International Law in The Hague, represented more than anyone else this type of cosmopolitan 'Euro-lawyer', having 'a state of readiness, a personal ability to make one's way into other cultures ... [and] a built-up skill in manoeuvring more or less expertly' within different systems of meaning.[28] Throughout his European career, from his taking part in the negotiations for the Treaty of Rome (on behalf of Luxemburg) to his presiding over the ECJ, he continued moving from country to country transcending with no apparent difficulty national frontiers and linguistic barriers within the Member States and discussing with ease the qualities of the respective national legal categories and theories.[29]

As striking as this sort of trajectory might be, one should not, however, overestimate the importance of this cosmopolitan legal capital. Certainly this new 'model of excellence' was influential: the creation within the EC institutions of the 'jurist-linguist', a civil servant at the Commission distinct from both the legal service and the translation service, gave some sort of institutional recognition to this mix of legal and linguistic competences.[30] Yet, clearly, the possession of this legal-linguistic asset was not equally necessary to all lawyers, as the national origin

28 Hanerz, U. (1996), 'Cosmopolitans and Locals in World Culture', in Hanerz, U., *Transnational Connections: Culture, People, Places* (London: Routledge), 102–11, 103. As Hanerz states: 'being on the move is not enough to turn into a cosmopolitan, and we must not confuse the latter with other kinds of travellers.'

29 Of the 15 members of Commission's legal service in the mid 1960s, at least five of them had received a degree in law from a foreign university (Collège de Bruges, the universities of Minneapolis, Yale, Cambridge and London).

30 As a result of this process, the so-called 'groupe de révision juridico-linguistique' of the Commission in charge of verifying the legal conformity of the texts in all EC official languages came to occupy a key position: all of the texts drafted by the General Directorates had to be authorized by the members of the Commission. Berlin, D. (1987), 'Organisation et fonctionnement de la Commission des Communautés européennes', in Cassese, S. (ed.), *L'administration européenne* (Institut Européen d'Administration Publique).

and the institutional/professional background also played a key role. As French sociologist Anne-Catherine Wagner has argued: 'in this international environment, the power struggle between the nations is not simply an abstraction; it has a direct influence on the positions the players occupy, on their trajectories and on the social relationships.'[31] And the considerable difference in value of the different European languages, diplomas and professional experiences is critical to understanding the investment which lawyers had (or did not have) to make at the transnational level. As a matter of fact, the major influence of the French lawyers during this early phase of the EC law can only be fully comprehended in the light of the following general structures of the emergent European construction:

i. The central position of the French diplomacy that allowed them to occupy key positions in the European legal space (general advocate or president at the ECJ, director of the legal services of the Commission and the Council and so on);
ii. the predominance of the French language within the EC at the time making it possible for them to be immediately and almost without effort impelled in the core of European legal discussions that were mostly being held in French;
iii. their common belonging (with only a few rare exceptions) to the French Conseil d'Etat, an institution whose prestige went far beyond the national borders (beginning with countries such as Italy or Belgium which both have a Conseil d'Etat and an administrative law based on the 'French model').

This powerful position of French lawyers was indeed reflected in their limited investments in 'legal cosmopolitanism'. Besides being less endowed with an international background in terms of education and previous career, they rarely directed their strategies towards the symbolic economy of multilingualism, publications in foreign languages, participation in foreign symposiums, and so on. In these respects, their investments in European-ness were far smaller than those of their Belgian, Italian or Luxembourgian counterparts, who, on the contrary, had manifested from the very beginning a developed European '*bonne volonté*'. Quite strikingly, France's first general advocate at the ECJ, Maurice Lagrange, had almost never left the 'cocoon' of the Conseil d'Etat before getting to the Court, and most of his publications during his stay at the Court were published in French or francophone journals. Yet, his very national profile did not prevent him from being considered a true 'spiritual father to the function of general advocate', a role he over the years made into 'one of the most distinguished seats of the EC law'.[32]

31 Wagner, A-C. (1997), 'Les stratégies transnationales en France', *Skeptron Occasional Papers* 13, 6.

32 'Eloge funèbre de Maurice Lagrange prononcé par le président Lord Mackenzie Stuart', in CJCE, *Aperçu des travaux de la Cour en 1986 et 1987 et audiences solennelles* (Luxembourg, 1988), 206.

As a result, legal cosmopolitanism actually appeared only as one specific, yet rare, road towards the constitution of an authority capable of speaking in the name of EC law. Since access to the EC positions (diplomatic, political, professional, academic and so on) was still heavily dependent on variegated forms of *national* cooptation, the building of an authority in this emerging ELF would essentially take place within national spaces.

### *National Cartels of Euro-lawyers*

Reaching one of the key positions in the ELF was limited to actors coming from a fairly restricted number of national institutions and legal circles.[33] In order to become a judge or a *référendaires* at the Court, a member or a director at one of the legal services (of the Commission or of the Council) required having close relations with the pole of 'state lawyers' with positions in both the bureaucratic and the legal realms. In France, the Conseil d'Etat had secured a quasi monopoly in this respect.[34] In Italy, institutions such as Consiglio del contenzioso diplomatico or the Avvocatura dello Stato constituted, at least initially, the main breeding grounds for Euro-lawyers. As a consequence, the ELF was first and foremost structured around *national communities of Euro-lawyers*. What made these communities consistent was both the density of networks and inter-personal relationships, and the fact that they were all at the same engaged in similar undertakings: promoting the value of their European experience on the national level and defending the importance of their own country's legal tradition in the European debates over the building of the general principles of Euro-law. The first EC law books were written by *national* legal experts of EC law.[35] The founding in each of the Member States of EC law journals during the first half of the 1960s,[36] as well as the activities of the national sections of the FIDE, also contributed to maintaining the type of solidarity that was

33 This predominance of national recruitment has for a long time been preserved within the cabinets of the members of the Commission. Concerning this issue, see Joana, J. and Smith, A. (2002), *Les commissaires européens. Technocrates, diplomates ou politiques* (Paris: Presses de Sciences Po).

34 Concerning the French networks around the EC institutions, see Mangenot, M. (2008), *De l'Etat à l'Europe. Les hauts fonctionnaires français aux origines des institutions européennes* (Strasbourg: Presses universitaires de Strasbourg).

35 The first commentary on the Rome treaties, the *Trattato istitutivo della CEE : commentario*, edited in Italy in 1962 by three professors of law, Roberto Monaco, Rolando Quadri and Albert Trabucchi, assembled 44 contributors, all Italian, who represented by their diversity the different arenas where EC law was being produced (professors of law, civil servants from the Commission, diplomats, legal experts from the different cabinets, lawyers and so on).

36 In Italy, *la Rivista di diritto europeo* from 1961, in the Netherlands and in Great Britain, the *Common Market Law Review* (1963), in Belgium, *Les Cahiers de droit européen* (1965), in France, the *Revue trimestrielle de droit européen* (1965) and in Germany, *Europarecht* (1966).

being constructed within these national legal circles.[37] Interestingly, these national gatherings of Euro-lawyers gave life to an intersectorial space of circulation in which jurists from different institutions and with variegated clientele would not only interact but also co-operate.

The following analysis of the career of the three of the most active Italian EC lawyers of this period (1950–70) – Nicola Catalano, Riccardo Monaco and Alberto Trabucchi – suggests that they were engaged in a game of role switching, pleading alternately 'in favour of' and 'against' *each* of the diplomatic, administrative and political interests present in the European construction. All three jurists were involved in an intense doctrinal legal activity (Catalano was indeed the head of the Italian section of the FIDE) and published – often together – the first Italian manuals on EC law, as well as numerous commentaries on the ECJ's jurisprudence.[38] All three were eventually appointed as judges at the Court of Justice during the period. Here they gained a reputation as pro-European lawyers defending the ECJ's 'supremacy' and 'direct effect' doctrine. Two of them (Catalano and Monaco), however, had previously acted as legal advisers to the Italian delegations during the inter-governmental conferences (Messina, Val Duchesse, and so on) where they in fact had fiercely defended Italian national interests. Throughout the period considered here (1950–70), they were also directly involved in the defence of the EC executives (Nicola Catalano was a member of the CECA legal service between 1953 and 1956), of Italian regions (Alberto Trabucchi defended the department of Bolzano versus the state of Italy at the Italian Constitutional Court in June 1956) and of private clients (in 1962, Nicola Catalano set up a legal practice specialized in EC law).

### *Lawyers as Europe's First Trustees*

These un-interrupted moves between the private and the public, between law and politics, and between the national and the Community levels would have seemed contradictive, even inconceivable if they had been carried out by other players of the European game, beginning with diplomats and public officials. But to the EC lawyers, this proclivity to change position appeared to be a sign of professional excellence, since it seemed to confirm the capacity to defend 'in the name of the law' all sorts of causes and interests. And when judge Monaco recalls the 'friendly legal fights before the European Court of Justice' with his friend Catalano (with

37 These legal circles were nevertheless composed differently in each Member State. The first French EC lawyers were thus inscribed in spaces that *a priori* were more divided (especially between the *conseillers d'Etat*, the lawyers and the law professors) than their Italian or German counterparts.

38 Among the numerous references, see in particular, Nicola Catalano (1962), *Manuel de droit des Communautés européennes* (Paris: Dalloz-Sirey), Riccardo Monaco, Alberto Trabucchi, et al., *Codice delle comunità europee*, and Riccardo Monaco, Alberto Trabucchi, et al., *Trattato istitutivo della Comunità economica europea*, 1965, etc.

whom he had co-authored important academic reports promoting European legal integration) – 'myself as the legal agent of the Italian government and him as a defender of the EC'[39] (acting as judge) – it comes across as a polite discussion between legal gentlemen who could easily have defended the opposite position. The ease with which lawyers crossed the frontiers of the European construction is incomprehensible if one does not refer to the fact that these lawyers from the different Member States shared a common legal *habitus* characterized by a specific readiness to defend contradicting social interests and to deal with competing social allegiances 'in the name of law'.[40] As a matter of fact, legal know-how is not just a purely technical competence, but should be understood equally as (intellectual) equipment inciting, and at the same time enabling, lawyers to handle variegated and often contradicting social loyalties. This required that a set of complex strategies were brought into play, that is, strategies that allowed them to maintain – in all situations – a distance to the roles played. This, however, had the in-built risk of sometimes causing misunderstandings in some of the borderline cases. A good example is the 'embarrassing' position of Riccardo Monaco when he argued his position in the highly divisive and controversial *Costa v. ENEL* case brought before the Court of Justice in July 1964. By being at one and the same time the legal agent of a country that bluntly intended to deny the Court's legitimacy on the matter, and a future judge of the Court (he was about to get the nomination) claiming the 'supremacy' of EC law over all national laws, he had no other solution than to withdraw from the case in order not to compromise his loyalty to both sides:

> Due to my function, I was supposed to represent the Italian government [in the *Costa* case]; but I did not in any case wish to assume alone all of the responsibility in this case. Therefore, I made the *Avvocato generale dello stato* appoint one of his best collaborators, the lawyer L. Tracanna, and I furthermore obtained that my renowned colleague and friend Massimo Severino Giannini could assume the Italian defence. ... The public hearing was important; it was assured by Tracanna and Giannini. The surprise was general when I declined taking the floor. But this could be justified; the rumour had already begun to spread that I would be appointed Judge at the Court in October.[41]

39 Monaco, R. (1984), 'Nicola Catalano 1910–1984', *Rivista di diritto europeo*, 103–4, 103.

40 The hypothesis of such a European legal *habitus* would find some confirmation in the various accounts of common European legal history (cf. authors like Ernst Kantorowicz or Paolo Grossi), as well as of a shared set of principles that organize that legal practice, particularly *vis-à-vis* the economic realm. Cf. Osiel, M. (1990) 'Lawyers as Monopolists, Aristocrats, and Entrepreneurs', *Harvard Law Review* 103:8, 2009–66.

41 Monaco, R., *Memorie di una vita, memorie per l'Europa* (Rome: Ledip), 158. Translation by author.

Certainly, modern legal science has progressively developed tools (particularly legal fictions such as the distinction between individuals and institutional roles, physical persons and legal entities) to facilitate the contacts between actors and the numerous social positions they occupy.[42] As technicians of these formalities, lawyers continuously divide their tasks between as many questions of fact as questions of law, between as many social causes as causes of law, between as many physical persons as moral persons. All this made them experts in organizing multi-personnel games, to the benefit of their clients whose ubiquitous presence in different arenas and organizations (through proxies) they helped organize. But also – and maybe even more so – to their own benefit in so far as they could accumulate clients having different and varying interests. This is actually one of the specific characteristics of the *legal representation* lawyers have codified over the course of history: through notions such as 'mandate', 'power of attorney' or 'delegation', it enabled lawyers to engage in the *defence* of specific interests and causes, while maintaining a *distance* from these groups by means of the act of re-translation *in legal terms*. If there can be said to exist a certain 'European legal identity', it may therefore be less the result of a European legal heritage than of this common professional predisposition to perform this subtle mixing of *closeness* to numerous profane interests they are to defend, and of *distance vis-à-vis* those very interests, in the name of a 'legal reason', that they collectively claim to embody as a professional corps.

If it is true that the EC polity is a multi-layered space made up of heterogeneous social interests without a state organizing them in a more or less stable way, one has to acknowledge that this legal *habitus* is particularly suited. This alchemy of distance and adherence made it possible for Euro-lawyers to both *intervene in* and *circulate between* all of the social games that constituted this nascent polity. With no doubt this is one of the essential conditions for the concentration of European legal capital in relatively few hands. The accumulation of resources that took place in this circulation in fact enabled the 'cartelization' of the European legal market around a limited number of players. This process is certainly never as apparent as in the case of those who – having been directly involved in the negotiations and the writing of the treaties of Paris and Rome – felt 'a bit responsible for the institutional system described in the Treaty of Rome'.[43] Being entitled to authoritatively refer to the 'spirit', the 'economy' or even the 'philosophy' of

42 Boltanski, L. (1973), 'L'espace multipositionnel: multiplicité des positions institutionnelles et habitus de classe', *Revue française de sociologie* 1, 3–26. In his analysis of the American 'ruling class', C. Wright Mills identified *lawyers* as 'professional go-between of economic, political and military affairs, and who thus act to unify the power elite'; but he had not analysed why lawyers could be considered as such skilful social actors, particularly well prepared for circulating and mediating between the different types of elites. Wright Mills, C. (1956), *The Power Elite* (Oxford: Oxford University Press), 288–9.

43 Catalano, *Manuel de droit des Communautés européennes*, 42.

the EC treaties gave them a great advantage when it came to accessing the legal positions they had helped frame as treaty-makers. As a matter of fact, six of the 16 judges and general advocates that succeeded one another at the Court of Justice between 1951 and 1969 had directly participated in writing the treaties, whereas the first directors of the legal service – Ernst Wohlfart for the Council of ministers and Michel Gaudet for the Commission – had both taken part in the negotiations of the Treaty of Rome.[44] Such a process can be observed in other segments of EC policies,[45] but it is undoubtedly of a special importance in the legal realm where lawful interpretation of legal texts is precisely what actors strive for.[46] The authority gained through direct participation in the drafting of the EC treaties was thus reinforced by that drawn from their practical experience of EC institutions. As such, they easily qualified as authentic 'founding fathers' of the European legal order.

What then made up this first European legal capital was a composite set of resources (national origin, institution, legal-linguistic competence, social capital and so on) enabling these actors to surpass the sectorial and national borders that delineated the nascent ELF. Transnational and cross-sectorial circulation, I would therefore argue, was a key element in the process of accumulating *Euro-legal* credentials. Armed with technologies perfectly adjusted to this weakly institutionalized European entity, the first EC lawyers thus were the first European brokers who ensured the contacts between a range of weakly connected sectorial and/or national spaces. It is our assumption that this genesis does not represent a pre-history of a long convergence process through which Euro-lawyers would progressively conform their national counterparts, as a teleological reading of European integration as a potential 'super-state' would suggest; but rather that it is a critical juncture were a *stable* relationship between law, lawyers and EU polity has been defined.

---

44 Such a list should also include Christian Calmes the first general secretary of the Council of Ministers and Carl Friedrich Ophuls the first representative of the German government at the Coreper, respectively doctor of law and professor of international public law. Both of them had been members of the group of legal experts that participated in the writing of the Treaty of Paris.

45 In fact, a large number of EC positions (members of the Commission, general directors, vice general directors) were attributed to former members of the various delegations, who had met during the 1950s within the framework of negotiating the treaties of Paris and Rome.

46 Their 'jurisdiction' (Abbott) over the interpretation of EC treaties was favoured by the fact that the Court of Justice had refused to recognize the '*travaux préparatoires*' as a relevant source for their exegesis. As the meaning of these treaties was not bounded by any explicit political guidelines, they were opened to a *legal* reinterpretation.

# PART 3
# LANGUAGE AS BARRIER AND CARRIER OF EUROPEAN LEGAL INTEGRATION

# Chapter 11
# Introduction: Language as Barrier and Carrier of European Legal Integration

Anne Lise Kjær

As suggested in the preceding parts of this book, studying European legal integration implies examining a number of processes: constitutionalization and democratization, or conversely, the dynamics of transnational market formation. Some of the authors describe legal actors as 'the missing link' in integration studies (Chs. 7, 9 and 10), yet this view does not cover the fact that jurists, judges and lawyers, the flesh and blood of legal integration, belong to a plurality of legal cultures and speak a multitude of different languages. Although often neglected in integration studies, the success of the European project heavily relies on the possibility of a mutual understanding of European legal actors and an ability to surmount the barriers caused by linguistic and cultural diversity and difference.

Thanks to the 'convergence' debate initiated by Pierre Legrand,[1] integration constraints relating to European legal cultures have been on the research agenda of comparative legal studies for the past decade. The question at issue is whether the diversity of legal cultures in Europe presents an obstacle to legal integration, or whether it might – paradoxically – also be a source of inspiration for the development of a European legal order. Some writers argue that differences between European legal traditions are irreducible.[2] Others maintain that differences are contingent upon practice and that increased interaction between jurists, judges and lawyers across the boundaries of domestic legal systems has the effect that

1 See in particular Legrand, P. (1996), 'European Legal Systems are not Converging', *International and Comparative Law Quarterly* 45, 52–81.

2 Legrand, 'European Legal Systems are not Converging'. A more modest stance is taken by, for example, Harlow, C. (2002), 'Voices of Difference in a Polyphonic Community: The Case for Legal Diversity Within the European Union', in Beaumont, P. et al. (eds), *Convergence and Divergence in European Public Law* (Oxford: Hart), 199–224; cf. Teubner, G. (1998), 'Legal Irritants: Good Faith in British Law or How Unifying Law Ends Up in New Divergences', *Modern Law Review* 61, 11–32.

cultures gradually converge, and that they do so 'faster than one is prepared to acknowledge'.[3]

Whereas the plurality of legal cultures has attracted some attention in research, linguistic diversity is not a major theme in the scholarly debate on legal integration. From the point of view of linguistics and translation studies, this is surprising. European multilingualism makes the ideal of a common legal language in Europe seem a contradiction in terms and calls for closer scrutiny. The relevance of the topic can hardly be ignored in view of the immense political efforts made to draft a common European constitution or develop common principles of private law – also considering the fact that several transnational research groups have set themselves the task of developing, in some form, a common legal language across the great variety of national legal languages.[4]

One plausible reason for the silent life of languages in integration studies might be the fact that research is conducted mostly by experts on law, politics and – increasingly – sociology. In these research traditions, language is rarely considered as a subject in its own right. Therefore, only a few writers have focused on the problems and potentials posed by the multiplicity of European legal languages.[5] Moreover, the role of language and translation in European legal integration has not yet been established as an independent and coherent research field. However, European legal linguistics[6] seems to be gaining more attention as a cross-disciplinary field, suggesting that the quiet and thorny working of

3 The quote stems from an early contribution to the debate: Markesinis, B.S. (1994), 'Learning from Europe and Learning in Europe', in Markesinis, B.S. (ed.), *The Gradual Convergence: Foreign Ideas, Foreign Influences, and English Law on the Eve of the 21st Century* (London: Clarendon) 1–32 (30). From the same period, see also Bell, J. (1995), 'English Law and French Law – Not so Different?', *Current Legal Problems* 48:2, 63–102.

4 For an overview, see Beale, H. (2006), 'The European Civil Code Movement and the European Union's Common Frame of Reference', *Legal Information Management* 4:11. A critical survey is given in Schepel, H. (2007), 'The European Brotherhood of Lawyers: The Reinvention of Legal Science in the Making of European Private Law', *Law & Social Inquiry* 32:1, 183–99.

5 Glanert, S. (2006), 'Zur Sprache gebracht: Rechtsvereinheitlichung in Europa', *European Review of Private Law* 14:2, 157–74; Heutger, V. (2003), 'Law and Language in the European Union', *Global Jurist Topics* 3:1, Article 3; Kjær, A.L. (2004), 'A Common Legal Language in Europe?', in van Hoecke, M. (ed.), *Epistemology and Methodology of Comparative Law* (Oxford: Hart), 377–98; López-Rodríguez, A.M. (2004), 'Towards a European Civil Code Without a Common European Legal Culture? The Link between Law, Language and Culture', *Brooklyn Journal of International Law* 29, 1195–220; Pazzo, B. and Jacometti, V. (eds) (2006), *Multilingualism and the Harmonisation of European Law* (Alphen aan den Rijn and London: Kluwer Law International).

6 See for example Burr, I. and Gréciano, G. (eds) (2003), *Europa: Sprache und Recht* (Baden-Baden: Nomos); Mattila, H. (2006), *Comparative Legal Linguistics* (Aldershot: Ashgate); Müller, F. and Burr, I. (eds) (2004), *Rechtssprache Europas. Reflexion der Praxis von Sprache und Mehrsprachigkeit im supranationalen Recht* (Berlin: Duncker & Humblot).

language and translation in transnational legal encounters is a fundamental pillar of European legal integration.

The four chapters of this Part examine the role of language and text in law from a plurality of perspectives. Although the interests, methods and theories of the writers differ, there is general agreement concerning one central point: language and text matter when dealing with law. From this starting point, the individual scholars pursue radically different goals.

Legrand presents theoretical arguments suggesting that linguistic diversity is an insurmountable barrier to European legal integration. Mattila describes how that barrier may be coped with in practice – by means of translation or the use of a *lingua franca*.

Twining discusses the relevance of the notion of 'surface law', a metaphor regularly applied in comparative legal studies for the kind of law that presents itself when only the texts and not the practices of law are considered. Weigand considers the nature of language and shows that texts of law cannot be separated from practices of law, and that legal language, like language use in all other cases, are dialogic interactions between language users.

When read in conjunction, the papers reveal two paradoxes of European legal integration relating to the role of language:

1. *Law and text*: Law is not a matter of text. Legal rules expressed in legal texts are surface law and only the tip of an iceberg. What actually matters is how people act and think in real life, and law cannot be reduced to a particular way of using language. Nevertheless, law relies heavily on the use of language and any legal practice is a mixed game, integrating language, mind and action. While law is not a matter of text, law cannot be separated from the texts in which law is practiced.
2. *Law and multilingualism*: Linguistic relativity and radical untranslatability of languages make full interlingual understanding improbable, and integration efforts are impeded because legal actors read, interpret and apply common rules differently. Nevertheless, language is the very medium in which mutual understanding occurs; it is through translation and in intercultural dialogue that legal actors agree on common rules and strive for harmonization of their different world views.

## Law and Text

The relevance of analysing the nature of language when studying the mechanisms of law seems obvious. 'Language is the medium through which law acts';[7] hence, the relationship between law and language is not a trivial one. However, the crux of

7 Bix, B. (1993), *Law, Language and Legal Determinacy* (Oxford: Oxford University Press), 1.

the matter is what one understands by 'language'. If language is identified only with the 'bare' words of legislative texts, it would belong to what Twining, in his chapter, calls 'surface law', not as important as those 'real' reasons that eventually govern the judge when deciding cases. If law is not considered to be very much a matter of reading, writing and interpreting legislative texts, then theories of language, in this understanding of the word, would seem to be of no particular use.

But, as Twining argues, the notion of 'surface law' may be misleading. It owes its existence to the sociology-of-law opposition of 'appearance' and 'reality' in law: law in books and law in action; paper rules and real rules; rules and results (outcome); rules and consequences ('impact'); rules and predictions, and so on. What these dichotomies misleadingly postulate, according to Twining, is that there exists a gap between the 'bare text' on one hand and the 'underlying' problems, principles, policies and rationale beneath the surface on the other. '[T]reating these familiar contrasts as binary and talk of "gaps" both suggest that the two poles of each dichotomy are separate, perhaps even unrelated alternatives.' However, '[w]hen rules are flouted, not enforced, manipulated, or misinterpreted the activity takes place with reference to those rules' and the underlying principles and policies 'are intimately related to "surface law"'.

From a linguistic point of view, the core problem of the contrasts between law in books and law in action is that they rest upon the presumption that such a thing as the 'bare text' or 'mere words' exists. Only few linguists today uphold a view of language as a self-sufficient system. The predominant view is that language cannot be described independently of people's use of language as a means of cognition and communication and that it is an integrated part of people's actions and interactions in real-life situations in time and space. The structuralist distinction between *langue* and *parole*, or competence and performance (which resembles the oppositions commented on in Twining's paper) has been widely abandoned since the pragmatic and cognitive turns in linguistics.

As Weigand states in her chapter, '[i]t is no longer controversial to state that competence, even communicative competence, is a methodological concept, and performance restricted to empirical 'data' does not do justice to the complex object of the mixed game. There is no bridge between a rule-governed system and ever-changing performance, or in legal terms, between the law and the case. The bridge is established in the minds of human beings, by their *competence-in-performance*'. She continues, '[l]aw and jurisprudence are not purely abstract logical systems which exist on paper independently of human beings. They are created by human beings by means of language and dialogue and have to be applied in each individual case.'[8]

8 The Mixed Game Model or the Theory of Dialogic Action Games was developed by Weigand as a holistic linguistic model capable of dealing with the complexity of dialogic interaction. Cf. Weigand, E. (2003), *Sprache als Dialog. Sprechakttaxonomie und kommunikative Grammatik*, 2nd rev. edn (Tübingen: Niemeyer).

When Twining's examination of the notion of 'surface law' is applied to the paradoxes of European legal integration, a multitude of important issues emerges. One problem is that what is dismissed as mere 'surface law' by a common law-judge, marks the binding starting point of legal reasoning for a civil law-judge. Therefore, even if the presumption that the judge functions only as *la bouche de la loi* is not upheld in civil law legal systems, there is no doubt that a civil law-judge will attach greater importance to the formal rules expressed in the 'bare' legislative texts than his colleagues from a case law-based legal system.

Another point to be considered is the fact that in a Europe of somewhat harmonized and unified law, there is a wealth of texts all of which may receive the stamp of 'surface law'. National legal rules co-exist with European legal rules, and European legal rules are phrased in just as many language versions as is required by the linguistic regime of the organization in question (in the case of EU law, that is, at the time of writing no less than 23). The question is if there is anything beneath the plural surfaces that binds them together and safeguards the coherence or consistency of the patchwork of surface texts. Some would assert that the underlying concepts, principles and policies are more or less the same across European legal languages and legal systems. This is the opinion voiced by most protagonists of a common European law, and it is the basic presumption of all integration initiatives referred to above (cf. note 4). Pierre Legrand opposes that presumption. For Legrand, what lies beneath the surface of legal rules is a *mentalité* of lawyers which is fundamentally and irreducibly intertwined with the culture of the national legal order to which they belong.[9]

A final issue is the translation of the common European legal texts. As Mattila explains in his chapter, '[a] legal translation must adequately express the relevant legal concepts behind the terms of the source language in the target language even in cases where no exact equivalent exists.' Hence, translation can never be a simple substitution of one 'bare text' for another 'bare text'; translation inevitably includes meaning and interpretation and thus makes it clear that the distinction between surface law and real law or text and meaning is misconceived from the outset.

## Law and Multilingualism

Legal language is culture-bound and dependent on one particular society and its legal system. In past centuries, Latin used to play the role of a common legal language which was applied across the boundaries of local law, but in today's Europe there is no such legal *lingua franca*. As illustrated by Mattila in his contribution, neither Latin nor international English (that is, 'not-common-law-bound legal English') are reliable as common legal languages. Therefore, even if there is a common core of Latin expressions and maxims that are known in

9 Legrand, 'European Legal Systems are not Converging', 60.

all countries and have an identical universal meaning established by long-time usage, there are also numerous expressions and maxims which are closely tied to particular legal cultures and which sometimes have a purely national character. As far as international English is concerned, it is just as deceptive, resting, as it often does, on inferences from the national legal languages of its speakers. It follows that lawyers belonging to different legal systems have no shared language. Expressing legal rules in a plurality of legal languages thus presupposes translation.

Jurists studying European legal integration are indebted to Pierre Legrand for bringing the subject of cultural diversity to the fore. In his contributions to the debate on the possibility and desirability of harmonization and unification of law and convergence between European legal cultures,[10] he has willingly played the role of the 'Devil's advocate'. Even if it may have given him the stamp of a 'bad European', as he suggests in his chapter in this book, he has never ceased stating that 'one-law' is not only undesirable but also impossible!

In his chapter, Legrand restates and refines this message with arguments drawn from the linguistic relativity thesis of von Humboldt, the hermeneutics of Gadamer, and the phenomenology of Derrida, and he adds that 'one-language' – the common European legal language that integrationists strive for – is impossible as well.

Language can be viewed as mainly a social phenomenon, implying that language is a counterpart to culture or human action or society. Yet language can also be understood in terms of *a* language or *many* languages, covering the plurality of mother- or 'father-tongues', as Legrand has it, spoken by people throughout the world.

Legrand clearly considers language in the second sense. He asks, 'Can a francophone ever see or hear the word "onerous" without the word "onéreux" intruding?' What kind of question is that? It cannot be a question of the *use* of those languages in time and space. No language user – francophone or otherwise – will ever experience in real life hearing words used in isolation. And no language user will experience reading words without a context or without an explanation, a translation or the possibility of asking, 'What did you mean by that?' As Weigand puts it in her contribution, '[l]anguage use is always dialogically oriented. Dialogue not only includes meaning and understanding, but also reacting, at least mentally.'

Thus, the comparison of 'onerous' and 'onéreux' that Legrand makes, must be a theoretical comparison of differences between the vocabularies of two *language systems*. What he claims is that languages are irreducibly different, and that interlingual understanding will consequently always be imperfect and approximate: 'To say that one's language is one's world-view does not mean, *pace* Donald Davidson, that one cannot identify a radically different language – and engage comparatively with it, for instance by purporting to "translate" it – inevitably approximately – into one's "own" language.'

10 See the collection of works in Legrand, P. (1999), *Fragments on Law-as-Culture* (Deventer: Tjeenk Willink).

Translation in the every-day reality of translators and legal actors, and the methods that they employ in order to cope with linguistic and conceptual differences described in Mattila's paper, are not in focus in Legrand's contribution. However, when studying European legal integration – not as a theoretical notion, but as an empirical fact – it is relevant to study language in practical use. Thus, Legrand exposes himself to misunderstanding, by failing to specify the *existence form* of language that is the object of his analysis: *langue* or *parole*, system or discourse, competence or performance, or using an analogy from the sociology of law: 'words in books' or 'words in action'?

In the scholarly debates on legal integration, linguistic and conceptual divergence attract increasing attention. But more often than not, comments are made on a God's eye basis that neglects the fundamental problems of translation, in both theoretical and practical terms.

The analysis of 'discretion', referred to by van Roermund in a book on divergent concepts in European law,[11] is illustrative of such forgetfulness of language and linguistic diversity: The author discusses the two notions of 'discretion' in German law; 'genuine discretion' and 'quasi discretion', without wondering whether *discretion* is a proper rendering in English of the German legal concept of 'Ermessen', which I suppose is what is meant. Likewise, he has seemingly no problem in concluding that at 'a fairly high level of abstraction' there is a 'core of discretion' common to all legal orders of the EU.

Van Roermund seems to forget that his abstractions are phrased in English and that this entails either an English-language perspective on the concepts that he is discussing or a deliberate use of an international Pidgin English, cleansed for meaning derived from English law. The problem is that a neutral, de-nationalized and standardized common language is not achievable. Hence, as shown by both Mattila and Legrand, in interlingual analysis one never escapes language; there is no neutral or formal language above languages from which to conduct the analysis. Or as stated by Derrida: there is the 'absolute impossibility of a metalanguage' and the 'impossibility of an absolute metalanguage'.[12]

The lack of a common language entails that '[t]ranslations often constitute one of the weakest links in international legal procedures', as Mattila has it. Therefore, 'the linguistic plurality of the European Union – a richness which needs to be protected – causes a major problem which endangers the results of European legal integration: imprecise, even entirely incorrect translations of legal documents in cases of an international nature.'

Nevertheless, in spite of the difficulties of mutual understanding caused by European multilingualism, it can hardly be denied that European legal actors are engaged in a perfectly meaningful dialogue across linguistic barriers. How can

11 van Roermund, B. (2008), 'Laws at Cross-purposes: Conceptual Confusion and Political Divergence', in Prechal, S. and van Roermund, B. (eds), *The Coherence of EU Law: The Search for Unity in Divergent Concepts* (Oxford: Oxford University Press).

12 Quoted from Pierre Legrand's contribution to this collection.

one explain why international legal communication seems to work in practice when theories of language and translation offer nothing but reasons why it does not and cannot? Are the theories wrong or is our judgement of practice wrong? Are we blinded by our deeply felt wish to understand each other across linguistic barriers when the truth is that we do not?[13] Or is the explanation much simpler? Is the reason why it is possible to cross linguistic barriers, as Cao states in a recent book on legal translation, 'that no exact equivalence or complete identity of understanding can be expected or is really necessary'?[14] Or in other words: theory is engaged in describing the ideal of absolute and perfect understanding; practice is content with less.

13 Compare the similar statement by Jackson, B.S.: 'any "legal vision of Europe" has to be recognised as resting upon an act of faith, and not merely reason – faith that despite epistemological difficulties, understanding is possible …', in Jackson, B.S. (1993); 'Legal Visions of the New Europe: *ius gentium*, *ius commune*, European Law', in Jackson, B.S. and McGoldrick, D. (eds), *Legal Visions of the New Europe* (London, Dordrecht and Boston: Kluwer) 3–35 (at 34).

14 Cao, D. (2007), *Translating Law* (Clevedon: Multilingual Matters), 35.

# Chapter 12
# Surface Law

William Twining[1]

## Introduction

I first met Henrik Zahle in Florence, where we were the only two lawyers at a conference on 'Complexity'. We immediately became friends. Later, I corresponded with him about his admirable work on legal polycentricity. Later still, in the autumn of 2005, we shared a desk in Bentham House at University College London. He was working on evidence, about which we had several interesting discussions. However, one day I floated some half-formed thoughts about the idea of 'surface law'. The starting-point was the suggestion that Alan Watson's thesis about legal transplants was both important and plausible, but that it only dealt with 'surface law'. This did not mean that Watson's thesis was superficial, but what did it mean? Henrik was interested. He encouraged me to develop the basic idea and invited me to contribute a paper on the subject to a conference he was organizing. I accepted the invitation because I hoped to continue our conversations in Copenhagen. Like many others, I was shocked by the news of his illness and premature death. I dedicate this modest contribution to his memory. It was he who encouraged me to develop the ideas, but I am very conscious that it misses the critical insights that he had promised me. At least, like the first site of our relationship, it conveys a message of complexity.

## Sophie's Problem

Once upon a time Sophie, a student of dispute processes, decided to investigate the handling of disputes in universities. Casual inquiry suggested to her that appointments and promotions of academic staff were a major source of regular and bitter conflicts in academic life. She decided to do a pilot study on the topic in the local university, an institution that broadly followed British patterns of academic governance.

Although her perspective was ethnographic, Sophie decided to start with the formal structure of authority and decision-making in the university. The annual calendar set out the texts of the Charter and Statutes of the University. A regularly

1 I am grateful to participants at the conference and to Hugh Beale, Caroline Bradley, Andrew Halpin and Neil MacCormick for useful comments and suggestions.

updated 'blue book' collected the main regulations of the central administration. From these sources she learned that all appointments to academic positions were made by the Governing Body (the Council) on the recommendation of the University Appointments Committee, chaired by the Vice-Chancellor or his deputy. The Committee consisted of 12 regular members and for each appointment just two representatives of the relevant department or subject area. Under the university statutes all 'permanent' academic vacancies had to be advertised, with formal applications addressed to the Registrar of the University.

Sophie obtained an interview with the Registrar. Before she saw him she studied all of the formal rules governing appointments that were published in the University's calendar and 'blue books'. She was sceptical whether these told the whole story. The Registrar outlined the procedures in terms that followed the published rules. He also showed her two sample files containing advertisements, referees' reports, and extracts from the minutes of the Appointments Committee. All seemed to conform to the rules. The Registrar expressed surprise that appointments might be considered contentious.

'The process works smoothly. The short-listed candidates are all interviewed on the same day. Decisions are made on the spot and, usually within 24 hours, the Vice-Chancellor contacts the preferred candidate with an offer, which is subject to confirmation by Council. In my ten years, Council has approved all such recommended appointments.'

The Registrar concluded: 'You are wasting your time. If you are looking for controversy or conflict, you would do better by looking at student discipline, salary disputes, or proposals for curriculum revision.'

Undeterred, Sophie went to see the Dean of the Faculty of Humanities and Social Sciences, who confirmed nearly everything that the Registrar had said and added little.

'But have you not had any controversial appointments?' asked Sophie.

'Of course, not all appointments are popular, especially among the younger staff, but this is a University matter and we have succeeded in keeping it that way. There was one minor incident two or three years ago in one department, when some of the staff tried to "democratize" the process. As soon as we learned about this, we clamped down on it.'

'How did you find out?' asked Sophie.

'A candidate who was not short-listed sent in a claim for expenses for an unauthorized visit', was the reply.

Sophie decided to move down to departmental level. But instead of contacting any more officials she chose to start with some of the younger members of staff. Borrowing from John Flood's approach to barristers' clerks, she met two of them in a pub.[2] When asked about the claim for unauthorized expenses, they laughed:

2 Flood, J. (1983), *Barristers' Clerks: The Law's Middlemen* (Manchester: Manchester University Press); Goffman, E. (1959), *The Presentation of Self in Everyday Life* (New York: Anchor).

'Oh, we are careful not to repeat that mistake. When candidates come down for informal visits we pay their expenses on the spot from the fund for visiting speakers – we ask them to give a seminar as well as interviewing them.'

'Who interviews them?'

'The Departmental Appointments Committee (DAC), in addition to individual interviews by interested colleagues'.

As recounted by these two informants the DAC had been in existence for a decade and still continued. It consisted of six elected members and the Head of Department *ex offici* . Both elections to the DAC and decisions on specific appointments were regularly contested. The DAC controlled the short list. The Head of Department was mandated to press for the appointment of the candidate(s) chosen by the DAC, whatever his or her views. Careful 'official' records were kept. On gaining access to these files, Sophie found a rich documentary record of over a decade of disputes with the names of dozens of further potential candidates who had not reached the university's short-lists. Her project was viable.

This is a familiar example of an 'unofficial institution' with quite elaborate interposed norms[3] and detailed written records of actual disputes, almost none of which reached the attention of the university authorities, who believed that they had a monopoly of power and authority over the whole process, when in fact they were nearly always merely rubber stamping decisions taken at earlier secret, 'democratic' and disputatious stages of the same process.

If Sophie had followed the advice of Llewellyn and Hoebel,[4] or of John Flood, she would have started in the pub and asked questions along the line: 'Had any good disputes lately?'[5] With co-operation of informants and access to records, she could have collected quite detailed case studies that would illustrate in a concrete way the existence of a highly institutionalized set of techniques, procedures, forms and devices and their interaction with the 'official' system of governance.

The documentary material supplemented by further interviews provided enough material for a doctoral thesis. Sophie began by analysing her data in terms of some standard traditional dichotomies: appearance/reality; aspiration/reality;

3 The *locus classicus* on interposition is Kadish, M.R. and Kadish, S.H. (1973), *Discretion to Disobey: A Study of Lawful Departure from Legal Rules* (Stanford, CA: Stanford University Press). Cf. the account of the local dispute process institutions tagged on to the colonial courts by the Basoga in Uganda in Fallers L. (1967), *Law Without Precedent* (Chicago, IL: University of Chicago Press).

4 Llewellyn, K.N. and Hoebel, E.A. (1941), *The Cheyenne Way* (Norman, OK: University of Oklahoma Press).

5 The Llewellyn-Hoebel 'case method', given classical shape in *The Cheyenne Way*, was designed to learn about actual institutions and practices in the context of informants who were inarticulate, or secretive, or did not think in general terms about rules, institutions and practices. The uses and limitations of the case method in legal anthropology have been extensively canvassed in the literature, see, for example, Epstein, A.L. (ed.) (1967), *The Craft of Social Anthropology* (London: Tavistock) or Twining, W. (2002), *The Great Juristic Bazaar* (Aldershot: Dartmouth), 157–70 and 192 n. 50.

paper rules/real rules; law in books/law in action; back stage/front stage; official/unofficial; theory/practice.[6] What these seductive dichotomies have in common is that they are often used to identify a 'gap' between each of the contrasted pairs.

It is tempting to say of this example that the official accounts of the appointments procedures was superficial, incomplete and misleading and that the university's Charter, Statutes, and other published rules were only 'surface law'. In this paper, I focus on this last phrase and suggest that in discussions of legal pluralism, or diffusion of law, or unification, harmonization or convergence of laws across jurisdictions – and many other topics – we need a more precise and sophisticated apparatus of analytic concepts and distinctions to give adequately differentiated accounts of some of these standard dichotomies and the relations between them.

Before analysing the phrase 'surface law', I shall introduce some more examples that illustrate the standard dichotomies in a variety of contexts: (a) The gap between 'aspiration' and 'reality' in relation to the international regime of human rights; (b) gaps between 'appearance' and 'reality' in discussions of legal realism and socio-legal studies; (c) different conceptions of what constitutes 'depth' in relation to convergence in comparative law; (d) the American experience of attempts at unification and harmonization of law and its possible relevance to recent projects to harmonize or unify European private law.[7]

## Aspiration and Reality: Universalism and the International Regime of Human Rights

The international human rights regime is nearly 'universal' at state level insofar as almost all members of the United Nations subscribe or are signatories to many, most or all of the main documents. A high level of formal acceptance by nation-states of much of the developing international human rights regime, including both 'hard' and 'soft' instruments, is indeed a remarkable achievement. But to treat this on its own as strong evidence of the universalization of human rights is too simple. In the view of some, most of the regime does not go beyond optimistic aspiration and surface law. Apart from the fact that formal acceptance and ratification is

6 She also considered using the Marxian distinction between base and superstructure, but decided that it did not fit her case study.

7 Pressure of space has necessitated omitting sections on: (e) hidden and neglected legal orders; (f) interlegality; and (g) diffusion of law and legal transplants; see Twining, W. (2008), General Jurisprudence (Cambridge University Press), Ch.10.

patchy and that significant reservations are common,[8] the following points are regularly made by commentators:[9]

1. formal acceptance and ratification may have been pressured, insincere, cynical, or perceived as a meaningless formality;
2. the norms may be given different meanings by different signatories;[10]
3. there are well-known differences about the relative importance and priorities given to different groups of rights (for example, civil and political / social and economic), to balancing conflicting rights, or to balancing rights and economic and other considerations;
4. international monitoring and reporting, let alone enforcement, is selective and uneven; it allows great scope to more powerful states to pursue their own interests under the guise of human rights and democracy; on the whole, the monitoring of civil rights is, so far, much more developed than for social, cultural and economic rights.[11]

---

8 On reservations, see Gardner, J.P. (ed.) (1997), *Human Rights as General Norms and a State's Right to Opt Out: Reservations and Objections to Human Rights Conventions* (London: British Institute of International and Comparative Law); Lijnzaad, L. (1995), *Reservations to UN-Human Rights Treaties: Ratify or Ruin?* (Dordrecht: Nijhoff); Sachleben, M. (2006), *Human Rights Treaties: Considering Patterns of Participation, 1948–2000* (New York: Routledge).

9 A useful alternative formulation is by Ann Kent: 'A major source of contention is the universality of the human rights regime, in the sense of universal acceptance of its norms and principles, the scope of its monitoring and the impartiality of its application. Although there is no doubt that the regime exists and that it is both formally accepted and applied by states, it is not clear that it holds the same meaning for all. Obstacles to universality of interpretation include (a) a lack of consensus about norms; (b) the need for norms to be processed and put in operation through institutions; and (c) the fact that the carriers of ideas in institutions are states.' Kent, A. (1999), *China, the United Nations, and Human Rights: The Limits of Compliance* (Philadelphia, PA: University of Pennsylvania Press), a work that I have found particularly helpful in writing this section. See, on China, Foot, R. (2000), *Rights Beyond Borders* (Oxford: Oxford University Press).

10 A common arena of contention is different interpretations of 'sovereignty' both in international law and in both internal and transnational political discourse.

11 Kent suggests that there is a continuum of at least five stages of international and domestic compliance: '(1) accession to human rights treaties, the acceptance of the norms that this entails, and acceptance by the target state of the right of UN bodies to monitor conditions and of its obligation to respond; (2) procedural compliance with reporting and other requirements; and (3) substantive compliance with the requests of the UN body, exhibited in international or domestic behavior. At the domestic level, the continuum extends to (4) *de jure* compliance, or the implementation of international norms in domestic legislative provisions; and (5) de facto compliance, or compliance at the level of domestic practice.' Kent (1999), *China, the United Nations, and Human Rights*, 23–5. Cf. Dembour, M-B. (2006), *Who Believes in Human Rights?* (Cambridge: Cambridge University Press) esp. ch. 5.

5. the signatories of human rights instruments are nation states, who may not be democratic or truly representative of their people;
6. the international regime applies mainly to states, to a lesser extent to regional groupings, and only patchily to non-state actors such as refugees and displaced persons, freedom fighters and transnational businesses;
7. there is often a large gulf between external acceptance of the international regime of human rights and internal law, attitudes, political and legal culture, and actual practices.[12]

This litany of obstacles and shortfalls, familiar to human rights lawyers, can be extended. An optimistic Universalist might reply: 'All of these points refer to a gap between aspiration and reality, which we readily concede. The important point is that there is a very broad worldwide consensus about the aspiration and this is based on values which are broadly, if not universally, shared and which are gradually converging towards a common set of standards that can be accepted, monitored and enforced.'

While some of the points relate specifically to treaties, the discourse of international lawyers is suggestive in considering surface law: acceptance, reservation, accession, ratification, enactment, implementation, enforcement, procedural compliance, substantive compliance (at both international and domestic levels), uniform interpretation and application, reporting and monitoring (to which one might add impact assessment) are familiar categories and distinctions which highlight points about the kinds of information that may often not be ascertainable from surface law.

## Appearance and Reality: Some 'Realist' Perspectives

Roscoe Pound and the early American Legal Realists are generally credited with developing a range of ideas around contrasts between 'appearance' and 'reality': law in books and law in action;[13] paper rules and real rules;[14] rules and results (outcomes in particular cases);[15] rules and consequences ('impact');[16] rules and

12 Kent (1999), *China, the United Nations, and Human* Rights, 7. On compliance Kent draws heavily on the pioneering work of Abram and Antonia Chayes, for example, (1996), *New Sovereignty: Compliance with International Regulatory Agreements* (Cambridge, MA: Harvard University Press).

13 R. Pound (1910), 'Law in Books and Law in Action', *American Law Review* 44, 12.

14 Llewellyn, K.N. 'A Realistic Jurisprudence: The Next Step', *Columbia Law Review* 30, 431, reprinted in Llewellyn, K.N. (1962), *Jurisprudence: Realism in Theory and Practice* (Chicago, IL: University of Chicago Press).

15 'If rules were results, there would be little need of lawyers' (Llewellyn, K.N. (1930, 1960 reprint), *The Bramble Bush* (New York: Oceana), 9).

16 For example Pound, R. (1917), 'The Limits of Effective Legal Action', *American Bar Association Journal* 3, 56. One of the common points of departure of Realists was,

predictions;[17] the idea of total processes; the distinction between process and outcome, and so on. Most of these ideas have been developed, refined and extended with some sophistication, mainly under the rubrics of 'Law and Society', 'Law in Context', 'Sociology of Law', and 'Socio-legal Studies'.[18] Concern with action, policy, process, impact and so on is now commonplace in legal scholarship and legal discourse generally. In the present context it should be sufficient to make a few observations relevant to the standard dichotomies and the idea of 'surface law'.

Most generalizations about 'the Realists' are false or trivial or both.[19] But by focussing on specific individuals and texts, we can remind ourselves of some non-trivial points.

First, for early Realists, such as Corbin and Llewellyn, 'rule-scepticism' did not entail the belief that 'talk of rules is a myth'.[20] Rather they made the point that articulations of rules in texts and judicial opinions tended to be misleading because they were too abstract and too 'formal'. In particular, they did not catch the 'real' reasons that influenced judges or justified their decisions. In short, surface rules were often not the operative rules. Corbin put it this way in a letter to Llewellyn: 'Pared-down principles there must, of course, be "the law"; but it seldom struck me that the ones I found in print were *the* ones.'[21]

---

according to Llewellyn: '(8) An insistence on evaluation of any part of law in terms of its effects, and an insistence on the worthwhileness of trying to find these effects.' ('Some Realism about Realism' (1931) reprinted in *Jurisprudence*, at 42, 55–7).

17 Insofar as some Realists conflated the concepts of rules and predictions, they have been rightly criticized; insofar as they emphasized the uses and limitations of rules as means to predicting and the importance of prediction in legal practice, their insights have often been ignored.

18 On the misleadingly sharp dichotomy between 'sociology of law' and 'socio-legal studies', which became an arena of contention in the 1970s, see Nelken, D. (1981), 'The "Gap Problem" in the Sociology of Law: A Theoretical Overview', *Windsor Yearbook of Access to Justice* 1, 35–61, discussed below.

19 Twining, W. (2002), 'Talk about Realism', in *The Great Juristic Bazaar*, ch. 5.

20 'It may seem strange that the contention that rules have a central place in the structure of a legal system could ever be seriously doubted. Yet "rule-scepticism", or the claim that talk of rules is a myth, cloaking the truth that law consists simply of the decisions of courts and predictions of them, can make a powerful appeal to a lawyer's candour.' Hart, H.L.A. (1961), *The Concept of Law* (Oxford: Oxford University Press), 133. Hart attributed 'rule scepticism' to Holmes and Llewellyn, but conceded that there were moderate versions of this position. On Llewellyn's attitude to rules see below.

21 Arthur Corbin to Karl Llewellyn, letter 1 December 1960 (quoted in Twining, W. (1973), *Karl Llewellyn and the Realist Movement* (London: Weidenfeld and Nicolson (hereafter KLRM) at p. 32). Cf. longer quotation from Corbin ibid. On Llewellyn's mature account of 'the steadying factors' that made appellate judicial decisions reasonably predictable, see (1960), *The Common Law Tradition: Deciding Appeals* (Boston, MA: Little, Brown).

Second, it was Llewellyn who in an early article drew his famous distinction between 'paper rules' and 'real rules'. This has often been misunderstood. His main concern was to distinguish between descriptions of judicial behaviour (what judges do and what influences them) and normative prescriptions (rules that guide and justify decisions):[22]

> 'Real rules' then, if I had my way with words, would *by legal scientists* be called the practices of the courts and not 'rules' at all .... The concept of 'real rule' has been gaining favor since it was first put into clarity by Holmes. 'Paper rules' are what have been treated , traditionally, as rules of law: the accepted *doctrine* of the time and place – what the books say 'the law' is ...[23]

The idea of 'paper rules' has often been interpreted to refer to rules that are not operative at all or are merely a façade. That was not Llewellyn's point. Rather it was that such surface rules are on their own not very informative:

> Are 'rules of law' in the accepted sense eliminated in such a course of thought? Somewhat obviously not. Whether they be pure paper rules, or are the accepted patter of the law officials, they remain present, and their presence remains an actuality – an actuality of importance – but an actuality whose *precise* importance, whose bearing and influence become clear .... First of all they appear as what they are: rules of authoritative ought, addressed *to* officials, telling *official* what the *official* ought to do. To which telling the officials either pay no heed at all (the pure paper rule; the dead letter statute; the obsolete case) or listen partly (the rule 'construed' out of recognition; the rule to which lip-service chiefly is paid, while practice runs another course) or listen to with all care (the rule with which the official practice pretty accurately coincides).[24]

Neither Corbin nor Llewellyn were strong 'rule sceptics'. Corbin worked on the first Restatement of Contracts. Llewellyn was Chief Reporter of the Uniform Commercial Code. He wrote a book (unpublished) on 'The Theory of Rules', and consistently argued for better, more informative 'Grand Style' rule formulations that 'carry their reasons on their face'.[25] If there is a core idea in Legal Realism it

22 In his early 'Realist' writings Llewellyn, like most American jurists, was strongly court-centred; however, his law-jobs theory allows for a much wider conception of 'legal action'.

23 Llewellyn, *Jurisprudence*, 21–2. Llewellyn was concerned to distinguish between authoritative prescriptions (rules for practice) and descriptions of practice (cf. the phrase, 'as a rule X does'). His main point is that the relationship between a prescriptive rule and practice relating to it is unclear on its face. So one needs to be sceptical of any implicit or explicit claims that a practice conforms to the rule(s). This scepticism is not about the existence of rules, but about the idea that they describe practice. The 'realistic' jurist needs to know about both the rules and the practice and their relationship.

24 Llewellyn, 'A Realistic Jurisprudence', 23.

25 KLRM, n. 23, Appendix B.

is that for most purposes in nearly all contexts talk of rules alone is not enough.[26] For Realists like Llewellyn and Corbin, the key feature of the idea of surface law is that on its own it is not very informative. The basic insight is that bare statements of legal rules are generally not self-enacting, self-interpreting, self-applying, self-invoking, self-enforcing or self-legitimating. For most theoretical and practical purposes the study of rules alone is not enough.[27] Of course, what is considered 'enough' depends on context and purpose and is regularly contested; similarly, without more, the idea of 'reality' begs a lot of questions.

Third, contrasts between the law in books and the law in action, real rules and paper rules, front-stage and back-stage have sometimes led to a temptation to shift attention to one branch of the dichotomy and to neglect the other. For example, to claim to be only concerned with real rules or the law in action or what goes on backstage. A healthy counter-balance is a classic article by Doreen McBarnet in which she criticized socio-legal scholars and criminologists for ignoring legal rules or treating them as unimportant.[28] McBarnet's point was that her colleagues had made a contrast between the proclaimed ideology of the criminal justice system and what went on in practice, ignoring the details of the law. Whereas, the more interesting contrast was between the ideological pretensions of the system and the detailed substantive rules. Here legal detail was hidden behind surface ideology.[29]

## Comparative Law: Three Perspectives on Convergence

> With the enactment of the Chinese Civil Code, systems of private law modeled on those of the West will govern nearly the entire world. Western legal systems, moreover, are much alike. Both 'common law' systems such as those of England and the United

26 See Twining, 'Talk about Realism'.

27 Twining, W. and Miers, D. (1999), *How to Do Things with Rules*, 4th edn (London: Butterworths) chs 2 and 3.

28 McBarnet, D. (1978), 'False Dichotomies in Criminal Justice Research', in Baldwin, J. and Bottomley, A.K. (eds), *Criminal Justice: Selected Readings* (London: Martin Robertson). More controversially, McBarnet argued that far from criminal justice norms embodying civil rights and due process, many of them subverted it: 'The operation of the law is not a subversion of the substance of the law but exactly what one would expect it to produce: the law in action is only too close a parallel to the law in books; due process is for crime control' (pp. 30–31). This was criticized as overstatement by Bob Roshier and Harvey Teff (1980), *Law and Society in England* (London: Tavistock), 16–17; cf. Nelken, 'The "Gap Problem" in the Sociology of Law', 41–2, n. 16.

29 A different, but related theme is developed in a well-known paper by David Nelken: 'The "Gap Problem" in the Sociology of Law'. This contains a brief, but useful, intellectual history of 'concerns about "discrepancies" or "disjunctions" between promises or claims held out for law and its actual effects' (p. 41). The significance of Nelken's paper in the present context is that 'the gap problem' refers to a variety of recurrent concerns, which are of considerable theoretical and practical significance, but which need to be differentiated.

> States and 'civil law' systems such as those of France, Italy and Germany have a similar doctrinal structure based on similar legal concepts. They divide private law into certain large fields such as property, tort and contract, and analyze these fields in a similar way .... The organization of the law and its larger concepts are alike even if particular rules are not. Accordingly, though answers may differ, the problem of whether a boy is liable for injuring a playfellow or a seller is liable for defects in his merchandise is analyzed in much the same way in Hamburg, Montpelier, Manchester and Tucson, or for that matter in New Delhi, Tel Aviv, Tokyo, and Jakarta.[30]

This is the opening paragraph of James Gordley's *The Philosophical Foundations of Modern Contract Doctrine*. It is intended to be provocative and at first sight it succeeds. This looks like a rash and superficial generalization about 'global law'. Apart from not providing evidence in support of this statement, it seems on the face of it to give a misleading account of how disputes and accidents are handled in different countries and cultures. Let us postulate a case in which a schoolboy seriously injures a playfellow in a school yard in Tokyo, or Jakarta or Montpelier or Tucson, Arizona. Can we assume that the reaction would be uniform in all places? Might not it be fatalistic in one place, the start of a family or clan feud in another, the basis for an insurance claim in a third, and an occasion for litigation in a fourth? Even if we think in terms of possible litigation, is it clear that questions about who might sue and who might be sued could be different (the playfellow or his parents, or his clan as plaintiff bringing action against the boy, his parents or clan, the school, a public authority or an insurance company)? Would fault be an issue in all places and would similar distinctions be drawn between accident, negligence, recklessness and intent? Would considerations of age, provocation, contributory negligence and so on be similar? And in respect of the People's Republic of China, to what percentage of the population is the Civil Code relevant as a practical matter?[31] In short, Gordley seems to be making a wildly misleading generalization about both the law in books *and* the law in action.

A more charitable reading, however, suggests that Gordley's thesis may well be correct on its own terms. First, he explicitly states that he is not generalizing about detailed rules, but about the underlying concepts of the law of obligations. Second, he is making no claims about enforcement, use, or litigiousness in different countries. Rather he is suggesting that if a jurist were presented with a hypothetical

30 Gordley, J. (1993), *The Philosophical Foundations of Modern Contract Doctrine* (Oxford: Oxford University Press), p. 1.

31 Remoteness of state law from the general population may not be a significant break with tradition. See Jones, W.C. (2003), 'Trying to Understand the Current Chinese Legal System', in Hsu, S.C. (ed.) (2003), *Understanding China's Legal system* (New York: New York University Press).

problem about a wrong, such as this, the basic conceptual tools for analysing the situation would be the same in most parts of the world.[32]

*The Philosophical Foundations of Modern Contract Doctrine* is an outstanding work of intellectual history. Gordley's thesis is that in the sixteenth and early seventeenth centuries Spanish neo-scholastics[33] achieved a synthesis of Roman contract doctrine and Aristotelian moral philosophy mediated by Thomas Aquinas. The result was a coherent system of contract based on the Aristotelian virtues of truthfulness (including promise keeping), liberality and commutative justice. In the seventeenth century the Aristotelian basis for this theory of contract was undermined by the criticisms of post-Enlightenment thinkers, but the doctrines themselves survived. 'Legal doctrine and moral philosophy began to drift apart.'[34] Later the doctrines were reformulated by the early modern natural lawyers, first Grotius and then Puffendorf, Domat and Pothier. Both the continental codes and common law cases drew heavily on these doctrines, shorn of their philosophical basis. Out of this evolved a positivistic and incoherent 'will theory' of contract detached from any theory of virtue or the Aristotelian idea of essences. In the twentieth century the inadequacy of the will theory has been widely recognized, but neither Kantian nor utilitarian theory nor economic analysis can provide a philosophical foundation for explaining 'why the law does not place the same value on all commitments or treat them in the same way ... Many jurists are now pessimistic about the very possibility of discovering general doctrines that can explain the rules of positive law or the results most people regard as fair.'[35]

Gordley's elegant thesis is a powerful argument about the intellectual roots of modern contract doctrine, its shared origins in the synthesis of Roman law and neo-Aristotelian ideas by the Spanish scholastics, and its decline into incoherence in both civil and common law systems. Gordley explicitly claims to be writing about contract theory rather than a history of the law of contract or its practical operation, which for most of the time was hardly influenced by the writers he discusses. Instead it is the story of the rise and decline of attempts to find a coherent philosophical foundation for the law of contract.

Gordley's generalization is not about surface law. It is not about the rules of private law, but rather about the shared historical origins of some basic concepts and the sad story of their losing touch with their ideological roots. He emphasizes structure, concepts and ways of thought rather than detailed rules and actual practice. His concern is with the interdependence of doctrine and underlying ideology. This can hardly be treated as shallow or superficial. But what lies under

32 However, he can be faulted for assuming that jurists in these scattered metropolitan centres all share the same *mentalité* (see below); cf. Pierre Legrand's critique of Gordley's 'reductionism' in another context: (1999) *Fragments on Law-as-Culture* (Deventer: Tjeenk Willick), 87–90.

33 Vitoria and his school.

34 Gordley, *The Philosophical Foundations of Modern Contract Doctrine*, 121.

35 Gordley, *The Philosophical Foundations of Modern Contract Doctrine*, 214.

the surface in this account is not social context or actual use or practical effects, but rather basic concepts and ideology at two or three removes from the 'surface'.

In the published version of his inaugural lecture at University College London in 2001 Professor (now Sir) Basil Markesenis contrasts differences between what is on the surface and what lies beneath from the point of view of a comparative lawyer.[36] His starting-point is a rejection of comparison of concepts (and by implication detailed legal rules):

> [C]omparison of systems through their concepts can lead to confusion and inaccuracies. For different concepts may conceal similar solutions and philosophies, and similar concepts may hide differences, which flow from other structural differences.[37]

The theme is a familiar one in comparative law, but Markesenis's interpretation is quite distinctive. First, he contrasts the surface concepts and rules of legal doctrine with the concrete solutions to problems that are reached in particular cases.

Second, exhibiting the *mentalité* of a common lawyer, he argues that the best method of comparison of the operation of legal doctrine in practice is through careful study of actual judicial decisions.[38]

Third, he differentiates a number of 'levels' which need to be distinguished in teasing out similarity and difference. At the risk of over-simplification I shall restate these as follows: First, there is the level of abstract legal doctrine – rules and principles. This is not very useful in making comparisons between common law and civil law doctrine as it operates in adjudication, because common law judges are not given to making precise formulations of legal rules. A second level, the explicit reasoning of judges is also not suitable, because of the generally more open style of common law judges in respect of policy arguments and the predominantly opaque style of most judges in the civilian tradition. Both exposition of legal rules and judicial reasoning are, for Markesenis, 'on the surface'.[39] A third level of inquiry is a search for policy reasons which may or may not have been

36 Markesenis, B. (2001), 'Unity or Division: The Search for Similarities in Contemporary European Law', *Current Legal Problems* 54, 591. Some of the themes in Markesenis's lecture were developed at greater length in essays collected in his (1997) *Foreign Law and Comparative Methodology* (Oxford: Hart).

37 Markesenis, 'Unity or Division', 595. Cf. Kahn-Freund, O. (1978), *Selected Writings* (London: Stevens), 285–7.

38 Markesenis, 'Unity or Division', 592: 'The study of a foreign legal system, especially through decisional law, has the advantage of putting one initially at ease. For invariably in such studies one is starting the journey of discovery by looking at litigated situations that are the same in most countries.'

39 Markesenis uses the word 'surface' explicitly several times (for example, 'Unity or Division', 602, 604, 612 (twice), 'deep' or 'deeper' (for example, 607 and 608), 'the superficial reader' (of judicial opinions) (610) and 'levels' several times. As I read him, he treats explicit concepts, rule statements, judicial reasoning, and even particular fact

made explicit in the reasoning of the judges concerned, but which may be inferred by careful analysis and some knowledge of the context. But there is a fourth level, which is to identify core issues of policy that any (modern) state must confront. 'At this level legal arguments become subservient to political, economic or moral ones, which now come to the fore'.[40] Markesenis concludes:

> [T]the core issues which confront our European systems are the same even though the answers they receive are different. The next realization is that if the answers differ it is not really because of the concepts or even the arguments used on the surface, but because of understandable and legitimate divergences at the core. … [h]owever at the core we do not find legal, and certainly not legalistic, arguments. On the contrary, we here encounter political, moral, social and economic issues. Because these issues are of wider import, lawyers cannot solve them. Moreover, and this is just as important, they are not issues that can be described as typically French, German, or English: they appear across borders and thus their very nature encourages comparison. Finally, individual systems – for instance, the French – can and have vacillated over what kinds of answers are appropriate to these fundamental questions …'[41]

Markesenis's method is a sophisticated variant of the 'functionalist' tradition in comparative law, which treats law in terms of responses or 'solutions' to problems and often suggests that civil and common law systems converge by arriving at similar solutions to shared problems often by different conceptual routes. This approach has been much criticized, but I am not here concerned with that controversy.[42] But Gordley and Markesenis may not be as different as they appear. Gordley is arguing that the law of obligations in both civil and common law traditions has quite similar conceptual structures that have shared historical

---

situations as all being on the surface in the context of his argument that in doing comparative analysis of judicial opinions one needs to dig beneath all of these.

40 Markesenis, 'Unity or Division', 608.

41 Markesenis, 'Unity or Division', 612. The passage continues: 'So the real differences between the systems do not lie at the surface where sets of similar facts lead to litigation – I call, this the first circle – but at the core – which I call the third circle. What stops us from realizing this phenomenon and where necessary, addressing it in an intelligent way (especially if the harmonisation of laws is our aim) are the arguments that take place in the second circle where concepts, notions, and legal reasoning reign supreme. … The proper understanding of the systems thus requires us to reduce the importance of the second circle and to locate and define the real issues which lurk in the third.' Markesenis's three 'circles' differ from my rendering in the text, because I am concerned to treat explicit rule statements, concepts and explicit reasoning as all being on the 'surface' as well as the 'sets of similar facts' he refers to in this passage. This fits in better with the other contrasts discussed in this chapter.

42 Hyland, R. (1996), 'Comparative Law', in Dennis Patterson (ed.), *A Companion to Philosophy of Law and Legal Theory* (Cambridge, MA: Blackwell); Graziadei, M. 'The Functionalist Heritage', in Legrand, P. and Munday, R. (eds) (2003), *Comparative Legal Studies: Traditions and Transitions* (Cambridge: Cambridge University Press), 100–127.

roots, but both have lost touch with the underlying ideology. Markesenis is arguing that conceptual differences are less important than underlying problems and that the 'deepest' level is basic issues of policy and ideological responses to these 'core' issues (the metaphor shifts) and that the ideology may be contested within as well as across legal systems. Both converge in treating ideology as lying 'deeper' than both detailed rules and basic legal concepts. Ironically they differ from McBarnet who in the 1970s treated the proclaimed ideology of the criminal justice system as being on the 'surface' for criminologists.

Gordley and Markesenis are also similar in emphasizing convergence and underlying similarities. Here, of course, they are part of the target of the fierce campaign by Pierre Legrand against 'traditional' comparative law. In a series of broadsides in papers with such titles as 'Legal Traditions in Western Europe: The Limits of Commonality',[43] 'European Legal Systems are Not Converging'[44] and 'Against a European Civil Code',[45] Legrand has attacked both plans for unification and harmonization of laws in Europe and, more generally, the tendency in comparative law to emphasize similarity rather than difference.[46]

I am not here concerned to enter into the merits of this debate. What is interesting is that for Legrand what lies beneath the surface of detailed legal rules, legal doctrine and legal concepts is 'legal culture' and the *mentalité* of lawyers, which are so fundamentally different within the broad common and civil law traditions that any attempts to unify, harmonize and claim convergence between the two traditions are bound to be superficial.[47]

## Unification and Harmonization of Laws

### *The American Experience*[48]

The American Law Institute (ALI), an alliance of leading judges, practitioners and academics, was founded in 1923 as a response by the organized legal profession

43 In R. Jagtenberg, R. et al. (eds) (1995), *Transfrontier Mobility of Law* (The Hague: Kluwer International), 63–84.

44 *International and Comparative Law Quarterly* 45 (1996), 52.

45 *The Modern Law Review* 60 (1997), 44.

46 Legrand, P. (2003), 'The Same and the Different' in Legrand and Munday, *Comparative Legal Studies*, 304–5.

47 I have argued elsewhere that as much as those he criticizes Legrand falls four square within the 'Country and Western Tradition of Comparative law' in that he largely confines his attention to state law in 'parent' common law and civil law systems and is still concerned with legal doctrine, although from an epistemic point of view. Twining, W. (2000), 'Comparative Law and Legal Theory: The Country and Western Tradition', in Edge, I. (ed.), *Comparative Law in Global Perspective* (New York: Transnational), 62–3.

48 This section is a condensed version of longer accounts in KLRM, 272–6 and Twining W. (1994), *Blackstone's Tower* (London: Sweet and Maxwell), 132–5.

to a number of perceived challenges to law in the United States: the need to adapt the common law to American conditions; the need to preserve the unity of the common law across a multiplicity of jurisdictions; the modernization of the law in the wake of social, economic and technical change; and the simplification of the sources of law in the face of the burgeoning output of authoritative materials by Federal and state legislatures, courts and other agencies. The ALI was also seen by some as an attempt by leaders of the legal profession to strengthen its control over the management and development of the administration of law by virtue of their technical expertise. The *Restatement* project offered academics, who would do most of the work, influence and status within the legal establishment.

The objectives were reformist, to improve, modernize and unify the common law, but they had to be presented as apolitical. The involvement of the judiciary, the desire to produce an authoritative text that would not be a code, and the desire to by-pass the state legislatures, required not only circumspection in describing the objectives but also procedures and a form that would not invite political criticism. For the enterprise to succeed it was essential that it should operate largely by consensus in a non-partisan mode, so that its products would be accepted by the legal profession and, if they were aware of it, by the general public as representing the agreed wisdom of experts on matters that were essentially technical.

Three main instruments were developed to further these ends: restatements, model codes and (in co-operation with the Commissioners for Uniform State Laws) uniform laws, of which by far the most important has been the Uniform Commercial Code (UCC). In the early years the *Restatement* project was given the highest priority. A series of code-like texts was to be prepared, designed in the words of the first Director, 'to present an orderly statement of the general common law of the United States ... The object of the Institute is accomplished insofar as the legal profession accepts the restatement as prima facie a correct statement of the general law of the United States.'[49]

Three main factors in combination virtually dictated the choice of some such solution: the first and overriding consideration was that the legislatures must be by-passed.[50] Secondly, practitioners and judges felt that they were drowning in a sea of precedent and the courts, partly because of their complicated structure, were failing as instruments of harmonization and simplification. What was wanted was a simple, clear, accessible text. Third, the *Restatements* would be authoritative only to the extent that they would in fact be used by the legal profession and the courts. To this end any suggestion of utopian or radical reforms would need to be discounted. The acceptability of the *Restatement* would be enhanced by being

49 Lewis, W.D. (1937), *Introduction to Restatement of Restitution and Unjust Enrichment* (Philadelphia, PA: American Law Institute), 9.

50 More frankly than most, at the First Meeting of the ALI, John W. Davis stated: 'None of us here, I fancy, certainly none of those who are familiar with Congress or the forty-eight legislatures of our states, anticipate that this labor shall be committed to their charge', ALI, *Proceedings*, II at 112 (1923).

primarily expository in form and style. 'The back stage' view was that the aim was simplification, unification, *and* improvement of American common law; 'the front stage' presentation was of an impartial and accurate distillation of existing uniformities.

Even those who accepted the main objectives, methods and underlying theory of the *Restatement* acknowledged that there were practical problems in providing a correct, simple statement of the common law of over 50 jurisdictions. What is the draftsman to do if there is no case in point, or the authorities are in conflict, or if there is no succinct judicial formulation of a rule? What if some states have changed the law by statute or if a recent case from a court of high authority in one jurisdiction purports to overrule or depart from previous authority? Or if local conditions are not uniform throughout the various states? When in doubt, is the conscientious draftsman to choose the predominant opinion or to predict what the courts are likely to do or to choose what s/he considers to be the 'best' opinion? And what if the law is clear, but the Reporter or professional opinion generally consider it to be bad for some reason?[51]

The *Restatement* form is a theoretical hybrid, glossing over the distinction between neutral exposition (description) of what the law is and statement of preference or recommendation as to what the law ought to be (prescription). One of the fundamental themes of realist jurisprudence is, of course, that the nature of authoritative legal materials is such that they do not always yield one correct answer as to what the law is, with the result that equating exposition of the law with a simple model of descriptions of the empirical world is misleading. The *Restatement*, while based on meticulous analysis of the authorities, recommends solutions with relatively few inhibitions when the authorities do not speak with a single tongue. The method is that of interstitial development of the law by simplification and by expressing choices between competing alternatives. Its value for practical purposes lies in its accessibility, its relative simplicity and its decisiveness. The two latter qualities reduce its value for the historian or for the theorist who is looking for a reliable contemporary 'description' of the state of the law at a particular moment of time, a quest which some would consider to be misconceived in any case.

The *Restatements* have come under fire from various quarters. To the radical reformer they are over-cautious as instruments of legal development since they only attempt to change in the absence of a consensus, and restrict themselves to choosing between alternatives that have already been adopted somewhere. The *Restatements* were also attacked for being undemocratic. In 1992 one Federal

51 Barton Leach, a Reporter, lamented: '[W]e can never adversely criticize a rule which we find we have to state. Such a by-law presents a very unpleasant dilemma to a Reporter. He must either state a good rule which he knows perfectly well is not the law; or he must state a bad rule and by his very statement entrench it further.' Leach, B. 'The Restatements as they were in the beginning, are now and perhaps thenceforth shall be', *A.B.A. Journal* 23, 517, at 519.

judge wrote that the ALI was an unelected, unaccountable elite involved in quasi-legislation 'without obtaining any input from Congress and/or the States legislatures, without obtaining input from the broad-based representative interests of the masses of ordinary citizens, and without giving any meaningful consideration of any kind to the social, economic and political interests of the various minority groups in this country'.[52]

While some Realists, such as Corbin, were involved in the project, others, from the start, attacked the whole enterprise as being theoretically unsound. The most common criticisms were levelled at four underlying assumptions: (a) that it is possible to describe the law as it is in neutral terms; (b) that it is possible to declare the principles of common law independently of authority; (c) that it is possible to make meaningful statements of legal rules without reference to their rationales; (d) that it is possible to make accurate and meaningful statements of legal rules without reference to the practical context of their operation.[53]

The value of the *Restatements* is still controversial. At the seventy-fifth Anniversary of the ALI, much was made of its success, including over 110,000 citations by the courts.[54] Whereas immense efforts had been devoted to drafting uniform laws and persuading state legislatures to adopt them, successes were largely confined to commercial law.[55] On the other hand Lawrence Friedman has lamented the enormous investment of efforts by leading scholars in a misconceived enterprise – a waste of talent on 'toys of the trade'.[56] In 2002 he returned to the attack:

> Another project, dominated by the treatise writers, was the heroic (and probably foolish) attempt to 'restate' the common law ... But the draftsmen ignored, for the most part, the social and economic meaning of the working common law. They made it logical and orderly, but at the cost of ripping out the living, pulsing heart of the system.[57]

One may interpret the Realist sceptics and Lawrence Friedman as dismissing the *Restatements* as merely surface law: divorced from any social, economic or

52 Simmons, P.A. (1992), 'Government by Unaccountable Private Non-Profit Corporation', *Journal of Human Rights* 10: 67.

53 A good survey of the early criticisms is Merryman, J. (1954), 'The Authority of Authority', *Stanford Law Review* 6, 613.

54 *The American Law Institute, 75th Anniversary 1923–98* (Philadelphia, PA: ALI, 1998).

55 'Uniform acts prepared by the Conference [of Commissioners on Uniform State Laws] not relating to commercial law have not been generally adopted by state legislatures' (*The American Law Institute, 75th Anniversary 1923–98*, 251).

56 Friedman, L. (1985), *A History of American Law*, 2nd edn (New York: Simon and Schuster), 674–6.

57 Friedman, L. (1973), *American Law in the Twentieth Century* (New Haven, CT: Yale University Press, 2002), 488; cf. (2005), *History of American Law* 3rd edn (New York: Simon and Schuster), 488. Friedman is one of Alan Watson's sharpest critics.

procedural context they were misleading as descriptions, uninformative about legal doctrine in action, feeble as attempts to modernize or reform, and of a limited practical value – an odd juristic hybrid, a common law quasi-code with at best limited persuasive authority. Perhaps the main objection was that the static code-like form was contrary in intention and spirit to the incremental development of the common law in the crucible of litigation.

Whether or not such criticisms are overdrawn, they apply far less clearly to American efforts to harmonize private law through uniform laws and model codes The story of efforts to promote uniform laws through legislation is different from the *Restatements* in respect of juridical form, the politics of enactment and practical impact. By far the most ambitious and influential project was the Uniform Commercial Code (UCC), which was jointly sponsored by the ALI and the Commissioners for Uniform State Laws. Hardly anyone thinks of that as merely 'surface law'. Of course, if one reads the UCC solely as text, it counts as such, even though it includes explicit guides to interpretation, statements of purpose and extensive comments normally presented as part of the text. But this is not how the UCC is read and used by American judges, practitioners, academics and students. The culture of the UCC is underpinned by a vast literature that recounts its origins, underlying jurisprudence, legislative history, judicial interpretation, and scholarly expositions, critiques and controversies. No more than 'The American Constitution' or 'the European Convention on Human Rights' refers solely to a document, the referent of 'the UCC' is not a bare legislative text. If outside the United States it were treated as such by students of comparative law or law reformers looking for legislative models, it would be subject to the same dangers of misunderstanding and misuse as unadorned surface law. The style of drafting, the form, the idea of a common law 'code', the underlying assumptions about judicial interpretation and the code's relation to commercial practice, all belong to the culture of common law, with a few Llewellynesque glosses.[58]

### *Projects for Unification and Harmonization of Eu opean Private Law: The 'Restatement' Model*

Interestingly, in efforts directed towards unification and harmonization of private law in the European Union, the *Restatements* have been used as an ostensible model in several leading projects.[59] To what extent do these classic American

58 More generally, Andrew Halpin argues for 'a richer notion' of legal doctrine, which includes not only formulations of rules, but also principles, differentiated conceptions of interpretive roles and sophisticated conceptions of the nature of legal materials – all of which are usually 'beneath the surface'. Halpin, A. (2004), *Definition in Criminal Law* (Oxford: Hart) ch. 1.

59 '[T]he Principles of European Contract Law has become well-known and strangely influential in the sense that they have spurred a veritable industry of restatements'. Beale, H. (2006), 'The European Civil Code Movement and the European Union's Common Frame

projects have any relevance to the contemporary European context? At first sight the differences are vast: apart from contingencies of time and space, one can point to some striking contrasts:

- in Europe the issues relate to unification of laws of different nation states rather than within one single, albeit federal, sovereign state; but in both instances there is an issue about the extent to which the states have sovereign power over private law;
- in the United States the Restatements and Uniform Laws were felt to be needed because under the Constitution private law was largely within the jurisdiction of the several states; in the European Union there is no such restriction and there is therefore more scope for initiatives channelled through a single, if complex, centre, subject to the principle of subsidiarity;[60]
- in Europe unification involves transcending several legal traditions (civil, common law, Scandinavian) and differences within those traditions; in the United States the problem was largely one of maintaining the unity (and dominance) of the imported English common law;
- in Europe the Member States chose to develop a multilingual community, so unification has to cope with a multiplicity of languages as opposed to American legal culture that was underpinned by one version of the English language;
- in Europe unification of laws is being attempted in a political context in which unity is strongly contested; in The United States after the Civil War national unity was not such an issue so far as law was concerned;
- in Europe unification is being attempted across diverse traditions, cultures and religions at a time when 'diversity' is more openly recognized than it was in the United States in the first half of the twentieth century;
- in Europe most of the efforts at unification are directed towards persuading the European Parliament and Council (usually via the Commission) to adopt measures of unification; in the United States, as we have seen, the *Restatements* were conceived as a means of by-passing the legislative and executive branches of the various states.

Despite these and many other differences, there are some apparent similarities that might justify treating the American and European efforts as analogous:

---

of Reference', *Legal Information Management*, 4–11, at 6. This sections draws heavily on this article, but any errors are mine alone.

60 However, the EU has been harmonizing regulatory law for a long time, but only in respect of consumer protection has it intervened significantly in respect of private law (in the narrow sense).

- the main focus of attention in both cases has been on private law, especially commercial law and contract – which are sometimes subsumed under the contested category of 'lawyers' law';
- some, but not all, of the main initiatives have come from non-governmental organizations and individuals;[61]
- apart from the movement for a European Civil Code (or a Code of Contract), many of the projects aim at constructing forms of 'soft law' short of legislation, several taking the form of 'restatements';
- most of the end-products seek to render existing doctrine as formal statements of legal principles or rules, some supplemented by notes similar to those of the American *Restatements*;
- most of the European projects are expressly directed to quite specific practical purposes rather than as academic exercises.[62]

There are thus some similarities between the American *Restatements* and some European projects on unification, especially in respect of juridical form, in having limited (though varied) practical objectives, in being concerned with rather cautious incremental legal development, and in being in large part the work of private sector organizations and academics. It is also tempting to suggest that the main initiators of the European projects are Euro-philes and the opponents and sceptics have been Euro-sceptics or legal nationalists, such as Pierre Legrand.[63] That may be partly true, but on its own it is too simple. So too is the argument that the outcome of such efforts will be merely surface law – obscuring local differences, misleading as descriptions, emphasizing superficial similarities, and likely to be of little practical importance.

---

61 A striking example is the Lando Commission, which broke away from UNIDROIT in 1980.

62 Some hope that their projects will be treated as preliminaries to codification. Others, who may be opposed to large scale codification, conceive of more limited practical uses. Beale, 'The European Civil Code Movement and the European Union's Common Frame of Reference', lists the following uses for some projects: (a) concretizing the *lex mercatoria*; (b) enabling parties to a transnational contract to adopt principles expressly (subject to any mandatory applicable national laws); (c) providing suitable models for legislation, sometimes by stating what is thought to be 'the best modern rule' (echoing an ALI dilemma, see above); (d) as a translation tool; (e) as guides to future sectoral harmonization, short of codification (as exemplified by existing EU Directives and regulations on consumer contracts).

63 The debate about codification is sometimes represented as a power struggle between representatives of the common law and civil law traditions. As Legrand argues, codification or large-scale unification would probably be dominated by the civilians. (Legrand, P. (1997), 'Acts of Repression' reprinted in *Fragments on Law-as-Culture*, ch. 9). That is probably too simple, but one might interpret the use of the 'restatement idea' as a concession to common law incrementalism. Cf. Legrand, P. (1997), 'Against a European Civil Code', *Modern Law Review* 60, 44–63.

The targets of such generalized scepticism are quite varied. They include the ideas that (a) there is a common core of principles and concepts of European contract, or more generally private law; (b) codification of European contract or private law is feasible and desirable; (c) a common European culture will develop over time.

There are strong grounds for arguing that such scepticism is over-generalized: first, as Hugh Beale has pointed out:

> In one sense we already have a European private law in the form of legislation from Brussels. Firstly, some of the articles of the Treaty, for example those dealing with competition, give direct rights of action to those who are injured by anti-competitive practices. Secondly, there are many regulations that affect matters of private law, for example, in the field of jurisdiction. And, thirdly, there are European Directives, which Member States are obliged to implement though the precise means of implementation is left to the Member State.[64]

This legislation, especially on competition and consumer law, can hardly be dismissed as unimportant, ineffective or a mere façade.[65]

Second, the European projects in the field are quite varied: UNIDROIT, the Trento Project, the Lando Commission, the European Commission on European Contract Law, the movement for codification of private law or contract, and the study group on Social Justice in European Law all have different agendas and methods.[66] Most have quite specific and nuanced objectives that fall short of codification. For example, the Common Frame of Reference, which is being developed for the European Commission, is likely to be used as a legislative and interpretive 'toolbox' of standard principles, concepts and terminology that will guide revision and extension of sectoral harmonization, but does not aim for codification. Indeed, some of those involved with this project and its predecessors are specifically opposed to codification.[67] The European Commission has backed away from ambitious legislative projects designed to replace national legislation in deference to the doctrine of subsidiarity; and some governments, including that of the United Kingdom, have opposed unifying legislation that would replace national laws – although a good deal of unifying has been done in respect of consumer protection.

Third, the processes involved and the conceptions of the enterprise are a good deal more complex and sophisticated than the original American *Restatements*.

---

64 Beale, 'The European Civil Code Movement and the European Union's Common Frame of Reference'.

65 Cf. European legislation in other fields.

66 These are usefully surveyed in Beale, 'The European Civil Code Movement and the European Union's Common Frame of Reference'.

67 Beale, 'The European Civil Code Movement and the European Union's Common Frame of Reference'.

One major difference is that the main strategic aim is to work with the European legislative authorities rather than to by-pass them. Even if the main preparatory work is quite abstract and technocratic in tendency, political concerns (for example protection of weaker parties), will have an opportunity to be weighed in an allegedly democratic legislative process.

Thus, although the main current projects on unification of European private law aim at the production of code-like statements of principles and/or rules, the processes involved and the institutional context are likely to make them less vulnerable to charges of 'formalism' or the production of mere 'surface law' than the ALI *Restatements*.

## Meanings and Referents of 'Surface Law'

I have so far avoided defining 'surface law'. The foregoing case-studies suggest that the standard dichotomies that we have explored are regularly used (often quite loosely) in a variety of contexts, that they reflect some persistent concerns that need to be differentiated, that what is treated as being on the surface varies, and that the vocabulary has a strong emotive bias along lines of 'we know best': deep/superficial; appearance/reality; what is meant to happen / what actually happens. It is also clear from these examples that familiar formalist/realist differences of perspective are a recurrent theme.

Of course, what appears 'on the surface' depends on standpoint. In order to keep things simple let us postulate as a paradigm case an outside observer (student, scholar or citizen) encountering a legal order for the first time in the form of legal rules articulated in formal texts such as codes, statutes, treaties, regulations, textbook statements, restatements and the like.[68] Let us treat as extensions other standpoints (for example a legal draftsman, or a 'foreign' lawyer or businessman visiting another legal system) and other legal phenomena such as ideologies, buildings, public legislative processes, trials and so on which may be what newcomers and others first encounter 'on the surface'.

Confining ourselves to legal texts and external observers simplifies the analysis. However, in the present context it is sensible to have a reasonably broad conception of 'law' because some of the standard contrasts are made between explicit statements of legal rules and something else: 'the law in action', 'real rules', 'unofficial law', hidden normative and legal orders, interposed norms and institutions, underlying principles, ideologies and so on. In diffusion a common

68 Since some of the most important contrasts have been between the surface and what lies beneath what judges say, it is sensible to include legal judgments or opinions. But, especially in the common law, these do not always embody 'rules in fixed verbal form'. An elusive category is 'official views', beloved of ironic sociologists. For example, generalized secondary accounts of the kind that McBarnet accused criminologists in the 1960s of relying on to make contrasts between 'appearance' and 'reality'.

contrast is often made between 'official' imported law and pre-existing 'unofficial law' – typically customary or religious normative orders that exist below the surface and the interaction with which is often overlooked.[69] So without entering into debates about definitions or conception of 'law', I shall here treat these contrasted phenomena as falling within the ambit of the 'legal'.[70]

### *'Surface' as Metaphor*

*The Oxford English Dictionary* devotes nearly three pages to usages of 'surface'. The definition that most closely catches its most common usage in the present context is figurative:

> Usually denoting that part or aspect of anything which presents itself to a slight or casual mental view, or which is perceived without examination; outward appearance often in such phrases as *on the surface* = superficially. Also, to scratch the surface ...[71]

'Surface' in this context is a metaphor suggesting that the exterior of a physical object or the top of a body of liquid (a lake, the sea, a cup of coffee). The liquid metaphor suggests a vertical plane, with an observer looking down on the surface.[72] There is a common, but not a necessary, suggestion that the surface is opaque and what lies beneath it may be different from what is observable on top. In that case it may be hidden, arcane, secret, invisible and more or less 'deep'. The metaphor can be dangerous in several obvious respects.

---

69 For example, Pistor, K. and Wellons, Ph. A. (1999), *The Role of Law and Legal Institutions in Asian Economic Development 1960–95* (Oxford: Oxford University Press). Of course, the converse can be the case, that is, it is state law that is the 'host'; for example, the growing interaction between Muslim law and custom and pre-existing state law in the United Kingdom (see Menski, W. and Pearl, D. (1998), *Muslim Family Law*, 3rd edn (London: Sweet and Maxwell), 51–83), or the interaction between Brazilian state law ('asphalt law') and 'upstart' Pasagarda law of the *favelas* (Santos, B. de S. (2002), *Toward a New Legal Common Sense* (London: Butterworths) ch. 4).

70 For a broad conceptualization of the 'legal' that would fit this contrast see Twining. W. (2003), 'A Post-Westphalian Conception of Law', *Law and Society Review* 37, 199 at 231–42, esp. 240–41 and Twining, *General Jurisprudence*, Ch. 4. The conception of law developed there or, more succinctly, MacCormick's conception of 'institutionalized normative order' will fit my purpose here (MacCormick, D.N. (2007) *Institutions of Law* (Oxford: Oxford University Press)) The argument in this chapter would not be changed radically if a narrower conception of 'law' were insisted on – for the standard contrasts could be expressed in terms of legal/non-legal phenomena. However, some examples, such as, the Cheyennes or Sophie's project, might be excluded from such an analysis because they do not involve 'law' so conceived at all.

71 *Oxford English Dictionary*, 2nd edn (1989).

72 Of course, the metaphor is sometimes mixed – for example, with veneer, façade, shell contrasted with core, heart, root.

First, it may suggest that the surface is opaque; but, of course, many liquids are more or less transparent.

Second, it suggests that what is below the surface is not or may not be the same. There is, of course, a whole spectrum of possibilities from the liquid having the same consistency throughout, as in a well mixed cocktail, to multiple layering (as with oil and water) or to a whole complex world of different phenomena hiding or hidden 'beneath the surface'. [73]

Third, what appears on the surface depends in part on standpoint. What is obvious or apparent to one may be hidden from another. In most of the examples used here it is reasonable to postulate an outside observer. But there are of course many other standpoints, including those in which what is first encountered is not a legal text but, for example, a fatal road accident, a policeman, a writ or summons, a standard form contract, a court building, an actual trial, or a courtroom drama – in all of which, the official legal rules are 'in the background'.[74]

Fourth, quite what conception of 'law' is adopted in the circumstances and what 'law' presents itself to a particular observer may vary. So, for example, it is rules embodied in texts that are most commonly treated as the law on the surface: the university's published rules in Sophie's project; formal human rights instruments; codes or doctrinal statements of contract rules; the texts of the American *Restatements* and Uniform laws; and so on. But, in his approach to comparative law, Markesenis treats judicial opinions rather than abstract rules as being on 'the surface' and contrasts the styles of common law and civil law judges in respect of openness about policy and willingness to articulate precise rules. Llewellyn, when talking about 'paper rules', was similarly contrasting what judges say and what they do in the context of common law adjudication. However, McBarnet's complaint against criminologists was that they focused on 'official' legal ideology (due process, the rule of law, defendant's rights) and contrasted this with what happened in practice, while ignoring the details of the intermediate formal legal rules.

### *Some Obvious Health Warnings*

In pursuing her research Sophie needs to bear in mind some salutary 'health warnings' about using, or at least over-using, these contrasts. Some of the important ones could be summarized as follows:

---

73 Cf. my exchange with Westbrook about diffusion: Westbrook, D.A. (2006), 'Theorizing the Diffusion of Law: Conceptual Difficulties', *Harvard International Law Journal* 47, 489 at 490–91 and Twining, W. (2006), 'Diffusion and Globalization Discourse', *Harvard International Law Journal* 47, 507, at 511.

74 Even in respect of legal texts there are variants from formal statements of legal rules to which other considerations might apply: for example, the Comments of the Uniform Commercial Code, 'the small print' in a standard form contract (is this 'on the surface'?), or judicial opinions (judgments) where there is no explicit 'holding' or *ratio decidendi*.

a. Do not be seduced by the emotive charge in these terms. Nearly all these dichotomies involve terms that privilege one branch of a dichotomy against the other: reality, real rules, action, practice, back stage, depth all imply some kind of superiority when contrasted with appearance, aspiration, paper rules, books, theory and superficiality. In the present context it is especially important to be wary of contrasts between superficiality and depth and not to confuse 'surface' with 'superficial'. If such contrasts are to be analytically useful, they need so far as is feasible to be purged of any strong emotive associations.
b. Because of (a) there may be a temptation to focus attention on one branch of the dichotomy and to neglect the other. For example, to claim to be only concerned with real rules or the law in action or what goes on backstage. A healthy corrective is McBarnet's criticism of socio-legal scholars and criminologists for ignoring legal rules or treating them as unimportant.[75]
c. Obviously, more than one kind of 'gap' is suggested by these contrasts, but they are often not clearly differentiated. Gaps between appearance and reality and aspiration and reality are quite different – and 'reality' is a notoriously question-begging term. The distinction between 'paper rules' and 'real rules' was originally used to draw a distinction between empirical description and normative prescription of judicial behaviour. Karl Llewellyn was careful to emphasize that even 'pure paper rules' remain an actuality in adjudication.[76] Similarly, the contrast between law in books and law in action is often used in ways that assume that law books only contain bare statements of rules of law and nothing else. That is hardly true of most law books, let alone books about law.[77] For some of us, a persistent challenge has been to get more of the action into the books.[78]
d. The extent of a 'gap' varies considerably. Gaps can be immense, minor or almost non-existent as a matter of continuous variation. In empirical inquiries nothing about the extent of a gap should be taken for granted.
e. Perhaps, most important, is the point that treating these familiar contrasts as binary and talk of 'gaps' both suggest that the two poles of each dichotomy are separate, perhaps even unrelated alternatives.[79] However, this is not the case with nearly all the alternatives considered here. When rules are flouted, not enforced, manipulated or misinterpreted the activity tales place with reference to those rules. 'Underlying' problems, principles, policies and rationales are intimately related to 'surface' law. 'Interposed' norms and institutions are inserted between surface phenomena and actual practices.

75 McBarnet, 'False Dichotomies in Criminal Justice Research'.

76 See above n. 22.

77 Abel, R. (1973), 'Law Books and Books about Law', *Stanford Law Review* 26, 175.

78 Twining, W. (1997), *Law In Context: Enlarging a Discipline* (Oxford: Oxford University Press), ch. 3.

79 I am grateful to Andrew Halpin for emphasizing this point.

> Overlooked or 'invisible' legal and normative orders may sometimes proceed independently and without reference to official or state law, but more often there is some interaction: the relationship can involve competition, conflict, co-existence, co-optatation, complementarity, subordination, repression or other forms of 'interlegality'.[80] To think of binary opposition or 'gaps' is misleading; the central point is that on its own, surface law is typically uninformative about interlegality.

If the concept of 'surface law' is to have any value as an analytical concept, it needs to be used in ways, which avoid the pitfalls of these crude but powerful dichotomies. In particular, we should try to dissociate the concept from a number of assumptions:

a. Surface law is not necessarily *superficia* or *only* on the surface. Rather accounts of surface law are typically uninformative about matters we need to know about if we are to make judgements about the meaning, importance, effectiveness and uses of legal rules.
b. Surface law is not necessarily *unimportant*. As anyone interested in cricket will know, information about the surface of a cricket ball (or pitch) is usually more important in predicting swing, spin and bounce than what lies beneath. Similarly, there are many reasons why the exact wording and text of legal rules may be very important indeed. And critics of phenomena like the *Restatements* regularly underestimate the power of conveniently accessible, simple, quotable texts. However, to say that a phenomenon is *only or merely* surface law does imply that it is superficial, unimportant and possibly ineffective.
c. Surface law is not necessarily 'hard' or 'soft'. The Universal Declaration of Human Rights and the Standard Minimum Rules for the Treatment of Prisoners are both 'soft', in the sense that they are not binding, but both have been very influential and of great symbolic significance. Conversely, some international conventions may be 'hard' in the sense of binding, but be ineffective, or insignificant, or dead letters.

## Conclusion

The practical importance and power of 'surface law' as interpreted here is easily underestimated. However, a recurrent theme of the examples discussed here is

80 'Our legal life is constituted by an intersection of different legal orders, that is, *interlegality*. Interlegality is the phenomenological counterpart of legal plurality, and a key concept in an oppositional postmodern conception of law.' Santos, *Toward a New Legal Common Sense* at 437; cf. 427–30. For a more prosaic interpretation see Twining, 'Diffusion and Globalization Discourse', 512–13.

that what lies 'beneath the surface' and how it relates to official legal doctrine as embedded in texts can be at least as or more important for most purposes of understanding and practical action, but it can easily pass unnoticed or be ignored or overlooked. In other words, if 'surface law' consists only of bare statements of legal rules, on its own it hardly provides enough information to understand, interpret, enforce or use the prescriptions still less to know how they work in practice or to evaluate their effects. At a general level, such observations can be dismissed as banal. Any reasonably sophisticated lawyer realizes that bare statements of rules are not very informative and that rules are not self-enacting, self-interpreting, self-applying, self-implementing and so on. Similarly recurrent debates about 'formalism' and 'realism' (and the like) are a familiar part of the juristic landscape. The 'health warnings' suggested above could be dismissed as no more than 'common sense'.

First, one can readily agree that 'surface law' and like terms are too ambiguous and too emotionally loaded to be of much use as analytical concepts. But some of the examples considered above suggest that there is a range of distinctions and concepts that can be useful in discussions of pluralism, diffusion, harmonization, convergence and so on. The differentiation of the range of levels in gaps between aspiration and reality in respect of international human rights (and in the literature on regulation and compliance) is suggestive. So are Llewellyn's nuanced differentiations between types of paper rules. So too are the different perspectives among comparative lawyers and students of diffusion about what might lie or be going on 'beneath the surface'.

Second, there is an important political dimension. The alleged universality of the human rights regime is open to more cynical interpretations in terms of Realpolitik and lip-service; critics of the American *Restatements* suggested that these were an example of technocratic and undemocratic private legislation by the organized bar, aided by compliant academic lawyers; Legrand treats enthusiasm for emphasizing similarity and convergence as ideologically driven; there is clearly a political motive behind some of the current efforts to construct a *ius commune* and to unify European private law but, as we have seen, the objectives of such efforts are quite varied and some of the leading participants in the projects are opposed to codification and supportive of broad interpretations of subsidiarity.

To sum up: (a) these recurring dichotomies are indeed significant, but they often reflect different underlying concerns; (b) accounts of 'surface law' are often on their own inadequate, mainly because they are uninformative ('the study of rules alone is not enough'); (c) 'surface' as a metaphor conceals a number of pitfalls, not least in the bias in terms such as superficial, deep, action, reality; (d) not all 'surface law' is superficial, soft or unimportant; (e) as I hope Henrik Zahle would have agreed, the idea of surface law is an important dimension of polycentricity; and, finally, (f) the various examples discussed contain some suggestive distinctions and ideas that are more nuanced than the crude standard dichotomies. That may help to inform discussions of convergence, unification and harmonization of law in the European context.

# Chapter 13
# Word/World (of Primordial Issues for Comparative Legal Studies)

Pierre Legrand*

'[W]hat is the word? What the wrong word?'– Beckett[1]

One, everyone, lives in world. No one lives anywhere else.

Although not reducible to any articulation (of it), world is articulable and is indeed articulated through the mediation of language. World cannot be approached other than through language. Any attempt to articulate a view of world can only manifest itself within language (as is the case with any attempt to articulate a view of law).

From Aristotle to Kant, there has prevailed a model whereby the workings of language have been explained in terms of the designation of objects, of the assignment of names to objects.[2] According to this predilection, language is a tool for re-presenting objects that exist independently from it. This is to say that language's role is to designate what are assumed to be extralinguistic entities. As such, language is apprehended as an instrument of communication remaining external to thought – which means, *inter alia*, that what 'there is' or what is 'present' or what 'signifies' precedes the 'system' of signification. The *Cratylus* is exemplary of the position holding that one must begin with world: '[I]t is far better to investigate [the things that are] and learn

---

* I am indebted to Dr Anne Lise Kjær for kindly inviting my participation to the colloquium that inspired this contribution. As I researched and wrote my text, I thought of Casimir and Imogene who may yet get to appreciate the difference between word (what they are told about how things are) and world (how things 'are'). Unless attributed, translations are mine.

1 Samuel Beckett, *Ill seen ill said*, in *The Grove Centenary Edition*, ed. by Paul Auster, vol. III (New York: Grove Press, 2006), p. 455 [1981]. The re-writing from the French is Beckett's own.

2 For a historical overview, see Peter T. Geach, *Reference and Generality* (Ithaca, NY: Cornell University Press, 1962).

about them through themselves than to do so through their names.'[3] The word's burden is thus to say world adequately, faithfully – to achieve what Schleiermacher famously calls a '*Dolmetschung*'.[4] On the view of language as an instrument for fixing and communicating world, linguistic diversity cannot be an objection against the unity of world and the universality of reason. Here, the unity of world resists the multiplicity of languages. Such is Hilary Putnam's claim: '[O]ur conceptual schemes *are* just different "descriptions" of what are in some sense "the same facts"', that is, 'two descriptions are descriptions of *one and the same world*'.[5]

But one can move from a paradigm of perception to a paradigm of understanding. Instead of a view of language as world-disclosure based on the model of designation of an object by means of a name, one can adopt a model whereby a property is attributed to an entity through which this entity is interpreted 'as something'. In other terms, the designation of entities by means of a name is no longer to be understood in the sense that something already known beforehand is given a name but in the sense that only through that meaning is it established that that entity is: 'Language is charged with the task of making beings manifest.'[6]

Thus, one can say with Heidegger that '[o]nly where there is language, is there world'.[7] Indeed, Novalis stigmatized the habitual 'logology' ('*Logologi[e]*'): 'The ridiculous error of people who imagine speaking for the things themselves is quite simply astonishing. But they all ignore the unique feature of language, which is that it is only occupied with itself.'[8] Already Gorgias, the expounder of what is perhaps the first theory of language in the Western tradition, had argued that word (what he called 'λόγος' or '*logos*') is 'a powerful ruler [whose] substance is minute

3 Plato, *Cratylus*, in *Complete Works*, ed. by John M. Cooper and transl. by C.D.C. Reeve (Indianapolis, IN: Hackett, 1997), p. 154. Although the matter has become controversial, this text is habitually assigned to Plato's 'middle period' (*c*. 387 – *c*. 367 B.C.E.).

4 Friedrich Schleiermacher, *ü ber die verschiedenen Methoden des Uebersezens*, in *Sämmtliche Werke*, vol. III/2 (Berlin: G. Reimer, 1838), pp. 209–10 [1813].

5 Hilary Putnam, *Renewing Philosophy* (Cambridge, MA: Harvard University Press, 1995), pp. 110 and 122, respectively [emphasis original].

6 Martin Heidegger, *Elucidations of Hölderlin's Poetry*, transl. by Keith Hoeller (Amherst, NY: Humanity Books, 2000), p. 55 [hereinafter *Elucidations*]. For the original text, see *Erläuterungen zu Hölderlins Dichtung*, in *Gesamtausgabe*, vol. IV (Frankfurt: Vittorio Klostermann, 1981), p. 37 ['*Der Sprache ist aufgegeben, das Seiende als solches im Werk offenbar zu machen*'] (hereinafter *Erläuterungen*).

7 Heidegger, *Elucidations*, *supra*, note 6, p. 56. For the original text, see *Erläuterungen*, *supra*, note 6, p. 38 ['*Nur wo Sprache, da ist Welt*'].

8 Novalis, 'Monolog', in *Schriften*, ed. by Richard Samuel, vol. II (Stuttgart: W. Kohlhammer, 1981), p. 672 ['*Der lächerliche Irrthum ist nur zu bewundern, daß die Leute meinen – sie sprächen um der Dinge willen. Gerade das Eigenthümliche der Sprache, daß sie sich blos um sich selbst bekümmert, weiß keiner*'] (1799).

and indivisible, but [whose] achievements are superhuman'.[9] For him, to begin with word rather than world is to uphold another regime of governance. Ceasing to operate under the aegis of ontology, no longer aiming to say what is as is, one works under the auspices of performance, which, through intertwined semantic and syntactic word-effects, makes world be. Word is no longer only a means, but a genuine force: it makes world come to language (apprehended as a sign-system). In his (lost) treatise, *On What Is Not, or On Nature*, Gorgias's critique of ontology shows how entities are not always-already there, how they are effectively but an effect of word.[10]

Here, the idea of language as designating objects, somehow already existing in themselves, is 'disconfirmed': 'Man lives primarily with objects, indeed, since feeling and acting in him depend on his presentations, he actually does so exclusively, *as language presents them to him*.'[11] And if word is a copy of anything, 'it is a copy, not of the object in itself, but of the image thereof produced in consciousness'.[12]

Contrary to the instrumentalist perspective, then, the role of language here begins long before any communication in the strict sense takes place – which means, *inter alia*, that the 'system' of signification precedes what 'there is' or what is 'present'

9 Gorgias, *Encomium of Helen*, ed. and transl. by D.M. MacDowell (London: Duckworth, 1982), § 8, p. 23 [*c*. 414 B.C.E.].

10 For a discussion of this work, see G.B. Kerferd, *The Sophistic Movement* (Cambridge: Cambridge University Press, 2001), pp. 93–100. What we know of Gorgias's text, written in 444–441 B.C.E., is attributable to detailed commentaries by Aristotle and Sextus Empiricus.

11 Wilhelm von Humboldt, *On Language*, ed. by Michael Losonsky and transl. by Peter Heath (Cambridge: Cambridge University Press, 1999), pp. 59–60 [my emphasis] (†1836) [hereinafter *Language*]. For the original text, see *ü ber die Verschiedenheit des menschlichen Sprachbaues und ihren Einfluß auf die geistige Entwicklung des Menschengeschlechts*, in *Gesammelte Schriften*, ed. by Albert Leitzmann, vol. VII/1 (Berlin: B. Behr, 1907), pp. 59–60 ['*nicht bestätigt*'/'*Der Mensch lebt mit den Gegenständen hauptsächlich, ja, da Empfinden und Handeln in ihm von seinen Vorstellungen abhängen, sogar ausschliesslich so, wie die Sprache sie ihm zuführt*'] (hereinafter *Kawiwerk*). Since Humboldt had intended this text to form the introduction to a multi-volume work on the Kawi language on the island of Java, it is commonly known, in German at least, as the '*Kawiwerk*'.

12 Humboldt, *Language*, *supra*, note 11, p. 59. For the original text, see *Kawiwerk*, supra, note 11, pp. 59–60 ['*(das Wort) ist nicht ein Abdruck des Gegenstandes an sich, sondern des von diesem in der Seele erzeugten Bildes*']. Cf. Ludwig Wittgenstein, *Zettel*, ed. by G.E.M. Anscombe and G.H. von Wright and transl. by G.E.M. Anscombe (Oxford: Blackwell, 1967), § 191, p. 33: 'The words are not a translation of something else that was there before they were' ['*Die Worte sind keine ü bersetzung eines Andern, welches vor ihnen da war*'] (1929–48). This bilingual edition has the German text facing the English translation.

or what 'signifies'.[13] Such is Richard Rorty's point: '[T]he world does not speak. Only we do.'[14]

On this conception, one must reject 'referential semantics' to explain the working of language (that is, the idea that language is related to world as name to object). Language does not have a passive character. Indeed, it asserts power – in Nietzsche's blazing assertion, '[i]t is the powerful who made the names of things into law'.[15] Consider the following illustrations of the performative character of word: 'They are seen as *black*, therefore they *are* black; they are seen as *women*, therefore, they *are* women.'[16] To be sure, 'what things *are called* is incomparably more important than what they are'.[17] Thus is Jacques Derrida vindicated: textuality, as it institutes through the word and in the word, is intrinsic 'to the world, to reality, to being'.[18] And '[l]anguage is [seen] not [to be] about description, but about *commitment.*'[19]

---

13 This is one of Derrida's main post-phenomenological arguments. For example, see Jacques Derrida, *La voix et le phénomène* (Paris: Presses Universitaires de France, 1967).

14 Richard Rorty, *Contingency, Irony, and Solidarity* (Cambridge: Cambridge University Press, 1989), p. 6.

15 Friedrich Nietzsche, *The Will to Power*, ed. by Walter Kaufmann and transl. by Walter Kaufmann and R.J. Hollingdale (New York: Vintage, 1967), III, § 513, p. 277 [†1901] (hereinafter *Will to Power*). For the original text, see *Der Wille zur Macht* [III–IV], in *Gesammelte Werke* [*Musarionausgabe*], vol. XIX (Munich: Musarion, 1926), p. 26 ['*Die Mächtigen sind es, welche die Namen der Dinge zum Gesetz gemacht haben*'] (hereinafter *Wille zur Macht*).

16 Monique Wittig, *The Straight Mind* (Boston, MA: Beacon Press, 1992), p. 12 [1981]. Cf. Friedrich Nietzsche, *Human, All Too Human*, transl. by Marion Faber and Stephen Lehmann (London: Penguin, 1994), I, § 11, p. 19: 'The shaper of language was not so modest as to think that he was only giving things labels; rather, he imagined that he was expressing the highest knowledge of things with words' [1878]. For the original text, see *Menschliches, Allzumenschliches*, in *Werke*, ed. by Giorgio Colli and Mazzino Montinari, vol. IV/2 (Berlin: Walter de Gruyter, 1967), pp. 26–7 ['*Der Sprachbildner war nicht so bescheiden, zu glauben, dass er den Dingen eben nur Bezeichnungen gebe, er drückte vielmehr, wie er wähnte, das höchste Wissen über die Dinge mit den Worten aus*'].

17 Friedrich Nietzsche, *The Gay Science*, transl. by Walter Kaufmann (New York: Vintage, 1974), II, § 58, p. 121 [emphasis original in English] (1882) [hereinafter *Gay Science*]. For the original text, see *Die fröhliche Wissenschaft*, in *Werke*, ed. by Giorgio Colli and Mazzino Montinari, vol. V/2 (Berlin: Walter de Gruyter, 1973), p. 98 ['*dass unsäglich mehr daran liegt, wie die Dinge heissen, als was sie sind*'] [1882] (hereinafter *Fröhliche Wissenschaft*).

18 Jacques Derrida, *Limited Inc.*, ed. by Elisabeth Weber (Paris: Galilée, 1990), p. 253 ['*au monde, à la réalité, à l'être*'].

19 Donna J. Haraway, *Simians, Cyborgs, and Women* (New York: Routledge, 1991), p. 214 [my emphasis]. Cf. Novalis, 'Poëticismen', in *Schriften*, ed. by Richard Samuel, vol. II (Stuttgart: W. Kohlhammer, 1981), p. 558: 'The entire language is a *postulate*' ['*Die ganze Sprache ist ein* Postulat'] (emphasis original) [1797].

Observe that '[t]o bring [world] to language is not to change it into something else, but, in articulating and developing it, to make it become itself.'[20]

'No thing is where the word is lacking.'[21]

As bearer of a totality of meanings, language fixes the categorical framework of everything that can be talked about.

That 'there resides in every language a characteristic *world-view*' is Humboldt's principal insight.[22]

As bearer of a world-view that circumscribes one's understanding, as constitutive of meaning, language partakes in the activity of thinking (rather than being incidental to it): 'Thought and language are therefore one and inseparable from each other.'[23] Language is the condition of possibility of all experience of world. *Pace* Hilary Putnam (*supra*), identity of referent can only be guaranteed indirectly through identity of meaning (which means that it cannot be guaranteed at all). What one experiences in world is actually *constituted* by language.

If language is constitutive of the understanding of that about which understanding must be reached, it cannot be envisaged as a mere instrument for achieving understanding about something that would exist independently of it.

---

20 Paul Ricoeur, 'Phenomenology and Hermeneutics', in *Hermeneutics and the Human Sciences*, ed. and transl. by John B. Thompson (Cambridge: Cambridge University Press, 1981), p. 115. This text was initially published in French in Germany.

21 Martin Heidegger, *On the Way to Language*, transl. by Peter D. Hertz (New York: Harper Collins, 1971), p. 60 [1959] (hereinafter *On the Way*). For the original text, see *Unterwegs zur Sprache* (Stuttgart: Günther Neske, 1959), p. 163 ['*Kein Ding ist, wo das Wort gebricht*'] (hereinafter *Unterwegs*).

22 Humboldt, *Language*, *supra*, note 11, p. 60 [emphasis original in English]. For the original text, see *Kawiwerk*, *supra*, note 11, p. 60 ['*in jeder Sprache (liegt) eine eigenthümliche Weltansicht*']. But this idea can be found already in the theory of 'point of view' ('*Sehe-Punckt*') developed in Johann Martin Chladenius's *Einleitung zur richtigen Auslegung vernünfftiger Reden und Schrifften* (Leipzig: 1742), § 308, p. 185. For an extensive discussion of Chladenius's work, see Peter Szondi, *Introduction to Literary Hermeneutics*, transl. by Martha Woodmansee (Cambridge: Cambridge University Press, 1995), pp. 14–66. More recently, the notion of 'world-view' has been claimed by Benjamin L. Whorf, *Language, Thought, and Reality*, ed. by John B. Carroll (Cambridge, MA: MIT Press, 1956), pp. 212–13.

23 Humboldt, *Language*, *supra*, note 11, p. 54. For the original text, see *Kawiwerk*, *supra*, note 11, p. 53 ['*(Die intellectuelle Thätigkeit) und die Sprache sind daher Eins und unzertrennlich von einander*'].

That language should be the condition of possibility of ascription of meaning entails that meaning can only be generated after acquisition of language and that meaning is always-already linguistically realized.

'It is the world of words that creates the world of things.'[24]

Language thus competes with the individual for authorship of the synthesis through which world is constituted. Not only does language 'restrai[n] [one] when [one] speak[s]',[25] but it claims against one, as a 'beyond-one', the authorship of operations constituting the individual's world-view.

(Utterances, thus, are no longer to be regarded as the most basic 'hermeneutic' unit. Rather, one must begin with the background of shared presuppositions, which involves an undifferentiated state of knowledge of both language and world – this is because one learns to look at world through the eyes of one's father-tongue and because, conversely, the development of one's linguistic capacity becomes articulated on the basis of world as it surrounds one. Otherwise, sentences would lack 'literal' meaning, that is, a speaker would not achieve illocutionary success. One understands an utterance when one knows what makes it acceptable. But knowledge of acceptability conditions depends on contingent background knowledge, which is implicit – hence not entirely expressible in propositional knowledge and not capable of being thematized at will – and ultimately predetermines the validity of the utterance itself.)

The self is a they-self: there is something like 'absorption in the world' in effect.[26] One's pre-ontological but existential way of being-in-the-world is of being-with-others, which is very much being like everyone else: such an inauthentic form of being-in-the-world is not an accident but a primordial phenomenon.[27]

---

24 Jacques Lacan, *Ecrits* (Paris: Le Seuil, 1966), p. 276 ['*C'est le monde des mots qui crée le monde des choses*'] (1956). Note that the thesis that meaning determines reference not only underlies the so-called 'linguistic turn' but also serves as a basis for the analytic tradition initiated by Frege and Russell. For example, see John Searle, 'Proper Names', (1958) 67 *Mind* 166.

25 Humboldt, *Language*, *supra*, note 11, p. 63. For the original text, see *Kawiwerk*, *supra*, note 11, p. 64 ['*es (ist) die Sprache selbst, von der ich dabei Einschränkung erfahre*'].

26 Martin Heidegger, *Being and Time*, transl. by Joan Stambaugh (Albany, NY: State University of New York Press, 1996), p. 121 [1927] (hereinafter *Being and Time*). For the original text, see *Sein und Zeit*, 18th edn (Tübingen: Max Niemeyer, 2001), p. 130 ['*Aufgehen in der Welt*'] (hereinafter *Sein und Zeit*).

27 Heidegger, *Being and Time*, *supra*, note 26, pp. 118–22.

'We do not merely speak *the* language – we speak *by way of* it.'[28] To speak implies 'letting something be said to us'.[29]

'*[L]anguage* speaks' (although its voice can be inaudible).[30] There is a 'speaking-to-us' ('*Zuspruch*') at work.[31]

Linguistic world-disclosure has priority over any conversation, which is why '[s]peaking is a listening not *while* but *before* we are speaking. This listening to language also comes before all other kinds of listening that we know, in a most inconspicuous manner.'[32]

This is (in part) what Jacques Derrida means when he suggests a move from 'ontology' to 'otology' pursuant to which one would be open (to language and to law-as-language), attentive, listening, receptive, hearkening, *lending an ear* to the claims of the text.[33]

---

28 Heidegger, *On the Way*, *supra*, note 21, p. 124. For the original text, see *Unterwegs*, *supra*, note 21, p. 254 ['*Wir sprechen nicht nur* die *Sprache, wir sprechen* aus *ihr*'] (emphasis original).

29 Heidegger, *On the Way*, *supra*, note 21, p. 124. For the original text, see *Unterwegs*, *supra*, note 21, p. 255 ['*Sichsagenlassen*'] (emphasis omitted).

30 Heidegger, *On the Way*, *supra*, note 21, p. 124. For the original text, see *Unterwegs*, *supra*, note 21, p. 254 ['die *Sprache* spricht'] (emphasis original).

31 For this translation from Heidegger's philosophical vocabulary, see James K. Lyon, *Paul Celan and Martin Heidegger* (Baltimore, MD: Johns Hopkins University Press, 2006), p. 223, note 14. The reference is to Martin Heidegger, *Holzwege*, in *Gesamtausgabe*, vol. V (Frankfurt: Vittorio Klostermann, 1977), p. 369 [1950].

32 Heidegger, *On the Way*, *supra*, note 21, pp. 123–4. For the original text, see *Unterwegs*, *supra*, note 21, p. 254 ['*das Sprechen nicht zugleich, sondern* zuvor *ein Hören. Dieses Hören auf die Sprache geht auch allem sonst vorkommenden Hören in der unscheinbarsten Weise vorauf*'] (emphasis original).

33 For example, see Jacques Derrida, *Politiques de l'amitié* (Paris: Galilée, 1994), p. 410 ['*otologie*']. Bultmann likewise advocates 'listening to the claims of the text': Rudolf Bultmann, 'Das Problem der Hermeneutik', in *Glauben und Verstehen*, vol. II (Tübingen: J.C.B. Mohr, 1952), p. 228 ['*(den) Anspruch (des Texts) zu hören*'] (1950). See also Martin Heidegger, *What Is Called Thinking* transl. by J. Glenn Gray (New York: Harper Collins, 1968), p. 128: '[W]e are compelled, as soon as we set out upon a way of thought, to give specific attention to what the word says' [1954]. For the original text, see *Was heisst Denken?* (Tübingen: Max Niemeyer, 1984), p. 88 ['*sobald wir uns auf einen Weg des Denkens begeben, (sind wir) schon daran gehalten, eigens auf das Sagen des Wortes zu achten*'].

(To say, like Humboldt, that thinking is 'inseparable' from language means that it is 'inseparable' from each specific language for 'language manifests itself in reality only as a multiplicity'.[34])

Note that one cannot (unlike Humboldt, for example) ground the constitution of linguistic world-disclosure in the activity of talking as such, that is, a world-view cannot be interpreted as the 'product' of the activity of the speaker. Rather, that activity is (unconsciously) dominated by the world-disclosing function of language. In other words, language as medium of understanding is subordinated to language as world-disclosure: it cannot be apprehended as the result of an individual activity, but as a necessary condition of possibility of that activity.

(Accordingly, any attempt to find a foundation prior to language is doomed as this would deny language's role of world-disclosure.)

(To say that one's language is one's world-view does not mean, *pace* Donald Davidson, that one cannot identify a radically different language – and engage comparatively with it, for instance by purporting to 'translate' it – inevitably approximatively – into one's 'own' language.[35])

The grasp of language as constitutive of thought amounts to a detranscendentalization of reason since it locates reason in the plurality of languages: reason is language. This means that there is no pure reason that exists independently of language, that reason cannot be separated from the actual, cultural conditions of its existence, that reason cannot be envisaged as alingual (or acultural).

---

34 Wilhelm von Humboldt, *ü ber die Verschiedenheiten des menschlichen Sprachbaues*, in *Gesammelte Schriften*, ed. by Albert Leitzmann, vol. VI/1 (Berlin: B. Behr, 1907), p. 240 ['*Die Sprache erscheint in der Wirklichkeit nur als ein Vielfaches*'] (1829). For Humboldt's statement on inseparability, see *supra* at text accompanying note 23. Cf. Gilles Deleuze and Félix Guattari, *Mille plateaux* (Paris: Editions de Minuit, 1980), p. 14: 'There is no language as such, nor a universality of language, but a concourse of dialects, of patois, of jargons, of special languages' ['*il n'y a pas de langue en soi, ni d'universalité du langage, mais un concours de dialectes, de patois, d'argots, de langues spéciales*'].

35 For a detailed and compelling refutation of Davidson's claim to the effect that one cannot be in a position to judge that others hold to a radically different conceptual scheme from one's own, see Michael N. Forster, 'On the Very Idea of Denying the Existence of Radically Different Conceptual Schemes', 41 *Inquiry* 133 (1998). For Donald Davidson's position, see his *Inquiries into Truth and Interpretation* (Oxford: Oxford University Press, 1984), pp. 183–98.

'[T]he idea of an absolute reason is not a possibility for historical humanity. Reason exists for us only in concrete, historical terms – i.e., it is not its own master but remains constantly dependent on the given circumstances in which it operates.'[36]

(Indeed, not only is language central to the capacity to think about world, but it is also the centre of reason's misunderstandings about itself.[37])

Now, the only 'there is' is that of plurality of words (not unity of world).[38] To translate is no longer a '*Dolmetschung*' but an '*ü bertragen*' – and the translator emerges as a '*Fahrensmann*'.[39] In Jacques Derrida's words, 'for the notion of translation, one must substitute a notion of *transformation*: the regulated transformation of a language by another, of a text by another.'[40] He adds: 'We will never have been involved and never have been involved in fact in the "transportation" of pure signifieds which the signifying instrument – or the "vehicle" – would leave intact and untouched, from one language to another.'[41] Instead of translation, there is *resignificatio* (apprehended as a performative move that is epistemically positive).[42]

---

36 Hans-Georg Gadamer, *Truth and Method*, 2nd edn transl. by Joel Weinsheimer and Donald G. Marshall (London: Sheed & Ward, 1989), p. 276 [1960] (hereinafter *Truth and Method*). For the original text, see *Wahrheit und Methode*, 6th edn (Tübingen: J.C.B. Mohr, 1990), pp. 280–81 ['*die Idee einer absoluten Vernunft überhaupt keine Möglichkeit des geschichtlichen Menschentums. Vernunft ist für uns nur als reale geschichtliche, d. h. schlechthin: sie ist nicht ihrer selbst Herr, sondern bleibt stets auf die Gegebenheiten angewiesen, an denen sie sich betätigt*'] (hereinafter *Wahrheit und Methode*). Cf. Nietzsche, *Will to Power*, *supra*, note 15, III, § 522, p. 283: 'Rational thought is interpretation according to a scheme that we cannot throw off' [emphasis omitted]. For the original text, see *Wille zur Macht*, *supra*, note 15, p. 522 ['*Das vernünftige Denken ist ein Interpretieren nach einem Schema, welches wir nicht abwerfen können*'] (emphasis omitted).

37 See J.G. Hamann, 'Metakritik über den Purismus der reinen Vernunft', in *Vom Magus im Norden und der Verwegenheit des Geistes*, ed. by Stefan Majetschak (Munich: Deutscher Taschenbuch, 1988), p. 208 [1784].

38 Cf. Humboldt at text accompanying note 34, *supra*.

39 Celan coined this 'nonexistent word that resides somewhere between a "traveling man" and a "ferryman"': Lyon, *supra*, note 31, p. 40.

40 Jacques Derrida, *Positions* (Paris: Editions de Minuit, 1972), p. 31 ['*à la notion de traduction, il faudra substituer une notion de* transformation: *transformation réglée d'une langue par une autre, d'un texte par un autre*'] (emphasis original).

41 Derrida, *supra*, note 40, p. 31 ['*Nous n'aurons et n'avons en fait jamais eu affaire à quelque "transport" de signifiés purs que l'instrument – ou le "véhicule" – signifiant laisserait vierge et inentamé, d'une langue à l'autre*'].

42 I borrow the notion of 'resignification' from the work of Judith Butler. Marshalling the inherent instability of linguistic meaning, 'resignification' allows for the alteration or redirection of a meaning having sedimented within a term on account of its pre-existing relationships. For example, see Judith Butler, *Bodies That Matter* (London: Routledge, 1993), p. 191.

'[W]hat Richard Rorty calls the "moral vocabulary" of Saint Paul and the "moral vocabulary" of Freud should be understood precisely as differences in vocabulary. We shouldn't [...] think of Saint Paul and Freud as holding competing "descriptions of the world," for then we should be moved to think of one of them as right and the other as wrong. Instead, we must think of them as playing what (following Wittgenstein) Rorty calls "alternative language games," in which case saying that Freud's beliefs are more true than Saint Paul makes as little sense as saying that German is more true than Hebrew.'[43]

In Heidegger's words, '[interpretation] is always based on a *fore-having*.' The 'unveil[ing]' is 'always done under the guidance of a perspective which fixes that with regard to which what has been understood is to be interpreted'. 'The interpretation is grounded in a *foresight* that "approaches" what has been taken in fore-having with a definite interpretation in view.' '[T]he interpretation has always already decided, finally or provisionally, upon a definite conceptuality; it is grounded in a *fore-conception*.'[44]

The Heideggerian notions of '*Vorhabe*' ('fore-having'), '*Vorsicht*' ('foresight'), and '*Vorgriff*' ('fore-conception'), as they foreground the Bultmaniann idea of 'pre-understanding' ('*Vorverständnis*') and the Gadamerian conception of 'prejudice' or 'prejudgment' ('*Vorurteil*'), suggest that only within the pregiven sign-system within which one is framed does one understand, does one ascribe meaning, does one experience what one may want to seize as 'truth'. In other words, there is a preliminary structure of understanding that is inherently constitutive of any understanding and, as such, that is a *condition* of understanding: how could one understand anything against a 'no-background' situation?[45]

---

43 Walter Benn Michaels, *The Shape of the Signifie* (Princeton, NJ: Princeton University Press, 2004), p. 43, referring to Rorty, *supra*, note 14, p. 5.

44 Heidegger, *Being and Time*, *supra*, note 26, pp. 140–41. For the original text, see *Sein und Zeit*, *supra*, note 26, p. 150 ['*(Die Auslegung) gründet jeweils in einer* Vorhabe. *(...) Die Zueignung des Verstandenen, aber noch Eingehüllten vollzieht die Enthüllung immer unter der Führung einer Hinsicht, die das fixiert, im Hinblick worauf das Verstandene ausgelegt werden soll. Die Auslegung gründet jeweils in einer* Vorsicht *(...). (...) Wie immer – die Auslegung hat sich je schon endgültig oder vorbehaltlich für eine bestimmte Begrifflichkeit entschieden; sie gründet in einem orgriff*] (emphasis original).

45 Bultmann, *supra*, note 33, p. 216; Gadamer, *Truth and Method*, *supra*, note 36, pp. 277–307 ('Prejudices as Conditions of Understanding'). For the original text, see *Wahrheit und Methode*, *supra*, note 36, pp. 281–95 ['*Vorurteile als Bedingungen des Verstehens*']. Cf. Wittgenstein, *supra*, note 12, § 234, p. 43: 'What happens is not that this symbol cannot be further interpreted, but: I do no interpreting. I do not interpret, because I feel at home in the present picture' ['*Nicht das findet statt, daß sich dieses Symbol nicht mehr deuten läßt, sondern: ich deute nicht. Ich deute nicht, weil ich mich in dem gegenwärtigen Bild heimisch fühle*'].

(To write 'like' Heidegger, one could refer to a constellation of fore-constraints or *Vorzwänge*.)

Because thinking is inextricably linked to an always-already-existing language that makes it possible, there cannot be a presuppositionless starting-point.

'[T]he essential link of thought to language [...] will never dispense with idioms.'[46]

There is the 'screen of words'.[47]

There is, then, 'the prisonhouse of language'.[48]

Law-thought is inextricably linked to an always-already-existing law-language that makes it possible, which means that there cannot be a presuppositionless starting-point.

There is, then, the prisonhouse of law (comparatists-at-law beware!).

There is no (scrutable) world-as-such (or 'is-ness') that would guarantee something like the 'objectivity' of knowledge about it. Since anything about which an agreement must be reached is not accessible as an entity in itself but is linguistically prestructured,[49] any understanding of it is unavoidably subject to interpretation.[50]

---

46 Jacques Derrida, *Donner le temps*, vol. I: *La fausse monnaie* (Paris: Galilée, 1991), p. 76 ['*le lien essentiel de la pensée (...) au langage (...) ne fera jamais l'économie des idiomes*']. Derrida further reflects on the 'impossib[ility] to bring out a concept of essence [...] that would transcend idiomatic difference': *ibid.* ['*impossib(ilité) de dégager un concept de l'essence (...) qui transcende la différence idiomatique*'].

47 Pierre Legendre, *Ce que l'Occident ne voit pas de l'Occident* (Paris: Fayard, 2004), p. 75 ['*l'écran des mots*'].

48 J. Hillis Miller, 'The Critic as Host', in Harold Bloom et al., *Deconstruction and Criticism* (New York: Continuum, 1979), p. 230. In its complete form, this (famous) Nietzschean formulation reads as follows: 'The most heroic effort to escape from the prisonhouse of language only builds the walls higher.'

49 Cf. Friedrich Nietzsche, 'On Truth and Lies in a Nonmoral Sense', in *Philosophy and Truth*, ed. and transl. by Daniel Breazeale (Atlantic Highlands, NJ: Humanities Press, 1979), p. 82: 'The "thing-in-itself" [...] is [...] something quite incomprehensible to the creator of language and something not in the least worth striving for' [1873]. For the original text, see 'Ueber Wahrheit und Lüge im aussermoralischen Sinne', in *Gesammelte Werke* [*Musarionausgabe*], vol. VI (Munich: Musarion, 1922), p. 79 ['*Das "Ding an sich" (...) ist auch dem Sprachbildner ganz unfasslich und ganz und gar nicht erstrebenswerth*'].

50 This is an opportunity to draw a crucial distinction. It is not that interpretation allows one to 'grasp' or 'get hold of' understanding. Interpretation is not an activity through

Because meaning (or the mode of re-presentation of the *designatum*) is a condition of access to 'any-referent-there-is', a 'referent' is understood through meaning – which is also fore-meaning.

'The only "objectivity" here is the confirmation of a fore-meaning in its being worked out.'[51]

The constitution of meaning must escape any attempt at objectification. Interpretation does not demonstrate 'the' meaning of what would be 'objectively' present, but rather clarifies what is 'always already' relevant.

The symbolically mediated character of one's relation with world prohibits the possibility of postulating a world-as-such that would be accessible through perception to all interpreters in an identical way. However, it does not prevent postulating a world-in-itself that would simply not be accessible. Assuming one wants to retain the possibility of objective experience (but why would one?), one must turn to the conditions of possibility of communication. The idea is that speakers who share a language would share a knowledge of meanings that constitutes the unitary framework for everything that can appear as world. Thus, the identity of meanings shared by speakers would guarantee the identity of reference of the signs they use. Even allowing for this highly problematic set of assumptions (why would the fact that two individuals speak French to one another ensure identity of meaning and identity of reference?),[52] how to generate the unity of the world

---

which one can enter into possession of understanding. Rather, interpretation channels understanding and thus is constitutive of understanding, such that each understanding must assume an interpretation, whether consciously or not. Through interpretation, 'understanding appropriates what it has understood in an understanding way': Heidegger, *Being and Time*, *supra*, note 26, p. 139 (for the original text, see *Sein und Zeit*, *supra*, note 26, p. 148: '*das Verstehen [eignet sich] sein Verstandenes verstehend zu*'). For example, speaking another langage than one's 'own' always involves translation no matter how well one speaks it and no matter, therefore, how sub-consciously this process operates. Indeed, this is the case within one's 'own' language also, for example when a twenty-first-century reader considers a sixteenth-century text. Although one tacitly apprehends the sixteenth-century 'rose' as a twenty-first-century 'rose' and thus fails to detect the ways in which 'the' text has changed on account of the 'foreignness' that temporality has introduced into it, the reader's blindness does not detract from the fact that a process of translation is effectively taking place.

51 Gadamer, *Truth and Method*, *supra*, note 36, p. 267. For the original text, see *Wahrheit und Methode*, *supra*, note 36, p. 272 ['*Es gibt hier keine andere "Objektivität" als die Bewährung, die eine Vormeinung durch ihre Ausarbeitung finde* '].

52 Cf. Friedrich Nietzsche, *Thus Spoke Zarathustra*, transl. by Graham Sparkes (Oxford: Oxford University Press, 2005), I, § 15, p. 5: 'Never did one neighbour understand the other' [1883]. For the original text, see *Also sprach Zarathustra*, in *Werke*, ed. by Giorgio Colli and Mazzino Montinari, vol. VI/1 (Berlin: Walter de Gruyter, 1968), p. 70 ['*Nie verstand ein Nachbar den andern*'].

linguistically disclosed through the plurality of historically-contingent world disclosures? The idea that identity of meaning could be guaranteed within the limits of a given linguistic world-disclosure means that at best reference (and truth) are turned into intralinguistic notions dependent on a prior and contingent constitution of meaning such that one must, here also, address the incommensurability of linguistic world-disclosures.

'The prejudices and fore-meanings that occupy the interpreter's consciousness are not at his free disposal.'[53]

'That is why the prejudices of the individual, far more than his judgments, constitute the historical reality of his being.'[54]

'In fact history does not belong to us; we belong to it.'[55]

('[I]t is literally more correct to say that language speaks us, rather than that we speak it.'[56])

In fact, language does not belong to us; we belong to it. (In Derrida's words, 'a language does not belong.'[57])

---

53 Gadamer, *Truth and Method, supra*, note 36, p. 295. For the original text, see *Wahrheit und Methode, supra*, note 36, p. 301 ['*Die Vorurteile und Vormeinungen, die das Bewußtsein des Interpreten besetzt halten, sind ihm als solche nicht zu freier Verfügung*'].

54 Gadamer, *Truth and Method, supra*, note 36, pp. 276–7. For the original text, see *Wahrheit und Methode, supra*, note 36, p. 281 ['*die Vorurteile des einzelnen (sind) weit mehr als seine Urteile die geschichtliche Wirklichkeit seines Seins*'] (emphasis omitted).

55 Gadamer, *Truth and Method, supra*, note 36, p. 276. For the original text, see *Wahrheit und Methode, supra*, note 36, p. 281 ['*In Wahrheit gehört die Geschichte nicht uns, sondern wir gehören ihr*']. Cf. Ludwig Wittgenstein, *On Certainty*, ed. by G.E.M. Anscombe and G.H. von Wright and transl. by Dennis Paul and G.E.M. Anscombe (New York: Harper and Row, 1972), § 94, p. 15: 'But I did not get my picture of the world by satisfying myself of its correctness; nor do I have it because I am satisfied of its correctness. No: it is the inherited background against which I distinguish between true and false' ['*Aber mein Weltbild habe ich nicht, weil ich mich von seiner Richtigkeit überzeugt habe; auch nicht weil ich von seiner Richtigkeit überzeugt bin. Sondern es ist der überkommene Hintergrund, auf welchem ich zwischen wahr und falsch unterscheide*'] (1950–51). This bilingual edition has the German text facing the English translation.

56 Gadamer, *Truth and Method, supra*, note 36, p. 463. For the original text, see *Wahrheit und Methode, supra*, note 36, p. 467 ['*insoweit ist es buchstäblich richtiger zu sagen, daß die Sprache uns spricht, als daß wir sie sprechen*'].

57 Jacques Derrida, *Apprendre à vivre enfi* , ed. by Jean Birnbaum (Paris: Galilée, 2005), p. 39 ['*une langue, ça n'appartient pas*'].

('There is no mother tongue, but a seizure of power by a dominant language within a political multiplicity.'[58])

In fact, law does not belong to us; we belong to it. (This is why 'any comparison is, at the outset, defective'.[59])

There is no extraworldly observer who could stand over against world. Rather, one finds oneself within a symbolically prestructured world within which one finds oneself always-already thrown.

The preclusion of an appeal to an extraworldly standpoint makes facticity into the obligatory (non-presuppositionless) starting-point: disclosedness is essentially factical.[60]

Language is at once arbitrary/contingent (it cannot be deduced as cultural reality since there is no *a priori* dimension to it) and necessary/indispensable (it is impossible to speak without speaking a language – and without speaking a language that is always-already structured).[61] Even the enrichment of language (say, through Heidegger's philosophical neologisms) takes place in/through language. It is conditioned by language.

Language is insurmountable.

The insurmountability of language is not only factual. It is also normative.

(There is, again, 'the prisonhouse of language' [*supra*].)

'Understanding is to be thought of less as a subjective act than as participating in an event of tradition, a process of transmission in which past and present are constantly mediated.'[62]

---

58 Deleuze and Guattari, *supra*, note 34, p. 14 ['*Il n'y a pas de langue-mère, mais prise de pouvoir par une langue dominante dans une multiplicité politique*'].

59 Stéphane Mallarmé, 'Quelques médaillons et portraits en pied', in *Oeuvres complètes*, ed. by Henri Mondor and G. Jean-Aubry (Paris: Gallimard, 1945), p. 528 ['*Toute comparaison est, préalablement, défectueuse*'] (1892). This text appeared on the occasion of the death of Tennyson.

60 Heidegger, *Being and Time*, *supra*, note 26, pp. 203–4. For the original text, see *Sein und Zeit*, *supra*, note 26, p. 221.

61 Hamann, *supra*, note 37, p. 211.

62 Gadamer, *Truth and Method*, *supra*, note 36, p. 290. For the original text, see *Wahrheit und Methode*, *supra*, note 36, p. 295 ['*Das Verstehen ist selber nicht so sehr als eine Handlung der Subjektivität zu denken, sondern als Einrücken in ein ü berlieferungsgeschehen, in dem sich Vergangenheit und Gegenwart beständig vermitteln*'] (emphasis omitted).

'Understanding is, essentially, a historically effected event.'[63]

'[W]e should learn to understand ourselves better and recognize that in all understanding, whether we are expressly aware of it or not, the efficacy of history is at work.'[64]

There is something like a 'history of effects' ('*Wirkungsgeschichte*') being 'refracted through language' such that '[t]here are no contexts of human understanding that are not constituted in terms of some linguistic framework and [that] when we understand the world, ourselves, or others, we do so in terms of that framework'.[65]

'[W]e are always already involved in an understanding of being.'[66]

'Whatever and however we may try to think, we think within the sphere of tradition.'[67]

Observe how saying that all understanding is prejudiced in that it is circumscribed by the light that the historical situation sheds on the interpreter himself, and indeed on that which the interpreter is trying to understand, is not necessarily negative. The work of prejudice can, in fact, prove empowering.[68] Thus, one can understand Marcel Duchamp's readymades as art because one belongs to a culture

---

63 Gadamer, *Truth and Method, supra*, note 36, p. 300 [emphasis omitted]. For the original text, see *Wahrheit und Methode, supra*, note 36, p. 305 ['*Verstehen ist seinem Wesen nach ein wirkunsgeschichtlicher Vorgang*'].

64 Gadamer, *Truth and Method, supra*, note 36, p. 301. For the original text, see *Wahrheit und Methode, supra*, note 36, p. 306 ['*daß man sich selber richtiger verstehen lerne und anerkenne, daß in allem Verstehen, ob man sich dessen ausdrücklich bewußt ist oder nicht, die Wirkung dieser Wirkungsgeschichte am Werke ist*'].

65 Brice Wachterhauser, 'Getting it Right: Relativism, Realism and Truth', in *The Cambridge Companion to Gadamer*, ed. by Robert Dostal (Cambridge: Cambridge University Press, 2002), p. 66.

66 Heidegger, *Being and Time, supra*, note 26, p. 4. For the original text, see *Sein und Zeit, supra*, note 26, p. 5 ['*(W)ir bewegen uns immer schon in einem Seinsverständnis*'].

67 Martin Heidegger, *Identity and Difference*, transl. by Joan Stambaugh (Chicago, IL: University of Chicago Press, 2002), p. 41 [1957]. For the original text, see *Identität und Differenz*, in *Gesamtausgabe*, vol. XI (Frankfurt: Vittorio Klostermann, 2006), p. 50 ['*Was immer und wie immer wir zu denken versuchen, wir denken im Spielraum der ü berlieferung*'].

68 For a 'positive concept of prejudice', see Hans-Georg Gadamer, *Philosophical Hermeneutics*, ed. and transl. by David E. Linge (Berkeley, CA: University of California Press, 1976), p. 9 [1966]. For the original text, see 'Die Universalität des hermeneutischen Problems', in *Gesammelte Werke*, vol. II (Tübingen: J.C.B. Mohr, 1986), p. 224 ['*einen positiven Begriff des Vorurteils*'].

that envisages art in a certain manner, that has an idea of what art is and of what art can be. Or, '[w]e can understand a certain text as a novel, for example, because we belong to a history and culture that knows what a novel is.'[69]

Not even anything like 'literal' meaning can be assessed 'as such'. Consider the four following statements by John Searle: 'the notion of the literal meaning of a sentence only has application relative to a set of background assumptions'; 'these background assumptions are not all and could not all be realized in the semantic structure of the sentence'; '[these assumptions] are not fixed and definite in number and content'; 'each specification of an assumption tends to bring in other assumptions, those that determine the applicability of the literal meaning of the sentence used in the specification.'[70]

If 'meaning' and 'truth' are never given independently of language, if they are epistemically constrained, they cannot be conceived as existing outside the limitations of a particular culture (or tradition) in a specific time and place. If there is something like '*Vorgriff*', there is a historical specificity to every act of understanding (whether because it reflects institutional conditions or resists forms of institutional appropriation).[71] If there is no account of truth not dependent at all upon the particular way in which it is experienced, there is, then, no sense

69 Georgia Warnke, 'Literature, Law, and Morality', in *Gadamer's Repercussions*, ed. by Bruce Krajewski (Berkeley, CA: University of California Press, 2004), p. 92. This argument does not exclude the possibility that one can develop an idiosyncratic view of the novel or of art. Indeed, I readily admit that there is a basic ability to deviate from an ingrained cognitive pattern in ways that are creative. Cf. William R. Everdell, *The First Moderns* (Chicago, IL: University of Chicago Press, 1997), where the author, focusing on the period from 1899 to 1913, illustrates the emergence of notions like recursion, radical subjectivity, multi-perspectivism, contingency and ontological discontinuity through narratives devoted to individuals who, although socialized into a particular constellation of ideas, became able to think in a different way than the one presented to them. Examples of persons offering what Everdell regards as disjunctive thought include Freud, Husserl, Strindberg, Kandinsky, Bohr and dozens of other such luminaries. *Adde*: Rorty, *supra*, note 14, p. 50: '[Human beings can] manipulate the tensions within their own epoch in order to produce the beginnings of the next epoch.' This, however, is '[t]he most they can do'.

70 John R. Searle, *Expression and Meaning* (Cambridge: Cambridge University Press, 1979), pp. 120, 120, 126, and 126, respectively. Cf. Wittgenstein, *supra*, note 12, § 716, pp. 123–4: 'What about these two sentences: "This sheet is red" and "this sheet is the colour called 'red' in English"? Do they both say *the same*?' [emphasis original] ('*Wie ist es mit den beiden Sätzen: "dieses Blatt ist rot" und "dieses Blatt hat die Farbe, die auf Deutsch 'rot' heißt"? Sagen beide* dasselbe*?*').

71 Indeed, Heidegger himself acknowledges that 'even the ontological investigation that [he] is now conducting is determined by its historical situation': Martin Heidegger, *The Basic Problems of Phenomenology*, transl. by Albert Hofstadter (Bloomington, IN: Indiana University Press, 1982), p. 22. For the original text, see *Die Grundprobleme der Phänomenologie*, in *Gesamtausgabe*, vol. XXIV (Frankfurt: Vittorio Klostermann, 1975),

in keeping truth as a heuristic goal.[72] In the words of Richard Rorty, 'how [can] ontological knowledge [...] be more than knowledge of a particular historical position?'[73]

The effort to convince others of the truth of one's interpretations must be redescribed as the effort to make them speak one's language.[74]

('The conviction that others are mistaken must be redescribed as dislike of the fact that they are different, and the desire to convince them of the truth must be redescribed as the desire to get them to be the same.'[75])

('Truth' is, ultimately, an artificial – and, often, not-so-innocent – attempt to confine contingency and creativity within set limits. It operates as an *exclusionary* tool.)

Different languages are in fact different world-views, strictly contingent and plural.

('Hebrew and German do not contradict each other, and insofar as Saint Paul's and Freud's moral vocabularies are like Hebrew and German, they don't contradict each other either [...]: they aren't disagreeing, they're just speaking different languages.'[76])

(The claim that 'in any language it is possible to express any series of ideas'[77] – which Humboldt also defends – cancels the specific sense of any assumption about

---

p. 31 ['*die ontologische Untersuchung, die wir jetzt vollziehen, ist durch ihre geschichtliche Lage bestimmt*'].

72 *Contra*: Karl-Otto Apel, 'Universal Principles and Particular Decisions and Forms of Life', in *Value and Understanding*, ed. by Raimond Gaita (London: Routledge, 1990), p. 81: '[T]he notion of a serious argumentative discourse implies the *regulative idea* of a universal consensus to be reached about all controversial validity-claims, as for example, those involving meaning, truth and even the rightness of norms' [emphasis original]. Along converging lines, see Jürgen Habermas, *Between Facts and Norms*, transl. by William Rehg (Cambridge, MA: MIT Press, 1996), p. 282: 'The law of a concrete legal community must, if it is to be legitimate, at least be compatible with moral standards that claim universal validity beyond the legal community' [1992].

73 Richard Rorty, *Essays on Heidegger and Others* (Cambridge: Cambridge University Press, 1991), p. 40.

74 See Haraway, *supra*, note 19, p. 173, who equates the 'dream of a common language' with the dream of 'a perfectly true language'.

75 Michaels, *supra*, note 43, p. 61.

76 Michaels, *supra*, note 43, pp. 45–6, referring to Rorty, *supra*, note 14, p. 5.

77 Wilhelm von Humboldt, *Ueber das vergleichende Sprachstudium in Beziehung auf die verschiedenen Epochen der Sprachentwicklung*, in *Gesammelte Schriften*, ed. by Albert Leitzmann (Berlin: B. Behr, 1905), vol. IV, p. 16 ['*in jeder (Sprache lässt sich)*

languages and world-views and shows that Humboldt's intellectual construction is not genuinely a theory.[78])

Different laws are in fact different world-views, strictly contingent and plural.

Specific languages (Babel's babblings!) – historically transmitted and irreducibly plural – prejudice one's experience through the world-views that they provide: '[T]he object of knowledge and statements is always already *enclosed* within the world horizon of language.'[79]

Specific laws – historically transmitted and irreducibly plural – prejudice one's experience through the world-views that they provide. Making Mallarmé's point again, this is why 'any comparison is, at the outset, defective' [*supra*].

To learn a new language is to adopt a new world-view. 'But because we always carry over, more or less, our own world-view, and even our own language-view, this outcome is not purely and completely experienced.'[80]

(Can a francophone ever see or hear the word 'onerous' without the word '*onéreux*' intruding?)

('Of all the stumbling blocks inherent in learning [French], the greatest for me is the principle that each noun has a corresponding sex that affects both its articles and its adjectives. [...] *Vagina* is masculine [...], while the word *masculinity* is feminine. Forced by the grammar to take a stand one way or the other, *hermaphrodite* is male and *indecisiveness* female.'[81])

---

*jede Ideenreihe ausdrücken*'] (1820). Cf. Roman Jakobson, 'On Linguistic Aspects of Translation', in *Language in Literature*, ed. by Krystyna Pomorka and Stephen Rudy (Cambridge, MA: Harvard University Press, 1987), p. 431: 'All cognitive experience and its classification is conveyable in any existing language.'

78 Cristina Lafont, *The Linguistic Turn in Hermeneutic Philosophy*, transl. by José Medina (Cambridge, MA: MIT Press, 1999), p. 37.

79 Gadamer, *Truth and Method*, *supra*, note 36, p. 450 [my emphasis]. For the original text, see *Wahrheit und Methode*, *supra*, note 36, p. 454 ['*Was Gegenstand der Erkenntnis und der Aussage ist, ist vielmehr immer schon von dem Welthorizont der Sprache umschlossen*'].

80 Humboldt, *Language*, *supra*, note 11, p. 60. For the original text, see *Kaviwerk*, *supra*, note 11, p. 60 ['*Nur weil man in eine fremde Sprache immer, mehr oder weniger, seine eigne Welt-, ja seine eigne Sprachansicht hinüberträgt, so wird dieser Erfolg nicht rein und vollständig empfunden*'].

81 David Sedaris, *Me Talk Pretty One Day* (New York: Little, Brown, 2000), p. 188 [emphasis original]. I am grateful to Dr Andreas Philippopoulos-Mihalopoulos for generously taking the time to contribute this quotation. Cf. Humboldt, *Kaviwerk*, *supra*, note 11, p. 621: 'Every language places definite boundaries upon the spirit of those who

(Research on neural mechanisms regulating the activities of different languages in bilinguals with specific reference to the inhibitory processes enabling the activation of the target language and the concurrent suppression of interaction from the language not then in use demonstrate that there is interference from the language not in use as regards the production of the target word both 'at the levels of lexical selection and phonological representation'.[82])

To learn a new law is to adopt a new world-view. Since one always carries over one's own law-view, the new standpoint is never fully experienced. Consider Montesquieu: 'If triangles created a god, they would give it three sides.'[83]

'It is enough to say that we understand in a *different* way, *if we understand at all.*'[84]

(In terms of word *vis-à-vis* world, there is always an 'excess' or a 'deficit' of meaning in the sign: whatever one refers to cannot be what one refers to, no matter how sophisticated one's language proves to be.[85] Consider Hannah Arendt: 'That the object that is there to underwrite the presentation of things can just as well be called "Tisch" or "table" means that there is something of the real essence of the things that we fabricate and name that escapes us.'[86])

---

speak it, and insofar as it provides a determinate orientation, excludes others' ['*Jede Sprache setzt dem Geiste derjenigen, welche sie sprechen, gewisse Gränzen, schliesst, insofern sie eine gewisse Richtung giebt, andre aus*'].

82 A. Rodriguez-Fornells, R. De Diego Balaguer, and T.F. Münte, 'Executive Control in Bilingual Language Processing', in *The Cognitive Neuroscience of Second Language Acquisition*, ed. by Marianne Gullberg and Peter Indefrey (Oxford: Blackwell, 2006), p. 139.

83 Montesquieu, *Lettres persanes*, in *Oeuvres complètes*, ed. by Roger Caillois, vol. I (Paris: Gallimard, 1949), LIX, p. 218 ['*si les triangles faisoient un Dieu, ils lui donneroient trois côtés*'] (1721).

84 Gadamer, *Truth and Method*, *supra*, note 36, p. 297. For the original text, see *Wahrheit und Methode*, *supra*, note 36, p. 302 ['*Es genügt zu sagen, daß man* anders *versteht,* wenn man überhaupt versteht'] (emphasis original). Cf. Humboldt, *Language*, *supra*, note 11, p. 63: 'all understanding is always at the same time a not-understanding.' For the original text, see *Kawiwerk*, *supra*, note 11, p. 64 ['*Alles Verstehen ist daher immer zugleich ein Nicht-Verstehen*'].

85 For a compelling expression of the idea that portrayal is betrayal, see José Ortega y Gasset, 'La reviviscencia de los cuadros', in *Obras completas*, vol. VIII (Madrid: Alianza Editorial, 1983), p. 493 [1946].

86 Cf. Hannah Arendt, *Denktagebuch*, ed. by Ursula Ludz and Ingeborg Nordmann, vol. I (Munich: Piper, 2002), p. 42 ['*Dadurch, dass der Gegenstand, der für das tragende Präsentieren von Dingen da ist, sowohl Tisch wie "table" heissen kann, ist angedeutet, dass uns etwas vom wahren Wesen des von uns selbst Hergestellten und Benannten entgeht*'] (1950).

('In the seventeenth century, Locke postulated [and condemned] an impossible language in which each individual thing – every stone, every bird, every branch – would have its own name; Funes once contemplated a similar language, but discarded the idea as too general, too ambiguous. [...] Two considerations dissuaded him: the realization that the task was interminable, and the realization that it was pointless. [...] [Yet,] [n]ot only was it difficult for him to see that the generic symbol "dog" took in all the dissimilar individuals of all shapes and sizes, it irritated him that the "dog" of three-fourteen in the afternoon, seen in profile, should be indicated by the same noun as the dog of three-fifteen, seen frontally.'[87])

Language is constitutive of one's relationship with world. Even access to individual experience from one's inner world can only be disclosed through language and propositional knowledge of it can only be had to the extent that the world-disclosing ability of language will allow. This is not to say that linguistic expressions must be held to determine what there is. 'Referents' exist independently of meaning and can be treated as being logically independent of any linguistic community's particular ways of conceiving them – which is to say that no 'referent' can be reduced to whatever description we offer of it (and which also means that it might be more productive not to conceptualize our accounts as 'descriptions' at all). In this respect, I agree with John Searle: '[J]ust as it does not follow from the fact that I see reality always from a point of view and under certain aspects that I never directly perceive reality, so from the fact that I must have a vocabulary in order to state the facts, or a language in order to identify and describe the facts, it simply does not follow that the facts I am describing or identifying have no independent existence.'[88] In this sense at least, world is logically independent of our ways of

87 Jorge Luis Borges, 'Funes, his Memory', in *Collected Fictions*, transl. by Andrew Huxley (New York: Penguin, 1998), p. 136 [1944]. For the original text, see *Ficciones* (Madrid: Alianza Editorial, 1995), pp. 133–4 ['*Locke, en el siglo XVII, postuló (y reprobó) un idioma imposible en el que cada cosa individual, cada piedra, cada pájaro y cada rama tuviera un nombre propio; Funes proyectó alguna vez un idioma análogo, pero lo desechó por parecerle demasiado general, demasiado ambiguo. [...] Lo disuadieron dos consideraciones: la conciencia de que la tarea era interminable, la conciencia de que era inútil. [...] No sólo le costaba comprender que el símbolo genérico* perro *abarcara tantos individuos dispares de diversos tamaños y diversa forma; le molestaba que el perro de las tres y carorce (visto de perfil) tuviera el mismo nombre que el perro de las tres y cuarto (visto de frente)*'] (emphasis original in Spanish).

88 John R. Searle, *Mind, Language, and Society* (New York: Basic Books, 1998), p. 22. Cf. Michael Dummett, *Thought and Reality* (Oxford: Oxford University Press, 2006), p. 92: 'We do not create the world; we must accept whatever it presents to us.' Indeed, 'we have no control over what we find it to be like'. Accordingly, I would disagree with those who contend that 'reality' is 'a reification of our own conceptual and cognitive nature, with no more claim to autonomy than a mirror image' as reported in Crispin Wright, *Realism, Meaning and Truth*, 2nd edn (Oxford: Blackwell, 1993), p. 2.

conceiving it. (Yet, 'the distinction between the real and the unreal and the concept of agreement with reality themselves belong to our language.'[89])

But language identifies what there *can* be for a linguistic community (or, which is another way of putting it, what a community can say that there is): language concerns the possibility of access to an understanding of an entity (and has nothing to say as regards the existence of an entity).

'[R]eference *is* nonsense except relative to a coordinate system.'[90]

(The practice of 'reference' does not presuppose the reality of one world, a single 'objective' world about which interpretations would differ. It presupposes the existence of world – which appears reasonable enough – but remains agnostic on whether one's reference to world is to the same world as other languages' references. It could very well be, but who would know?)

(Admittedly problematically, assume 'English law'. There is no way in which a French comparatist's 'English law' could legitimately be said to be referring to an 'English law' that would be the same as an Australian comparatist's 'English law', both of which would be apprehended as interpretations of something that can possibly, reasonably be said to exist as 'English law'.)

If the French language cannot say 'fairness', it does not mean that fairness does not exist in France, but that it cannot exist for this linguistic community (or that this community cannot say that fairness exists, that it cannot epistemically access fairness). So, it is not that what is, contingently, linguistically, pre-structured in each historical language determines what entities are, but that it determines what entities can be for a linguistic community, that it delineates the frontiers of scrutability of reference. (So, it is not that what is, contingently, legally, pre-structured in each historical law determines what entities are, but that it determines what entities can be for a legal community, that it delineates the frontiers of scrutability of reference.)

No interpretation of world can make world not-independent of this interpretation (in this sense, world is always constituted by interpretation, exists and can only exist intralinguistically and intratheoretically) and no interpretation of world can

89 Peter Winch, *Ethics and Action* (London: Routledge and Kegan Paul, 1972), p. 12.

90 W.V. Quine, *Ontological Relativity and Other Essays* (New York: Columbia University Press, 1969), p. 48 [hereinafter *Ontological Relativity*]. See also 'The Elusiveness of Reference', in *Sprache, Theorie und Wirklichkeit*, ed. by Michael Sukale (Frankfurt: Peter Lang, 1990), p. 22: '[M]eaning determines reference within each fixed ontology'; *Word and Object* (Cambridge, MA: MIT Press, 1960), p. 53: '[T]erms and reference are local to our conceptual scheme.'

make world not not-independent of this interpretation (world is whatever it is irrespective of whatever one says about it).

(If one wanted to understand another language, one would have to step out of one's 'own'. But, assuming this to be possible – which it is not –, one would no longer have a language with which to do any understanding.)

(Everything that is contributing to experience of world is very much a part of it. As one sees world, where one is, when one is, and who one is affects world: it is part of what world is. It is not just that reading *The Merchant of Venice* in the twenty-first as opposed to the sixteenth century does not mean the same thing. It is also that the meaning of the play varies: the mark that is the play has different meanings (or is made to perform different meanings, what the text means being subsumed by what it does). It is, therefore, that the play varies (and only in a superficial, and therefore inadequate, way is it said to be the same play). In this sense, the play is not an object. And 'objecthood' is defeated even as reading is irreducibly re-presentational: the difference between interpretations becomes a difference between plays and the difference between plays concerns a difference between the individuals who are interpreting the plays. It is not so much that there is disagreement between two individual positions since there is nothing, no fact of the matter, to disagree about (as there would be, say, if two individuals were debating the square root of 625). Rather, there is agreement about differentiation. The difference is a conflict of interpretations around determinacy/indeterminacy of meaning – what Jacques Derrida aptly calls a 'conflic[t] of force': different things are meant by those who hold one position (or speak one language) and those who hold another (or who speak another language).[91] Ultimately, the difference is a difference in what the interpreters are. It is a difference about identity.[92])

There is always, then, the *differend* between self and other.[93] (If one can only refer to world in an interpretive fashion, this means that world only acquires meaning within a differential process.[94])

91 Derrida, *supra*, note 18, p. 267 ['*conflits de fo ce*'].

92 For this argument, see Michaels, *supra*, note 43, pp. 19–81.

93 I borrow the neologism 'differend' from the English translation of Jean-François Lyotard, *Le différend* (Paris: Editions de Minuit, 1983). See *The Differend*, transl. by Georges Van Den Abbeele (Minneapolis, MN: University of Minnesota Press, 1988).

94 See Derrida, *supra*, note 18, p. 273. For an exploration of Derridean differance with specific reference to language and translation, see Kathleen Davis, *Deconstruction and Translation* (Manchester: St. Jerome Publishing, 2001), pp. 10–19.

(The differend continues even as the self purports to subject the other to the rule of his self-identity, for example through an extension of his own way of life.)[95]

(And the differend continues even as I decide that things between us cannot go any further, that your divergent view can remain what it is, for this is a determination that I make on the basis of my own set of assumptions.)

('[I]f the Arabs call Mars Qahira and the Japanese call it Kasei, they are not disagreeing. It can only make sense to say that people who give Mars different names are disagreeing if they think that the name they are giving it is not merely its name in their language but its right name – its name for itself. And even if – to imagine an instance of "cultural change" – the people who call Mars Qahira should begin calling it Kasei, it wouldn't be because they had been argued out of the old name.'[96] The process is rather one of 'resignification': 'Resignification understands giving things new names as giving them the names you want them to have, rather than as giving them what seem to you the right names.'[97])

The fact that the meaning of terms used by speakers and hearers do not coincide because of a difference in their background knowledge need not imply that they cannot be referring to the same entity. Assume a statute prohibiting the wearing of conspicuous religious signs or '*signes religieux ostensibles*' at school. The (French) speaker and the (Canadian) hearer may mean something different by '*signes religieux ostensibles*'. Let us say one means 'X' and the other means 'Y'. Yet, although no one could possibly know this, it could be that 'X' and 'Y' overlap point for point. Even the fact that the speaker's account does not coincide with the hearer's account does not mean that both accounts do not, in fact, identify overlapping 'referents' or, even, an identical 'referent' such that both interlocutors could be, strictly speaking, talking about 'the same thing' (one way of making this argument is to say that different extensions need not entail different intensions). Again, though, one could never possibly know, and one must be content with a working understanding. The fact that speaker and hearer offer different accounts (the speaker has in mind one meaning of '*signes religieux ostensibles*' and the hearer has in mind another) does not mean that there cannot be negotiation so that one can defer to the other's meaning not because it is right but as part of a process of resignification. In this sense, epistemologization of reference, that is, the thesis that 'referring' means 'identifying', is perhaps best understood as 'identifying provisionally' or 'identifying under reserve' such that any identification of 'referents' can be resignified (this seems much more reasonable than denying an

---

95 For the view that '[s]eriously to study another way of life is *necessarily* to seek to extend our own – not simply to bring the other way within the already existing boundaries of our own', see Winch, *supra*, note 89, p. 33 [my emphasis].

96 Michaels, *supra*, note 43, p. 120.

97 *Ibid.*

epistemic dimension to reference, than de-epistemologizing reference so as to make it non-epistemic, the point being that linguistic contact with the 'referent' does not necessarily exhaust the matter of epistemic contact with it).

Language being responsible for world-disclosure, that is, for the constitution of entities that can 'appear' to individuals, it predetermines what can/cannot be predicated meaningfully of these entities. Hence, it predetermines beliefs about them rather than their truth or falsity.

The hermeneutical insight into the pre-judgemental structure of understanding is not the ontologization or hypostatization of tradition as truth. For one thing, one is aware that any 'consensus' within tradition can have been achieved through distortion and compulsion. Jacques Derrida refers to 'the colonial structure of every culture' and mentions the 'terror' wrought by culture, whether 'soft, discreet, or screaming'.[98] In the words of John Caputo, 'tradition is largely the story of the winners while the dissenters have been excommunicated, torched, castrated, exiled, or imprisoned.'[99]

The normative presuppositions underlying the constitutive character of language do not imply the epistemic postulate of immediate access to the entity 'as such'. Rather, the epistemic content concerns the entity 'under a certain account'. One can meaningfully commit oneself to the existence of a 'referent', but not to the particular way in which it is described by other speakers. Consider the word 'law' envisaged as an indexical or implicitly indexical expression. It does not contain any descriptive conditions that must necessarily and sufficiently be satisfied by 'entities' in order to allow reference to them as 'law'. Reference to an 'entity' belonging to 'law' cannot be equated with ascription to it of a determinate property that would be regarded as a criterion for 'membership'. While a green lemon is still a lemon and a three-legged tiger is still a tiger, 'law' is that which bears a certain relation to 'law' *around here at this time* (to paraphrase Wittgenstein, law is what explanation of law explains).[100] In other words, law's extension is partly determined indexically but in important ways, it is fashioned culturally.

98 Jacques Derrida, *Le monolinguisme de l'autre* (Paris: Galilée, 1996), pp. 69, 45 and 45, respectively ['*la structure coloniale de toute culture*'/'*terreur*'/'*douce, discrète ou criante*'].

99 John D. Caputo, 'Gadamer's Closet Essentialism: A Derridean Critique', in *Dialogue and Deconstruction: The Gadamer-Derrida Encounter*, ed. by Diane P. Michelfelder and Richard E. Palmer (Albany, NY: State University of New York Press, 1989), p. 264.

100 I refer to the definition of 'meaning' propounded by Wittgenstein, who, in this regard, claims that 'what the explanation of meaning is […] will be the meaning': Ludwig Wittgenstein, *The Blue Book*, in *The Blue and Brown Books* (Oxford: Blackwell, 1958), p. 1 [1933].

Approaching the matter from an intercultural perspective, it is not, then, that there is not the same reality for speakers of different languages but that these speakers can only 'mean' it in idiosyncratic ways, which entails that there can be no communication across languages. Let us refer to this implication as the incommensurabilist consequence. Each language having developed through contingent historical, traditional, epistemological, social – that is, cultural – processes, there is no *characteristica universalis*.

(Gorgias's lost treatise, *On What Is Not*, 'offered proofs of three propositions: (a) nothing is; (b) even if it is, it is incomprehensible to man; (c) even if it is comprehensible, it is incommunicable to the next man' – which entails that 'speech cannot communicate the truth'.[101])

In the absence of meta-language, the differend remains immune to the logic of 'objective' adjudication and cannot be brought to the bar of some tribunal of universal rationality. The differend is not truth-apt. It is, in fact, an abyss.[102]

I apprehend the articulation of difference as suspended in a spectral dimension between presence – what one sees (for example, the signifier) – and absence – what one does not see, but what is there nonetheless (for example, the *trace*, be it 'historical', 'economic', 'sociological', or whatever, which an archival *analysis* can elucidate).[103] (Here, 'analysis' follows '[t]he most ancient usage', that which, according to Heidegger, can be found in Homer's *Odyssey* and which refers to 'what Penelope did night by night, namely, unravel the fabric she had woven during the day'.[104] Cf. 'comparative *analysis* of law', that is, comparison-at-law as an unweaving, dismantling, unbinding, emancipating, liberating intervention

101 D.M. MacDowell, 'Introduction', in Gorgias, *supra*, note 9, pp. 11 and 14, respectively.

102 The word 'abyss' ('*Abgrund*') appears in Celan's correspondence with specific reference to the separation between languages: Lyon, *supra*, note 31, p. 37.

103 For an exploration of 'difference' within comparative legal studies, see Pierre Legrand, 'The Same and the Different', in *Comparative Legal Studies: Traditions and Transitions*, ed. by Pierre Legrand and Roderick Munday (Cambridge: Cambridge University Press, 2003), pp. 240–311 [hereinafter *Same and Different*]; Pierre Legrand, 'Sur l'analyse différentielle des juriscultures', *Revue internationale de droit comparé*, 1999, p. 1053. See also Pierre Legrand, 'On the Singularity of Law', 47 *Harvard International Law Journal* 517 (2006) [hereinafter 'Singularity']. The notions of 'spectrality' and 'trace' are, of course, key Derridean motifs.

104 Martin Heidegger, *Zollikon Seminars*, ed. by Medard Boss and transl. by Franz Mayr and Richard Askay (Evanston, IL: Northwestern University Press, 2001), p. 114 [23 November 1965]. For the original text, see *Zollikoner Seminare*, ed. by Medard Boss (Frankfurt: Vittorio Klostermann, 1987), p. 148 ['*(Der älteste Gebrauch des Wortes Analyse) wird dort gebraucht für das, was Penelope nächtlich tut, nämlich für ihr Auflösen des Gewebes, das sie tagsüber gewebt hatte*'].

– and, therefore, as a risk.) Difference marks relatedness ('A' is different *from* 'B'), which is a connection.[105] Against that background, I approach incommensurability as being primordially a relational concept which concerns the intrinsic flux and tension between differentials of force.

(The comparatist-at-law bears witness to the differend. He acknowledges singularity – although he knows that it must remain opaque to language since no language can account for singularity – and strives to give expression to the discontinuity of experience, thereby revealing an ethical commitment to recognition and respect.)

(Note that there is nothing here to suggest that the differend is immune to critique. The point, though, is that because any understanding is a 'participating understanding' ['*teilnehmende(s) Verstehen*'],[106] whatever critique is brought to bear is *situated*.)

Incommensurability is the unthought of law. As such, the fact of linguistic incommensurability remains unacknowledged,[107] as does the fact of legal incommensurability.[108] But this reaction is complex, for lawyers, just as they overlook linguistic and legal incommensurability, simultaneously register it. Thus, linguistic and legal incommensurability is at once (empirically) present and (ideologically) absent. In other words, lawyers know how languages and laws differ, but act as if they did not know it: knowledge and not-knowledge are, somewhat perversely, operating concurrently. This oscillation between the fact of incommensurability, on the one hand, and the fantasy of translatability/communicability applied like a patch on the fact of incommensurability found to be ideologically objectionable, on the other hand, offers an illustration of what Freud, examining one's relation to world, called 'ego-splitting' ('*Ichspaltung*').[109] But why the disavowal of incommensurability? Why the rejection of the differend? Freud

---

105 See Gilles Deleuze, *Différence et répétition* (Paris: Le Seuil, 1968), p. 154, who observes that 'difference relates immediately to one another the terms that differ' ['*la différence rapporte immédiatement les uns aux autres les termes qui diffèrent*'].

106 Bultmann, *supra*, note 33, p. 221.

107 But see Simone Glanert, 'Zur Sprache gebracht: Rechtsvereinheitlichung in Europa', (2006) 14 *European Review of Private Law* 157; 'La langue en héritage: réflexions sur l'uniformisation des droits en Europe', *Revue internationale de droit comparé*, 2006, p. 1231.

108 See Pierre Legrand, 'Comparative Legal Studies and the Matter of Authenticity', (2006) 1 *Journal of Comparative Law* 365.

109 For example, see Sigmund Freud, 'Splitting of the Ego in the Process of Defence', in *The Standard Edition of the Complete Psychological Works of Sigmund Freud*, transl. by James Strachey, vol. XXIII (London: Hogarth Press, 1964), pp. 271–8 [†1940]. For the original text, see *Die Ichspaltung im Abwehrvorgang*, in *Gesammelte Werke*, vol. XVII (Frankfurt: S. Fischer, 1941), pp. 57–62.

famously claimed that the source of this resistance was 'unknown'.[110] I argue that the key to an understanding of the negative apprehension of the differend lies in the fact that what Jacques Derrida terms 'differance' ('*différance*') – understood here as the force that generates effects of difference – is regarded as strange/uncanny and generates fear and hostility.[111] Indeed, Nietzsche refers to 'injury, assault, exploitation, destruction' being intrinsic to difference.[112] The generally defensive response to differentiation must be envisaged in relation to the way in which, on account of the interpellation generated by 'more-than-one' meaning, difference as it is brought to the psyche is linked to the tension and pain that are congruent with upheaval (of one's fixity of meaning) and indeterminacy (of meaning).

An encounter with what is other than oneself (the differentiating other) is primordially uncanny. Since the other is not part of what I consciously consider to be my self and yet since it emerges from within me (*I* see it), it has to provoke the feeling that it is at once 'not-me' and 'me'. It leaves one structurally undecided about whether the other means 'x' or 'not-x'. It leaves one vertiginously undecided in relation to the most basic question: Is it me? Is it not me? *What about me?*

(An elderly gentleman, Uncle Theo, is sitting with his twin niece and nephew while they play on the seashore. The beach is a source of acute discomfort to Uncle Theo. Although the children's noise and exuberance bother him, what really makes Uncle Theo most anxious is the manifold variety of things. As if twinness was not enough of an ontological disturbance, there are all those pebbles on the beach. Because each pebble is clamouring in its particularity, the totality of them is threatening the intelligibility and the manageability of world. Uncle Theo is a man who can only negotiate the possibility of plurality if the many can be reduced to a few or, best of all, to one. While the twins display a childlike delight in variety, Uncle Theo exhibits a plethoraphobic distaste for multiplicity and randomness. His preoccupation with perceptual and conceptual tidiness shows Uncle Theo as the

110 Sigmund Freud, *Group Psychology and the Analysis of the Ego*, in *The Standard Edition of the Complete Psychological Works of Sigmund Freud*, transl. by James Strachey, vol. XVIII (London: Hogarth Press, 1955), p. 102 [1921]. For the original text, see *Massenpsychologie und Ich-Analyse*, in *Gesammelte Werke*, vol. XVII (Frankfurt: S. Fischer, 1941), p. 111 ['*unbekannt*'].

111 For a sophisticated investigation of the motifs of 'difference' and 'differance' in Derrida's work, see Rodolphe Gasché, *Inventions of Difference* (Cambridge, MA: Harvard University Press, 1994).

112 Friedrich Nietzsche, *On the Genealogy of Morals*, ed. by Walter Kaufmann and transl. by Walter Kaufmann and R.J. Hollingdale (New York: Vintage, 1989), p. 76 [1887] (hereinafter *Genealogy*). For the original text, see *Zur Genealogie der Moral*, in *Werke*, ed. by Giorgio Colli and Mazzino Montinari, vol. VI/2 (Berlin: Walter de Gruyter, 1968), p. 328 ['*ein Verletzen, Vergewaltigen, Ausbeuten, Vernichten*'] (hereinafter *Genealogie*).

typical lawyer, that is, as someone who is dismayed and disturbed by difference, who *wishes it away*.[113])

'The law becomes a sort of reality imposed upon the social data, shaping it, and becoming in the end more "real" than the facts.'[114]

Anchoring themselves firmly in nonrelatedness to world,[115] lawyers earnestly seek tranquillization against any differential disruption wrought by the insistent existentiality of languages and laws. Freud refers to 'Eros' – or the pleasure principle – as 'the force that introduces disturbances into the process of life'.[116]

Specifically, there is (or there must be) one-law, the matter of the language or languages in which this one-law is written somehow, in lawyers' eyes, not affecting the 'oneness' sought by them. It is as if the oneness of law, by virtue of the intellectual and aesthetic authority it is deemed to command, expelled linguistic pluralism from the realm of relevance and conferred upon it a kind of 'excremental' value.[117] One-law is here revealed as an inherently theological

---

113 Iris Murdoch, *The Nice and the Good* (London: Vintage, 2000), pp. 152–3 [1968]. I follow closely Elizabeth V. Spelman, *Inessential Woman* (London: Women's Press, 1988), pp. 1–2.

114 Jacques Ellul, *Histoire des institutions*, 9th edn, vol. III (Paris: Presses Universitaires de France, 1982), p. 27 ['*Le droit devient une sorte de réalité imposée au donné social, le mettant en forme, et finissant en somme par devenir plus "vrai" que les faits*']. Cf. D.50.17.207: 'A matter judicially decided is treated as true' ['*Res judicata pro veritate accipitur*']. My quotation is based on *The Digest of Justinian*, ed. by Alan Watson and transl. by various authors, vol. IV (Philadelphia, PA: University of Pennsylvania Press, 1985), p. 969 [533].

115 For example, see Pierre Schlag, *The Enchantment of Reason* (Durham, NC: Duke University Press, 1998), p. 128: 'Not only must the legal self be severed from its objects of inquiry, but it must also be separated from its formative and environmental contexts.' See also Theodor W. Adorno, *Negative Dialectics* (London: Routledge, 1973), p. 309: 'For the sake of an unbroken systematic, the legal norms cut short what is not covered, every specific experience that has not been shaped in advance; and then they raise the instrumental rationality to the rank of a second reality *sui generis*' [1966]. For the original text, see *Negative Dialektik* (Frankfurt: Suhrkamp, 1966), p. 304 ['*Die Rechtsnormen schneiden das nicht Gedeckte, jede nicht präformierte Erfahrung des Spezifischen um bruchloser Systematik willen ab und erheben dann die instrumentale Rationalität zu einer zweiten Wirklichkeit sui generis*'].

116 Sigmund Freud, *The Ego and the Id*, in *The Standard Edition of the Complete Psychological Works of Sigmund Freud*, transl. by James Strachey, vol. XIX (London: Hogarth Press, 1961), pp. 46–7 [1923]. For the original text, see *Das Ich und das Es*, in *Gesammelte Werke*, vol. XIII (Frankfurt: S. Fischer, 1940), p. 275 ['*die Libido (...), die Störungen in den Lebensablauf einführt*'].

117 See Claude Lévesque, 'Au nom du réel', in *Jacques Derrida*, ed. by Marie-Louise Mallet and Ginette Michaud (Paris: L'Herne, 2004), pp. 215–16.

enterprise, a religion as closed system basing itself on an axiomatics, expressing itself apodictically, resting on a neo-Kantian distinction between the true and apparent worlds,[118] a dogma that cannot question its faith in unity and which, therefore, halts before the factual and renounces the challenge of facticity.[119] This commitment to one-law involves a fetishistic process, a kind of compromise with world: it repudiates the registered multiplicity within world and the corollary requirement for interpretation of proliferous meaning (a fact) and substitutes for it willed unity and the corresponding expectation of fixity of meaning (a fantasy). Making a positivistic or formalistic move, lawyers locate truth in translatability (which is a variation on the theme of linguistic monism) and in communicability (which is also a variation on the theme of linguistic identity). One-law thus

---

118 According to Ugo Mattei, there exists, and there can be discovered, a 'common core of efficient principles hidden in the different technicalities of [...] legal systems': *Comparative Law and Economics* (Ann Arbor, MI: University of Michigan Press, 1997), p. 144. *Adde*: Mauro Bussani and Ugo Mattei, 'The Common Core Approach to European Private Law', 3 *Columbia Journal of European Law* 339 (1997–98), p. 340: '[C]ommon core research is a very promising tool for unearthing deeper analogies hidden by formal differences.'

119 For a formulation of this aspiration to unity which takes the form of a desire to kill proliferation of meaning within local law, see Rodolfo Sacco, *Introduzione al diritto comparato*, 5th edn (Torino: UTET, 1992), p. 47: 'One tends to see, within a legal order, the will of the legislator, who creates the norm, and scholarship and judicial decisions that interpret and apply this will. In principle, the various rules (legal, scholarly, or judicial) should be identical. If there is a difference, it must be ascribed to an error on the part of the interpreter' ['*si tende a vedere, all'interno di un ordinamento, una volontà del legislatore, che crea la norma, e una dottrina ed una giurisprudenza che interpretano e applicano questa volontà. Le varie regole (legale, dottrinale, giudiziaria) sarebbero, in via di principio, identiche. Se una difformità esiste, ciò si deve imputare ad un errore dell'interprete*']. As Sacco underlines, '[t]his course of logic is of no use to the comparatist' ['*Questo iter logico non è fruibile dal comparatista*']. If comparatists-at-law pursue this unitary drive, the deterritorialization that they are claiming becomes strictly territorial (they are indeed looking beyond national law) and not at all intellectual (they are acting like national lawyers). This deterritorialization, then, becomes a 'false exit': Jacques Derrida, *Marges – de la philosophie* (Paris: Editions de Minuit, 1972), p. 162 ['*fausse sortie*'].

decreases the tension and avoids the pain associated with difference.[120] There is at work a massive tension-reducing pleasure principle.[121]

For Lacan, there exists a constitutive antagonism lying at the heart of identity that concerns the Other rather than the other. One may find that the other's contribution is enriching (consider the other's culture or language), while showing, for instance at the political level, a fierce resistance to pluralism. This is because there is the Other, inherently inhuman – and thus unpersonalizable or resolutely abstract – and unerasable. While the individual can achieve an attenuation of the space that divides him from the other, his relation with the Other is insusceptible of this kind of accommodation. It is indeed the irreducibility of the Other that grounds the psychoanalytical conception of the unconscious. In the words of Lacan, 'the unconscious is the discourse of the Other.'[122] This Other is the symbolic Other that impinges upon the subjectivity of the individual, that deprives him of his pleasure. And this symbolic Other is the order of language, which organizes itself according to its internal articulations in a realm apart from the individual, from which the individual is excluded (although he is represented therein, for instance on account of the pronoun 'I'), but through which the individual constructs himself: 'Symbols embrace the life of man in a network so complete that they join those who will engender him "through bone and flesh" before he comes into the world, that they bring upon his birth with the gifts from the stars, if not with the gifts from the fairies, the design of his destiny.'[123] What would be traces of the Other, this pseudo-person who begets language?[124] Consider how the frustration of desire is located in a primordial impossibility since the perfect coincidence between desire and its

120 Famously, Descartes excluded all facticity in order to sustain the view that a piece of wax that 'has just been taken from the honeycomb' and that has subsequently been put 'by the fire' remains the same wax: 'Any doubt on this issue would clearly be foolish.' I have explored the connection between such anti-heterogeneous scientificization and the adjudicative work of the French *Cour de cassation* in Pierre Legrand, 'Perspectives du dehors sur le civilisme français', in *Le droit civil, avant tout un style?*, ed. by Nicholas Kasirer (Montreal: Thémis, 2003), pp. 153–83. The quotations are borrowed from René Descartes, *Meditations on First Philosophy*, ed. and transl. by John Cottingham (Cambridge: Cambridge University Press, 1996), pp. 20 and 22 [1641]. The text originally appeared in Latin.

121 I have addressed this matter elsewhere: Pierre Legrand, 'The Return of the Repressed: Moving Comparative Legal Studies Beyond Pleasure', 75 *Tulane Law Review* 1033 (2001).

122 Lacan, *supra*, note 24, p. 16 ['*l'inconscient, c'est le discours de l'Autre*'] (emphasis omitted).

123 Lacan, *supra*, note 24, p. 279 ['*Les symboles enveloppent en effet la vie de l'homme d'un réseau si total qu'ils conjoignent avant qu'il vienne au monde ceux qui vont l'engendrer "par l'os et par la chair", qu'ils apportent à sa naissance avec les dons des astres, sinon avec les dons des fées, le dessin de sa destinée*'].

124 Lacan, *supra*, note 24, p. 9.

object can only be a myth: there is the incapacity for the individual to express what he wants to say. Thus, the autonomy of the individual is under threat since all must go 'through the parades of the signifier'.[125] It is because the self confuses the Other and the other that he comes to think that it is the other who has deprived him of what he is missing and to feel resentment towards him. While it is language which is in effect depriving him, the individual gets to think that he must blame the other.

As much as the intense anxiety experienced by lawyers may make translatability/communicability feel like a fact, it remains a fantasy. Linguistic incommensurability is actively differentiating and generates a factical fragmentation that lawyers do not want to see. Preferring the flight from the anxiety generated by facticity, choosing to move away from integration with environment, from a bindingness with world that raises tension levels, from relation (again, difference is a force of relation), lawyers refuse to internalize difference (it would cause anguish) and choose to engage in dedifferentiation as a kind of auto-immune response to world, as a counterpoint to the trauma wrought by the life of languages,[126] as a denial of the vital differences that emerge from the fact of languages in world (again, each difference is a force). In the end, lawyers display a submissive, nihilistic attitude to life: they evince a desire for an ascetic ideal, for a nondifferentiated state of rest or equilibrium, a kind of world-negating principle, a oneness which is also a nothingness, a '*degré zéro*' of complexity.

The lawyers' 'no' to world, or to life, boasts ancient antecedents. Consider the Platonic notion of ideal forms situated in a supersensuous beyond. This philosophical doctrine is at the root of all devaluations of the sensuous, its most important offspring being Christianity.[127] Now, as soon as a supersensuous beyond

125 Lacan, *supra*, note 24, p. 628 ['*par les défilés du signifian*']. See generally Jacques Lacan, *Le séminaire*, vol. XVI: *D'un Autre à l'autre*, ed. by J-A. Miller (Paris: Le Seuil, 2006).

126 For an excellent illustration of this intellectual and emotional move, see Jean-Paul Sartre, *Nausea*, transl. by Lloyd Alexander (New York: New Directions, 1964), pp. 126–32 [1938]. I address this text in relation to the French *Cour de cassation*'s apodictic strategy in Legrand, *supra*, note 120.

127 For an argument to the effect that the history of philosophy in the West is the history of a philosophy of the same whose hidden purpose has always been to find a means to attenuate the shock of alterity, see Paul Feyerabend, *Farewell to Reason* (London: Verso, 1987), p. 116: 'Almost all [philosophers] praised oneness (or, to use a better word, monotony) and denounced abundance. Xenophanes rejected the gods of tradition and introduced a single faceless god-monster. Heraclitus heaped scorn on *polymathi'e*, the rich and complex information that had been assembled by commonsense, artisans and his own philosophical predecessors, and insisted that "what is Wise is One". Parmenides argued against change and qualitative difference and postulated a stable and indivisible block of Being as the foundation of all existence. Empedocles replaced traditional information about

is posited, true value (or the value of truth) finds itself rooted in the beyond. When ultimate value (whether in Platonic or Christian terms) is located in the nonmaterial beyond, life itself, in all its variegated manifestations, becomes the negative fall away from the good – hence, the familiar condemnation of the sensuous, of the body and sexuality, of facticity, of diversity, of difference. Unity becomes the original good lost in the fall into the body and its hunger (showing itself through the drives). Ideals (say, 'one-law') appear as a defensive distortion of the drives, that is, they allow the good to be interpreted as a reaction against the bad of the drives (and of the body and of life).[128] Through the 'artifice' of the ideal,[129] through the oblivion of facticity, life moves away from the 'yes' to 'more-than-oneness' or difference, which is also a 'yes' to pain, as absence of suffering becomes the supreme good.[130] A 'yes' to ideals is a 'no' to multiplicity or difference, that is, to pain. It is a 'no' to facticity, to all the factical traces that are symptomatic of linguistic incommensurability. It is a move away from the uninterpretability-as-one built into difference. It is also a move away from the encounter with the impossibility or the limit of the interpretation of difference.[131]

---

the nature of diseases by a short, useless but universal definition. Thucydides criticized Herodotus's stylistic pluralism and insisted on a uniform causal account. Plato opposed the political pluralism of democracy, rejected the view of tragedians such as Sophocles that (ethical) conflicts might be unresolvable by "rational" means, criticized astronomers who tried to explore the heavens in an empirical way and suggested tying all subjects to a single theoretical basis.' See also Emmanuel Levinas, *En découvrant l'existence avec Husserl et Heidegger*, 3rd edn (Paris: Vrin, 2001), pp. 261–82. Indeed, for all their critical edge, even Heidegger's ontological analysis of 'Being' and Gadamer's reconciliative hermeneutics ultimately fail to escape this pattern. But see, for a very influential interpretation of Nietzsche as a philosopher of difference, Gilles Deleuze, *Nietzsche et la philosophie*, 3rd edn (Paris: Presses Universitaires de France, 1999) [1962].

128 See Paul Ricoeur, *De l'interprétation* (Paris: Le Seuil, 1965), pp. 40–44.

129 Nietzsche, *Genealogy*, *supra*, note 112, p. 120. For the original text, see *Genealogie*, *supra*, note 112, p. 384 ['*ein Kunstgriff*'].

130 See Nietzsche, *Genealogy*, *supra*, note 112, pp. 129–34.

131 Historically, laws derived from the Roman model have favoured a monistic framework. On the understanding that if law is interpreted there is differentiation, interpretation (specifically, judicial and scholarly interpretation) has been devalued and denied. Already, the Digest deemed itself uninterpretable. See generally Fritz Pringsheim, 'Justinian's Prohibition of Commentaries to the Digest', in *Gesammelte Abhandlungen*, vol. II (Heidelberg: Carl Winter, 1961), pp. 86–106 [1950]. Other notable statements against interpretation include the injunction of *conseiller d'Etat* Pussort in his 1665 memorandum to Louis XIV: 'To prohibit the reference to any statute or ordinance other than the new one after its publication; the making of any annotation, commentary or collection of cases, under pain of punishment' ['*Défendre de citer aucune loy ou ordonnance autre que la nouvelle après sa publication; de faire aucune note, commentaire, ni recueil d'arrests, à peine de punition*']. For a fuller exposition of the memorandum, see Jacques Vanderlinden, *Le concept de code en Europe occidentale du XIIIe au XIXe siècle* (Brussels: Editions de l'Institut de Sociologie de l'Université Libre de Bruxelles, 1967), p. 360. A further opinion

along these lines surfaced in von Cocceji's draft *Corpus Juris Fridericianum* of 1749: *Code Fréderic*, trans. from the German by A.A. de C.[ampagne], vol. I (n.pl.: n.publ., 1751), part I, bk I, tit. II, art. 10: 'We prohibit the making [*sic*] commentaries or dissertations on the whole body of law, or on any part of it. For most commentators, ignorant of the spirit and reason of the law, only occasion useless disputes.' The text is lifted from the English translation which, based on the French text, was published as *The Frederician Code*, vol. I (London: Richardson, 1761). Contempt for interpretation is possibly nowhere more apparent than in a royal cabinet order dated 14 April 1780, where Frederick the Great refers in the same breath to 'learned law' ('*Rechtsgelehrten*') and 'junk full of subtleties' ('*Subtilitatenkram*'): *Corpus Juris Fridericianum* (Berlin: Königlichen Akademie der Wissenschaften, 1781), p. xii. Indeed, the apotheosis of Frederick's casuistic enterprise, the *Allgemeines Landrecht für die preußischen Staaten* of 1794, made it clear that scholarship remained out of favour: 'Of the opinions of scholars, or of the old remarks of judges, no consideration shall be taken for future decisions.' For the original text, see *Allgemeines Landrecht für die preußischen Staaten*, ed. by C.J. Koch, vol. I (Berlin: Guttentag, 1878), 'Einleitung', art. 6 [old art. 8], p. 22 ['*Auf Meinungen der Rechtslehrer, oder ältere Aussprüche der Richter soll, bei künftigen Entscheidungen, keine Rücksicht genommen werden*']. Napoleon is reputed, upon the appearance but a few years later of the first scholarly commentary on the French *Code civil*, to have exclaimed, 'My code is lost' ('*Mon code est perdu*'). I have been unable to find any reference to support the claim. What is clear, according to Las Cases, one of Napoleon's companions on St Helena, is that the Emperor was less than enthusiastic toward the whole idea of scholarly commentaries. For views attributed to Napoleon, see [E.] de Las Cases, *Mémorial de Sainte-Hélène: Journal de la vie privée et des conversations de l'empereur Napoléon à Sainte Hélène*, vol. III (London: Colburn/Bossange, 1823), VI, p. 235: 'No sooner had the code appeared that it was followed almost immediately, as if by way of supplement, by commentaries, explanations, developments, interpretations, and what not! And I used to exclaim: Sirs, we have cleansed the Augean stables, in the name of God let us not fill them once again!' ['*A peine le code eut paru, qu'il fut suivi presque aussitôt, et comme en supplément, de commentaires, d'explications, de développemens, d'interprétations, que sais-je? Et j'avais coutume de m'écrier: Eh! Messieurs, nous avons nettoyé l'écurie d'Augias, pour Dieu ne l'encombrons pas de nouveau*']. In France, more than two hundred and fifty years after Montesquieu ('the judges of the nation are but the mouthpieces that utter the words of the law, inanimate beings that can modify neither its strength nor its rigour': *De l'esprit des lois*, in *Oeuvres complètes*, ed. by Roger Caillois, vol. II [Paris: Gallimard, 1951], bk XI, ch. 6, p. 404 [1748] ['*les juges de la nation ne sont (...) que la bouche qui prononce les paroles de la loi; des êtres inanimés qui n'en peuvent modérer ni la force ni la rigueur*']), nearly two hundred years after Royer-Collard ('The only true judgments are those that are inscribed in advance in the statutes': [Prosper] de Barante, *La vie politique de M. Royer-Collard*, 2nd edn, vol. I (Paris: Didier, 1863), p. 347 [1817] ['*Il n'y a de vrais jugements que ceux qui sont écrits d'avance dans les lois*']), the position remains 'an administrative conception of the judge': Pierre Legendre, 'Qui dit légiste, dit loi et pouvoir', *Politix*, 1995, no. 32, pp. 30–31 ['*une conception administrative du juge*']. For a discussion of codification as a means for 'the political power of the state to assert a central will uniformly in the whole of the community', see Csaba Varga, *Codification as a Socio-historical Phenomenon*, transl. by Sándor Eszenyi et al. (Budapest: Akadémiai Kiadó, 1991), p. 334. 'Codification has to do with discipline': Pierre Bourdieu, *Choses dites*

In a very important sense, though, a 'no' to difference – that is, to the life of languages – wishes to be transmuted into a 'yes' to life itself. In the end, this is why 'slave morality' (Nietzsche's formula) says '[n]o to what is "outside", what is "different", what is "not itself"',[132] why it is opposed to any noble affirmation of difference, that is, of the sensuous, such that any affirmation of difference becomes evil for the slave. Along the way, the ideal purports to cancel hermeneutics – the brand of hermeneutics-as-energetics that cannot be divorced from the drives, since it is required to ascribe meaning to (variegated) world, and that is no longer required in the realm of ideals. (As Paul Ricoeur reminds us, hermeneutics is not only motivated by 'obedience' but also by 'suspicion', by a desire to challenge meaning – a 'destructive' and 'iconoclastic' vocation that can only sit uneasily with the proponents of 'no-difference'.[133])

Nietzsche perspicuously observes that ideals have been around for a long time. Given that this is the case, he surmises that there must be a necessity of the first order within life itself promoting this '*life-inimical* species',[134] prompting life to 'turn against itself, *deny itself*'.[135] Nietzsche's conclusion is that through the ideal, life wishes to protect itself from itself. Thus, the ideal emerges as a conserving or 'yes'-force of life,[136] something which assumes a strategy of dedifferentiation.[137]

(Paris: Editions de Minuit, 1987), p. 98 ['*La codification a partie liée avec la discipline*']. Most fascinatingly, interpretation is resisted by the interpreters themselves. But see, for a denunciation of the 'connivance' ('*connivence*') between scholars and the lawmaker and a critique of scholarship's predilection for a monistic approach to law, Philippe Jestaz and Christophe Jamin, 'L'entité doctrinale française', D.1997.Chron.167, p. 172. For a reply, see Laurent Aynès, Pierre-Yves Gautier and François Terré, 'Antithèse de "l'entité"', D.1997. Chron.229: *Quod erat demonstrandum.*

132 Nietzsche, *Genealogy*, *supra*, note 112, p. 36. For the original text, see *Genealogie*, *supra*, note 112, p. 284 ['*Nein zu einem "Ausserhalb", zu einem "Anders", zu einem "Nicht-selbst"*'].

133 Ricoeur, *supra*, note 128, p. 36 ['*obéissance*'/'*soupçon*'/'*destructeur*'/ '*iconoclaste*'].

134 Nietzsche, *Genealogy*, *supra*, note 112, p. 117 [emphasis original in English]. For the original text, see *Genealogie*, *supra*, note 112, p. 381 ['*diese lebensfeindliche Species*'].

135 Nietzsche, *Genealogy*, *supra*, note 112, p. 117 [emphasis original in English]. For the original text, see *Genealogie*, *supra*, note 112, p. 380 ['*es sei denn, dass es sich etwa gegen sich selber wende, sich selbst verneine*'].

136 See Nietzsche, *Genealogy*, *supra*, note 112, pp. 120–21.

137 Indeed, so powerful is this ideal that even comparatists-at-law whose very *raison d'être* lies in diversity, espouse the goal. I illustrate this specific commitment in Legrand, 'Same and Different', *supra*, note 103, pp. 245–50. It is still fair to say that within comparative legal studies, registration and repudiation of difference remains the basic unconscious – and not-so-unconscious – process at work, no more so than when a comparatist observes 'how similar our laws on tort are or, more accurately, how similar they can be made to look with the help of some skilful (and well-meaning) manipulation': Basil

(Nietzsche adds, though, that on account of the ideal, the individual wish to preserve oneself by avoiding pain simultaneously emerges as 'a limitation of the really fundamental instinct of life which aims at *the expansion of power*' – something which, in effect, only *opening oneself to pain, raising tension*, will ultimately allow.[138])

(Correlatively, the differentialists' dissatisfaction with idealists aims to be turned against the differentialists themselves: 'the direction of *ressentiment* is *altered*.'[139] In this way, the differentialists' instincts are kept in check – one is reminded of Freud's 'superego', which features both an opposition to sexuality and the internalized destructiveness of guilt. The way in which the defenders of a Europe of multiple laws are branded as bad Europeans is one example of the manner in which advocates of multiplicity/difference are made to suffer from guilt or bad consciousness.)

Assume a meeting of different forces, say, the force of resistance to pluralism versus the force of what this resistance encounters. How does the law-mind typically react to the differentiating opening of pathways (in Freud's parlance, '*Bahnungen*')?[140] The abundance of pathways generates an increase of tension, a pain, which itself prompts an automatic unconscious tendency to relieve such tension via the pathway already opened, that is, already familiar to one. Mental energy wishes to travel down the pathway of the experience of satisfaction, which here must mean one-law. As it leaves behind the abundance of pathways and its attendant tension, one-law thus becomes tension-relieving or trauma-relieving law. The conscious association of perception (of one-law) with tension relief becomes a function of the (conscious or unconscious) elimination of the prior, tension-raising opening of differential pathways (that is, other laws). Through one-law, lawyers seek an 'unbinding' from world (which must also be understood as a discharge of tension). The 'bindingness' with world had raised tension levels. 'Unbinding' from world – that is, finding refuge in an 'artificial' or utopian one-law – is very

S. Markesinis, 'Why a Code is Not the Best Way to Advance the Cause of European Legal Unity', (1997) 5 *European Review of Private Law* 519, p. 520.

138 Nietzsche, *Gay Science*, *supra*, note 17, V, § 349, p. 291 [emphasis original in English]. For the original text, see *Fröhliche Wissenschaft*, *supra*, note 17, p. 267 ['*einer Einschränkung des eigentlichen Lebens-Grundtriebes, der auf Machterweiterung hinausgeht*'].

139 Nietzsche, *Genealogy*, *supra*, note 112, p. 128 [emphasis original in English]. For the original text, see *Genealogie*, *supra*, note 112, p. 393 ['*die Richtung des Ressentiment (ist) verändert*'].

140 See Sigmund Freud, *Project for a Scientific Psychology*, in *The Standard Edition of the Complete Psychological Works of Sigmund Freud*, transl. by James Strachey, vol. I (London: Hogarth Press, 1966), pp. 295–343, *passim* [1895/†1950]. For the original text, see *Entwurf einer Psychologie*, in *Gesammelte Werke*, vol. XIX (Frankfurt: S. Fischer, 1987), pp. 373–486, *passim*.

much a discharge of tension. It is a conversion of energetics into unbindingness. The tension-relieving effect depends on perceptual identity in the sense that only perception of 'oneness' can prompt the (sentiment that there has been) elimination of difference. (Observe that the awakening of consciousness about the virtues of one-law, including tension-relief, depends on the very differentiating process that it seeks to eliminate.)

Evidently, there can be no question of leaving local laws to stand in juxtaposition as so many monads for although law is nowhere but in its inscription it cannot be reduced to that inscription. The goal for comparatists-at-law must thus be to 're-inscribe' (or 'deconstruct') the locality of law beyond any spatio-temporal facticity (and to do so at another level than the metaphysical, whether celestial or tellurian) in order to make it amenable to cross-legal/cross-cultural/cross-traditional negotiation. Quite apart from partaking in an inexhaustible quest the outcome of which is marked by the comparatist's exhaustion (or the editor's final deadline), this process of 're-inscription' is, of course, an act of violence. But it is emphatically a 'lesser' violence than that wrought on the 'legal' by the metaphysician masquerading as comparatist-at-law and wielding the sticks of deracination and transcendentalization (or is it panoptic control?) through the invocation of a *praesumptio similitudinis* that is but the dedifferentiating positing of an identification which conceals its own violence-as- concealment (of the traces).

The alternative 'model' thus demands sensitivity to the matter of alterity without renouncing the ambition of knowledge. It must eschew the semblance of understanding that comes with the re-presentation of otherness-in-the-law in familiar, domestic terms, something which – under the guise of 'dialogue' – is an inadvertent invitation to the subjugation of others into a frame of reference that is actually alien to them and that can only result in the distortion of cultural meaning. A key point that must be readily appreciated is that I am not addressing this question in terms of any specific individual's idiosyncratic subjectivity – the kind of subjectivity that could be avoided if one did one's homework properly with a competent dose of fair-mindedness. The understanding into which the other is appropriated is not locked into the consciousness of an individual subject such that it would be of the appropriating individual's own making. When the interpreter comes to the other's law and purports to make sense of it, the anticipation of meaning that he brings to bear to the act of ascription is, in fact, profoundly historical and, in that sense, deeply traditional. The meanings that the interpreter brings to the act of interpretation were internalized by him as he was thrown into a tradition (linguistic, legal, and otherwise) that constituted him as the individual that he is (and as a member of the tradition). The basic point is that the individual's sphere of understanding is, in important ways, inherited and that it arises irrespective of any subjective preferences. One can, in fact, take matters one step further. Understanding does not emerge despite this historical situatedness or traditionary embeddedness but is made possible because of it. How could any understanding happen without anticipation of meaning? And how could there be anticipation of meaning without belongingness to a tradition or culture? 'An expectation is embedded in a situation from which it takes its rise.'[141] This is, if you like, the work of history. But, of course, the basic question resurfaces. If history works to fashion my understanding of the world, how can I ever make sense of a law having come from 'elsewhere' (i.e., from another language, another history, another set of institutions, another array of social practices) other than on perspectival terms? The complication is compounded by the fact that foreign law too partakes in a vantage point that was shaped by a history, a politics, a society, and so forth. How can foreign law, which is situated, be accessible to my understanding which is itself situated, albeit within a different episteme? In other words, how can inter-traditional or inter-cultural understanding happen? 'The great problem in [...] a hermeneutical approach [when the distance to overcome, needed for any understanding, is not just a distance within one single culture (...) or a temporal one (...), but rather the distance between two (or more) cultures, which have independently developed in different spaces (*topoi*) their own methods of philosophizing and ways of reaching intelligibility along with their proper categories] is the peculiar type of preunderstanding necessary to cross the boundaries of one's own philosophical world.'[142] Something like this difficulty already exists within a single culture. But, according to my hypothesis, we have something specifically different. Here, comparatists-at-law find themselves operating under a different *mythos* or horizon of intelligibility. Even assuming that understanding is possible while one is operating within one's hermeneutic circle (that is, intra-hermeneutically), how can one ever understand something that does not belong to one's circle, how can one ever ascribe meaning to an indigenous declension of the 'legal' expressing itself *elsewhere*? The short answer, in my view, is that one simply cannot do so. This is a crucial idea embodied in the notion of 'incommensurability' – which wants to fight the received view that there exists a law-text that would present itself in its ontological self-sameness both to those operating locally and to those operating elsewhere, that the same law-text would come to language in different traditions and yet would somehow 'unite' traditions

141 Wittgenstein, *supra*, note 12, § 67, p. 14 ['*Eine Erwartung ist in einer Situation eingebettet, aus der sie entspringt*'].

142 See Raimundo Panikkar, 'What Is Comparative Philosophy Comparing?', in *Interpreting Across Boundaries*, ed. by Gerald J. Larson and Eliot Deutsch (Princeton, NJ: Princeton University Press, 1988), p. 130. For an argument showing the limits of Gadamerian hermeneutics with specific reference to cross-cultural understanding, see Marina Vitkin, 'The "Fusion of Horizons": On Knowledge and Alterity', 21 *Philosophy & Social Criticism* 57 (1995). Cf. Arendt, *supra*, note 86, p. 43: 'Within a homogeneous human community, the essence of the table is indicated unequivocally by the word "table", and yet as soon as it arrives at the frontier of the community, it vacillates' ['*Innerhalb einer homogenen Menschengemeinschaft wird das Wesen des Tisches durch das Wort Tisch vereindeutigt, um doch gleich an der Grenze der Gemeinschaft ins Schwanken zu geraten*'] (1950).

even as they bring the law-text to language across cultural boundaries. It is not that there is 'something' (a law-text) that the local interpreter would see in one aspect and that the foreign interpreter – let us say, the comparatist – would see in a different aspect as allowed by his own perspective. It is, rather, that there is no 'unique' law-text or – which is another way to put the matter – that the law-text is inherently historically and linguistically constituted in the sense that it can only exist from within a historical and linguistic perspective, from within an episteme, and that it cannot be envisaged as existing otherwise. The law-text, and the law *tout court*, cannot transcend perspective. In the words of Alasdair MacIntyre, '[t]here is no standing ground, no place for enquiry, no way to engage in the practices of advancing, evaluating, accepting, and rejecting reasoned argument apart from that which is provided by some particular tradition or other.'[143] What is said of moral philosophy can be said of law, that is, that 'the evaluative and normative concepts, maxims, arguments and judgments [...] are nowhere to be found except as embodied in the historical lives of particular social groups and so possessing the distinctive characteristics of historical existence: both identity and change through time, expression in institutionalized practice as well as in discourse, interaction and interrelationship with a variety of forms of activity.'[144] Like language, for example, which can only name in such a way, law is tied to what it names. The fact is that '[w]e have not *got* a language which will serve as a permanent neutral matrix for formulating all good explanatory hypotheses, and we have not the foggiest notion how to get one.'[145] And the further fact is that we have not got a neutral law either: any purported metalanguage exists 'in' a language. Any claim about law is made in the terms of *a* law (and of *a* language): there is the 'absolute impossibility of a metalanguage' and the 'impossibility of an absolute metalanguage'.[146]

---

143 Alasdair MacIntyre, *Whose Justice? Which Rationality?* (Notre Dame, IN: Notre Dame University Press, 1988), p. 350.

144 Alasdair MacIntyre, *After Virtue*, 2nd edn (Notre Dame, IN: University of Notre Dame Press, 1984), p. 265.

145 Richard Rorty, *Philosophy and the Mirror of Nature* (Princeton, NJ: Princeton University Press, 1979), pp. 348–9 [emphasis original].

146 Derrida, *supra*, note 98, p. 43 ['*impossibilité absolue de métalangage*'/ '*Impossibilité d'un métalangage absolu*']. There is '[n]o historical metalanguage [that can] bear witness in the transparent element of some absolute knowledge': Jacques Derrida, *Fichus* (Paris: Galilée, 2002), p. 57 ['*Nul métalangage historique pour en témoigner dans l'élément transparent de quelque savoir absolu*']. I have explored the matter of idiomaticity in Pierre Legrand, 'Issues in the Translatability of Law', in *Nation, Language, and the Ethics of Translation*, ed. by Sandra Bermann and Michael Wood (Princeton, NJ: Princeton University Press, 2005), pp. 30–50; Legrand, 'Singularity', *supra*, note 103. Like Derrida, 'I never cease to decapitate metalanguage or rather to plunge its head back into the text': Jacques Derrida, *Glas* (Paris: Galilée, 1974), p. 132 ['*je ne cesse de décapiter le méta-langage ou plutôt de lui replonger la tête dans le texte*'].

How far can a comparatist who has assimilated the epistemological assumptions of a legal tradition as actively forged and reinforced through a legal-cultural system of schooling within which he has been immersed come to edge understanding – in the strong sense of the term – closer to the experience of another legal culture and away from mere ventriloquism about that culture? Such is Dan Sperber's argument: '[Y]our understanding of what I am saying is not a reproduction in your mind of my thoughts, but the construction of thoughts of your own which are more or less closely related to mine.'[147] As Laurence Thomas observes, '[n]o amount of imagination in the world can make it the case that one has the subjective imprimatur of the experiences and memories of another.'[148] In effect, 'there is [...] *always* a remainder, much that I do not understand about the other person's experience and perspective.'[149] Acquired knowledge, then, is inevitably derivative or contingent, which is why linguistics teaches that 'the phonetic boundaries of bilingual speakers are never exactly the same as those for corresponding monolinguals'; in other words, the bilingual 'never reaches the ideal goal of a new phonological norm'.[150] Clearly, idealizing descriptions of extensive commonalities and co-operative mutualities supposedly presupposed by human communication obscure epistemological differences amongst verbal agents not least as regards the significant operation of asymmetrical relations between comparatists-as-observers and their interlocutors-as-observed. Is there then a reconstructive approach that would allow the comparatist to escape the situation in which he has always already been thrown? The answer cannot have much to do with 'contact' – that is, with anything like 'immersion'. The hermeneutic difficulty lies elsewhere for the issue concerns the absence of shared episteme. No quantity or intensity of contact can change anything to that dissonance: the law under scrutiny by the comparatist will continue to have been produced by a tradition and a culture that differ from the tradition and the culture having constituted the comparatist and within which he continues, perhaps unwittingly, to dwell. Both traditions and cultures still do not share an object.

147 Dan Sperber, *Explaining Culture* (Oxford: Blackwell, 1996), p. 58. This formulation reminds one of Homi K. Bhabha, *The Location of Culture* (London: Routledge, 1994), p. 31: 'the Other text is forever the exegetical horizon of difference, never the active agent of articulation.'

148 Laurence Thomas, 'Moral Deference', 24 *Philosophical Forum* 233 (1992), p. 235.

149 Iris Marion Young, 'Asymmetrical Reciprocity: On Moral Respect, Wonder, and Enlarged Thought', 3 *Constellations* 340 (1997), pp. 354–5 [my emphasis].

150 Ellen Bialystok and Kenji Hakuta, *In Other Words: The Science and Psychology of Second-Language Acquisition* (New York: Basic Books, 1994), p. 16. A fascinating study on the limits of acculturation is James P. Lantolf, 'Second Culture Acquisition', in *Culture in Second Language Teaching and Learning*, ed. by Eli Hinkel (Cambridge: Cambridge University Press, 1999), pp. 28–46. See generally Rod Ellis, *The Study of Second Language Acquisition* (Oxford: Oxford University Press, 1994), pp. 299–345. See also *supra*, note 82 and accompanying text.

('[T]here are limits to the degree of ultimate disagreement that can exist within a society (for without some degree of moral homogeneity it would not be a society); but there are no limits [...] on disagreement between societies.'[151])

The very notion of 'dialogue' – which assumes that two interlocutors are speaking the same language – makes Jacques Derrida uncomfortable and prompts him to assert that he prefers the idea of *negotiation*.[152] For him, the language that one hears is always another language. (One is unaccountably reminded of Beckett referring to 'the simple and necessary and yet so unattainable proposition that their way of being we, [is] not our way and that our way of being they, [is] not their way'.[153]) Of course, this is not to deny the intersections that unite Jacques Derrida and Hans-Georg Gadamer around an anti-positivist stance.[154] Derrida agrees with Gadamer that when it comes to language, the individual is *not in charge* and that, if anything, it is rather the other way around.[155] Yet, ultimately, Gadamer impels one '[t]o recognize one's own in the alien' and claims that 'to become at home in [the alien] is the basic movement of spirit, whose being consists only in returning to itself from what is other'.[156] It is precisely this projection of self into the other, which means that knowledge of the other ultimately constitutes a way of achieving a deeper knowledge of self, that Derrida rejects. For him, such a Hegelian manifestation of the will to appropriate and assimilate the other to self, such symbolic violence being visited on the other, is inadmissible: 'the same is the same only by being

151 Bernard Williams, *Morality* (Cambridge: Cambridge University Press, 1972), p. 19. In my view, it would be more helpful to refer to 'differentiation' across societies than to 'disagreement': *supra*, note 92 and accompanying text.

152 Jacques Derrida (with Pierre-Jean Labarrière), *Altérités* (Paris: Osiris, 1986), p. 85. Cf. Pierre Legendre, *Le désir politique de Dieu* (Paris: Fayard, 1988), p. 183: 'dogmatic systems as such do not dialogue, [...] they can only negotiate' ['*les systèmes dogmatiques comme tels ne dialoguent pas, (...) ils ne peuvent que négocier*'] (emphasis omitted). *Adde*: Novalis, *supra*, note 8, p. 672: 'Authentic dialogue is naked word-play' ['*das rechte Gespräch ist ein bloßes Wortspiel*'].

153 Samuel Beckett, 'The Capital of the Ruins', in *The Complete Short Prose*, ed. by S.E. Gontarski (New York: Grove Press, 1995), p. 277 [1946]. Cf. Heidegger, *Being and Time*, *supra*, note 26, p. 222: 'we are at best always just "there" too.' For the original text, see *Sein und Zeit*, *supra*, note 26, p. 239 ['*Wir (...) sind höchstens immer nur dabei*'].

154 It is no doubt such commonalities that have allowed Derrida to praise hermeneutics as a form of deconstruction. See Derrida, *supra*, note 119, pp. 162–3.

155 Diane Michelfelder and Richard Palmer, 'Introduction', in Michelfelder and Palmer, *supra*, note 99, p. 2.

156 Gadamer, *Truth and Method*, *supra*, note 36, p. 14. For the original text, see *Wahrheit und Methode*, *supra*, note 36, pp. 19–20 ['*Im Fremden das Eigene zu erkennen, in ihm heimisch zu werden, ist die Grundbewegung des Geistes, dessen Sein nur Rückkehr zu sich selbst aus dem Anderssein ist*'].

sensitive to the other.'[157] According to Derrida, I do not hear the other when I claim to understand him since 'the will to understand [constrains] the other to yield, to conform himself to the schemes of thought that I inflict on him and that by-pass *his* specificity'.[158] Since understanding is always, despite itself, structurally so to speak, a prisoner of schemes and signs, 'to understand' is inevitably to integrate the other *nolens volens* into one's system. To the extent that it claims an 'interpretive totalization',[159] hermeneutics must therefore be resisted. Indeed, Derrida opines that '*Verstehen*' must concern not so much a continuous relation of mediation, but rather the *interruption* of such relation.[160] This interruption must manifest itself as 'the condition of understanding'.[161] For Derrida, the Gadamerian thesis of 'understanding' and his own claim of 'non-understanding' are 'absolutely irreconcilable'.[162] Consider the two positions. According to Gadamer, '[o]ne must look for the word that can reach another person. And it is possible for one to find it; one can even learn the language of the other person. One can cross over into the language of the other in order to reach the other. All this is possible for language as language.'[163] But Derrida objects to this brand of consensualism, this Gadamerian/Hegelian 'fusion of horizons' ('*Horizontverschmelzung*'),[164] which happens even if the other is remarkably different. The Gadamerian '*Aufhebung*' suggests that the differentiation of horizons is merely a transitory phase destined to 'sublate' itself in a consensus or fusion.[165] For his part, Derrida asserts that sameness between *interpretans* and *interpretandum* cannot be envisaged: there is

157 Derrida, *supra*, note 13, p. 95 ['*le même n'est le même qu'en s'affectant de l'autre*'].

158 Jean Grondin, *L'herméneutique* (Paris: Presses Universitaires de France, 2006), p. 103 ['*la volonté de comprendre (contraint) l'autre à se plier, à se conformer aux schèmes de pensée que je lui impose et qui passent, par le fait même, à côté de* sa *spécificit* '] (emphasis original).

159 Jacques Derrida, *Schibboleth* (Paris: Galilée, 1986), p. 50 ['*totalisation interprétative*']. In 1986, in a note added to *Truth and Method*, *supra*, note 36, p. 299 (for the original text, see *supra*, note 36, p. 305), Gadamer showed sensitivity to this argument. Grondin, who was a close disciple of Gadamer, discerns here the possible influence of Derrida: *supra*, note 159, pp. 104–5.

160 Jacques Derrida, 'Three Questions to Hans-Georg Gadamer', transl. by Diane Michelfelder and Richard Palmer, in Michelfelder and Palmer, *supra*, note 99, p. 53.

161 Jacques Derrida, *Béliers* (Paris: Galilée, 2003), p. 21 ['*la condition de la compréhension*'].

162 Jacques Derrida, *L'écriture et la différence* (Paris: Le Seuil, 1967), p. 427 ['*absolument inconciliables*'].

163 Hans-Georg Gadamer, 'Destruktion and Deconstruction', transl. by Geoff Waite and Richard Palmer, in Michelfelder and Palmer, *supra*, note 99, p. 106.

164 For Gadamer's recognition of a Hegelian influence on his thought, see *Wahrheit und Methode*, *supra*, note 36, p. 312. This reference is lost in the English translation: *Truth and Method*, *supra*, note 36, p. 307.

165 See generally Jean Grondin, 'La fusion des horizons', *Archives de philosophie*, 2005, pp. 401–18.

only 'iterability' (even what is repeated is never the same) and 'differance' (even what signifies never has a fixed or fixable meaning) – two idiosyncratic notions that allow one to open oneself to the idea of the singularity of the text and to the further idea of the strangeness of the text, that is, to the decolonization of difference coercitively assimilated to sameness. For Derrida, 'equivocity is in fact always irreducible': 'words and language in general are not and can never be absolute *objects*.'[166] There is more, for according to Derrida 'we cannot – and *must* not – exclude, when someone is speaking, privately or publicly, when he teaches, publishes, preaches, orders, promises, or prophetizes, informs or communicates, that some force within him also efforces itself *not* to be understood, approved, accepted within the consensus.'[167] While Gadamer in the end seeks to eliminate everything having to do with specificity, that is, with difference – according to him, 'whatever is alienating in a text, whatever makes the text unintelligible, is to be overcome and thereby cancelled out by the interpreter',[168] which means that 'understanding is, in the end, always possible'.[169] When Gadamer asserts that understanding must seek to fashion itself in conformity with the things themselves, for example, with 'the *matter* of the text', that is, with 'that which the formal arrangement of the text mediates',[170] and when he claims that understanding must therefore 'keep something at a distance [...] as soon as it is rejected by the sense of the text itself',[171] Derrida, although also concerned with the idea of fidelity (he writes that 'reading cannot legitimately transgress the text toward something else

166 Jacques Derrida, 'Introduction', in Edmund Husserl, *L'origine de la géométrie*, transl. by Jacques Derrida (Paris: Presses Universitaires de France, 1962), p. 106 ['*l'équivocité est en fait toujours irréductible*'/'*les mots et le langage en général ne sont et ne peuvent jamais être des* objets *absolus*'] (emphasis original) [1954].

167 Derrida, *supra*, note 33, p. 246 ['*nous ne pouvons – ni ne* devons – *exclure, quand quelqu'un parle, en privé ou en public, quand il enseigne, publie, prêche, ordonne, promet ou prophétise, informe ou communique, que quelque force en lui s'efforce aussi de* ne pas *être compris, approuvé, accepté dans le consensus*'] (emphasis original).

168 Hans-Georg Gadamer, 'Text and Interpretation', transl. by Dennis J. Schmidt and Richard Palmer, in Michelfelder and Palmer, *supra*, note 99, p. 41 [1983]. For the original text, see 'Text und Interpretation', in *Gesammelte Werke*, vol. II (Tübingen: J.C.B. Mohr, 1986), p. 350 ['*Das Befremdende, das einen Text unverständlich macht, soll durch den Interpreten aufgehoben werden*'].

169 Gadamer, *Truth and Method, supra*, note 36, p. 217. For the original text, see *Wahrheit und Methode, supra*, note 36, p. 221 ['*am Ende (gelingt) immer wieder das Verstehen*'].

170 Paul Ricoeur, *Du texte à l'action* (Paris: Le Seuil, 1986), p. 368 ['*(l)a* chose *du texte*'/ '*ce que l'agencement formel du texte médiatise*']. Gadamer refers to 'the meaning of the text' as 'the thing itself': *Truth and Method, supra*, note 36, p. 465. For the original text, see *Wahrheit und Methode, supra*, note 36, p. 469 ['*der Sinn des Textes*'/'*die Sache selbst*'].

171 Gadamer, *Truth and Method, supra*, note 36, p. 465. For the original text, see *Wahrheit und Methode, supra*, note 36, p. 469 ['*etwas fernzuhalten (...), sobald es von dem Sinn des Textes selbst verweigert wird*'].

than itself'[172]), defends the view that the 'real' and, specifically, the 'reality' of the text is out of reach and inappropriable and, indeed, that it cannot be shown 'as such' or 'in and of itself'.[173] Reading, for Derrida, must '*produce*' a 'signifying structure', that is, '[it] must always aim toward a certain relation, overlooked by the writer, between what he masters and what he does not master of the schemes of the language he is using.'[174] 'What guides me', observes Derrida, 'is always untranslatability.'[175]

'Peter' is not a translation of 'Pierre'.[176]

'Law' is not a translation of '*droit*' (how *could* 'law', which emerges in an idiographic legal culture such as England's, be a translation of '*droit*', which is the product of a nomothetic legal culture like that governing in France ?).

('And there stand those stupid languages, helpless as two bridges that go over the same river side by side but are separated from each other by an abyss. It is a mere bagatelle, an accident, and yet it separates.'[177])

In other words, 'X is translatable as Y' does not relate to the idea of sameness or synonymy of meaning. (The point is reminiscent of Quine's indeterminacy argument: it is not that no translation can ever be achieved but that no translation

---

172 Jacques Derrida, *De la grammatologie* (Paris: Editions de Minuit, 1967), p. 227 ['*(la lecture) ne peut légitimement transgresser le texte vers autre chose que lui*'].

173 Jacques Derrida, *Voyous* (Paris: Galilée, 2003), p. 198 ['*comme tel*'/'*tel qu'en lui-même*'].

174 Derrida, *supra*, note 172, p. 227 ['produire'/'*structure signifiant* '/'*toujours viser un certain rapport, inaperçu de l'écrivain, entre ce qu'il commande et ce qu'il ne commande pas des schémas de la langue dont il fait usage*'] (emphasis original).

175 Jacques Derrida, in Aliette Armel, 'Du mot à la vie: un dialogue entre Jacques Derrida et Hélène Cixous', *Magazine littéraire*, April 2004, p. 26 ['*Ce qui me guide, c'est toujours l'intraductibilité*'].

176 Jacques Derrida, *Psyché*, 2nd edn (Paris: Galilée, 1998), p. 209. Cf. Wilhelm von Humboldt, 'Aeschylos Agamemnon', in *Gesammelte Schriften*, ed. by Albert Leitzmann, vol. VIII (Berlin: B. Behr, 1909), p. 130, who makes the point that languages 'necessarily feature differences' ['*Es muss nothwendig Verschiedenheiten darbieten*'] (1816).

177 *Rilke Briefe*, ed. by the Rilke-Archiv in Weimar, vol. I (Frankfurt: Insel, 1950), p. 41 ['*Und da stehen nun diese dummen Sprachen hilflos wie zwei Brücken, die nebeneinander über denselben Fluß gehen, aber durch einen Abgrund voneinander getrennt sind. Es ist nur eine Bagatelle, ein Zufall, und es trennt doch ...*']. Rainer Maria Rilke's letter to Clara Rilke is dated 2 September 1902 and written from Paris. In it, the poet comments on the difficulty of communicating with Rodin on the occasion of his visit to him. Note that the word 'abyss' ('*Abgrund*') is also found in Celan, *supra*, note 102.

can ever be correct – and one reason for this has to do with the fact of inscrutability of reference, another Quinean thesis).[178]

Jacques Derrida's deconstruction refutes the normalizing procedure that organizes a unique 'logos' of communication and preserves the idea of 'conversation'.[179] Derrida does not believe in the fusional understanding that animates Hans-Georg Gadamer. He does not believe in an exchange that would be finite and definite, in an agreement: 'I am not convinced that we ever really do have this experience that Professor Gadamer describes, of knowing in a dialogue that one has been perfectly understood or experiencing the success of confirmation.'[180] Alterity is insurmountable. In the midst of 'an unmasterable polytonality, with grafts, intrusions, interferences',[181] 'a thousand possibilities will always remain open even as one understands something of this sentence that makes sense.'[182] Paradoxically, it is this hermeneutics of resistance to univocity of meaning – this hermeneutics of polyphony, of heteroglossia, of dissemination, of 'destinerrance'[183] – which assists in conferring to deconstruction its affirmative dimension in that it asserts 'the possibility, for the other tone or for the tone of another, to come at any time to interrupt a familiar music'.[184] Deconstruction, as a gesture of heteronomic confidence, of Deleuzian deterritorialization, is '*more*

178 See Quine, *Ontological Relativity*, *supra*, note 90, pp. 26–68. Two significant contributions introducing Quine's ideas are Peter Hylton, 'Quine on Reference and Ontology' and Robert Kirk, 'Indeterminacy of Translation', in *The Cambridge Companion to Quine*, ed. by Roger F. Gibson (Cambridge: Cambridge University Press, 2004), pp. 115–50 and 151–80, respectively. See also Hans-Johann Glock, *Quine and Davidson on Language, Thought and Reality* (Cambridge: Cambridge University Press, 2003).

179 Cf. Martin Heidegger, *Nietzsche*, transl. by David F. Krell, vol. II (New York: Harper & Row, 1984), p. 181: 'Yet we must guard against the presumption that we now belong among those who really understand. Perhaps we too are mere onlookers' [1961]. For the original text, see *Nietzsche*, vol. I (Pfullingen: Günther Neske, 1961), p. 445 ['*Doch hüten wir uns zu meinen, wir seien damit schon Verstehende; vielleicht schauen wir nur zu*'].

180 Derrida, in Michelfelder and Palmer, *supra*, note 99, p. 54.

181 Jacques Derrida, *D'un ton apocalyptique adopté naguère en philosophie* (Paris: Galilée, 1983), p. 67 ['*une polytonalité immaîtrisable, avec greffes, intrusions, parasitages*'].

182 Derrida, *supra*, note 18, p. 122 ['*Mille possibilités resteront toujours ouvertes, alors même qu'on comprend quelque chose de cette phrase qui fait sens*'].

183 This neologism is frequent in the work of Derrida. It wishes to convey the idea, intrinsically aporetic, according to which a meaning, although destined for an addressee, errs – which means, for instance, that it sometimes travels from the addressee to the addressor.

184 Derrida, *supra*, note 181, pp. 67–8 ['*la possibilité pour l'autre ton ou le ton d'un autre, de venir à n'importe quel moment interrompre une musique familière*']. The idea of 'deterritorialization' occurs frequently in the work of Deleuze. For example, see Gilles Deleuze and Félix Guattari, *L'anti-Oedipe* (Paris: Editions de Minuit, 1972); Deleuze and Guattari, *supra*, note 34.

*than one language*'.[185] And comparison, as a gesture of heteronomic confidence, of Deleuzian deterritorialization, is more than one law.

(As it allows for ethical space, that is, for the other's point of view, incommensurability enhances agency. It forces one to select one's 'truths'.[186])

What strategy, then? I claim that one or two (major) correctives to established comparative research about laws can be implemented. They will not solve the conundrum of incommensurability, which to my mind is insoluble. But they will significantly alleviate its impact. Accepting that the absence of epistemological commensurability cannot be taken to imply the lack of all referential interface (even though there can be no question of an identity of referents in terms of their extension or of an ascertainable identity of 'referents' in terms of their intension), any movement across different frames of references must avoid any ascription of truth-in-the-law. It must also eschew any attempt at synthesis – which, as it implements the synthesizer's standard of rationality, entails an (undue) appropriation and assimilation of the other's law and of the other-in-the-law. Indeed, any synthesis can only be achieved from within one (anticipatory) frame of reference and will inevitably lead to a partial dissolution of the other, that is, to an annexation.[187] A synthesis is, ultimately, a *thesis*. Rather, a relationship to what is meant, to what is being spoken of, must be arranged in the light of the determinative-disclosive function of (non-neutral) language. This must mean keeping the interference with the activity performed by the *interpretandum* itself to the minimum. I argue that the optimal way to achieve this limited-intrusion policy is to trace the *interpretandum* to the episteme whose construct it is. Note that, in this respect, the idea is not to restore 'the' meaning of a law-text but to pay attention to its constitution, that is, to recover the range of 'things' of which the law-text speaks. Only then can the comparatist avoid the worst implications of reductionism (cabining, domesticating and distorting the other's voice) and dogmatism (elevating one's position to measure the other's). Only then can one eschew, to an extent at least, receptivity to the other as already-imported, as already-and-irrevocably reduced to self. Only

---

185 Jacques Derrida, *Mémoires pour Paul de Man* (Paris: Galilée, 1988), p. 38 ['plus d'une langue'] (emphasis original).

186 See Joan C. Williams, 'Rorty, Radicalism, Romanticism: The Politics of the Gaze', [1992] *Wisconsin L.R.* 131.

187 Cf. Alasdair MacIntyre, *Three Rival Versions of Moral Enquiry* (Notre Dame, IN: Notre Dame University Press, 1990), p. 117: 'It is not that the adherent of one particular standpoint cannot on occasion understand some rival point of view both intellectually and imaginatively, in such a way and to such a degree that he or she is able to provide a presentation of it of just the kind that one of its own adherents would give. It is that even in so doing the mode of presentation will inescapably be framed within and directed by the beliefs and purposes of one's own point of view.'

then is comparison attuned to the voice of the other. Only then does comparison *listen*. Only then is comparison *other-wise*.

Although incommensurability is necessary to understand world as the relatedness of differentials of force, one can read the history of comparative legal studies as the forgetting of incommensurability of languages and of laws. Not to understand this forgetting is to remain mired in positivism despite claims to be going beyond it. It is to confine oneself to a Derridean 'false exit' (*supra*).

In a text devoted to Virginia Woolf's *To the Lighthouse*, Gayatri Spivak writes at the outset that '[her] essay is not necessarily an attempt to illuminate *To the Lighthouse* and lead us to a correct reading'.[188] When will comparisons-at-law, finally mocking the illusory security that referential fixity of meaning would provide, defend the cause of another textuality by beginning their research on, say, the English law of estoppel with a sentence that could look like this: 'This essay relating to the English law of estoppel is not necessarily an attempt to illuminate the English law of estoppel and lead us to a correct reading of it.' When will comparatists-at-law finally admit that there cannot be inscription of law irrespective of them?

'[F]rom time to time I have the consolation [...] of sinning willy-nilly against a foreign language, as I should love to do with full knowledge and intent against my own.'[189]

When will comparatists-at-law learn to sin against foreign law and against their 'own' law or, more accurately, when will they learn to accept that they have always-already been sinning against law?

Untranslatability is not so much the fact of no-translation as it is that of the incessant not-translation.

One can say of laws what Humboldt said of languages: that the genuine significance of their study lies in their participation 'in the formation of representation'.[190]

Comparison is the incessant not-comparison. As such, it addresses – and must address – the endless exploration of *differends*. It must address legal cultures as constellations of radically different singularities-in-the-law, as sites for the

188 Gayatri Chakravorty Spivak, *In Other Worlds* (London: Routledge, 2006), p. 41 [1987].

189 Samuel Beckett, *Disjecta*, ed. by Ruby Cohn (New York: Grove Press, 1984), p. 173. This is Martin Esslin's English translation of a letter written in German by Beckett on 9 July 1937. For the original text, see *id.*, p. 54.

190 Humboldt, *supra*, note 34, p. 119 ['*an der Bildung der Vorstellungen*'].

exploration of incommensurable dissensus (across cultures) and of indomitable dissent (within cultures).

Individuals socialized in the law 'have long been accustomed to think of law as something apart': 'The grand ideals of justice, of impartiality and fairness, have seemed to remove law from the ordinary, disordered paths of life.'[191] The habitual, unexamined assumption is that if one has culture, one cannot have justice (or reason). In other words, the claim is that cultural erasure is a pre-requisite to *justice* (justice cannot emerge from localism, which is deemed to be prejudiced or biased – 'prejudice', of course, being considered a bad thing). But, if there is eradication or annihilation, how can there really be justice? The first order of business for comparatists trained as lawyers must be to value a justice that is neither eradicating nor annihilating and to appreciate that '[t]o say that the law is cultural does not by itself dismantle the force of the idea of justice'.[192] On the contrary, as Emmanuel Levinas has observed, 'justice is impossible unless he who renders it finds himself within proximity.'[193] For lawyers, to turn to culture is to acknowledge that *recognition of local specificity is the condition for justice*, the justice that is due to the other's law and to the other-in-the-law.[194] This is not to say, of course, that comparative interventions purporting to elucidate difference across laws do not also imply a measure of violence. After all, the comparatist-at-law is implicated in the construction of difference: he works on the laws and engages them in a process of differential 're-inscription'. This is, of course, an act of violence – and, to this extent, violence permeates every comparison. But 'a word that would manifest itself without any violence would be saying nothing.'[195] From the moment there is an '*articulation*',[196] there cannot be non-violence. As he ceaselessly questions violence as part of his aspiration to justice, what the comparatist can/must do is to choose a lesser violence than that wrought on the 'legal' by positivists and formalists, those who claim to bear the authority of a justice already attained. By edging his way toward what there is – there *are* laws – the comparatist, while he may still fall short of anything like justice 'as such', ameliorates injustice.

191 Robert Post, 'The Relatively Autonomous Discourse of Law', in *Law and the Order of Culture*, ed. by Robert Post (Berkeley, CA: University of California Press, 1991), p. vii.

192 Carol J. Greenhouse, 'Just in Time: Temporality and the Cultural Legitimation of Law', 98 *Yale L.J.* 1650 (1989), p. 1650.

193 Emmanuel Levinas, *Autrement qu'être ou au-delà de l'essence* (Paris: Livre de Poche, 2001), p. 202 ['*La justice est impossible sans que celui qui la rend se trouve lui-même dans la proximité*'] (1974).

194 For a challenging exploration of the irreducible connections between 'justice' and 'singularity', see Jacques Derrida, *Force de loi* (Paris: Galilée, 1994), pp. 11–63.

195 Derrida, *supra*, note 162, p. 218 ['*Une parole qui se produirait sans la moindre violence (...) ne dirait rien*'].

196 Derrida, *supra*, note 162, p. 219 ['*articulation*'] (emphasis original).

(Any comparison that restricted itself to understanding law 'objectively' would be engaged in the dedifferentiating, tranquillizing flight from pain or the uncanny into the realm of narcotizing ascetic ideals – such as truth. Theories which only view comparison as being concerned with 'objects' – say, representations as opposed to re-presentations – remain mired in sterile debates about the 'objectivity' of their practice. They constantly purport to escape from the inescapable tie to the comparatist as *interpretans* and to the diverse law as *interpretandum*: they cannot think of interpretation as differential relating.)

Yet, bearing in mind the difficulties associated with the production of a fully-fledged presence of the law, which must feature even what is seemingly absent from it but which haunts it nonetheless and, therefore, inhabits it – in other words, which must allow for the *spectrality* of the 'legal'[197] – one must be content with something like comparative minimalism, a kind of *comparatisme malgré tout* or Beckettian 'comparing *on*' that allows one to move beyond parochialism and yet preserve a sound measure of epistemic modesty.[198] In an important sense, one compares because the alternative is worse. On the one hand, it would be unacceptably easy to say that since no full transcultural understanding can be had, one might as well remain confined to one's own world. On the other hand, it would be oh-so-facile to fall for the utopia of one-law. The comparatist's contrarian challenge is thus to recognize and to respect alterity. It is to foster a relationality across laws/languages as singularities. It is to develop knowledge that heralds '[a] new kind of arrangement which will not be that of a harmony, a concordance, or a conciliation, but which will accept disjunction or divergence as the infinite centre from which, through speech, a relation must be created – an arrangement which does not compose but juxtaposes, that is, leaves *outside* one another the terms coming into relation, respecting and preserving this *exteriority* and this distance as the principle – always already undermined of all meaning[:] [j]uxtaposition

---

197 Derrida refers to 'a quasi-logic of the ghost that one ought to substitute, because it is stronger, to an ontological logic of the presence': Derrida, *supra*, note 194, p. 68 ['*une quasi-logique du fantôme qu'il faudrait substituer, parce qu'elle est plus forte qu'elle, à une logique ontologique de la présence*'].

198 The preposition 'on' is one of the most important motifs in Beckett's work. For an exploration of this theme, see *The Grove Companion to Samuel Beckett*, ed. by C.J. Ackerley and S.E. Gontarski (New York: Grove Press, 2004), p. 421.

and interruption here assume an extraordinary force of justice'.[199] One compares because, well, how could one not?[200]

199 Maurice Blanchot, *L'entretien infin* (Paris: Gallimard, 1969), p. 453 ['*Un arrangement d'une sorte nouvelle, qui ne sera pas celui d'une harmonie, d'une concorde ou d'une conciliation, mais qui acceptera la disjonction ou la divergence comme le centre infini à partir duquel, par la parole, un rapport doit s'établir: un arrangement qui ne compose pas, mais juxtapose, c'est-à-dire laisse* en dehors *les uns des autres les termes qui viennent en relation, respectant et préservant cette* extériorité *et cette distance comme le principe – toujours déjà destitué – de toute signification. La juxtaposition et l'interruption se chargent ici d'une force de justice extraordinaire*'] (emphasis original). Blanchot was referring to René Char's verse.

200 In his well-known paper on world literature, Moretti claims that there is 'no other justification for the study of world literature [...] but [...] to be [...] a permanent intellectual challenge to national literatures': Franco Moretti, 'Conjectures on World Literature', *New Left Review*, Jan.–Feb. 2000, p. 68. In other words, the point of comparativism is to refute nationalism.

# Chapter 14
# Towards a Common European Legal Thinking: A Dialogic Challenge

Edda Weigand

## Addressing the Complex Goal

As the 25 Member States of the extended European Union have agreed to cooperate closely in order to achieve a strong, free and democratic union, it will be necessary to act in a joint European interest on a political, economic and legal level. With respect to the legal level, the European Union is in need of a shared legal basis. When faced with this challenge we must more than ever try to achieve an awareness of cross-national differences which are rooted in the diverging national histories of law and its application. To my mind, there are two questions to be tackled: first, the issue of how to arrive at a common European thinking when starting from different national legal systems; and second, the issue in principle of whether there is an independent concept of thought at all.

The first question concerning the route from national differences to common European thinking not only refers to different European languages, that is, to multilingualism. As languages are embedded in cultures, it refers more basically to multiculturalism, which can include multilingualism. Moreover it is a question which presupposes that a common European legal thinking is a goal worth striving for. Such a presupposition has come under attack by those who voted against the European constitution and consider it a step towards a universalistic politics which would undermine the legitimacy of different cultures.[1]

The second question concerning an independent concept of thought refers to a cross-disciplinary debate about human abilities which, to my mind, has finally been decided by recent neurological experiments which demonstrate that human abilities operate in an interactive way.[2] Consequently, thinking is an integrated part of human action and behaviour and turns out to be a dialogic challenge.[3] The

1 See, for example, Sampson, G. (2007), 'Minds in Uniform: How Generative Linguistics Regiments Culture, and Why it Shouldn't', in Grein, M. and Weigand, E. (eds), *Dialogue and Culture* (Amsterdam and Philadelphia, PA: Benjamins), 3–25.

2 Damasio, A. (2000), *The Feeling of What Happens: Body, Emotion and the Making of Consciousness* (London: Vintage).

3 Weigand, E. (2000), 'The Dialogic Action Game', in Coulthard, M. et al. (eds), *Dialogue Analysis VII: Working with Dialogue* (Tübingen: Niemeyer), 1–18, and Weigand,

path from national differences to a common European thinking will thus be a long and difficult process of arguing and negotiating and will aim to reconcile national differences at a superordinate European level (see Figure 14.1):

different national legal systems → common European legal thinking

*arguing and negotiating*

**Figure 14.1**

The ultimate objective of this process will be an agreement about a high degree of legal bindingness and about joint principles of application that guarantee effective legal action in the interests of the people of the European Union.

## Legal Thinking as a Dialogic Challenge

Law and jurisprudence are not purely abstract logical systems which exist on paper independently of human beings. They are created by human beings by means of language and dialogue and have to be applied in every individual case. Whereas the classical methodology of jurisprudence did not question the law as a set of pre-given norms and as juridical decisions which have been derived from them in a logical process, modern theorizing in jurisprudence starts from the natural phenomenon of legal action and focuses on human beings trying to settle their affairs on the basis of legal norms.[4] The *law* therefore has the function of a *tool* in dialogic processes and is to be re-considered within the concept of *language as dialogue*.[5] Such a concept is based on the assumption that language use is always dialogically oriented. Dialogue not only includes meaning and understanding but also reacting, at least mentally (see Figure 14.2).

What we call legal thinking is an integrated part of the legal action game. We do not think and speak and communicate separately. Even thinking without

E. (2002), 'The Language Myth and Linguistics Humanised', in Harris, R. (ed.), *The Language Myth in Western Culture* (Richmond, Surrey: Curzon), 55–83.

4 See, for example, Perelman, Ch. (1976), *Logique juridique. Nouvelle rhétorique* (Paris: Dalloz); Viehweg, Th. (1974), *Topik und Jurisprudenz. Ein Beitrag zur rechtswissenschaftlichen Grundlagenforschung* (München: Beck), 5th edn.

5 Weigand, E. (2003), *Sprache als Dialog. Sprechakttaxonomie und kommunikative Grammatik*, 2nd edn (Tübingen: Niemeyer); Haft, F. (1999), *Juristische Rhetorik* (Freiburg/ Breisgau, München: Karl Alber), 1st edn 1978.

speaking happens in an inner dialogue as, for instance, Wilhelm von Humboldt already emphasized.[6] In the end, the central reference point of every scientific enterprise is human beings. There is no explanation of the world independent of human beings, no truth to be found as such in the external world, only claims to truth expressed by human beings or truth in the eye of the observer.

*Dialogical Principle proper*

ACTION ↔ REACTION

**Figure 14.2**

If we consider the human species as the dialogic species, the legal action game will be a '*mixed game*' not only with respect to the interaction of different types of communicative means – verbal, cognitive, perceptual – but also with respect to human beings' double nature as social individuals.[7] Human beings always have to regulate their individual interests with their social-dialogic purposes. Social purposes are culturally shaped. Human action, including legal action, is thus sociobiologically determined by the interaction of human nature and culture (see Figure 14.3).[8]

To my mind, human behaviour is in the end based on the two fundamental mental states of *belief and desire*. Consequently, all types of human action have to be derived from these basic mental states.[9] It is in the end beliefs and desires which are argued for and negotiated in legal games with reference to the code of the law.

If we describe human action as mixed games, we need an action-theoretic basis that goes beyond classical theorizing in terms of systems or separate levels. According to Searle, the history of linguistics is mainly characterized by two strands: the strand of competence pursued by 'searchers after hidden laws' and the

6 Humboldt, W. v. (1827/1963), 'Ueber den Dualis' (Gelesen in der Akademie der Wissenschaften am 26. April 1827), in Wilhelm von Humboldt, *Schriften zur Sprachphilosophie* (Darmstadt: Wissenschaftliche Buchgesellschaft) (Wilhelm von Humboldt. Werke in fünf Bänden, hg. von Andreas Flitner und Klaus Giel. III), 113–43.

7 Weigand, E. (2003), 'Argomentazione giuridica, uno sguardo europeo', in Mariani Marini, A. (ed.), *Teoria e tecnica dell'argomentazione giuridica* (Milano: Giuffrè) (Consiglio Nazionale Forense), 23–32 and Weigand, E. (2006), 'Argumentation: The Mixed Game', *Argumentation* 20:1, 59–87.

8 Wilson, E. (1978), *On Human Nature* (Cambridge, MA and London: Harvard University Press).

9 Cf. Weigand, *Sprache als Dialog*.

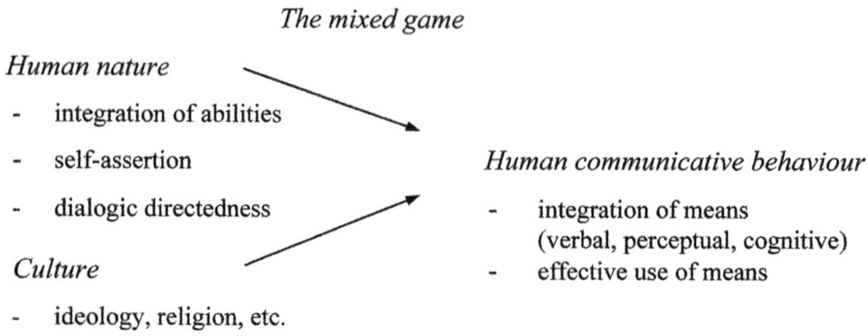


**Figure 14.3**

strand of performance which scrutinizes ever-changing authentic texts.[10] It is no longer controversial to state that competence, even communicative competence, is a methodological concept, and performance restricted to empirical 'data' does not do justice to the complex object of the mixed game. There is no bridge between a rule-governed system and ever-changing performance, or in legal terms between the law and the case. The bridge is established in the minds of human beings, by their *competence-in-performance*.[11] It is their legal competence-in-performance by means of which they create a code of law and apply it to cases of performance in a process of interpretation and argumentation which is dependent on different cultural evaluation. A theory of the mixed game implies a change from reductionism to holism,[12] from systems based on abstraction to human beings' interactively dealing with their needs and purposes. Theory can therefore no longer be separated as an artificial field but will have to be applicable to practice.

## Legal Action Games

The field of legal action comprises multiple games. They can be structured according to their primary purpose in speech act theoretic terms

- as representative games dealing with beliefs,
- as directive and explorative games dealing with desires,
- as declarative games dealing with creating validity by the institution of the law.

10 Searle, J.R. (1972), 'Chomsky's Revolution in Linguistics', *The New York Review of Books* 18:12, 16–24.

11 Weigand, *Sprache als Dialog*.

12 Simon, H.A. (1962), 'The Architecture of Complexity: Hierarchic Systems', in *Proceedings of the American Philosophical Society* 106, 467–82.

I am going to focus on representative games and will make a few remarks on the other types of legal games.

*Representative Games of Belief*

*The issue of argumentation* Representative games of belief are argumentative games.[13] Human beings express their beliefs in representative speech acts as claims to truth. As they are different individuals they have to negotiate diverging claims by means of arguments.

Argumentation has been dealt with in philosophy and linguistics either within logical theories or within rhetorical models of persuasion. In recent years we can see a tendency in philosophy and linguistics to overcome the separation of logic and rhetoric, for instance, in Pragma-Dialectics by the procedure of rhetorical manoeuvring[14] or by a procedure called the marriage of rhetoric and pragmatics.[15] These procedures however do not result in a consistent unified model. The persuasive model includes the audience but the audience is only seen from the perspective of the speaker. Dialogue however starts with the sequence of action and reaction. This is not a totally arbitrary sequence but is based on the functional structure of the initiative act.

What we need is an *open model of dialogic interaction* which is capable of describing what is going on in the mixed game by combining rationality and persuasion. Actions of arguing are to a high degree shaped by culture. Whereas in Western cultures argumentation means effective arguing in one's interest, there are other cultures which consider arguing as impolite.

Despite many attempts to clarify and define the concept of *persuasion*, the issue has not yet been settled. Persuasion still remains a concept which needs to be elucidated. Perelman to some degree grasped a crucial feature of the concept by focusing on what he called *adherence*, even if he stuck to logical syllogisms.[16] Adherence means aiming at acceptance. This is precisely the core of persuasion, namely trying to exert influence on the interlocutor in a way that is favourable for the speaker and promises acceptance. To my mind, it is due to human beings' nature as social individuals that they are *persuasive beings*. In this general sense, persuasion covers not only persuading in the narrow sense, that is, in directive games, but also convincing in representative games. Meaning, from the very outset, is persuasion (see Figure 14.4).[17]

---

13 Weigand, 'Argumentation'.

14 van Eemeren, F.H. and Houtlosser, P. (1999), 'Strategic Manoeuvring in Argumentative Discourse', *Discourse Studies*, 479–97.

15 Dascal, M. and Gross, A.G. (1999), 'The Marriage of Pragmatics and Rhetoric', *Philosophy and Rhetoric* 32:2, 107–30.

16 Perelman, *Logique juridique. Nouvelle rhétorique.*

17 Burke, K. (1950), *A Rhetoric of Motives* (New York: Prentice-Hall).

Meaning is persuasion

| REPRESENTATIVE | DIRECTIVE |
|---|---|
| ASSERTION ↔ ACCEPTANCE | REQUEST ↔ CONSENT |
| illocutionary claim to truth | illocutionary claim to volition |
| perlocutionary effect of *convincing* | perlocutionary effect of *persuading* |

**Figure 14.4**

Consequently, argumentation will never really be totally free from any trait of persuasion. Nonetheless we can distinguish three types of argumentation:

- so-called *neutral* or non-party argumentation which we expect, for instance, from expert reports or from legal commentaries,
- *biased* argumentation in court by advocates and prosecution,
- *comparative* argumentation, which tries to mediate between different points of view as we expect from the judge's argumentation in court.

*Legal argumentation* means argumentation with reference to the law. The way the law is referred to and interpreted inevitably brings in rhetorical principles as an important integrated component of the action game. Whereas *persuasion* belongs to meaning, *rhetoric* determines the choice of effective communicative means (see Figure 14.5):

| Meaning | | Means |
|---|---|---|
| | ↔ | |
| Persuasion | | Rhetoric |

**Figure 14.5**

Human beings try to negotiate their positions as effectively as possible. Biased argumentation will clearly use persuasive means of any kind, neutral argumentation will consider clarity and rationality as effective means. For jurists a special focus will be on the effective use of the law as a tool in dialogue. Modern jurisprudence seems to be aware of the fact that any *legal action* is in the end dialogic action.[18] Even establishing a correlation between the norm and the case represents a dialogical and rhetorical action. Haft therefore concludes: '... man kann der Rhetorik nicht entgehen; man kann nur danach trachten, sie zu beherrschen [it is not possible to avoid rhetoric; we can only strive to be in control of it] ...'.[19] It becomes very clear that such a complex object of study as legal action needs the cooperation of different disciplines which have agreed on the same premises: language as dialogue, language as action, language as effective rhetorical action.

Classical models of argumentation follow the line of rationality,[20] and even models of New Rhetoric stick to a logical basis. Rethinking human dialogic interaction means taking account of the restrictions of traditional models and trying to overcome them by going beyond rationality and including new results from research into neurology.[21] The *Theory of Dialogic Action Games* I developed over the last few years is a model which claims to address the complex by means of Principles of Probability.[22] As the action game is conceived of as a cultural unit, the theory of dialogic action games allows us to account for cultural differences which inevitably bear on the principles of dialogic action. For legal action games, the following points are crucial:

1. Legal argumentation is *dialogic* argumentation which negotiates different claims to truth and volition (see below). Rhetorical principles are inherent components.
2. Legal argumentation is an integrational activity or a *mixed game* of logic and rhetoric, of reason and persuasion.
3. Legal argumentation is dependent on *different legal systems and different legal cultures*. Neither reason nor persuasion are universal concepts but are influenced by the cultural environment.

Rhetoric as the effective use of communicative means deals with verbal means of communication such as lexis and utterance forms, together with the sequencing of moves and underlying dialogic schemata and strategies, that is, with cognitive

18 See, for example, Ballweg, O. and Seibert, Th. (eds) (1982), *Rhetorische Rechtstheorie* (Freiburg/Breisgau, München: Karl Alber) and Rodingen, H. (1977), *Pragmatik der juristischen Argumentation* (Freiburg/Breisgau, München: Karl Alber).

19 Haft, *Juristische Rhetorik*.

20 Cf. Toulmin, S.E. (1958), *The Uses of Argument* (Cambridge: Cambridge University Press).

21 Cf. Toulmin, S.E. (2001), *Return to Reason* (Cambridge, MA: Harvard University Press); Dascal, M. (1996), 'The Balance of Reason', in Nudler, O. (ed.), *La racionalidad. Su poder y sus limites* (Buenos Aires, Barcelona, Mexico: Paidos), 363–81; and Damasio, *The Feeling of What Happens*.

22 Cf., for example, Weigand, 'The Dialogic Action Game'; Weigand, 'Argumentation'; Weigand, E. (forthcoming), *Theory of Dialogic Action Games* (Amsterdam and Philadelphia, PA: Benjamins).

means, and all the associated parameters, among them cultural ones, which influence the use of these means. All these communicative means are integratively used for specific purposes and interests in the action game.

To conclude this section on representative games of belief I would like to give an example of what I consider crucial for human affairs in general, namely that truth is a matter of belief. Wittgenstein expressed it as a question: Mustn't we say at every turn I *believe* this to be true?[23] The example I am referring to is an expert report which played a major role in an authentic trial.[24] It is a case about a used car. This car becomes a controversial issue with reference to its empirical appearance. According to the plaintiff it shows signs of rust and even extensive rust, first signs of which must have already existed and were then only painted over at the time of purchase. According to the defendant there are only minor rust stains which did not exist at the time of purchase. Both parties justify their view with an expert report. We thus have two different expert reports referring to a seemingly simple empirical question. Obviously there are not even empirically objective facts. Consequently the court orders a further expert report specifying precisely the points to be clarified, among them:

> to ascertain whether the car delivered to the plaintiff has extensive rust on the underbody which has also affected load-bearing parts of the bodywork.

Representative speech acts are defined by a claim to truth, that is, not by an absolute truth value but by an individual claim on the part of the speaker depending on their knowledge and experience. It can therefore be strengthened by the status of the speaker. Representative speech acts made by an expert are more liable to be believed. Experts are expected not to be biased in favour of any party. Even if we presuppose that they only follow their expert knowledge, different expert reports may come out differently, depending on different knowledge and evaluation, as was the case in our trial.

*The lexical issue of the law and the case* As this example demonstrates, describing the relation between the law and the case is an intricate task. It is not only an issue of representative speech acts but primarily a lexical issue. In the history of science, a very interesting *convergence of jurisprudence and linguistics* can be observed insofar as both demonstrate a similar change in theorizing, from classical methodology restricted to rationality and codes, to a modern methodology which goes beyond abstract rule-governed patterns. It is 'the end of certainty'[25] which is

23 Wittgenstein, L. (1972), *On Certainty* (New York: Harper & Row).

24 Here quoted in English translation; cf. the court records in Altehenger, B. (1996), *Forensische Texte* (Hamburg: Buske), 289ff.

25 Prigogine, I. (1997), *The End of Certainty: Time, Chaos, and the New Laws of Nature* (New York: The Free Press).

recognized not only in physics but in other disciplines as well and requires a new type of open theorizing.

The first question to be posed by jurists is the question of *what the case is*. Is it, for instance, to give a popular example, 'intent' or 'negligence'? From the very beginning, juridical and linguistic thinking converge: what jurists discuss in terms of 'structural thinking',[26] linguists discuss in terms of lexical semantics. Whereas linguists can refer to the concept of indeterminacy of meaning for words of everyday use, jurists have to fix the relation between the case in performance and the normative concept of the law and to establish a high degree of legal bindingness. The infinite variation of performance has to be reduced to the structure of the law in the mind of the jurist.

Already this first step of deciding what is the case, is a *step of arguing* which is dependent on individual *evaluation*. The individual position taken in this step will then be brought to bear in a dialogic argumentative process of confirming, defending and attacking arguments inside and outside of court.

For both disciplines *rethinking language and the law* means abandoning one-sided models of traditional methodology and searching for a methodology which is capable of bridging the gap between competence and performance in the 'mixed game' of competence-in-performance. Whereas from the juridical point of view the focus is on the *effective use of the law as a tool*, from the linguistic point of view the focus is on the *effective use of language and communication in legal affairs*. The two juridical areas of 'structural thinking' and 'argumentative thinking'[27] correspond to the two linguistic areas of 'lexical semantics' and 'language as dialogue'.

What jurists discuss in terms of *the law and the case*, linguists discuss *in terms of word meaning*. For almost a century of modern linguistics language was considered to be a sign system. Having now arrived at a general turning point in science where the limited explanatory power of fixed rule-governed systems is increasingly being recognized,[28] far-reaching consequences have to be drawn. For lexical semantics, this means the end of artificial models which are based on defining the meaning of the sign.[29] In performance it is human beings who use words in order to predicate how they perceive the world. Human beings are not isolated hermits but social beings who have to settle their diverging views in the case of conflicts. Where negotiation of diverging views cannot be settled in everyday argumentation, a level of superordinate validity, that is, the institution of the law, is called for. The law and its technical terms try to fix reality, reduce multi-faceted and ever-changing performance to a generally valid pattern. But even at

26 Haft, *Juristische Rhetorik*, 'Strukturdenken'.

27 Haft, *Juristische Rhetorik*, 'Strukturdenken und Argumentdenken'.

28 Cf. Harris, R. (1981), *The Language Myth* (London: Duckworth).

29 Cf. also Kjær, A.L. (2007), 'Phrasemes in Legal Texts', in Burger, H. et al. (eds), *Phraseologie. Phraseology. Ein internationales Handbuch der zeitgenössischen Forschung*, Vol. 1 (Berlin and New York: de Gruyter), 506–16.

the level of the law, argumentation is, in principle, based on interpretation of the law and evaluation of the individual case.

The history of lexical semantics started with artificial models of single signs and lead to pragmatic models of words-in-use. It is a history characterized by changing concepts of the lexical unit, from the single word,[30] via the word in context,[31] to words-in-use or multi-word units.[32] In everyday language use words gain their meaning in phrases, and it is phrases from which the utterances are built up. Whereas the meaning of single words is characterized by indeterminacy, the meaning of phrases is more definite.[33] Words are used for predicating, that is, for expressing how the speaker perceives and identifies the world. In languages for specific purposes, such as the language of the law, words or terms are intended to identify an object as precisely as possible. Vocabularies for specific purposes, for example, vocabularies of legal terms, are therefore characterized by a *semantics of definitio* , whereas vocabularies of everyday use are characterized by a *semantics of use*.[34] A semantics of terms is not enough to decide what is the case. To take the example of the German term *leihen* as defined by law and the ordinary language use of the word *leihen*. In ordinary language, we use *leihen* for a variety of events, we can borrow a book, a car, for payment or not, we can borrow words, ideas, methodologies and so on. In the language of law, there are clearly defined conditions for the event of borrowing.

Jurists need technical terms which are to some degree defined, that is, whose conditions of use are restricted. Whereas, for instance, the meaning of the word 'violence' in everyday language is dependent on the speaker, on what the speaker considers to be violence, the language of the law must attempt to define the meaning of the word speaker-independently by changing the everyday word to a technical term. Nevertheless the gap remains between the case and the term. Here the jurist has to start with interpretation and evaluation for every individual case.

It is the linguist's task to develop a lexical semantics that is able to deal with everyday semantics-in-use and with the semantics of technical terms as well. Communication however is not a matter of single words or terms, it is a matter of utterances. Words and terms are used in utterances for different speech acts.

---

30 For example, Saussure, F. de (1974), *Cours de linguistique générale, fasc. 4*, ed. by R. Engler (Wiesbaden: Harrassowitz); Wierzbicka, A. (1972), *Semantic Primitives* (Frankfurt am Main: Athenäum).

31 For example, Mel'čuk, I.A. and Wanner, L. (1994), 'Lexical Co-occurrence and Lexical Inheritance: Emotion Lexemes in German: A Lexicographic Case Study', *Lexikos* 4, 88–160.

32 For example, Sinclair, J. (1998), 'The Lexical Item' in Weigand, E. (ed.), *Contrastive Lexical Semantics* (Amsterdam and Philadelphia, PA: Benjamins), 1–24 and Weigand, E. (1998), 'Contrastive Lexical Semantics', in Weigand, *Contrastive Lexical Semantics*, 25–44.

33 Weigand, E. (2006), 'Indeterminacy of Meaning and Semantic Change', in Love, Nigel (ed.), *Language and History. Integrationist Perspectives* (London and New York: Routledge), 79–98.

34 Wittgenstein, L. (1958), *Philosophical Investigations* (Oxford: Blackwell).

Speech acts are moves in dialogue, specific moves in argumentative dialogue, not autonomous on their own but dialogically oriented acts of human beings.[35] From the very beginning the individual view of the speaker, his/her evaluation and culturally different interpretation of the world comes in, enters even the meaning of terms. It is not one communicative competence which underlies dialogue but different competences-in-performance that are negotiated in dialogue by different interlocutors. Understanding cannot be presupposed but occurs in the process of dialogue. Evaluation can be explicitly expressed by words in the utterance. In large measure it is a cognitive phenomenon which lies behind the verbal sequence of utterances and determines the way the world is presented.

### *Directive and Explorative Games of Desire*

Legal action is not only argumentative action based on beliefs; it is also action based on desire which is expressed as a *claim to volition*. The claim to volition may relate to getting as much as possible in directive games or to detecting what really has happened, that is, to knowledge in explorative games. Negotiation of divergent directive claims is the purpose of games outside the court played by the parties' advocates who aim at achieving as good a position as possible for their clients. Again evaluative arguments and different positioning of an event play an important role and characterize the rhetoric of these games. Games of negotiation are games of power, not only rhetorical power. The points that are introduced in favour or against a position depend on evaluation and differ greatly with respect to different lifestyles in different cultures.

Explorative legal games of detecting what really has happened are mostly part of more complex games, for instance, cross-examination in a trial.

### *Declarative Games of Creating Validity*

The central goal of legal action can be considered to be to create legal validity through the text of the law. Human life as a matter of 'living with uncertainty'[36] needs an intersubjective benchmark to settle the different interests involved. Where conflicts cannot be solved by the conflict parties themselves, some superordinate legal power is required to decide the issue at stake. The verdict of the judge will not solve the conflict in the sense of reconciling the opponents but will end the conflict by making a decision. Legal texts, among them contracts, are central to this process. They are the result of argumentative games and create intersubjective validity by their declarative power. As texts they are not autonomous but components in the legal action game. As ordinary citizens we can refer to legal texts and request their validity. However, in the end controversial affairs will be decided by the judge in a trial.

35 Cf. Weigand, *Sprache als Dialog*.

36 Toulmin, *Return to Reason*.

On the way towards a common European legal thinking it will be crucial to design legal texts, including contracts, that are acknowledged by the individual partners. To my mind, this process cannot be conceived of as achieving one pattern of action equally valid in all countries but has to cater for national differences within a common framework. Essential points will have to be fixed in a way that grants some leeway for individual cultural evaluation. In the end, it will be hard political interests which will decide what a common European law looks like.

## From Differences to a Common Game

Let us now focus on the basic differences which have to be settled on the way towards a common European legal thinking. These differences, to my mind, are threefold: different procedures in court according to different legal systems, multiculturalism and multilingualism.

### *Different Legal Systems: Rule-based and Case-based Systems*

Concerning the European issue, legal argumentation will have to mediate between the two existing legal systems, the rule-based and the case-based system of regulation. Rule-based systems like those in France or Italy tend to focus on abstract codifications and the effectiveness of statutes; courts are mainly regarded as 'la bouche de la loi'. Case-based systems like Great Britain or Ireland concentrate on law as an argumentative process which takes place in front of a court; justice is regarded as an iterative way of deciding individual cases. The two models have merged due to the EU efforts to harmonize law, so that hybrid systems combining rule- and case-based systems are emerging. Nevertheless the two approaches still greatly influence legal reasoning and the effect of rhetorical aspects in court. The new EU Member States, in particular, had links to the different models, such as Malta and its relationship to the UK legal system or Latvian roots in the German philosophy of law. The ultimate objective of the EU efforts will be to arrive at a high degree of coincidence in a joint system of regulation which will accept cultural differences within a common framework.

### *Different Legal Cultures*

Apart from different legal systems the most important differences to be settled are cultural differences. For any action game a crucial parameter will be that human beings are cultural beings. Culture is not only an external system of values which we can apply or reject. Culture is also internalized according to the sociobiology of human behaviour. The so-called language–instinct debate, which considers language to be determined either by biology and genes[37] or by external culture,[38] is played at the extremes. The Theory of Dialogic Action Games is based on the sociobiology of language and human action, which is situated between these two extremes.[39]

Different legal cultures also imply different rhetorical means and strategies. *Rhetoric* is not an independent art but a skill that is learned within a *cultural* framework. As effective use of communicative means, it depends on what can count as effective in a certain culture. Rhetoric is thus not a universal system of conventions and strategies, for example of rationality, but is culturally embedded. If the cultural framework changes, 'recontextualization' is needed.[40] Even rationality does not represent a fixed universal value but turns out to be a Western concept.[41] The same is true of the 'criterion of legitimacy' in the institutional legal game of a trial. It can be applied to determine whether an argumentative move can count as acceptable or is to be rejected as not legitimate or inadmissible.[42] This leads in particular to the question of how a criterion such as 'acceptable' can be justified. It will in any case depend on the cultural value system.

Cultures in the end evolve from the fact that people set up different evaluative benchmarks for their specific conditions of life.[43] Value systems are externally comprehensible in different habits and customs and in the code of law. They are also internalized in human minds. Culture thus determines from the very outset what can count as acceptable or what can be conceived of as effective. Rhetoric and culture are not separate systems but interacting forces of human dialogic interaction. A model which is capable of describing the complex network of language, culture and rhetoric has to start from the complex and to deal with the interactions of various subsystems that constitute the hierarchy of the complex whole.[44] The whole means human beings' competence-in-performance in the mixed game. Human beings decide in the mixed game what they consider to be effective

37 For example, Chomsky, N. (1968), *Language and Mind* (New York: Harcourt Brace and World) and Pinker, Steven (1994), *The Language Instinct: The New Science of Language and Mind* (New York: William Morrow).

38 Sampson, G. (2005), *The 'Language Instinct' Debate*, rev. edn (London and New York: Continuum).

39 Wilson, *On Human Nature*; Weigand, E. (2007), 'The Sociobiology of Language', in Grein, M. and Weigand, E. (eds.) *Dialogue and Culture* (Amsterdam/Philadelphia: Benjamins), 27–49.

40 Kjær, A.L. (2008), 'Recontextualization of Concepts in European Legal Discourse', in Weigand, E. (ed.): *Dialogue Analysis and Rhetoric* (Amsterdam: John Benjamins), 251–266.

41 Weigand, E. (2007), 'The Sociobiology of Language' in Grein and Weigand, *Dialogue and Culture*.

42 Cf. Cattani, A. (2001), *Botta e risposta. L'arte della replica* (Bologna: Il Mulino).

43 Weigand, E. (2007), 'The Sociobiology of Language' in Grein and Weigand, *Dialogue and Culture*.

44 Simon, 'The Architecture of Complexity.

means. Their decision will thus in any case be their own decision; nonetheless it depends on the legal culture involved.

Legal cultures are based on traditions and the code of law. Across Europe, different traditions of legal culture and rhetoric have evolved over the centuries. Their differences have to be made transparent and reconsidered in developing a common European legal thinking. A common view requires us to reflect on and to decide what can be considered European values. In a more general sense, behind any evaluation there is the perspective of ideology or of a philosophy of law. On the one hand, there is the question of how far biased argumentation can be allowed to go, and on the other hand, there is the question of purpose and degree of punishment. Can it be a deterrent? Is there an obligation to rehabilitate a criminal offender? In any case, a European system of values will have to be conceived of as an open system, not as a fixed code. Not only ethical values but also hard political interests and power will play their role in achieving a common understanding.

Human beings cannot simply change their cultural identity and ignore values they have lived with from birth. A clear example is the high value placed on the concept of the family in southern European countries. Addressing the ever-changing complexity of life cannot mean trying to achieve an equal code for all. Common European thinking will posit respect for cultural differences and dealing with them open-mindedly at the level of joint European interests. European culture is not only determined by the past, it has to take account of changing conditions and future challenges. European identity and a common European legal thinking will have to be created and will never be fixed concepts.

### *Different Terms*

Besides the differences in legal systems rooted in European multiculturalism there are the obvious differences resulting from different languages. The fact that human beings communicate in different languages is not in itself a problem. Languages can be translated, and translations function efficiently as far as they refer to common states of affairs. Problems arise when these states of affairs are differently conceptualized. As legal language tries to minimize the 'uncertainty' of meaning in ordinary language use and to define its lexical units, different terms arise not only as different expressions but as expressions for different meanings. This brings in the lexical issue of creating *terminological bridges*, which is the most important issue to be settled in the field of multilingualism.

A common European legal practice depends on an ever-growing number of conceptual and terminological bridges that establish relationships of content equivalence between different national and supranational legal systems. Thus, the emergence of common legal practice is accompanied by the evolution of cross-linguistic and cross-systemic conceptual and terminological knowledge. In order to ensure stable and dependable legal practice, this knowledge must be consolidated.

The new discipline of knowledge management is increasingly focusing on the issue of the consolidation of evolving knowledge.[45]

Each country in Europe, and elsewhere, has its own legal system. This system is accessible through its specific terminology. The terms denoting legal concepts, however, are linked to everyday language. They have to be understood by the lay people who are subject to the law. In the long run, people will not accept a legal system that is entirely opaque. A legal concept such as murder cannot be defined entirely independently from what the general language word 'murder' means. Therefore legal terms are not as language-independent as the terms we find, for instance, in mathematics or in chemistry.

This does not mean, though, that legal concepts cannot, to some extent, differ from the meanings of their everyday language counterparts. The law may define its terms, for example *property* or *trust*, in a way that may differ in certain details from the way these words are described in dictionaries. Thus, in the end, legal terms are based on a semantics of definition, in contrast to the semantics of use for words of everyday language.

How a legal concept is applied to a particular case is, however, not part of the definition of legal concepts. It is a matter of negotiation. In his discussion of legal hermeneutics, Gadamer therefore rejects the notion that there is an immediate, perspectiveless, ahistoric procedure that would make each judgement a mere process of subsumption leading to a pre-established outcome.[46] Similarly, Dworkin sees adjudication as a special case of hermeneutical understanding.[47] Still, there is an interplay between legal concepts and the cases they are applied to. If sufficient similar cases are adjudicated in a comparable way, this may lead to a re-definition of the concept.

Legal systems viewed as conceptual and terminological ontologies are nation-specific. The legal concept 'Eigentum' is found in the Austrian, the Swiss and the German legal systems; in each of them it is defined in slightly different ways. The same may well be true for the concept 'property' defined variously in the English, the Irish and the Scottish legal systems. If a nation is bilingual (for example, Ireland) or trilingual (for example, Switzerland), efforts will be made to make sure that the definitions of the concepts are as equivalent as possible.

As legal terms are always linked to the homonymous general language words, language plays an important role. The word *property* is not entirely co-referential with the word *Eigentum*, because in German there is also a related concept, *Besitz*, usually (mis-)translated as *possession*. In a European court ruling involving these concepts, straightforward translations may well be misleading. The differences in

45 Ahmad, K. and Gillam, L. (2002), 'Scientific Texts and the Evolution of Knowledge', in Koskela, M. et al. (eds) (2001), *Scientiae I. Proceedings of the 13th LSP, Vassa, Finland, August 20–24th 2001* (Vassa: University of Vassa Publications Unit), 123–35.

46 Gadamer, H.-G. (1965), *Wahrheit und Methode: Grundzüge einer philosophischen Hermeneutik*, 2nd edn (Tübingen: J.C.B. Mohr).

47 Dworkin, R. (1986), *Law's Empire* (Cambridge, MA: Harvard University Press).

the legal concepts will have to be explained, and a common application to the case in question may have to be negotiated. Such negotiations will make ample use of explications, descriptions, exemplifications and more or less partial definitions. All these clarifications can be seen as paraphrases of the language- and nation-specific legal term, and it is these case-specific clarifications which form the bridges between the incommensurate concepts of different legal systems.[48] Each bridge adds new legal knowledge to the relationship between the legal systems involved.

The common legal system evolving in Europe is best described as a subsidiary system that does not render the existing national legal systems obsolete. The terminological knowledge concerning European Community law can be regarded as consolidated.[49] The concepts are strictly defined, and termbanks supply the equivalents in the EU languages. Yet while Community law may to some extent replace national law, the national legal systems remain fully autonomous as long as they are not challenged by the Commission or a partner country. Whenever this occurs, the primordial task is to negotiate the equivalence between the case descriptions in the legal systems involved. This is done through the bridges mentioned above. To the extent that these bridges are re-used in comparable cases, they constitute increasingly consolidated legal knowledge of the equivalents obtaining between the legal systems involved.

There are various ways to describe the evolution of transnational legal knowledge. In the framework of cultural anthropology we can posit that the members of legal communities engage in Wittgensteinian language games. Within one community, these interactions lead to the consolidation of legal knowledge through the refinement of interpretative devices (for example, law commentaries, court verdicts), an ongoing process which can be viewed as a continuous improvement of the national legal system. In the exchange of knowledge across different communities, communication becomes problematic, as the dialogue must accommodate heterogeneous interpretative assumptions. Such a negotiation between different discursive realities can be a source for innovation, that is, the creation of new knowledge. The emergence of European Community law can be seen to be the result of such a negotiation.

In the ethnomethodologist school of anthropology, knowledge is seen as practice.[50] Here, the evolution of knowledge is the result of interplay between consolidated local practices by the establishment of 'boundary practices' enabling

48 Cf. Teubert, W. (2003), 'Writing, Hermeneutics, and Corpus Linguistics', *Journal of Logos and Language* 4:2, 1–17.

49 Cf. Borchardt, K.-D. (2000), *The ABC of Community Law*, 5th edn (Luxembourg: Office for Official Publications of the European Communities).

50 Cf. Mead, G.H. (1934), *Mind, Self and Society* (Chicago, IL: Chicago University Press).

us to bridge meanings across communities and systems.[51] The creation of case-specific bridges between different legal systems will lead to dependable boundary practices to the extent that the cases involved are treated as precedents which are invoked in subsequent cases. The evolving knowledge contained in the bridges will then lead to a consolidation of the new knowledge.

Methods of textual analysis will reveal the bridges. A suitable example is the adaptation of a national (in this case, British) statute to Community law, as discussed in the British Parliament:

> [T]he English law concept of a 'letting' or a 'leasing' as necessarily involving an interest in rem in land is not *reflecte* in the legal systems of most of our *Community partners*. The words ['any license to occupy land …'] were included in order to try and *achieve consistency across the Community* and to *implement*, using English *terminology*, the article 13B exemption relating to 'the leasing or letting of immovable property'. (www.parliament.the-stationary-office.co.uk/pa/ld200001/ldjudgmt/jd010607/collies-2.htm)

The words and phrases in italics are indicators of a bridging negotiation. In this example, the issue is the formulation of a new law. It creates an English equivalent for a concept used on the Continent, but not heretofore in Britain, in connection with the concepts of 'letting' and 'leasing'. This bridge, the words 'any license to occupy land …', will probably be re-used in applicable subsequent cases.

Texts in which we find bridges of this kind include, among others, national and European parliamentary proceedings, certain European Commission documents with a legally binding force, transnational commercial contracts and, very importantly, the rulings of the European Court of Justice. Taken together, they will provide an answer to the question how transnational legal knowledge in Europe evolves and to what extent it becomes consolidated. Corpus linguistics provides the methodology to compile appropriate (multilingual parallel) corpora of these texts and to extract the relevant terminological knowledge from them.[52]

## Conclusions

Very interestingly, the basic issue of the law, the relation between the case and the law, re-appears as a basic issue of linguistics in terms of 'performance' and 'competence'. For both disciplines the question is how to bridge the gap between these completely different phenomena. In my view, it can be bridged only in the minds of human beings by their competence-in-performance, which has to be developed as a *European competence-in-performance*. What is needed is a shared

51 Cf. Wenger, E. (1998), *Communities of Practice: Learning, Meaning and Identity* (Cambridge: Cambridge University Press).

52 Cf. Halliday, M.A.K. et al. (2004), *Lexicology and Corpus Linguistics* (London: Continuum).

basis of European law and a joint procedure of interpretation and argumentation which relates to a common system of values but tolerates certain differences.

Arriving at a common European legal thinking will not happen by itself. Joint effort in theory and practice is needed in consciously *deciding about* what can count as common values and in negotiating individual cultural differences. It will be a dialogic and specifically European challenge to cater for cultural differences in a common European House.

I would like to thank Wolfgang Teubert (Birmingham) for cooperating with me on an earlier draft of the section on terminological bridges.

# Chapter 15
# European Integration and Legal Communication[1]

Heikki Mattila

It is often presumed that Latin expressions and maxims form a useful means to transmit legal messages in the communication between lawyers of various countries where divergent languages are in use. According to this view, the key terms included in legal texts may be given in Latin, so that it is not necessary to translate them from one modern language to another when legal messages are sent across linguistic borders. In effect, a proposal has even been made to restore Latin as the *lingua franca* of Europe, to be used as the main tool of communication in the European Union.[2] In the first part of the present chapter, the author aims to show that Latin has some value for international communication, but this value, however, is quite limited. Therefore, translation of terms between the modern languages of law is needed today and will also be needed in the future, which means that the basic problems of legal translation cannot be avoided. These problems will be discussed in the second part of the chapter.

## Legal Latin as a *Lingua Franca*[3]

### *Latin in the History of Occidental Legal Systems*

Besides the great literary works of Antiquity and the Middle Ages, the scientific studies of various disciplines form an important part of the written heritage of Latin. In addition to the Latin works of the philosophers and theologians, those of

---

1 The language of this chapter has been checked by Mr Michael Hurd of the University of Lapland to whom the author expresses his warmest thanks.

2 Sturm, F. (2002), 'Lingua Latina fundamentum et salus Europae', *The European Legal Forum – Forum iuris communis Europae* 6, 313–20.

3 This part of the chapter reproduces, in an updated and somewhat enlarged form, the author's keynote address in French at the XVII World Congress of the International Federation of Translators (FIT) in 2005. See Mattila, H. 'Latin juridique et traduction', in Salmi, L. and Koskinen, K. (eds) (2005), *Proceedings of the XVII World Congress. International Federation of Translators – Actes du XVII^e^ Congrès mondial. Fédération Internationale des Traducteurs* (Paris), 20–26.

the natural scientists and mathematicians of the beginning of the modern era are particularly worthy of mention. The names of Kepler, Newton, Galvani, Gauss and Linné are known all over the world.

The importance of Latin as a scientific language also extends to the science of law. The great jurists of ancient Rome used Latin as the language of Roman law. In the Middle Ages, and much later in modern times, Latin was used in the administration of the Catholic Church and in the application of Canonical Law. The law faculties of the universities, too, worked only in Latin. Even the legislators, administrators and law courts of various countries often utilized Latin, not only in the Middle Ages but also after this period. Certainly, this was not a democratic solution: ordinary people were unable to follow the procedures in which their affairs – and, in extreme cases, their lives – were judged. But democracy was not the intention either. According to a great English lawyer of the beginning of the seventeenth century, it is better that plain people understand nothing about judicial proceedings (due to the language barrier) because, in any case, they would understand everything wrongly.

Thus, the use of Latin prevented – sometimes intentionally – communication between lawyers and ordinary people. It facilitated, however, the contacts not only between states but also within state boundaries in countries which were not linguistically united. Simultaneously, Latin guaranteed linguistic neutrality and equality between diplomats representing states in which divergent languages were in use. However, Latin was abandoned in administrative and judicial matters, in part already at the end of the Middle Ages and, to a much greater degree, in the beginning of modern times. It was eliminated entirely from legal circles in the eighteenth and nineteenth centuries. This was due to several reasons. In the field of diplomacy, the main reason was the increased power of France. In place of Latin, which was supported by the Pope and the Emperor of the Holy Roman Empire – that is, the German Emperor – the King of France insisted, with more and more energy, on the use of French. In effect, from the end of the seventeenth century on, French became the dominant language of diplomatic affairs. Among other reasons that explain the disappearance of Latin from legal circles, as far as domestic matters are concerned, are the strengthening of the idea of the nation-state, the increase in the number of original statutes promulgated in each state (due to this strengthening) and the accentuation of the ordinary person's position as an active player in the society during the Enlightenment.

In legal science, Latin was gradually replaced by modern languages quite late: in the eighteenth and nineteenth centuries. In exceptional conditions, Latin was still occasionally used in the nineteenth century in administrative and judicial dealings. This was the case in certain parts of the Austrian Empire: Latin functioned there as a kind of bulwark against the introduction of the language of the centre of power. In effect, in Hungary and in the south of Poland (Calizia), the authorities and the courts of law remained true to Latin in order to prevent the adoption of German, which was expansive at that time. Ironically, in Croatia, which was subject to the Crown of Hungary, Latin was used to repulse the Hungarian language.

Even today Latin is not entirely dead as a language of administrative and judicial dealings: the *Codex juris canonici* (1983), the legal code of the Roman Catholic Church, exists, it is true, in various vernaculars, but its Latin text is the only authentic version. The continuing viability of Latin as a language of administration and legal matters within the Roman Catholic Church can also be seen in the General Regulations of the Roman Curia of 4 February 1992. These Regulations prescribe that the dicasters of the Curia draw up their acts in Latin; they are authorized, however, to use the most widespread languages for correspondence or, according to needs, for preparing documents.

We can thus state that the transition period from Latin to modern languages in European legal circles took centuries. As for the Catholic Church, this transition is still taking place. One important consequence of the long period of time during which diverse languages have coexisted is language mixing. Generally speaking, gradual language changes are often characterized by long periods of language mixing. It is therefore easy to understand that all over Europe the legal languages were earlier teeming with Latin quotations. Besides the texts of legal scholars, this applied to legislation and other practical legal documents as well. Let us cite a fragment (Book IV, Chap. 15, Art. 12) of the *Codex Maximilianeus Bavaricus* (1756), compiled, in principle, in German: *unter folgenden drei Requisitis: weder Mora noch Culpa aut Facto Debitoris*. The phrase contains eleven words in all – of which no less than five are Latin![4]

*Extent of the Use of Legal Latin Today*

During the last three centuries, Latin expressions and maxims in legal texts have become less frequent, but their use has not been entirely abandoned. Far from it! Generally, it can be said that Latin quotations are much more numerous in legal science than in practical juridical documents (statutes, judgments, administrative decisions, private-law documents and so on). Legal scholars all over the Western world use Latin quotations. For instance, according to a study carried out by our research team, some 600 Latin expressions and maxims are still in use in Finnish legal circles.[5] The widespread use of Latin quotations is discernible even in certain non-European legal languages which have been under the influence of Western legal cultures.

However, the differences between various countries in the use of Latin are important, notably in the field of practical lawyering. There are countries, like

---

4 A summary of the international history of legal Latin is presented, in more detail, in Mattila, H (2006), *Comparative Legal Linguistics* (Aldershot: Ashgate), 125–36.

5 See (in Swedish) Mattila, H. (2000), 'Latinet i den finländska juridiska litteraturen', *Tidskrift utgiven av Juridiska Föreningen i Finland*, 288 *et seq*., and the same text – somewhat abridged – in Russian (2003), 'Latinskii iazyk v finskoi iuridicheskoi literature' (Латинский язык в финской юридической литературе), *Ius antiquum – Drevnee pravo* (Древнее право), 12:2, 152–64.

the Nordic countries, where statutes and court decisions never contain any Latin quotations – this in order to guarantee the comprehensibility of laws and judgments and, consequently, the principle of linguistic democracy. During the past few decades, language specialists of most Western countries have underlined the disadvantages of the use of Latin quotations in legal texts. Due to their efforts, many governments, like the French one, have taken express measures to reduce this use. Nevertheless, the legislators, judges, administrators and advocates of many countries, like the Anglo-Saxon countries and Italy, still use Latin expressions and maxims in their texts. It is also known that certain advocates general of the Court of Justice of the European Union often use Latin in their opinions.

It is particularly interesting to note that nowadays legal authors in Eastern Central Europe and in Eastern Europe are inclined to increase the number of Latin expressions and maxims in their texts, rather than reduce it. Following the collapse of socialism, these authors want, by using the classical language of jurists, to insist on the fact that their countries are parties to the common legal tradition of Europe.

It is symptomatic that the most important part of the great codification of Roman Law, the Digest of the *Corpus Juris Civilis*, is now being published in Russia in the form of a bilingual edition in which the Latin text and Russian texts appear side by side.[6] In Poland, a country of great Latin traditions, eight dictionaries of legal Latin (if one includes the abridged ones) have appeared during the past few years.[7] In Estonia, the tendency towards an augmented use of Latin expressions in legal texts has been noted in empirical research: in 1993, the articles published in the Estonian review *Juridica* contained 66 Latin expressions and maxims in all (that is, slightly more than one Latin expression per article). In 2002, the number of Latin expressions and maxims had increased to 448 (or more than five Latin expressions per article) – a substantial rise.[8]

### *The Functions of Latin Quotations*

One can thus note that legal scholars, like the legislators, administrators, judges and advocates of certain countries, still use Latin quotations. Why? There are several reasons. As already pointed out above, medieval (and later) lawyers wanted to

6 Kofanov, L.L. (Кофанов, Л. Л.) (ed.) (2001–), *Digesta Iustiniani* I– / Digesty Iustiniana I– (Дигесты Юстиниана I–). Centrum iuris romani investigandi – Tsentr izucheniia rimskogo prava (Центр изучения римского права), (Moscow: Statut & Konsul'tant Plius / Москва: Статут & Консультант Плюс).

7 These are enumerated in Mattila, H. (2002), 'De aequalitate Latinitatis jurisperitorum. Le latin juridique dans les grandes familles de droit contemporaines à la lumière des dictionnaires spécialisés', *Revue internationale de droit comparé* 3, Note 44, and in Mattila, H. 'Latin juridique et traduction'.

8 See (in Estonian) Ristikivi, M. (2003), 'Ladina keel ajakirjas Juridica 1993–2002', *Juridica* X, 727–32.

maintain their monopoly of vocational knowledge by using an esoteric language – a human frailty which has appeared in all professions throughout the ages. It is certain that the lawyers of the world today are no more free of this frailty than their predecessors. At the same time, the distinctive language of a group, prison slang as well as legal Latin, is apt to strengthen the ties between the members of the group. According to Ernst Kramer, Latin expressions and maxims form a 'beloved folklore' of lawyers – a folklore quickly absorbed by law students, though Latin is no longer among the subjects of the university curriculum.[9] However, the use of Latin quotations can also be explained by cultural reasons and the needs of communication.[10]

*Rhetorical and display functions* As in the case of the use of Latin quotations in general, lawyers often use Latin for rhetorical purposes. This particularly applies to locutions of a cultural nature: *sed contra*, *prima facie*, and so on. Expressions and maxims drawn from the classical languages raise the stylistic level of the text and give a splendour to it – no matter whether the listeners or the readers understand them or not. According to Viktor Klemperer, 'Das Fremdwort imponiert, es imponiert um so mehr, je weniger es verstanden wird' ['A word of foreign origin impresses; the less it is understood, the more it impresses']. Frequently, a Latin quotation serves as a kind of exclamation mark: when it is appropriately placed, the reader or listener is startled and his or her attentiveness increases. Consequently, a legal writer may add a Latin expression before a passage where the reasoning abruptly turns in the opposite direction or where an apparent conclusion proves to be false.

The rhetorical function of Latin is often mixed with another function: display. Latin quotations in the texts of legal writers may have a display as well as rhetorical function. In such cases, Latin takes on a symbolic meaning: legal science and judicial activities are linked to Roman law, the source of the common traditions of the European legal systems. However, as far as this display function is concerned, one must above all mention the use of Latin maxims on the walls of the palaces of justice, in the seals of judicial authorities, and in the emblems of public bodies and associations of lawyers. The most fascinating example of the past few years is the new palace of the Polish Supreme Court in Warsaw, inaugurated in 1999. Certain walls of this palace are bordered on the outside by a row of pillars, each of which is decorated with a Latin inscription. The first pillar, for instance, is trimmed with the famous maxim against the corruption of public servants: *Qui munus publice mandatum accepta pecunia ruperunt, crimine repetundarum postulantur* ('Those who violate their public responsibility of office by taking money, are liable to

9 Kramer, E. 'Lateinische Parömien zur Methode der Rechtsanwendung', in Cagianut, F. and Vallender, K.A. (eds) (1995), *Steuerrecht. Ausgewählte Probleme am Ende des 20. Jahrhunderts. Festschrift zum 65. Geburtstag von Ernst Höhn* (Bern: Paul Haupt), 141–2.

10 The functions of Latin quotations are discussed in Mattila, *Comparative Legal Linguistics*, 136–46.

criminal charges of corruption', D.48.11.9). There are 86 pillars in all, each inscribed with a maxim.[11]

*Expressing legal concepts and principles* From the point of view of communication between lawyers, it is essential that Latin expressions and maxims also express legal concepts and principles. This is particularly important in cases where there are no established equivalents in the modern languages involved and in cooperation between lawyers of various countries. International organizations and fields of law which have an international nature are worthy of special mention.

International private law may be cited as a good illustration. According to a study carried out by our research team,[12] there are some twenty Latin expressions that appear in practically all manuals and treatises written in this field of law in various countries. The most popular of these expressions is *lex fori* ('the law of the court'). It is repeated dozens of times in any treatise or textbook on international private law. Another example is arbitration in international commerce. In Article 33, paragraph 2, of the arbitration rules of the United Nations Commission on International Trade Law (UNCITRAL), for example, there appears the expression *ex aequo et bono* ('according to what is right and good'). Like other Latin expressions that are frequently used in this context, one may cite *aequitas mercatoria* ('commercial fairness') and *bona fide* ('good faith').[13] As for legal science, new legal phenomena of an international nature often acquire a Latin name. For instance, the new pan-European law (notably created by the activities of the European Union) is sometimes called *jus commune novum* ('the new common law'), and a company formed under community legislation is designated a *societas Europaea* ('European company').

### *Problems Related to the Use of Latin Quotations in Legal Texts*

Taking into account the examples above, it is not surprising that some scholars underline the importance of Latin in international communication between lawyers: Latin has been called the *lingua franca* of lawyers. As these examples demonstrate, legal circles throughout the world recognize and understand numerous Latin

11 See (in Polish) Wołodkiewicz, W. (2001), *Regulae Iuris. Łacińskie inskrypcje na kolumnach Sądu Najwyż-szego Rzeczypospolitej Polskiej* (Warsaw: Wydawnictwo C.H. Beck), 13–14 and 17–21.

12 See (in French) Mattila, H. (2005), 'Jurilinguistique et latin juridique', in Gémar, J.-C. and Kasirer, N. (eds), *Jurilinguistique: entre langues et droits- Jurilinguistics: Between Law and Language* (Brussels and Montreal: Bruylant and Les Éditions Thémis), 83–8. A summary of the study is given in English in Mattila, H. (2006), 'Comparative Jurilinguistics: A Discipline in statu nascendi', in Pozzo, B. and Jacometti, V. (eds), *Multilingualism and the Harmonisation of European Law* (Alphen aan den Rijn: Kluwer Law International), 29–31.

13 Meyer, R. (1994), *Bona fides und lex mercatoria in der europäischen Rechtstradition* (Göttingen: Wallstein Verlag), 14.

expressions. The list could easily be made longer: *animus donandi*, *audiatur et altera pars*, *causa*, *de facto*, *de jure*, *ex offici* , *ratio legis*, *vis major*, and so on.

However, sceptical voices have also been heard. Some specialists say that the international use of legal Latin is hindered by serious problems. These specialists refer to the fact that the legal orders of various countries are divergent for historical reasons. Therefore a Latin expression or maxim does not always express an identical concept or principle in different countries. The sceptics also stress that the Latin expressions and maxims in use within various legal orders may be externally dissimilar even in cases where the concepts and principles are identical. This is explained by the fact that no terminological work of an international nature concerning legal Latin has ever been compiled. For this reason, opinions on the matter are divergent. Which point of view is the correct one?

*International incoherence of legal Latin* Earlier, no empirical studies had been carried out on the international communication value of legal Latin. This is why legal scholars and other specialists have disputed this value. In order to throw light upon the matter, our research team carried out, at the end of the 1990s, a study on the international homogeneity of legal Latin. In this research, we compared the contents of specialized dictionaries of various countries (dictionaries of legal Latin or general legal dictionaries) containing a large number of Latin expressions and maxims. The results were published in French in 2002 and, in a summarized form, in English in 2006.[14]

Our research revealed important differences, notably between the common-law countries and Continental Europe: for instance, three quarters of the Latin expressions in the English and American dictionaries studied are different from the Latin expressions in the dictionaries published in the German linguistic zone. Furthermore, there are divergences within Continental Europe as well. The legal Latin used in Spain (and in the Spanish linguistic zone in general) is particularly distinctive. On the contrary, the content of the Polish dictionaries of legal Latin closely resembles that of the dictionaries published in the German-speaking countries, despite the complex history of the relations between Poland and these countries.

However, even in this last case, the coherence is relative. In Poland, for instance, there are Latin expressions and maxims in use that have a purely national character. This is well illustrated by the maxim *lex retro non agit* ('the law does not operate retroactively') – a maxim particularly popular in Polish law courts nowadays. The legal principle expressed by this maxim forbids, for instance, the punishment of any person for an act which was not an offence at the moment it was committed. The maxim *lex retro non agit* was not formulated by the Romans of antiquity, nor

14 Mattila, H. (2002), 'De aequalitate Latinitatis jurisperitorum. Le latin juridique dans les grandes familles de droit contemporaines à la lumière des dictionnaires spécialisés', *Revue internationale de droit comparé* 3, 717–58, and Mattila, *Comparative Legal Linguistics*, 150–57.

by the medieval jurists of Bologna or Paris. This linguistic formulation is purely Polish, and it does not appear in any dictionaries of legal Latin outside Poland (though the principle in itself is naturally observed in all rule-of-law states). This maxim was probably formulated by a Polish specialist of Roman law, Stanisław Wróblewski, at the beginning of the twentieth century.[15]

In certain fields of law, the lack of unity of legal Latin is particularly striking. This applies, for example, to the law of inheritance – a field where the author of these pages has recently carried out a study in which all Latin quotations were picked from leading treatises on the law of inheritance in certain countries.[16] The research materials included, *inter alia*, a comprehensive French treatise and a comprehensive Finnish treatise (both approximately of the same size: some one thousand pages).[17] In the texts of these two treatises, one can find almost exactly the same number of Latin quotations: about eighty. However, not a single one of these quotations is identical![18] In consequence, Latin is clearly alive in the law-

15 See (in Polish) Wołodkiewicz, W. (2001), 'Lex retro non agit', in W. Wołodkiewicz and J. Krzynówek (eds), *Łacińskie paremie w europejskiej kulturze prawnej i orzecznictwie sądów polskich* (Warsaw: Liber), 154–5.

16 The study was published in Finnish in 2006. See Mattila, H. (2006), 'De Latinitate recentiorum doctrinarum ad iura hereditaria pertinentium', in Aarnio. A., Kangas, U., Korhonen, R., Mattila, H. and Mikkola, T. (eds), *Syntymästä kuolemaan, oikeudesta informaatioon. Ahti Saarenpää 60 vuotta* (Suomalaisen Lakimiesyhdistyksen julkaisuja) (E 17), 113–36.

17 The Finnish work (three volumes) is: Aarnio, A. and Kangas, U. (2002), *Perhevarallisuusoikeus* (Helsinki: Kauppakaari) and (1999 and 2000) *iidem*, *Suomen jäämistöoikeus* I and II (Helsinki: Kauppakaari). The French work is: Terré, F. and Lequette, Y. (1997), 'Droit civil', in *Les successions. Les libéralités*, 3rd edn (Paris: Dalloz).

18 In Terré and Lequette, 'Droit civil', one finds: *a contrario, a fortiori, a matre, a non domino, a pari, a patre, ab irato, ad nutum, ad probationem, ad solemnitatem, ad validitatem, animus donandi, ante mortem, brevitatis causa, contra, cum onere, cum viribus, de cuius, de lege ferenda, de plano, de residuo, dimidium paternis, dimidium maternis, ex causa antiqua, ex causa nova, exceptio non adimpleti contractus, exequatur, fructus augent hereditatem, gens, habilis ad nuptias, habilis ad nuptias, habilis ad pacta nuptialia, habilis ad nuptias (...), in favorem, in fin , incertus ex certis personis, infans conceptus (...), infans conceptus pro nato habetur quoties de commodis eius agitur, infra, instrumentum, intra vires, intra vires hereditatis, intuitu personae, intuitus personae, ira, is de cuius successione agitur, litteris, ne varietur, negotium, nemo liberalis nisi liberatus, nemo plus iuris (...), pars bonorum, pars hereditatis, pater familias, paterna paternis, materna maternis, pendente conditione, per saltum et omisso medio, post mortem, post mortem testatoris, prior tempore potior iure, pro herede, propter nuptias, ratio legis, re, re et verbis, res perit debitori, res perit domino, resoluto iure dantis (...), resoluto iure dantis, resolvitur ius accipientis, sine onere, solvens, stricto sensu, sui generis, supra, ubi lex (...), ultra vires, ultra vires hereditatis, ultra vires successionis, verbis, verbis tantum, votum mortis.*

In Aarnio and Kangas, *Perhevarallisuusoikeus*, one finds: *ad hoc, ad pias causas, adoptio filii loco, adoptio minus plena, adoptio plena, ambiguitas contra stipulatorem est, animus revocandi, animus testandi, benigna interpretatio, calatis comitiis, cautela Socini,*

of-inheritance literature in both France and Finland – but in the form of entirely divergent expressions and maxims.

In cases where the same expression or maxim is in use in various countries, its meaning is normally identical or, at least, similar. However, we could state that there is a difference of meaning in 5 to 10 per cent of cases. A good example is the word *exitus*. In the legal orders of the German linguistic zone (as well as, for example, in the Nordic countries) *exitus* means, solely or principally, 'decease' or 'death'. However, common-law lawyers give it the sense of 'children', 'offspring', 'the rents, issues, and profits of lands and tenements', 'an export duty', and 'the conclusion of the pleadings'.

The external variation of Latin expressions and maxims is a particularly interesting phenomenon. It is well-known that Western legal cultures (or individual authors) diverge in the use of the letters 'i' and 'j' (*ius – jus*) and the letters 't' and 'c' (*condicio – conditio*). However, there also are important variations of other types. Our research team found external variations in approximately 10 per cent of the expressions and maxims researched. Sometimes the same maxim appears in five variants: *Quod ab initio non valet in tractu temporis non convalescet*; *Quod ab initio non valet in tractu temporis non convalescit*; *Quod ab initio vitiosum est, tractu temporis convalescere non potest*; *Quod initio vitiosum est, non potest tractu temporis convalescere*; *Quod nullum est nullo lapsu temporis convalescere potest*. All these variants convey exactly the same juridical idea – 'What is invalid from the start, does not become valid with time' – despite the variation in the verbal forms, in the use of nouns and in the word order.

These external variations are often explained by the changes of Latin in the Middle Ages. For instance, the expression *a contrario* ('from the opposite', 'from the contrary'), sometimes a part of the longer expression *argumentum a contrario* ('argument from the contrary'), comes from scholastic Latin. This form is used in the Romance countries, in the Anglo-Saxon countries, in Poland, in Russia, and

---

*clausula rebus sic stantibus, computatio canonica, computatio civilis, conditio si testator sine liberis decesserit, contra bonos mores, Corpus iuris civilis, dementia, dementia senilis, desuetudo, donatio post obitum, ex analogia, exheredatio, falsa demonstratio non nocet, favor testamenti, forum, forum domicilii, forum hereditatis, forum rei sitae, ignorantia iuris nocet, in abstracto, in concreto, in dubio contra preferentem, in dubio contra stipulatorem, inter vivos, ipso iure, ius accrescendi, ius representationis, lex Falcidia, lex specialis derogat legi generali, lis pendens, lucida intervalla, mater semper certa est, mater semper certa est etiamsi vulgo conceperit, modus qualificatu , mortis causa, mutatis mutandis, non scriptum, numerus clausus, occupatio, omne testamentum morte consummatum est, pacta sunt servanda, pater est, Pater vero is est quem nuptiae demonstrant, portio legitima, portio portioni accrescit, psychosis delusionalis, res nullius, retorsio, successio ab intestato, successio ascendentium, successio descendentium, successio graduum, successio in capita, successio in stirpes, successio ordinum, testamenta plene ad voluntatem, testantium interpretatur, testamentum correspectivum, testamentum mysticum, testamentum reciprocum, testamentum simultaneum, testamentum tempore pestis conditum, traditio, ultima voluntas, una caro, voluntas ambulatoria est usque ad mortem.*

so on. The more classical form of the expression (*e contrario*), which has exactly the sense, dominates in the German-speaking countries, in the Nordic countries, and so on.

An entirely different problem, important from the point of view of oral communication, is the differences in the pronunciation of Latin. Among Finnish lawyers, for example, the reconstructed classical pronunciation is dominant. This pronunciation makes a clear distinction between long and short vowels, and the letter 'c' always has the phonetic value of 'k'. On the contrary, in most Continental countries, the lawyers pronounce Latin in accordance with post-classical or medieval paragons, diverging somewhat in different countries: the letter 'c' may be pronounced as 's', 'ts' or 'tsh'. For Continental lawyers, it is difficult to communicate, by means of Latin, with their British or American colleagues: the common-law lawyers pronounce Latin almost in the way they pronounce English (the so-called *Anglo-Latin*). For instance, the expression *amicus curiae* is pronounced, according to *Black's Law Dictionary* – 'əmáykəs kyúriyiy' or 'əmíykəs kyúriyay'. Sometimes a Continental lawyer does not even understand that his or her British or American colleague is using Latin expressions if he or she is not used to hearing Anglo-Latin pronounced.

*Limited transparency of the expressions and maxims of legal Latin* In addition to the problems arising because of the differences between various legal cultures, the comprehension of Latin expression and maxims is often made more difficult by their limited, or even nonexistent, transparency from the point of view of ordinary Latin. Firstly, these expressions or maxims may appear in an abbreviated form. Secondly, the literal translation of an expression or maxim, even when it is written in its entirety, does not always give any idea of its legal content.

The ancient Roman lawyers used many abbreviations, and this use increased in the Middle Ages. Even today, lawyers continue to use abbreviated forms of Latin expressions and maxims in their writings. The abbreviated words may belong to common Latin, like *ibid.* = *ibidem* ('in the same work', 'in the same passage'), *id.* = *idem* ('the same', 'the same person') or *et seq.* = *et sequentes* ('and those following' [when the author mentions only the page on which the reference begins]), but it is sometimes a question of an expression of legal Latin in the proper sense of the word. In the titles of court decisions of the common-law countries, one finds, for instance, the abbreviation *v.* or *vs.* = *versus* ('against') between the names of the plaintiff and the defendant. Another example is *ex rel.*, which means *ex relatione* ('from the account or information [of another person]').

It is particularly unsettling for outsiders that lawyers frequently express Latin expressions and maxims consisting of several words by writing out only one word, or two or three words from the beginning of the expression or maxim in question. As an example, let us mention the maxim *de minimis non curat lex/ praetor* ('the law / the praetor does not concern itself / himself with trifles'). This maxim means, for instance, that the plaintiff cannot bring an action in cases where the interest of the suit is insignificant. Common-law lawyers often express this maxim by using only two words: *de minimis*. They say, for example, 'the *de minimis* rule' or '*de minimis* doctrine'. The literal translation 'rule of trifles' says very little to uninitiated people. Certainly, common-law lawyers are not the only ones to use this kind of abbreviation. A Nordic lawyer may speak about '*pater (is) est rule*'. The translation 'rule of "the father is (the one who)"' has no information value for outsiders. Only when this maxim is written out in its entirety does it become understandable for people who read Latin: *pater (is) est quem nuptiae demonstrant* ('marriage makes the father (of a child) presumed'; literally: 'the (identity of the) father (of a child) is demonstrated (implied) by the fact of marriage').

As pointed out above, it is also possible that many Latin expressions and maxims are not transparent from the point of view of uninitiated readers even in cases where they are written out in their entirety. An expression or maxim sometimes has a legal content that is not at all apparent in its literal translation. The Italian lawyers – as well as their Portuguese- and Spanish-speaking colleagues – sometimes use the expression *fumus boni juris*. This expression means, in literal translation: 'fragrance of a good right' – a most poetic expression, but quite opaque! The specialized dictionaries of legal Latin make it understandable: the expression *fumus boni juris* refers to situations where the plaintiff (or the applicant) possesses already at first sight a right so plausible that the court of law (or the administrative authority) in question agrees to consider the claim and examine the case in detail. Sometimes, this expression also appears in a shortened form, consisting of the single word *fumus*. For instance: *Accertata l'esistenza del fumus, va riscontrata l'esistenza del periculum in mora nella obiettiva difficoltà per* , and so on.[19]

In the common-law countries, a similar example is the expression *amicus curiae*, already cited above for its pronunciation. This expression frequently appears in British and American court decisions. The literal translation 'friend of the court' is totally opaque to outsiders: the expression *amicus curiae* refers to a natural or legal person (like an organization for the protection of civil rights) who/which – without being a party to the case – is authorized by the court of law to give specific legal information in the case or to draw the attention of the court to matters which fall within the public interest.

### *The Consequences for International Legal Communication*

The analysis above shows that legal Latin is an instrument of international communication – but one which is sometimes deceptive. On one hand there is, in this Latin, a common core, a 'solid nucleus': certain expressions and maxims are known in all countries and have an identical universal meaning established by long-time usage. On the other hand, there are also numerous expressions and maxims which are closely tied to particular legal cultures and which sometimes have a purely national character. In addition, the comprehension of the expressions and maxims of legal Latin is frequently difficult because of their abbreviated

---

19 Tribunale di Taranto, 23 August 2004, on the internet.

or otherwise shortened form; some of these expressions and maxims remain opaque even in cases where they are written out in their entirety if the reader is not initiated, even if he or she has a command of ordinary Latin. Finally, the expressions and maxims of legal Latin do not always appear in the same external form in all countries.

Given these conditions, it is essential to ask how comparative lawyers and legal translators obtain reliable information on the meanings of the Latin expressions and maxims they are supposed to understand and/or translate. The answer is obvious: they have to consult specialized dictionaries. As the empirical studies mentioned above indicate, important dictionaries of legal Latin exist in all major legal cultures, and frequently in small countries as well.[20] This applies to the English-speaking world, the French-speaking world, the German-speaking countries, the Spanish- and Portuguese-speaking world, Italy, Russia, Poland, Greece and – to mention a more exotic example – Indonesia.[21] Among the smaller countries, Estonia could be mentioned.[22] Besides dictionaries including expressions and maxims of legal Latin only, it is worth mentioning that some general dictionaries of legal terminology contain a great deal of Latin. In some cases the number of Latin expressions and maxims in these dictionaries is much larger than in the specialized dictionaries of legal Latin.[23]

It is particularly important that comparative lawyers and legal translators are conscious of the fact that they must always consult a dictionary of legal Latin published in the framework of the legal culture from which the source text comes. It is dangerous to try to understand or translate, for example, the Latin expressions of a German juridical text on the basis of an English or American dictionary of

20 A list covering a number of dictionaries of legal Latin published in major legal cultures (English linguistic zone, French linguistic zone, German linguistic zone, Spanish and Portuguese linguistic zone, Italy, Russia and Greece) can be found in Mattila, H. (2006), *Major Legal Languages* (Aldershot: Ashgate), 157–8. In Mattila, 'Latin juridique et traduction' one also finds some dictionaries of legal Latin published in smaller and more exotic countries (25–6).

21 Hamzah, A. (1985), *Istilah dan peribahasa hukum bahasa Latin* ('Legal Terms and Maxims in Latin') (Bandung: Penerbit Alumni).

22 Adomeit, K. Ristikivi, M. and Siimets-Gross, H. (2005), *Ladina-eesti õigussõnastik* ('Latin–Estonian Legal Glossary') (Tallinn: Eesti Keele Sihtasutus).

23 Notably, this concerns *Black's Law Dictionary*, 7th edn (St Paul, MN: West Publishing, 2000). The number of Latin expressions and maxims in the book is not given by the author, but in connection with our study (mentioned above) we calculated this number in an earlier edition. It is some eight thousand. In the two works by Guillermo Cabanellas, taken together, there are even more Latin expressions and maxims: approximately 9,600 (this number has also been calculated by our research team). See Guillermo Cabanellas and Luis Alcalá-Zamora y Castillo (1992), *Diccionario enciclopédico de derecho usual I–VIII*, 16th edn (Buenos Aires: Editorial Heliasta) and Guillermo Cabanellas (1992), *Repertorio jurídico de principios generales del derecho, locuciones, máximas y aforismos latinos y castellanos*, 4th edn (ampliada por Ana María Cabanellas. Buenos Aires: Editorial Heliasta).

legal Latin, and *vice versa*. For the same reason, the internet, which is often very useful, may also be dangerous as a source of information if the origin of the page consulted is uncertain. In the case of Latin expressions and maxims, as in all data retrieval, the use of adequate information sources is one of the most important virtues of comparative lawyers and legal translators. They have to master, so to say, the informatics of legal Latin.

## Basic Problems of Legal Translation

The examination above demonstrates that problems of international legal communication can be solved by using Latin expressions and maxims only to a limited extent. Therefore, legal terms need to be translated between modern languages. The problems encountered in doing so will be examined in the following section.

### *Need for the Translation of Legal Documents*

*European integration and legal cooperation across borders* During the past decade, European integration has made considerable progress. On one hand the structures of the European Union have been strengthened, and on the other hand the geographic area covered by the Union has been enlarged. Consequently, people, services, capital and goods move freely between Union countries. Logically, the principle of free movement has produced the multiplication of all kinds of legal relationships across state boundaries.

In such cases, disagreements between parties are decided by different bodies (arbitration tribunals, national courts of law, and so on). This involves procedures of an international nature, often leading to the enforcement of relevant decisions abroad. To resolve the problems of border-crossing lawsuits and enforcement, the European Union first drafted conventions of international private law (covering both conflicts of law and procedural matters). The Amsterdam Treaty (1999) later transferred essential sectors of the co-operation on justice and home affairs to the competence of the European Community. Hence, the competence of the Community was enlarged in the field of international private law, including international law of procedure (notably international legal assistance and enforcement of judgments). Following this, legislative work in this branch of law has been very active. A comprehensive system based on directly applicable regulations has been developed or is in preparation.[24] In the field of international criminal law, too, EU cooperation is extensive.[25]

*Increase of legal translation* The multiplication of lawsuits and other procedures of an international nature has caused a corresponding increase of legal documents from various countries: writs of summons served abroad, testimonies before a foreign court, statements of the contents of foreign law, judgments from other countries to be enforced, requests for extradition, and so on.[26] Legal documents are normally drafted in the official language of the country of origin.[27] This applies not only to the documents of official bodies but to many categories of private instruments as well: for example, in the field of family law and the law of inheritance (marriage settlements, deeds of partition of matrimonial property or estate distribution, and so on). If the language of the document is not the language of the procedure in another country, it must be translated.[28]

Translations often constitute one of the weakest links in international legal procedures – despite the fact that legal translators certainly do their best. Two major

24 The so-called Brussels I regulation, officially Council Regulation (EC) No. 44/2001 of 22 December 2000 on jurisdiction and the recognition and enforcement of judgments in civil and commercial matters, is worth special mention. Since family law (except maintenance recovery) was left out of this regulation, a new regulation covering the essential sectors of this field, the so-called Brussels II Regulation (No. 1347/2000), was drafted. This has recently been replaced by the Brussels IIa Regulation No. 2201/2003 of 27 November 2003 concerning jurisdiction and the recognition and enforcement of judgments in matrimonial matters and matters of parental responsibility in which child law is included more widely than before. Judgments on child maintenance are covered by the Brussels I Regulation, but in December 2005 a draft for a new regulation facilitating the enforcement of maintenance judgments (and other documents) and making international legal assistance in these matters more effective was prepared.

25 For this cooperation a special European judicial network has been created. See <http://www.ejn-crimjust.eu.int/>.

26 The translation of European Union documents is a different question. Official EU documents must be translated into all Member-State languages. Since there are 23 languages in the Union, the principle of linguistic equality creates a huge need for translations. In 2002, over three thousand translators were permanently employed by the European Community, and, in addition, a great number of freelancers were hired. Within the Community institutions, over three million pages were then translated. Within the European Court of Justice alone, the number of translated pages of a legal nature was over 450,000. The ECJ employs special staff for this – lawyer-linguists – who have legal training and solid linguistic competence. There are about twenty-five for each Union language.

27 Commercial documents and arbitration awards form an exception. In these documents, international languages, mostly English, are used. The same can be said of documents establishing the contents of foreign law in conflict-of-laws cases.

28 At present, the Brussels I Regulation presupposes that the petitioner presents a translation of the foreign judgment to be enforced (Article 55 (2)). The same applies to the Brussels IIa Regulation. According to reform plans, this requirement will be dropped

reasons can be mentioned.[29] Firstly, there are important conceptual differences between various legal systems, which means that a juridically exact translation is sometimes impossible. Secondly, the human and material resources available for translating are often limited, notably in areas outside commercial matters where big money is not involved. Let us consider first the problem of conceptual differences, following which, the resource problem.

*Conceptual Differences in Legal Translation*

*Overview* In spite of European integration, there are a great number of conceptual differences between the legal orders of the countries of the EU, some of them considerable, many others only minor. In legal documents to be translated in practice, legal concepts dating back to the *jus commune* period or unified by measures of integration and the original concepts of each legal order intertwine in a complex way. This occurs particularly in translation between traditional legal English – that is, common-law language – and continental languages expressing civil-law thinking. Even if a large number of legal rules have been unified by European integration measures, it is not clear to what extent common law and civil law are really converging. Furthermore, the conceptual differences between various continental countries also lead to serious translation problems. Differences in court structures and procedural techniques are especially worth mentioning. The following presentation on various strategies of legal translation includes examples of this kind of conceptual problem.

*Alternative translation strategies* A legal translation must adequately express the relevant legal concepts behind the terms of the source language in the target language even in cases where no exact equivalent exists. To do this, the translator has alternative strategies, including direct quotations, rough equivalents, term-

in cases concerning judgments on child support: only a standard form must be filled in. An important reason for this reform is that the translation of judgments is very expensive. In maintenance matters in which no large amounts of money are involved, it has been possible to obstruct the enforcement of foreign judgments by means of excessive translation requirements.

29 As for the theory of legal translation, see generally Arntz, R. (ed.) (1995), *La traduzione. Nuovi approcci tra teoria e pratica* (Bolzano: Accademia Europea Bolzano / CUEN,), Gémar, J.-C. (1995), *Traduire ou l'art d'interpréter. Langue, droit et société. Eléments de jurilinguistique*. Vol. 2: *Application* (Sainte-Foy: Presses de l'Université du Québec), and Šarčević, S. (1997), *New Approach to Legal Translation* (The Hague etc.: Kluwer Law International). As for the theory of EU translation, see Kjær, A.L. 'Legal Translation in the European Union: A Research Field in Need of a New Approach', in Kredens, Krzysztof and Goźdź-Roszkowski, Stanisław (eds) (forthcoming), *Language and the Law: International Outlooks* (Frankfurt am Main: Peter Lang).

like explanations, enumerative translations[30] and neologisms.[31] The first three strategies are common in practice, and they will be briefly discussed in the following section.

*Direct Quotations* The strategy of direct quotations means that a foreign term is not translated or adapted to the target language but is left as it is to symbolize an original foreign legal concept.[32] *Common law* and *equity* are famous English-language examples appearing as such in legal texts in various languages. Also *trust* may turn up, for example in the French versions of international conventions.[33] French examples can also be presented,[34] like *Conseil d'État*. This institution has been received in several countries, such as Greece, where its name is a direct calque: *Symvoúlio tis Epikrateías* (Συμβούλιο της Επικρατείας).[35] Hence, in legal

30 Different legal languages sometimes express hierarchies of concepts in different ways. It is possible that certain abstract terms of one language are lacking in another language. In this case, the translator may be obliged to enumerate a number of terms which together cover the contents of a single term in another language. For instance, in French one has to enumerate three terms (*lois, décrets et autres règlements*) to cover the Finnish *säädös*, which includes all kinds of statutes or enactments.

31 A translator may create a neologism to express a foreign concept. He or she then has three possibilities: a modification of the original foreign word adapted to the orthography and pronunciation of the target language, a direct calque (loan translation), or a neologism based on the functions of the institution or the characteristics of the concept in question. In ordinary translation, neologisms should only be created after careful consideration. Normally, this task should be left to terminology specialists. However, many neologisms are created in connection with EU translation in which translation work and terminology work are often combined. See in more detail Mattila, *Comparative Legal Linguistics*, 117–21, where the translations of *acquis communautaire* and *avocat général* in various languages are discussed.

32 Translators often add an explanatory note when using a direct quotation. This applies, *inter alia*, to the names of various law courts. When *Landgericht* is not translated, a translator may add a note explaining the hierarchical position of this German court and its competence *ratione materiae*.

33 Trust appears as a quotation in, for example, the French version of the Hague Convention on the Law Applicable to Agency. Article 3 (b) reads: le *trustee* n'est pas considéré comme un intermédiaire agissant pour le compte du *trust*, du constituant ou du bénéficiaire (the words trustee and trust are printed in italics in the original text).

34 To express original concepts of EC law, French quotations are common in Union languages. A good example is *acquis communautaire*.

35 *Symvoúlio* = 'council' and *Epikráteia* = State. See in more detail Kerameus, K.D. and Kozyris, P.J. (1998), *Introduction to Greek Law* (Athens: Sakkoulas), 26.

literature in English the *Symvoúlio tis Epikrateías* has sometimes been referred to as 'the *Conseil d'État of Greece*'.[36]

Exceptionally, an internationally well-known quotation may also derive from a small legal language. One of the most famous examples is the Swedish term *ombudsman* (lit. 'representative'[37]). This institution of supervision of legality, originally Swedish, has been adopted in many countries throughout the world, and specialists normally use the original term (*ombudsman*) when discussing this institution in any country, even if the official name is different, like *Parliamentary Commissioner for administration* in the United Kingdom, *médiateur* in France, or *rzecznik praw obywatelskich* (lit. 'civil rights agent') in Poland.

In many cases, the use of direct quotations depends on the target group. If the readers or listeners are experts in the field, this solution is natural. For instance, in some German *Länder* the inheritance of farms is regulated by special rules treating the farm as a separate unit which does not belong to the dead person's estate in general. This special branch of law is called *Anerbenrecht*. If the translation is aimed at specialists of inheritance law, notably in Central Europe, this term may be used to designate comparable farm inheritance systems in other countries. This was done, for example, by the author of these lines in his doctoral thesis in French in the case of an analogous Finnish legislative project.[38]

Legal Latin forms a particular case. As pointed out above, only a small number of Latin expressions and maxims in law are known everywhere. Therefore, it is often problematic to leave the Latin expressions and maxims of the source text as they are, that is, as direct quotations, with no translation in the target text. Foreign readers may have great difficulties to understand the exact legal content of these expressions and maxims since they are not always included in the dictionaries of legal Latin in their home countries, or – what is worse – the sense given to them may be different in these dictionaries. Hence, Latin expressions and maxims should be translated in brackets, using dictionaries of legal Latin in the legal culture where the source text has been produced.[39] This principle is followed, for example, by the Finnish translation unit of the European Court of Justice. An exception may be made in cases where the Latin term is commonly known, like the *common law* term *amicus curiae* (discussed above).

36 See, for example, H. Kanninen (2002), 'General Report on the Colloquium Subject: The Preliminary Reference to the Court of Justice of the European Communities', in *Association of the Councils of State and Supreme Administrative Jurisdictions of the European Union, 18th Colloquium* (Helsinki), 27. Very often, *Conseil d'État* and calques based on it, like *Consiglio di Stato* (Italy) or *Symvoúlio tis Epikrateías* (Greece), are directly translated into English as 'Council of State'.

37 See, for example, R. Anderson (1977), *Anglo-Scandinavian Law Dictionary* (Oslo, etc.: Universitetsforlaget).

38 H. Mattila (1979), *Les successions agricoles. Une étude en droit comparé* (Helsinki: Juridica), 112–13, 118–23.

39 As mentioned above, dictionaries of legal Latin in various countries are enumerated and partly described in Mattila, *Comparative Legal Linguistics*, 157–8.

*Rough equivalents* It is only a slight exaggeration to say that all legal translation means finding rough (approximate) equivalents: legal concepts crystallize legal rules, and legal rules always differ when we go deep enough into the details of legal institutions. The essential legal content of a rough equivalent may be the same as that of the original term, but there is some difference. Therefore, in translation theory, legal translation has been compared with a conflicts-of-law qualification: that is, the equating of a foreign legal concept with a domestic one when foreign law is applied.[40]

Let us take the French court name *Cour de cassation*. In normal legal translation, where the focus lies on the fact that it is a court of last resort, the designation 'Supreme Court of France' is precise enough.[41] If, however, the procedural system of the country is being examined, the matter is different. When it is a question of whether, in addition to issues of a legal nature, the facts of a case may also be decided by the highest jurisdiction, and under what conditions this jurisdiction may remand cases to lower courts, the translation 'Supreme Court of France' is too imprecise. Then a designation based on the original French name, 'Court of Cassation', is to be preferred.

The Finnish system of legal supervision gives a very illustrative example of the difficulty in finding an exact translation for original institutions. In Finland, in addition to the Ombudsman, there is another high official involved in the general supervision of legality in the country. The name of this official can be directly translated into English as *Chancellor of Justice*. He has several tasks. Firstly, he supervises the legality of the activities of the government and the President of the Republic. He is therefore present at plenary sessions of the cabinet. In practice, this also means giving advice to the government as to the legality of its acts. Secondly, parallel to the Parliamentary Ombudsman, the Chancellor of Justice supervises the legality of administrative activities in the country in general. Any citizen may, without any formalities, lodge a complaint to the Chancellor if he or she feels that he or she has been treated in an illegal way. This supervision also covers the activities of advocates. The Chancellor of Justice may order an inquiry in the case and, when appropriate, give an admonition to the civil servant in question or, in more serious cases, have charges brought against him. Earlier, up until the 1990s, the Chancellor of Justice also headed the Finnish corps of prosecutors, but this is no longer true: the office of the Prosecutor General now fulfils this purpose.

40 M. Galdia (2003), '*Juridisten tekstien kääntäminen erityisesti suomalais-saksalaisen vertailun näkökulmasta*' (Lakimies), 14.

41 For instance, 'supreme court' appears in the translation given for *Cour de cassation* by J. Baleyte et al. (1977), *Dictionnaire juridique français–anglais et anglais–français / Legal Dictionary French–English and English–French* (Paris: Éd. de Navarre): 'judiciary committee of the House of Lords', [U.S.] 'Supreme Court' (the translation is preceded by the sign # indicating that it is not a perfect equivalence).

This combination of tasks is original, compared with the situation in other countries, which has made the translation of the name very difficult. Let us examine some of the equivalents given in the Finnish Government Glossary.

In certain languages, like English, the designation is translated literally: *Chancellor of Justice*, *Justizkanzler* (German), *Kanselier van Justitie* (Dutch), *Chancelier de la Justice* (French), and so on. However, in Greek and Italian, the principle of literal translation has been abandoned, and the translator has tried to find, on the basis of the principle of functional translation, a rough equivalent for the name. Hence, in Greek the translation of the Finnish name in the Glossary is *Genikós Eisangeléas* (Γενικός Εισαγγελέας); *eisangeléas* is translated in Greek–French and Greek–English legal dictionaries as *procureur* and *public prosecutor*.[42] The Greek translation gives the impression that it is a question of a high prosecuting authority. Even earlier this was only one part of the truth, and today the translation is directly misleading since the Chancellor of Justice no longer heads the corps of prosecutors. In Italian, on the contrary, the name has been translated as *giureconsulto del governo*. The term *giureconsulto* refers to 'legal scholar'[43] – derived from the Latin name *jurisconsultus*, learned men who gave legal opinions in Ancient Rome. Consequently, the impression given by this translation is 'legal adviser of the Crown'. In effect, there is some truth in this since the Government often asks for the Chancellor's advice when it is not clear whether an act is legal or illegal. However, the task of general legal supervision, in relation to both the Government and the administration of the country or the corps of advocates, is entirely left out in this translation.

This dispersion of translations shows how difficult it is sometimes to find even a rough equivalent for legal institutions. In the case of 'Chancellor of Justice', the designations taken directly from foreign institutions overshadow some aspects of the Finnish institution. On the other hand, the literal translations say nothing about the tasks of this high official.

*Term-like explanations* Another technique the translator may use it to replace the original term with a short explanation (paraphrase) which expresses the most important conceptual elements of the term and which can be used in the target-language text like a term. Let us examine an original Spanish institution: *derechos forales*.

The term *derecho foral* has a long history. During the Arab occupation of the Iberian Peninsula, the Christians managed to retain certain areas in the northern parts of the Peninsula. Small Christian kingdoms were created: Leon, Castile,

---

42 Gadis, V. (*sine anno*), *Dictionnaire français–grec et grec–français des termes juridiques* (Athènes: Eptalofos), Chiotákis, M. (2000), *Ellino–anglikó lexikó nomikís kai emporikís orologías* (Ελληνο–αγγλικό λεξικό νομικής και εμπορικής ορολογίας) (Athens: Sákkulas) and Chiotákis, M. (*sine anno*), *Dictionnaire français–grec/grec–français des termes juridiques, économiques, commerciaux et E.U.* (Athens: Sakkoulas).

43 (1961) *Grande dizionario della lingua italiana* VI.

Navarre, Aragon, Catalonia, and so on. These kingdoms had their own legal systems which, notably in the field of civil law, were conserved and developed after the *Reconquista* of the Peninsula. These legal systems are called *derechos forales*.[44] When the new Civil Code (*Código civil*) of 1889 was promulgated for the whole country, the special civil-law systems of the former kingdoms were kept in force.[45] In these areas, the Spanish Civil Code is applied only in a complementary way.[46] Some *derechos forales* have been considerably reformed under the new Spanish Constitution (special mention should be made of the new Catalan civil-law system from the 1990s).

The Spanish *derechos forales* cover, *inter alia*, matrimonial property law and the law of inheritance. This term therefore appears, for instance, in Spanish deeds of partition concerning matrimonial property after divorce. The opposite term is *derecho civil común* which refers to the system of the Spanish Civil Code. In (former) Spanish deeds, one may find, for example, the expression *la regionalidad del marido era la común*. This expression may be explained by the necessity of pointing out whether the rules of the general Civil Code or those of one of the *derechos forales* are applicable to the partition; earlier, this was determined by the domicile of the husband.

Since the division between general civil law and regional civil laws is typically Spanish,[47] a term-like explanation is a good solution. One can say, for instance, 'Spanish regional civil law' or 'the Spanish regional civil-law system'.

*Difficulties in the choice of strategy* The examples above show that it is not easy to choose the right translation strategy in each particular case. As for foreign quotations (or neologisms), it is difficult to decide in advance how well-known the quotation in question is: who are the addressees of the text and will they all

---

44 The word *foral* originally derives from the Latin word *forum*.

45 Many old provisions of these systems had mainly symbolic importance. According to Article 103 of the earlier Catalan civil-law compilation, the inhabitants of the city of Barcelona and the diocese of Genora, when travelling outside their home locality, could even make their will orally in the presence of two witnesses, which is normally not possible. If the testator died during the trip, the witnesses in question had to swear the authenticity of the oral testament at the altar of the Saint Cross of the church Santos Justo y Pastor, before the statue of St Felix (*testamento sacramental*). After this, the will was transformed to an official written form by the court of law. See (1982), *Compilación del derecho civil especial de Cataluña* (Ley 40/1960). *Compilaciones del derecho civil foral. Cataluña – Aragon – Baleares* (Editorial Civitas), 58–9.

46 Ibán, I. (1995), *Introducción al derecho español* (Baden-Baden: Nomos) 135–6).

47 A leading legal dictionary of Spanish and English explains: '*Derecho foral* = local traditional law applicable in some parts of Spain as contrasted with civil code law. This distinction emanates from the ancient regional division of Spain such that in certain areas general *derecho civil* did not apply.' No direct translation is given for *derecho foral* in this dictionary (Gabanellas, G. and Hoague, E. (1991) *Diccionario jurídico español–inglés / Spanish–English Legal Dictionary* (London: Butterworths)).

understand the quotation? In the case of rough equivalents, the translator has to ponder whether the concepts expressed by the two terms (the source-language term and the target-language term) are similar enough to avoid the danger of fallaciousness. Finally, term-like explanations often make the text more awkward, in some cases this may be unavoidable. There is no method which will give an automatic answer in the decision-making process: legal translation is not a mechanical activity. The translators of legal texts have to resolve questions that presuppose vast expertise, a great deal of experience and good ability to judge cases where lines of demarcation have to be drawn. High-level competence is demanded of translators in such situations. The following paragraphs show that it is difficult to guarantee such competence.

*Lack of Competence and Resources in Legal Translation*

In practice, the problems of competence and resources are very demanding in legal translation. The translator should master not only two languages but also two legal systems (except in translations within bilingual unitary states). As Philippe Rémy has pointed out, 'Le vrai problème n'est pas tant le bilinguisme que le bijuridisme'. If this mastery is lacking, translations become useless or even misleading. However, a correct translation is always possible in these cases: the translator has simply made a mistake.[48]

Notably, in the application of foreign law and in the enforcement of judgments abroad, legal translation is often one of the weakest links in the process. This particularly applies to the area of the European Union with its many languages. Following the latest enlargement (Bulgaria and Romania), the number of Union languages – including Irish – is 23, which results in more than 500 different language combinations in legal translation (Danish–Greek, Latvian–Portuguese, German–Estonian, and so on). At the same time, there is only a limited amount of resources, particularly in small Member States.[49] The number of authorized translators is tiny for many language combinations. Sometimes, it is more or less impossible to find an authorized translator between two small languages. Furthermore, these translators do not often have legal training. Finally, translators between small languages are often obliged to translate from their mother tongue into a foreign language, which is far more difficult than in the opposite direction.

All this is visible in the quality of legal translations. The translators may be intelligent and hard working but they do not always have adequate training. They do their best, but legal texts, notably the texts of judgments, are often very technical

48 Many names of law courts are particularly misleading for historical reasons. A striking example is the fact that there are several courts called 'supreme court' in the State of New York. Despite their name, these courts are placed under the Court of Appeals.

49 This also applies to EU translation in the proper sense of the word. Even though the European Court of Justice possesses a number of highly qualified translators trained in law (lawyer-linguists), the problem of resources appears there as well.

and difficult. This makes fatal errors possible. Sometimes a legal translation is so misleading that it is impossible to get an idea of the subject of the text. For instance, the French court designation *Tribunal de grande instance de Paris* ('the court of first instance of Paris') has been translated into Finnish using an expression which would mean in English 'Supreme court (of France) seated in Paris'. Similarly, the expression '*de (plein) droit*' ('*ipso jure*') has been translated using the words 'with full reason'. Similar mistakes can easily be cited in the case of Spanish. The expression '*sentencia firm* ' ('final judgment'[50]) has been translated as 'stable statement'. A good example is also the terminology of *derecho foral* discussed above. The expression mentioned earlier, *la regionalidad del marido era la común* ('the general Civil Code / civil law of Spain was applicable to the husband') has been translated as 'the residence of the spouses was common'.[51]

The problems of legal translation have been discussed in international fora like the Hague Conference of Private International Law. However, it is very difficult to eliminate these problems. At least in small countries, it is impossible to require that all translators of legal texts have legal training, and special training in legal translation cannot be arranged for linguists in all cases (even if there are important programmes in many countries).

## Conclusion

Despite the considerable difficulties mentioned above, certain remedies are possible. One important remedy is creating better term sources. In addition to monolingual and multilingual legal dictionaries and glossaries,[52] various term banks are becoming more and more important. The new general term bank of the European Union, IATE – a fusion of the earlier terms banks, notably Eurodicautom and TIS – is worthy of special mention.[53] It includes a large amount of vocabulary

---

50 See for example Alcaraz Varó, E. and Hughes, B. (2006), *Diccionario de términos jurídicos inglés–español • Spanish–English*, 9th impr. (Barcelona: Editorial Ariel).

51 Today, the term *regionalidad* has been replaced by the term *vecindad civil*. In court decisions one may find expressions like: *Que don José Antonio Getino Fernández, de vecindad civil común, y doña María Pilar Domingo Calleja, de vecindad catalana, contrajeron matrimonio en Cambrils (Tarragona) el día 3 de febrero de 1984 sin otorgar capitulaciones matrimoniales* (STC 2002-039), or the grounds of a judgment may read: *... la redacción del antiguo artículo 14.4 del Código Civil, por la cual la esposa seguía la vecindad civil del marido, aunque en el presente caso, tampoco habría cambiado la solución, pues la vecindad civil de la esposa era la común como la del marido* (Sentencia de la Sec. 3ª de la A.P. de Tarragona de 13 de abril de 2004, Rollo 141/2003).

52 As for lacks, see de Groot, G.-R. and van Laer, C. (2006), 'The Dubious Quality of Legal Dictionaries', *International Journal of Legal Information* 34, 65–86.

53 See Mattila, H. (2007) 'Multilingual Term Banks of Criminal Law', a paper read at the *Nordisk Workshop för straffrätt*, University of Lapland, 23 March 2007. IATE

that is useful in all legal translation, not only in the translation work of Union institutions.

It is also important to rectify translation strategies. In the translation work of certain Union institutions, notably the Court of Justice, link translation (chain-link translation) will no doubt be used more and more frequently in the future. This will certainly be necessary in other translation activities as well (judgments of national law courts, private legal documents, and so on) despite the growth of translation costs in consequence. The link translation method has been discussed at, for example, the Hague Conference of Private International Law.[54] Link translation means that a legal document in a small language is first translated into a major language and from this major language into another small language needed in the matter in question. It is well-known that link translation may distort the message and, therefore, the final text must be checked carefully. However, when both stages of a legal translation (small language no. 1 → major language; major language → small language no. 2) are done by people who have solid legal and linguistic competence, the result is much more reliable than in the case of a direct translation between the two small languages made by a person who has limited competence only.

In case of link translations, a lawyer may control the correctness of the message transmission between his or her language and the major language used as a link if he or she has sufficient legal and linguistic knowledge. It is therefore useful to examine the need for lawyer training in the area of legal linguistics.

### *Lawyers' Training in Legal Linguistics*

*Linguistic abilities required of lawyers in the world today* As seen above, the linguistic plurality of the European Union – a richness which needs to be protected – causes a major problem which endangers the results of European legal integration: imprecise, even entirely incorrect translations of legal documents in cases of an international nature. In practice, legal documents are often translated by people who do not have a lawyer's background. In these cases, linguistic competence is an important instrument of control which can be used by the lawyers involved: judges, advocates, civil servants and others may verify the correctness of translations if they know legal languages and are conscious of the danger of message distortion in connection with translations. In cases where the content of the document in the target language is suspicious-looking, one should make sure that the message has not been changed. In effect, translators are not the only ones who should worry about translation errors. From the point of view of legal protection, these errors

can be freely used via the address: <http://iate.europa.eu/iatediff/SearchByQueryLoad.do?method=load>.

54 This strategy is also used in regular EU translation.

constitute a major danger comparable to other types of misunderstandings in cases of an international nature.

In order to be able to exercise a control function in legal translation, lawyers should have more knowledge about legal languages. Firstly, they need information concerning the characteristics and terminology of legal language in general. This presupposes that they understand the basic properties and conditions of use of all human language. A young lawyer may easily attach too much weight to the external aspect of a text and not make a clear distinction between a legal concept and the term expressing this concept – despite the fact that synonymy and polysemy are frequent phenomena in legal language. Secondly, European lawyers should have knowledge about major legal languages, particularly legal English but also legal German and French (as well as languages like Russian and Spanish). There are innumerable legal documents to be translated in Europe into or from German and French, and even today these languages are often used as link languages. Unfortunately, in many countries, like Finland, lawyers' knowledge of French and German has weakened during the past few decades.

On the other hand, it is becoming more and more important in international lawyering to know the relevant vocabulary sources. When reading or translating texts in foreign languages, a lawyer has to use suitable dictionaries or term banks. As for legal English, for instance, the growth of the so-called European legal English has to be taken into account. In this case, the adequate term sources are not always traditional common-law dictionaries but the glossaries and term banks of the European Union.

*The study programme of the University of Lapland* Consequently, specific training in legal languages should be given in European law faculties: no lawyer can avoid dealing with matters where foreign legal and linguistic knowledge is required. Many law faculties have become conscious of this.[55] In Finland, a special programme in legal linguistics has been created by the University of Lapland (Rovaniemi). Law students obtain cultural competence for international legal cooperation through teaching which gives them information about the history and characteristics of major legal languages, as well as about their mutual relations and international use, notably within the European Union.[56] Legal English and legal French occupy a special position in the programme, and legal Latin is also discussed in detail to give a solid background for language use today.

55 For instance, the Riga Graduate School of Law has started, in 2007, a new M.A. programme in comparative legal linguistics. See: <http://www.rgsl.edu.lv/index.php?part=jurd&page=j34>.

56 To advance and support this teaching, relevant study materials are needed. For this purpose, the author of these pages has written a general treatise on the subject (Mattila, *Comparative Legal Linguistics*).

# PART 4
# EXCEPTIONALISM AND NORMALIZATION: AMBIGUITY AND HONOUR IN EUROPEAN INTEGRATION PROCESSES

# Chapter 16
# Introduction: Exceptionalism and Normalization: Ambiguity and Honour in European Integration Processes

Hanne Petersen

Integration processes are difficult – as is well known especially from the field of national immigration law and practice. Most European nation states have had difficulties integrating immigrants within their own borders and most EU Member States have difficulties integrating themselves into the European communities, be it the EU or the Council of Europe with its Human Rights focus.

Both integration processes also require a changing understanding of law. The interest in several Nordic countries in legal polycentricity, which took off from the late 1980s, was related to this need for a changing understanding of law. Sociologists of law had long dealt with legal pluralism, but few academic lawyers and theorists had grappled with the implications of a much more varied legal landscape for the understanding of law. The ambition of legal polycentricity was to approach legal science from within and to reach another understanding – and practice – of law; to reform law from within. It was Henrik Zahle, who had originally coined the phrase 'legal polycentricity'. According to Surya Prakash Sinha, who became a friend of Zahle and myself after having participated in a conference on the topic, the advantages of adopting a legal polycentric approach were that it might maximize the legitimacy of legal orders, promote tolerance, non-coercive methodology and stability, provide a framework for understanding domination and resistance, as well as avoid the Marxist contradiction and the pluralist fallacy claimed by the single-value approach.[1]

Two of the three initiators of the research project on Legal Polycentricity had dealt with women's law and Sinha was the first Indian lawyer to become a professor of international law in the United States. He became a strong supporter of this project and approach[2] which appealed to what have from a Western and a

1 Sinha, S.P. (1995), 'Legal Polycentricity', in Petersen, H. and Zahle, H. (eds), *Legal Polycentricity: Consequences of Pluralism in Law* (London: Dartmouth), 31–71.

2 Surya Prakash Sinha subsequently published a book inspired by the cooperation: (1996), *Legal Polycentricity and International Law* (Durham, NC: Carolina Academic

nation-state perspective been considered 'peripheries' and 'minorities'. For the modern, national and, until a few decades ago, mostly male lawyer, there was no need to move beyond the national centre and the national approach to law.

Modern representatives of the legal profession have never been trained to seek out their legal identities, claims Kjell Åke Modéer in his contribution to this volume, subtitled 'Scandinavian Exceptionalism in Legal Cultures'. The national identity of lawyers was a given and so clear that there was no need to reflect on it. Giving up this identity, role and status in an uncertain and long-lasting process of integration into a European community and an 'ever closer union' has noticeably been difficult and a challenge not only for Scandinavian lawyers, but also for Scandinavian states and society at large.

Lawyers – and law – were considered important artisans and tools in *nation building* and in the development of *modern (welfare) societies*. That (Scandinavian) lawyers should be serving the development of *European* legal communities which limit and weaken the role of the nations which they had also served and gained privileges from serving is therefore both a paradox and a challenge.

Several of the Scandinavian countries are Lutheran constitutional monarchies and have considered themselves culturally relatively homogenous societies for centuries. This cultural homogeneity and associated 'value monism' has during the twentieth century been a strength which might very well in the twenty-first century turn into a constraint. All the Scandinavian countries have small populations but ambitions to be influential internationally and globally: 'Norway wants to present itself as a humanitarian great power.'[3] As small countries considered geographically peripheral they have, especially during the twentieth century, gone from a status of belonging to the poorer nations in Europe, experiencing large populations migrating to the new world, to becoming very affluent societies. This has allowed them not only to create modern welfare states at home but also to develop a certain sense of international humanitarian and moral superiority legitimized through relatively high development aid. However, it has also led to the 'iconization of the Scandinavian welfare state', as Kjell Åke Modéer writes.

For about a century – until 1972 – the Scandinavian countries upheld close contacts and undertook mutual action in many legislative areas. This cooperation was eased by the linguistic familiarities of the Scandinavian societies, which at the same time represented linguistic inaccessibility for outsiders. Sweden at one point opted out, wanting to increase development individually. Since the period of the oil crisis and the Danish membership of the EEC from 1973, the countries have increasingly moved in different directions and with different speeds. But they have all (except Finland) upheld a reluctant attitude especially to the European Union, with or without membership.

---

Press). He kept in contact with me and especially Henrik Zahle until Sinha's early death in July 2005.

3 Ministry of Work and Inclusion (2006), *Velkommen som ny statsborger* [Welcome as a new citizen].

This paradox of 'small state status' and 'moral superiority' is perhaps one reason for the reluctant Scandinavian attitude towards Europe. The fear of disappearing and losing influence as small countries and of losing exceptional (moral) status seems especially strong in relation to the European Economic Community turning into the European Union. None of the Nordic countries were members of the EEC from the beginning, but all of them became members of the Council of Europe and ratified the European Convention on Human Rights from the very beginning.

Modéer quotes a Swedish diplomat as having stated that the Swedish attitude towards Europe has been dictated more by the fear of being left out than by the pleasure of participating.

The 'fear of disappearing' in Europe has been felt stronger by the Scandinavian countries (Sweden, Norway, Denmark) than by Finland (a Nordic but not Scandinavian country). Finland's extensive border with the Soviet Union always nourished a strong sense of Realpolitik, which has made it adjust itself quickly and enthusiastically to the Union, including the Euro. The Scandinavians have kept a distance towards the European symbols and have upheld, and perhaps even strengthened, their own national and legal symbols. In Norway and Denmark, the (old) constitutions (from 1814 and 1849) have acquired quasi-sacred status.

Nationalist sentiments have grown especially in Denmark since the turn of the century and have been strongly directed against Muslim immigration, displaying the consequences of globalization within the community in the form of a new contested value pluralism and religious pluralism which had hardly ever been experienced before. The ambivalence towards value pluralism, legal pluralism and consequences of economic globalization has led to a strong defence of modernity and modern values in large parts of the Scandinavian communities. The Cartoon crisis in 2006 demonstrated the quasi-sacred status of 'freedom of expression' in Denmark; not adhering to this modern value was considered almost heretical.

Scandinavian legal realism always placed parliament high above the judiciary, but with the rising importance of the European economic, legal and human rights communities, this position of national legislatures is increasingly questioned. According to Kjell Åke Modéer, a break from the nationalistic legal culture began in the 1980s with the increasing influence of the European Court of Human Rights. Even if Scandinavian Legal Realism can no longer be described as a realist understanding of law, it still has a very large grip on the lay and professional understanding of law in the Nordic countries. In a sense, modernity has become not only an icon, but also a unitary ideal to stick to with almost fundamentalist commitment.

In Italy, on the contrary, the ambition has not been to uphold exceptional status but rather to become 'normal' and 'fully modern'. Italy has, in a European context, suffered from a sense of being 'backward' and its status as not fully 'modern' has led to shamefulness, as repeatedly mentioned in David Nelken's chapter.[4] Where

---

4 For similar arguments see Capussotti, E. (2007), 'Modernity versus Backwardness: Italian Women's Perception of Self and Other', in Passerini, L. et al. (eds), *Women Migrants*

the Scandinavian states perceive themselves as 'small but modern', Italy's self-image might perhaps be described as 'big but backward.'

Italy and Scandinavia may demonstrate some of the 'collective sensitivities' which are at stake and which produce some of the paradoxical situations in the processes of European (legal) integration. Neither the 'not yet modern' nor the 'fully modern' members are completely at ease with the European communities. Italy's pride in its great history has to a large degree been upheld in spite of fascism in the beginning of the twentieth century, contrary to Germany, which experienced a moral collapse that is not yet fully overcome in an expanded European Union. Italian shame of insufficient modernity is contrasted with its pride in the cultural past. Where it seems very difficult for the modern Scandinavian states to adapt to a pluralist, heterogeneous and globalized world, the Italian state and communities may perhaps find that easier.

David Nelken examines the processes by which law produces integration and suggests that we ask what is being integrated, by whom, how, why and with what results. Nelken defines legal culture as '"one way of describing relatively stable patterns of legally oriented social behaviour and attitudes". ... legal culture is about who we are not just what we do'. '"European ways of law" differ [and] it makes less and less sense to think of "domestic" norms as forming part of distinct national jurisdictions' than of their interaction with transnational norms, which modify local behaviour. There is, thus, a need to revise our ideas about integration. 'Large-scale interdependencies' may lead to 'unplanned as well as intended moves towards greater convergence. ... legal culture tends ever more to become ... subjectively "relational" rather than objectively "embedded."' These relations may be relations of attraction, as well as repulsion, from others.

Nelken underlines the need to explore who gains and loses through the proposed introduction of common standards. The interests of the elites and the population at large will not coincide. This is an insight which especially Danish politicians have had to make repeatedly during the 1990s where several issues were rejected at public referenda and which the EU as a whole experienced when French and Dutch voters voted 'no' to the European Constitutional Treaty.

Nelken quotes Roger Cotterell who has suggested that the process of unifying law between different legal systems could be compared to the process of assimilation between different cultural groups within a society. According to Cotterell, productive integration requires not assimilation, but mutual acceptance and mutual learning about the other in a framework of universal respect for human dignity and autonomy. It borders on the paradoxical, writes Nelken, that one of the key conditions *imposed* on candidate countries in the name of mutual acceptance is that they show more willingness to tolerate diversity.

---

*From East to West: Gender, Mobility and Belonging in Contemporary Europe* (Oxford: Berghahn Books), 195–211.

The example of Italian court delays and normalization processes demonstrates that it may be necessary and possible to question the European ambitions and standards for integration.

It is a source of shame and concern about image in Italy that court delays are so prevalent and lengthy. The European Convention on Human Rights has 40 signatories, but 36 per cent of all decisions handed down by the European Court of Human Rights were findings holding Italy responsible for unreasonable delay in its trial processes. Italy is not yet near to coming into line with the European norm – of somewhat more speedy processes.

But here another paradox appears. What is 'too slow' from one point of view can be 'too fast' from another – rhythms of time differ. The exceptional court delays of the Italian legal system also reflect the high level of independence from political control enjoyed by its judges and prosecutors.

'Speed is not everything' claims Nelken and asks why the Strasbourg Court gives so little attention to the speedy trials against immigrants caught *in flagrant* , as a breach of human rights.

In a final chapter, we have included a eulogy to Henrik Zahle written by Ditlev Tamm. Henrik Zahle, who initiated this project, sadly passed away during the summer of 2006, only nine weeks after having been diagnosed with cancer. Ditlev Tamm's very personal portrait of Henrik Zahle as a colleague and great legal scholar demonstrates some of the ambiguities of a personal and political nature, which has shaped one of the important Nordic legal personalities who came to work on European legal integration. It reminds us of what might be self-evident but often forgotten, namely that integration processes are part of human lives and are carried out by humans beings. This should not be forgotten in academic presentations and we wish to draw attention to both this aspect and to Henrik Zahle's personal contributions with the last chapter in this book.

As the son of a father who was director of the Museum for Applied Art in Copenhagen and a mother who was an art historian, Henrik Zahle was from a very early age familiar with European art heritage. He had visited Italian museums long before mass tourism started out – at a time when guardians had to be fetched to unlock the doors to the exhibition halls. Professionally, he mainly dealt with Nordic law until the late 1980s and early 1990s. When in 1986 he published his later frequently cited article on legal polycentricity in a Norwegian *Festschrift*,[5] it was also a reflection of the break from a nationalistic legal culture which Modéer addresses in his article. In 1990 Henrik Zahle received a research grant for a project on 'Law in a polycentric and ecological perspective' with Kirsten Ketscher and myself. This project had a combined focus on changing forms and changing

5 Zahle, H. (1986), 'Polycentri i retskildelæren' [Polycentricity in the theory of legal sources], in Bratholm, A., Opsahl, T. and Aarbakke, M. (eds), *Samfunn, rett, retferdighet – festskrift til Torstein Eckhoffs 70-årsdag* (Oslo: Tano).

values underpinning a pluralist understanding of law.[6] In 1991 Henrik Zahle and his family decided to move to Florence for a semester. He had contacts both at the University of Florence and at the European University Institute in Florence. In a short and witty article, 'The Thorny Road of Internationalization', he described the many technical and bureaucratic difficulties related to this move – somewhere between the tourist trip and emigration, but with bureaucratic requirements resembling those for emigration.[7]

In the beginning of his career, Henrik Zahle was an influential member of the Marxist inspired Nordic milieu of critical legal scholars and he considered himself a socialist in a broad sense until his death. The Danish left wing was generally very critical of the European Economic Community and the EU, and it was not until the end of the Cold War that also Zahle's views began to change in favour of Europeanization. His return to Denmark after the semester in Florence coincided with the heated discussions before the July 1992 Danish referendum on the Maastricht Treaty.

In 1989 he had published the first edition of his three volumes on Danish Constitutional Law (*Dansk Forfatningsret* I–III). This was still a very nationally oriented analysis of Constitutional Law – the European Community was only really mentioned in the second volume on Government and Administration. However, in the third edition of the work, published in 2003, international and supranational human rights had moved from being a short third *last* chapter in the 1989 edition, to a more prominent position as the third chapter in the volume on human rights.[8] The process of Europeanization was no longer an external and political matter, but had become an internalized issue of legal science.

In 1998 he published a small book on 'EU and the Danish Constitution' at a time when a court case was pending at the Danish supreme court about the compatibility of the Danish membership of the EU with the Danish constitution. This was a controversial act as Nordic university professors have not considered it 'politically correct' to interfere with interpretations while cases – especially Supreme Court cases – are pending. That Henrik Zahle was usually very 'correct' only underlined the urgent nature of this intervention.

In the initial chapter of the book, on 'Tradition', he concludes upon an important dilemma:

> Danish independence has always had to respect the limitations following from international law. That the autonomous may bind itself and thus become less autonomous

6 Zahle, H. (1994), 'Ecologization of Law: Introductory Remarks to a New Perspective: Law and Ecology', *Retfærd*, Special Issue on Law and Ecology.

7 Zahle, H. (1991), 'Internationaliseringens tornede vej', in *Årsberetning* (Retsvidenskabeligt Institut B, Københavns Universitet). Republished in Henrik Zahle (2007), *At forske ret. Essays om juridisk forskningspraksis* (Copenhagen: Gyldendal).

8 Zahle, H. (1989, 1995 and 2003), *Dansk Forfatningsret* Vols I–III [Danish Constitutional Law, Vols I–III] (Copenhagen: Chr. Ejlers Forlag).

> is not only a paradox, but also an expression of autonomy: Only by binding oneself may the autonomous establish stable and mutual relations to others. This is valid for treaty law, which requires state consent, and is valid for customary law in as far as it is confirmed by state practice.[9]

Henrik Zahle came to underline the importance of law and lawmaking as *relations* between humans during his last years. He increasingly turned towards value issues related to an understanding of legal forms and processes, especially in his quite personal essays on justice in legal practice based upon his experiences from 1999 to 2002 as a Supreme Court judge.[10] This move from a state-centred to a personal focus on the making of law and justice could perhaps be described as another important element in the process of legal integration. 'Care for Justice' requires personal responsibility, not just following law, be it state law or European law.

9 Zahle, H. (1998), *EU og den danske grundlov* (Copenhagen: Chr. Ejlers Forlag), 10.

10 Zahle, H. (2003), *Omsorg for retfærdighed. Essays om juridisk praksis*. [Care for Justice. Essays on Legal Practice] (Copenhagen: Gyldendal).

Chapter 17

# Adjustment or Reluctance? Scandinavian Exceptionalism in Legal Cultures

Kjell Å. Modéer

## I

Within a year, two of my close colleagues and friends in this field, Alexander Peczenik and Henrik Zahle, passed away. Both of them were suddenly and brutally taken from us. I will remember Henrik as a person who always invited dialogue. He was a colleague who listened. In the spring of 2006 we were engaged in several dialogues on law and religion, on legal history and on his project on a practical legal philosophy. This chapter is a contribution to continuing dialogues with Henrik's legal heritage. It must be continued in the years to come.

## II

The Nobel laureate in literature in 2006, Orhan Pamuk, has compared himself and his role as an author with James Joyce. In his works Pamuk describes his home town Istanbul as a part of Europe in the same way as James Joyce describes Dublin. Istanbul and Dublin, two gateways to and from Europe, one on the eastern edge, the other on the western, both belonging to the European peripheries. One of the focuses of this book is the relations between centre and periphery, between coherence and divergence within European legal thinking. My own periphery of Europe is defined as that of the Scandinavian countries. To what extent do the Scandinavian countries represent a periphery in northern Europe in relation to other European peripheries like Istanbul in the east and Dublin in the west?

Reading Pamuk and Joyce, one notices that in their works they undergo an important process by writing about Istanbul and Dublin – they are identifying their own culture. They use the mirror for self-reflection. They are describing what it means to be from Istanbul and Dublin. I believe lawyers can learn a great deal by reading their auto-biographical works and by comparing the method of writers of fiction to ours as legal professionals. How many Scandinavian lawyers have reflected on their identities within the law? And how many have compared their cognitive structures with those of other times and in other countries? The medieval jurists had to make the comparison between two equal legal systems, *ius commune* and *ius patrium*,[1] as did the appellate judges in early modern Scandinavia (in the seventeenth century) who tried to adapt the European legal knowledge they had acquired during their *peregrinatio academica* to the national territory wherein they had to make their legal decisions. By making comparisons, they constructed their national legal identity. The Swedish law professor David Nehrman-Ehrenstråle, a law Professor at Lund University during the first part of the eighteenth century, gave his students such an identity by teaching them in Swedish – not in Latin – about the Swedish law, and by urging them to be reluctant to apply the Roman law but rather to be good Christians in their professional work.[2] Modern representatives of the legal profession, however, have never been trained to find their legal identities. The modernity of the twentieth century closed the gates for such cognitive processes to create identities. The national identity should be so clear and evident that reflecting on it is not necessary. Today, however, in this late modernity of ours, we again have to make some sort of reflection, just as our former colleagues did in medieval times and in early modern Europe. Today, it really ought to be an obligation for law faculties to include such a discursive theme in the law curriculum! This chapter is an essay in this kind of self-reflection. It is an attempt to identify the characters of Scandinavian legal cultures in a time of transition and to see how this transition is related to the ongoing Europeanization of legal science.

My contribution will start from the current discourse on Scandinavian exceptionalism, initiated among others by Martin Shapiro at the University of California at Berkeley. Shapiro has written substantially on 'state exceptionalism' and has especially observed Scandinavian exceptionalism in his works on European law and European constitutional law.[3] The main question currently is to what extent one can talk about Scandinavian exceptionalism in the same manner as 25–30 years ago. An outsider in relation to European legal thinking – like Shapiro – explores European regionalism and observes that there is something particular in the countries of the northern part of Europe, with their values and their legal cultures, which makes them different from other regions in continental Europe. Also Konrad Zweigert and Hein Kötz in their *Introduction to Comparative Law* – now in its third edition – identified a special Nordic legal family within the legal families of Western civilization, which can be described as either those of the *civil law* or those of the *common law* countries. They do not base their legal system on

---

1 Glenn, P. (2006), 'The Aims of Comparative Law', in Smits, J. (ed.), *Elgar Encyclopedia of Comparative Law* (Cheltenham: Edward Elgar), 57–65.

2 Modéer, K.Å. and Nehrman-Ehrenstråle, D. (1979), 'En inledning', *Acta Societatis Juridicae Lundensis* 35, XX. Nehrman, D. (1729), *Inledning Til Then Swenska Iurisprudentiam Civilem* (Lund), §§ 44–5, 14.

3 Shapiro, M. (2002), 'Rights in the European Union: Convergent with the US?', in Shapiro, M. and Stone Sweet, A. (eds), *On Law, Politics, and Judicialization* (Oxford: Oxford University Press).

a continental-European codification and they do not have a case law-system. On the other hand, their legal systems are dominated by statutes, and in some of the Scandinavian countries a jury-system is used in the courts. So they have some sort of character of their own, they are *in between*; and throughout modernity they have been regarded as exceptional.[4]

As law faculties are greenhouses for upcoming generations of lawyers, legal ideologies and theories taught at these institutions have been very important for the creation of what can be identified as the Nordic legal paradigm of the twentieth century. Modern legal positivism and 'Scandinavian legal realism' were the dominating discourses in these countries during the greater part of the twentieth century. 'Scandinavian legal realism' in particular was a dominating Nordic discourse which has been of great importance for the scientific climate at the law schools in Sweden, especially in the postwar era 1945–1980.[5] Scandinavian legal realists questioned legal science as a science; they looked upon themselves as *social engineers* and regarded their professional work as a value neutral technique. Increasingly they regarded the political drafts of legislation as important legal sources. Within constitution reform the sovereignty principle of the people was regarded as superior to that of the separation of power. Scandinavian legal realism was the dominating legal school of thought throughout modernity, and it was not until the critical legal schools appeared at the law schools in the 1970s that legal realism – with a new generation of law professors – slowly began to fade out.

Today, we have – more or less – left the modernity of the twentieth century behind us and we have entered into the contemporary late-modernity of the early twenty-first century. Some say this change occurred thanks to post-modernity. I would say that the concept of polycentricity, which was introduced in Scandinavia by Henrik Zahle and Hanne Petersen some fifteen years ago, demonstrated how to find the way out of the homogenous national concept of law.[6] I will, however, not use the term 'postmodern' when I describe the contemporary Scandinavian legal paradigm which now is under construction. I prefer to call it 'late modern'. The current late modern analysis looks more for divergences and differences than for convergences and similarities within Scandinavian legal cultures.[7] An important context for an identification of Scandinavian legal culture and for the ongoing

---

4 This exceptionalism was emphasized by the Nordic lawyers who went to the Anglo-American countries after the Second World War and described different aspects of the legal system in the 'Scandinavian' welfare state. Modéer, K.Å. (2007), 'Young Men Go West! Nordiska jurister, deras studieresor till efterkrigstidens U.S.A. samt den rättskultur de mötte', in *Vänbok till Axel Adlercreutz* (Lund: Juristförlaget).

5 Scandinavian visibility in Anglo-American legal discourses after the Second World War can also be one explanation for this identification. Modéer, 'Young Men Go West!'.

6 Petersen, H. and Zahle, H. (eds) (1995), *Legal Polycentricity: Consequences of Pluralism in Law* (London: Dartmouth).

7 Cf. Grosswald Curran, V. (1998), 'Cultural Immersion, Difference and Categories in U.S. Comparative Law', *The American Journal of Comparative Law* 46:1, 43–92.

transformation is the iconization of the Scandinavian welfare state since the democratic breakthrough and the implementation of social welfare programmes in the period between the First and Second World Wars. 'American exceptionalism' is a term used to identify regional divergences in the United States, of which 'Southern exceptionalism' (segregation, lack of commitment regarding welfare and public education) is one example. Another example is the contemporary US administration's policy positions to global discourses on unilateralism. How does Scandinavian exceptionalism compare with this concept of American exceptionalism?

During modernity, Scandinavian exceptionalism became a part of its constitutional identity. Even if core values like democracy, solidarity and egality were related to education, social security and public health and were common in the Scandinavian countries, there were also differences and exceptions between the countries. Traditions and modern reforms are intertwined. Denmark, Norway and Sweden are still constitutional monarchies, while Finland and Iceland, the twentieth-century newcomers to the modern Nordic entity, are republics. Traditionally, all the Nordic countries had Lutheran state churches. Today Sweden is an exception, as The Church of Sweden in 2000 was separated from the state. The Church of Sweden still maintains a special status and still 77 per cent of the population are members. In Finland the constitution upholds two state religions, the protestant and the orthodox. Also, with regard to membership in the European Union, there is no Scandinavian unity. Norway and Iceland are not members, but Norway has ratified the Schengen treaty and adopted many of the directives of the European Union, and the Nordic countries are members of NATO, Sweden being the one exception.

So in relation to other European regions and to traditional civil law–common law-concepts, Scandinavian exceptionalism can actually be characterized by an internal exceptionalism. Scandinavia is in several respects 'in between'. The traditional myth of the homogeneous Scandinavian icon has cracked.

Why? To be able to understand the current late-modern situation in the Nordic countries one needs to draw comparisons in time and in space.

## III

Let me first draw you the geo-political map, and its transitions. First of all there is an internal diversion within the Nordic countries related to their legal history. Denmark and Norway were for centuries united in one kingdom, and Sweden and Finland in another. Thus the ruins of one west-Nordic and another east-Nordic legal culture can still be observed. In the nineteenth century there was a great romantic interest in the Nordic legal systems from German legal historians. The representatives of the German Historical School of law found interesting similarities between the medieval codes in Germany and those in the Nordic countries. The medieval Scandinavian codes were edited in new text-critical editions and monographs were written about the northern German legal sources, 'die nordgermanischen Rechtsquellen'. German legal historians like Karl von Amira and Konrad Maurer showed a lot of scientific interest in these Nordic legal sources.[8] This resulted in an ongoing interaction between German and Nordic legal scientists and involved a lot of its representatives in Scandinavian legal science in the sphere of German legal science. Up to the Second World War this interactive interest was of great importance to the development of the Nordic legal cultures. After the War the older generations of law professors tried to keep up relations with their continental-European colleagues. The younger generations, however, turned west and were inspired by Anglo-American legal culture.

The convergences between the Scandinavian legal systems also had their peak at the end of the nineteenth century and the first part of the twentieth century. Pan-Scandinavianism was an unsuccessful movement which started out in Lund in 1829. In the 1840s–60s this movement was strongly supported by students and intellectuals and had the naïve aim to merge the Scandinavian countries into a political unity, which could better compete with Germany, the increasingly strong neighbour on the southern rim of the Baltic Sea. The Scandinavianists pleaded for liberalism and constitutional reform. In 1845 the Swedish author Carl Jonas Love Almquist gave a talk in Copenhagen on 'The Practicability of Scandinavianism'.[9] It is a document filled with the spirit of its time. It was also a statement filled with pleas for harmonization of the legislation in the Nordic countries in several legal areas.

Liberty became a key word for Scandinavian constitutional and legal reform. As Eivind Smith demonstrated in his research regarding the Norwegian High Court, the separation of power principle on which the Norwegian constitution of 1814 was based made it possible for its justices to introduce judicial review in Norway in the 1850s.[10] A Swedish judge of the time, Johan Gabriel Richert, one of the pioneers within Swedish liberalism, urged for equality for all citizens in the courtrooms, not privileges for a few. He was also one of the supporters of the reformation of the legal system with help from a new codification like the French one. The conservatives, however, mobilized their forces, and the liberals lost this competition.[11] In all the Scandinavian countries, the judiciaries (in constitutional praxis) up to 1914 created independence and autonomy within their profession. It was the same case among the professional lawyers who formed free lawyer's

8 Björne, L. (2002), *Den konstruktiva riktningen. Den nordiska rättsvetenskapens historia. Del III* (1871–1919) (Lund: Rättshistoriskt Bibliotek, Vol. 60).

9 Almqvist, C.J.L. (1950), *Om skandinavismens utförbarhet: Föredrag hållet i Det skandinaviske selskab i Köpenhamn den 4 februari 1846* (Göteborg: O. Isacson).

10 Smith, E. (1993), *Høyesterett og folkestyret: prøvingsretten overfor lover* (Oslo: Universitetsforlaget Oslo).

11 Warburg, K. and Richert, J.G. (1905), *Hans lefnad och uttalanden*, Förra delen (Stockholm: P.A. Norstedt & Söners Förlag), 98.

associations inspired by the German model of professional independence, *die Freie Advokatur*.

Many of Almquist's generation of young liberals pioneered as students in this Scandinavianism movement. As mature and high-ranking civil servants they became the founding fathers of the Conventions for Nordic Jurists (*Nordiska juristmötet*), an institution founded in Copenhagen in 1872, which still convenes every third year in one of the five Nordic capitols. Starting with these Nordic conventions, the harmonization of Nordic legislation was initiated in several fields of law, for example in commercial law, contracts, maritime law, family law, security law and intellectual property law.

So Scandinavianism as a modern construct goes back to the constitutional liberalism of the 1840s–50s and with its legal implications for the legal culture it traces back to premodernity. I use the term 'premodernity' here as a general term for the time of introduction of the European modernity of the twentieth century within the law.[12] The modernization of society and the creation of the social state as a reaction to *laissez faire* liberalism characterized the period between 1870 and the Great War. The 'Social Question' became an essential discourse in Europe in general and also in the Scandinavian countries. The Swedish author August Strindberg is an intellectual representative of his time who in his works eloquently described this period of social transition. In his well-known poem 'The Boulevard System' (*Esplanadsystemet*), he used this metaphor to describe the evolution of the modern urban environment. By tearing down the old houses belonging to the old régime, the modern man could create the Boulevard system, to be able 'to get air and light'.

## IV

'Scandinavian Legal Modernity' started at the beginning of the 1910s. Axel Hägerström, professor of philosophy at Uppsala University, held his inaugural lecture in 1911. This lecture is often quoted as having been the foundation for the modern Scandinavian legal paradigm: Scandinavian legal realism instrumentalized by the Uppsala School of Legal scientists (Vilhelm Lundstedt, Östen Undén, Karl Olivecrona and Per Olof Ekelöf were their most important representatives in Sweden). This modern legal cognitive structure was pragmatic, realistic and anti-metaphysical in its nature; it emphasized the concept of 'valid law' and was preached from the Swedish academic pulpits from the 1920s onward. It suited the reform policy of the social-democratic party, which wanted to introduce a well regulated welfare-state. Law and politics interacted in this upcoming, strong welfare-state.

12 Wandel, T. (2005), 'Issues and Agenda: Too Late for Modernity', *Journal of Historical Sociology* 18:3, 256.

The concept of legal modernity is also closely related to the concept of the strong, democratic, Scandinavian social-democratic welfare-state. In particular the New Dealers in Franklin D. Roosevelt's United States were impressed by this Scandinavian model. In 1936 the journalist Marquis W. Childs published his most-read book *Sweden – The Middle Way*, in which the upcoming corporative Swedish welfare-state was described in positive terms.[13] Sweden was an archetype, according to Childs, for peace and prosperity – and could be an important model for the United States. Thurman W. Arnold at Yale Law School, who belonged to the think-tank of New Dealers, criticized Childs's idealistic view of Sweden. Sweden could be a more pleasant country to live in than the national socialistic Germany, but Sweden did not serve as a model for the United States, Arnold argued. The Swedish non-profitable enterprises, co-operative associations and companies subsidized by the state, were not constructs adaptable for the United States. 'Today the metaphor of the wild Russian and the cruel German has an emotional relevance for the U.S., which the metaphor of the light blond Swede hasn't.' By instinct, the explanation for the Swedish success story was that the country had a homogeneous population. 'This way to choose allegories, when you are evaluating the Swedish institutions, makes you run away from facts, which contradict our theories', Arnold concluded.[14] Today, 70 years after this comment, one may argue that Arnold made an interesting point. The homogeneous Swedish population, transformed from an old-fashioned farmer state into a modern industrialized and urbanized state, was an important part of Swedish exceptionalism. This observation was also relevant for the other Scandinavian countries.

Childs's book was also criticized in Swedish conservative media. Childs is an American researcher with blinders, they wrote. After his book was published, a large number of American tourists made a pilgrimage to Sweden to study the co-operative enterprises and the co-operative movement as a whole, as a mainstay of the Swedish economy. The media reported a female American tourist who, in front of an interesting Swedish church, interrupted the tourist guide to say 'I'm not here to see churches. I want to see a co-operative store!'[15]

## V

The European postwar situation was traumatic. Europe was laid to ashes and ruins in order to eliminate the Hitler state. The reconstruction of postwar Western Europe had not been possible without US economic support. It could also not be

13 Childs, M.W. (1936), *Sweden: The Middle Way* (New Haven, CT: Yale University Press).

14 Arnold, T.W. (1937), *The Folklore of Capitalism* (New Haven, CT: Yale University Press); Weber Waller, S. (2005), *Thurman Arnold: A Biography* (New York: New York University Press).

15 'Amerika studerar Sverige', *Svenska Dagbladet*, 22 July 1938, 4, col. 1.

done without the renaissance of traditional natural law concepts. The late 1940s created not only the universal UN Declaration of Human Rights in 1948, but also the German Basic Law in 1949 with its preamble emphasizing human dignity, and the European Convention on Human Rights (ECHR) adopted in 1950.

Within the Nordic countries Sweden now played the role of being exceptional. Sweden was the only Nordic country which did not take part in the war activities. Sweden and Switzerland were the so called 'neutral' countries in Western Europe. When, after the war, European countries that had been occupied by the Germans organized a legal reckoning of their past – *eine Bewältigung der Vergangenheit* – there was no reason (or time) for this in Sweden. After the war, Sweden in comparison with other European countries had an extraordinarily strong economy. In the summer of 1945 the social-democratic government could push the start button to continue its construction of the strong, modern welfare state. This model included private industries like Volvo, Saab and Ericsson, a progressive high tax system, strong corporative labour unions, and an increasing social welfare platform paid by taxes. When Swedish legal scholars went to conferences in Germany together with their Nordic colleagues in the early 1950s they felt like aliens. They noted that many of the discourses were about 'natural law' concepts. When law professor Per Olof Ekelöf from Uppsala, one of the Swedish legal realists, reacted against these metaphysical debates to one of his Nordic fellows, he received the response:[16] 'I don't think you understand, as you didn't participate.'

Sweden was – due to its neutrality – excluded from this common European mentality. The Swedish pragmatic position in the postwar period related to foreign politics, and in international public law questions followed the same line of neutrality and policy of non-alignment.

The postwar generation of Scandinavian jurists was the first to implement fully the modernity of the law. The last generation of the Scandinavian judiciary, which belonged to an older idealistic tradition, left the scene in the 1960s–70s.

There are differences between the characters of the judiciaries in the Nordic countries. The different roles of the jurists during the war period are important in that respect. Evidently the judiciary of the Swedish legal realists became a part of the secularization of the Swedish society. In Norway, on the other hand, there was still a more idealistic approach within the judicial culture. This was very much an effect of the independence the Norwegian High Court demonstrated in 1940 – affiliated to the exile government in London and not to the occupying Nazi regime.

## VI

Sweden is by population the largest of the Nordic countries and as such it also commands a strong position in inter-Nordic relations. The harmonization of the

16 Ekelöf, P.O. (1953), 'Juristkongress i Berlin', *Svensk Juristtidning* 38, 75.

Scandinavian legislation which started already in the 1880s continued during the postwar period and became a major element of the legal cooperation between the Nordic countries up to the 1970s.

Sweden, with its strong national welfare state and its distinct egalitarian welfare policy during the postwar period, however, changed the scenario. At the centenary celebrations of the Nordic convention for jurists, held in Helsinki 1972, the Swedish deputy minister of Justice, Carl Lidbom, addressed the audience by saying that Sweden congratulated the Nordic convention on one hundred years of cooperation, but from then on Sweden did not want to participate in a legislative harmonization of the law. The Nordic consensus strategy had become obstacle for the Swedish welfare state legislation. Sweden could not wait each time until the legislators in the most reluctant of the Nordic countries at last adopted the legal reform. Sweden wanted to speed up the modernization of its laws. If any of the Nordic countries were willing to join Sweden in its policy of reform they were most welcome; if not: thank you for the coffee!

The event in Helsinki 1972 resulted in a heated discussion among jurists in the Nordic countries.[17] It became the starting-point of a paradigm shift in modern Scandinavian legal history. Divergent national identities and legal cultures were prioritized to harmonization and convergence on the Nordic level. Since 1972 Nordic legal culture has no longer been upholding a traditional construct of convergence. Already in 1973 Denmark became a member of the European Community and focused more on Brussels than on the Nordic heartland. The new geo-political map in Europe after 1989–90 resulted in applications from three Nordic countries for membership of the European Union, and in the autumn of 1994 referenda were held in these three countries. Finland's popular vote decided on membership; one month later Sweden also decided to enter the Union but much more reluctantly, and if the referendum had been held today, Sweden presumably would have rejected membership. A well-reputed Swedish diplomat formulated it as: 'For several decades the Swedish attitude to Europe has been dictated more by the fear of being left out than by the pleasure of participating.'[18]

In Norway, two attempts to enter European entities by referendum have failed. The first in 1972 was related to membership of the European Community and the second in 1994 to membership in the European Union. Iceland did not even have a referendum. So the current political map of the Nordic Countries shows a diversity of patterns. Finland has adjusted well to the European agenda – the Finns also joined the European Monetary Union in 1999. Sweden did not, and the Swedes want to be missionaries for the Swedish model within the Union more

17 Modéer, K.Å. (2004), 'Östersjöområdets rättsliga kartor – rättskulturella konstruktioner i förändring', in Kekkonen, J. et al. (eds), *Norden, rätten, historia: festskrift till Lars Björne* (Helsinki: Finska juristföreningen), 193.

18 Modéer, K.Å. (2001), 'The Ongoing Dream: Legal and Political Culture in Postwar Sweden', *Studia Europaea* 8, Koninklijke Vlaamse Academie van Belgie voor Wetenschappen en Kunsten (Brussels), 45.

than to accept European subsidiarity. Denmark has, like England, a membership in the Union with special conditions. And Norway and Iceland are the outsiders. The Nordic countries of today are actually showing more diversity than when Scandinavianism began almost two centuries ago. European integration and supranational institutions have overruled the harmonization and convergence policies in these countries.

## VII

The current situation within the Nordic legal cultures is diverse not only between the countries. The legal professions within each country have also changed dramatically. The period of modernity was dominated by public law and the public servants. In the east-Nordic countries an administrative court system was introduced in the 1970s to handle the legal problems of the welfare-state and its social-security regulation. In Sweden high-ranking positions within the judiciary were increasingly given to jurists working in the Department of Justice or other political institutions. It became extremely difficult to obtain a judgeship in the High Court without having had some experience of drafting reform legislation within the government or in parliamentary committees. Furthermore, in Denmark affiliation to the Department of Justice was a stepping-stone to be recruited to the High bench. In Sweden even state-owned law firms with state-employed lawyers were introduced during the peak of modernity in the 1970s.[19]

In the 1980s the break-up of this nationalistic legal culture began. The supranational courts in Strasbourg and Luxembourg increasingly influenced the legal profession, even if there was a deep reluctance to give jurisdictions for the citizens to the European Court of Human Rights. Swedish Prime Minister Olof Palme in 1984 called this court 'a kindergarten' for human rights activists. This attitude has slowly been changed, especially since the Nordic countries incorporated the ECHR into their national legislation. The courts have also adjusted to this supranational pattern. In November 2005 the Swedish High Court made a judicial review related to Article 9 on religious freedom in the convention. Even if the freedom of religion clause in the Swedish constitution should have sentenced the defendant, he was acquitted due to the fact that he would have been acquitted if the case had been taken to the court in Strasbourg.[20]

Within this process of transition in late modern legal cultures the renaissance of the separation of power principle within the constitutional discourses in the Nordic countries is to be noted. The claims for judicial review are an example of this. As mentioned, Norwegian legal culture adopted judicial review of parliamentary norms already in the mid nineteenth century. In the other Nordic

19 Modéer, K.Å. (1994), *Den svenska domarkulturen – europeiska och nordiska förebilder* (Lund: Corpus iuris förlag).

20 (2005) *Nytt Juridiskt Arkiv I*, 87, 805.

countries, however, there has been a reluctance to give the judiciary such political power. Even if judicial review today is included in the Nordic constitutions, there is still reluctance within the judiciaries to take on this task. The incorporation of the ECHR also changed the scenario in the courtrooms as lawyers are increasingly urging the courts/judges to take a stand in this respect.

Private law firms have also adjusted slowly to the international format. European law firms grew into Americanized multi-law firms – so did the Scandinavian, even if the change has been slower. International corporate law firms were introduced and the boards of the Bar association in each Nordic country have been transformed from having being dominated by representatives from small- or mid-sized law firms into being dominated by corporate lawyers from larger law firms.

This also means that the conflict-solving models have turned increasingly from public to private with arbitration and later also mediation as alternative dispute resolutions. Within private law this universal change has also affected the number of cases brought to the public courts. The number of civil cases brought to the public courts has diminished dramatically.

The open boundaries have also affected legal science and the mobility of younger members of the academia. The earlier generations of law professors had their common networks within the Nordic academic environment. Since the 1970s an increasing number of graduate, PhD and post-doctorate students are spending a year abroad. To some extent the members of the academy are the most international part of the legal profession of today. In the long run, this internationalization will have a great impact on the legal cultures in the Nordic countries.

The drafting of the European constitutional treaty has brought the discourse of federalism into the European context. Federal and federalistic constructs are as such a part of the European constitutional history. Countries like Germany, Austria and Italy are familiar with federal solutions, and many of the current 25 Member States, especially the ten new ones, feel comfortable with the development of the European Union in the direction of a federation. The Scandinavian countries have demonstrated that they are reluctant and critical towards such solutions.

The Maastricht Treaty on the creation of the EU was approved in December 1991 and entered into force on 1 November 1993. In its cultural section it emphasized the importance of European cultural divergences related to history and languages on which the national or regional identity is based. The Maastricht treaty actually upheld the cultural divergences. When the earlier versions of the European treaty were drafted, the discourse went in another direction, especially regarding the preamble of the treaty. The core values of the Member States had to be identified and the question was raised if there is a common supranational 'European creed'. Keywords related to human rights, rule of law and welfare state regulation were mentioned in that respect. From the Mediterranean countries (like Italy), a proposition was made that references to God and Christian values should be included in the preamble.[21] For secular countries, like the Scandinavian, such references were regarded as very peculiar and odd, and have underlined a sceptical view towards the European project as a whole.

From a European constitutional perspective, the concept of Scandinavian exceptionalism demonstrated to a great extent the Jeffersonian attitude to federalism in the United States. The contemporary welfare state concept is under evaluation and transformation. Privatization has brought the responsibility of the welfare systems from the state to the society.[22] New liberal politics have – like in the United States – provided traditionally liberal and conservative parties the initiative for the reformation of the welfare-state. Interestingly enough, the social democrats today do not represent the progressive but the 'traditional' view of the welfare state, that is, that of the time of modernity. Scandinavian exceptionalism is eroding both from the inside (due to the different relationships to the European project) and from the outside (due to the divergences within the Nordic countries). German sociologist Ulrich Beck talks about the late-modern concept as the 'Second Modernity' (*die Zweite Moderne*). Within the 'Second Modernity' there is no categorical *either–or*, there is instead an '*as well as*' situation.[23] This means that a plurality of norms is competing for validity and jurisdiction in the late-modern welfare state: European directives as well as traditional welfare regulation. Not only Scandinavian welfare states are under reconstruction – their legal cultures are also in transition. Perhaps we within the legal community need authors like Orhan Pamuk and James Joyce to be able to identify these complex identities.

21 'EU Urged to Leave God Out Of Constitution', *National Liberty Journal*, 2003-MAR, at: <http://www.nljonline.com/>.

22 Hacker, J. (2002), *The Divided Welfare State: The Battle over Public and Private Social Benefits in the United State* (Cambridge: Cambridge University Press).

23 Beck, U. (2004), *Entgrenzung und Entscheidung: Was ist neu an der Theorie reflexiver Modernisierung* (Frankfurt am Main: Suhrkamp).

# Chapter 18
# Normalizing Time: European Integration and Court Delays in Italy

David Nelken

> Although groups and identities are necessarily fluid, the legal culture remains the cement that binds normality and normativity (Pierre Legrand 1: 1)[1]

I would like to dedicate this chapter to the memory of Henrik Zahle. I got to know Henrik quite well over the years; we visited with our families, and I taught with him in Copenhagen for one semester. I valued him as a friend who had a rare capacity to inspire one to be a better person, by example even more than by word. He is and will be much missed.

In his scholarship Henrik exhibited a versatility born of a strong curiosity about the role of law in everyday life. Though primarily a legal theorist and specialist in constitutional law, he was particularly keen for theorists to take notice of what social scientists have to tell us about the different roots and sources of law (including power, custom, tradition, communal life, the sense of reciprocity and natural justice). As a theorist of legal pluralism, his book (edited with Hanne Petersen) about legal polycentricity[2] is particularly relevant to the multifaceted themes of this volume, including as it does, discussions of such topics as 'legal integration as disintegration of national law'. Henrik also had the unusual experience of moving from academia to the Danish Supreme Court – and back again. Drawing on this personal exposure to the task of judging, his recent work was concerned to show that judges should treat rationality and emotion not as opposites but rather as complimentary sources of insight in deciding cases. But the search for such balance also characterized the way he lived his life.

Of the varied themes which the organizers of the workshop from which this volume emerged set out for discussion I shall be concentrating on the one they characterize as 'the encounter of legal cultures in Europe'. For the workshop they provided the following background remarks and questions:

> Does the diversity of legal cultures in Europe make out an obstacle to legal integration and to the possibility of developing a common European law? In theories of comparative

1 Legrand, P. (1995), 'Comparative Legal Studies and Commitment to Theory', *Modern Law Review* 58: 2, 262–273 at 264.

2 Petersen, H. and Zahle, H. (eds) (1995), *Legal Polycentricity: Consequences of Pluralism in the Law* (London: Dartmouth).

law, opinions differ. Some would argue that the differences between legal cultures are irreducible, others that they are not particularly deep, but contingent on practice and that they may consequently change, if legal actors want them to. Others endorse the view that legal cultures are discursively constructed or imagined and used only as a convenient excuse for not wanting to change the way that law is usually being practiced within the confines of the national legal system. The term 'encounter' is intended to cover all the varieties of this phenomenon: the contacts of legal cultures, traditions, and theories of law in the process of European integration; their interactions; their dialogue, conflict, collision; and the inheritance relations between them.

To begin to provide answers to these important questions we have to clarify the concepts involved and their theoretical implications. But we also need to examine case-studies of different types of given encounters. My aim here is to raise a number of questions that can help us get beyond a narrow focus on thinking about harmonization and diversity in terms of the implementation of and compliance with EU directives. In this chapter I shall focus in particular on the need to relate European integration to the larger context of 'the imposing and signalling of conformity' a process which is increasing in importance because of greater global interconnectedness. I shall first discuss what is involved in studying the relationship between integration and legal culture. I shall then offer a case study of the way the European Court of Human Rights attempts to harmonize, or as I would prefer to describe it, to 'normalize', court times in Italy. I shall not have space to do justice fully to either of these matters. The point of the exercise is rather to show the need to bring together topics which tend to be examined separately.

## On Integrating Legal Cultures

If we want to study the processes by which law produces integration we need above all to break the question down into a number of distinct enquiries. We can ask, for example, what is being integrated, by who, how, why and with what results? We need to distinguish talking about national jurisdictions, larger entities such as common and civil law traditions, or smaller contexts such as regions, courts or professions or trade practices. Does integration (as a means and as an end) involve changing institutions, constitutions, codes, principles, directives, regulations, procedures, rules, values, practices or ideas? What is the difference between relying on 'hard law' or 'soft law'?[3] What about *lex mercatoria*, *corpus juris*, *acquis communataire*, or other ways of encouraging common or best laws and practices?

---

3 For a recent analysis of 'soft law' in the context of European integration see Lange, B. (2007), 'How to Conceptualise Law in European Union Integration Processes: Perspectives from the Literature and Empirical Research', in Gessner, V. and Nelken, D. (eds), *European Ways of Law* (Oxford: Hart), 255–76.

But is law integrated? And if not how can different legal systems be integrated? The contributions to Petersen' and Zahle's book teach us a great deal about why national law is not and cannot be integrated. In studying any given legal system it makes more sense to talk of legal cultures in the plural.[4] But even given branches of law may often themselves be best described as 'chaotic'.[5] Boundaries of law do not coincide with national jurisdictions. We know that lawyers specializing in given fields such as commercial law often have more in common with lawyers in other jurisdictions than they do with those working in other fields in the same jurisdiction. Law varies in its dependence on the wider culture. But we still should not be too quick to assume that it is easier to integrate, for example, commercial law in different jurisdictions than it is to unify family law. Each can have aspects which link them to wider aspects of culture.[6] To a large extent, then, when practitioners assume that a legal system is an integrated whole this should be seen as no more than the (defeasible) claim to coherence being made by some official or legal actor whose task it is to find, make and justify such coherence.[7]

On the other hand, a great deal depends on what is being integrated, and in relation to what. For some authors it makes sense even to speak of 'European Ways of law', if the point of comparison is the type of 'adversarial legality' found in the United States.[8] Arguably, social science discussions would be more plausible if they were willing to rethink what was being integrated not so much in terms of legal jurisdictions or other types of legally categorized units, but in socio-legal categories (at local, national and transnational levels) such as 'fields',[9] 'communities'[10] or the 'interlegality' connected to different areas of social and economic life.[11]

---

4 See Bell, J. (2001), *French Legal Cultures* (Cambridge: Cambridge University Press). But more work needs to be done on the relationship between the idea of internal diversity within any national culture and the diversity that characterizes legal culture.

5 Dewar, J. (1998), 'The Normal Chaos of Family Law', *Modern Law Review* 61:4, 467–85.

6 Contrast Foster, N.D.F. (2007), 'Comparative Commercial Law: Rules or Context', in Orucu, E. and Nelken, D. (eds), *Comparative Law: A Handbook* (Oxford: Hart), 263–86, who argues that commercial law does have cultural specificity, with the confidence of Antokolskaia, M. (2007) 'Comparative Family Law: Moving with the Times?', in Orucu and Nelken, *Comparative Law*, 241–62, in the possibility of identifying 'better law' as a way towards realizing a common European family law.

7 Webber, J. (2004), 'Culture, Legal Culture, and Legal Reasoning: A Comment on Nelken', *Australian Journal of Legal Philosophy*, 25–36.

8 Gessner and Nelken, *European Ways of Law*.

9 Bourdieu, P. (1987), 'The Force of Law: Toward a Sociology of the Juridical Field', *Hastings Law Journal* 38, 805–13.

10 Cotterell, R. (1997), 'A Legal Concept of Community', *Canadian Journal of Law and Society* 12, 75–92.

11 Sousa Santos, B. de (1995), *Towards a New Common Sense* (London: Routledge). This term describes 'a highly dynamic process' where different legal spaces are 'nonsychronic'

Insofar as integration is possible, or is at least attempted or claimed, who or what is doing the integrating? In much of the academic and policy literature the focus is squarely on the implementation of European directives or other norms and the question is examined from the perspective of the European commission (most obviously by those whose research of those works is sponsored by the Commission). Compliance with given measures and, more generally, greater harmonization in Europe is considered both attainable and valuable. Such research tells us that different types of law are likely to be more or less easy to harmonize and places different countries in Europe in categories which indicate their willingness to collaborate.[12] But it is important to note that integration will not always be a matter of deliberate design on the part of the European Commission, or any other agency. And, just as efforts by design can 'succeed' or 'fail', other processes that proceed independently, or even in opposition to these efforts, can have varying or unexpected outcomes.

The language of implementation and compliance is likely to be less conceptually adequate for tracing these processes. In their outline statement the organizers of the workshop spoke mainly about 'encounters'. But they also referred to contacts, interactions, dialogue conflicts, collisions and so on. To study larger processes of harmonization or normalization we also need to add other terms such as 'convergence'[13] or 'diffusion'.[14] Different metaphors may be useful for pointing to different processes and it is difficult – perhaps impossible – to avoid using any metaphors. But this makes it all the more important to recognize that the metaphors we adopt carry implications. They may, for example, appeal to mechanical, organic or discursive analogies.[15] It is important that these implications should be exposed and not simply allowed unquestioningly to substitute for well-grounded theory.[16] But, on the other hand, we also need to be aware that authors who use terms like 'irritation' which seem like metaphors, may in reality be employing

---

and thus result in 'uneven and unstable combinations of legal codes (codes in a semiotic sense)' (p. 473).

12 For a 'state of the art' survey, see for example Sverdrup, U. (2005), 'Implementation and European Integration: A Review Essay', Working Paper No. 25, October 2005, <http://www.arena.uio>.

13 Friedman, L.M. (1994), 'Is there a Modern Legal Culture?', *Ratio Juris*, 117.

14 Twining, W. (2005), 'Social Science and Diffusion of Law', *Journal of Law and Society* 32, 203–40.

15 Nelken, D. (2001), 'Beyond the Metaphor of Legal Transplants? Some Consequences of Autopoiesis Theory for the Study of Cross Cultural Legal Adaptation', in Priban, J. and Nelken, D. (eds), *Law's New Boundaries: The Consequences of Autopoiesis* (Aldershot: Dartmouth), 265, and Nelken, D. and Feest, J. (eds) (2001), *Adapting Legal Cultures* (Oxford: Hart).

16 The organizers of the workshop seem to prefer mechanical and discursive metaphors to organic ones.

theoretical 'terms of art' whose meaning derives from their place in carefully defined theoretical language.[17]

What are we studying when we explore legal culture as an object, vector or outcome of integration? As I have argued elsewhere, legal culture, in its most general sense, can be defined as 'one way of describing relatively stable patterns of legally oriented social behaviour and attitudes'. The identifying elements of legal culture range from facts about institutions such as the number and role of lawyers or the ways judges are appointed and controlled, to various forms of behaviour, such as litigation or prison rates, and, at the other extreme, more nebulous aspects of ideas, values, aspirations and mentalities. Like culture itself, legal culture is about who we are not just what we do.[18] A valuable distinction introduced by Lawrence Friedman, when he defined the concept for the sociology of law, is that between on the one hand, 'internal legal culture', the culture of, for instance, lawyers, judges, legal academics, and on the other hand, 'external legal culture' – the attitudes (and actions) of those outside the official system who bring their expectations and demands to bear on it.[19]

Those who choose to use the term legal culture most often use it to refer to national legal cultures or to the time-honoured 'families of law' studied by legal comparativists. But they are increasingly being asked to face a number of serious objections.[20] In the first place, talking of legal culture presupposes that we know what we mean when we talk of culture. But, though reference to culture has become increasingly central in many disciplines, anthropologists, who originally developed the term, have found its common meanings less and less illuminating for the purpose of their explanations. As Sally Merry has explained, anthropology has elaborated a conception of culture as unbounded, contested, and connected to relations of power. The contemporary anthropological understanding of culture envisions a far more fluid, contested and changing set of values and practices than that provided by the idea of culture as tradition, and meaning is produced by institutional arrangements and political economy. Culture is marked by hybridity and creolization rather than uniformity or consistency. Local systems are analysed in the context of national and transnational processes and are understood as the result of particular historical trajectories.[21]

---

17 Teubner, G. (1998), 'Legal Irritants: Good Faith in British Law or How Unifying Law Ends Up in New Divergences', *Modern Law Review* 61, 11.

18 Nelken, D. (2004), 'Using the Concept of Legal Culture,' *Australian Journal of Legal Philosophy* 29, 1–28.

19 Friedman, L.M. (1975), *The Legal System: A Social Science Perspective* (New York: Russell Sage).

20 Nelken, D. (2006), 'Rethinking Legal Culture', in Freeman, M. (ed.), *Law and Sociology* (Oxford: Oxford University Press), 200–224, and Nelken, D. (2007), 'Three Problems in Employing the Concept of Legal Culture', in Bruinsma, F. and Nelken, D. (eds), *Explorations in Legal Culture*, Special issue of *Recht der Werkelijkheid, the Netherlands*.

21 Merry, S.E. (2003), 'Human Rights Law and the Demonization of Culture (and Anthropology along the Way)', *Polar* 26, 55–77.

Care must be exercised in employing any concept which makes reference to culture so as to avoid reifying national or other stereotypes. We need to recognize that much that goes under the name of culture is no more than 'imagined communities' or 'invented traditions'. It is easy to fall into the opposed vices of 'Occidentalism' or 'Orientalism', making other cultures seem either necessarily similar or intrinsically 'other'. If culture is always , to a large extent, a matter of struggle and disagreement, the purported uniformity, coherence or stability of given national or other cultures will often be no more than a rhetorical claim projected by outside observers or manipulated by elements within the culture concerned. Legal culture, like all culture, is a product of the contingencies of history and is thus always undergoing change.[22] In a period of globalization the problem is accentuated. When seeking to mark the limits of 'culture', it becomes ever more difficult to set boundaries to our imaginations and expectations: 'we inhabit' Rosemary Coombe tells us, a 'deterritorialized world'.[23] We participate via the media in other communities of others with whom we have no geographical proximity or common history. Hence, 'all totalising accounts of society, tradition and culture are exclusionary and enact a social violence by suppressing contingent and continually emergent differences'. Instead we must face the 'challenges of transnationalism and the politics of global capitalism or multiple overlapping and conflicting juridiscapes'.[24]

We should therefore be cautious about assuming any necessary correspondence between legal and general culture within any given national setting. How far it is thought appropriate that the 'internal legal culture' of legal professionals should correspond to the 'external legal culture' of groups and individuals in the wider society[25] is also itself a cultural variable (and one not sufficiently emphasized in work on legal culture by those scholars in the United states who take for granted the common-law emphasis on democratic participation in legal institutions which makes a virtue of the permeability of internal legal culture, as compared for example to the top-down conception of law and state found in many continental European countries). But it is the Anglo-American type of legal culture and conception of the term, which is increasingly being spread as if it was universally appropriate.

For many observers the most important question to ask about European integration has to do with the factors which shape the outcome of efforts to achieve more of it. It would be unrealistic to assume state, group or individual behaviour could ever completely conform to international commitments, especially as global

22 Nelken, D. (1995), 'Disclosing/Invoking Legal Culture' in Nelken, D. (ed.), *Legal Culture, Diversity and Globalisation*, special issue of *Social and Legal Studies* 4, 435.

23 Coombe, R.J. (2000), 'Contingent Articulations: A Critical Studies of Law', in Sarat, A. and Kearns, T. (eds), *Law in the Domains of Culture* (Ann Arbor, MI: University of Michigan Press), 21–64.

24 Appadurai, A. (1996), *Modernity at Large: Cultural Dimensions of Globalization* (Minneapolis, MN: University of Minnesota Press).

25 Friedman, *The Legal System.*

pressures are ongoing and changeable. But we also need to keep in mind that there can be disagreement about what is meant by and who defines success.[26] Is European integration a means to an end (and to what end?), or is it an end it itself? Because moves towards greater integration depend on the actions and motives of those promoting, using and being subject to such efforts, it can be difficult to generalize. The degree of conformity in each case will depend on the interests and values at stake.

On the one hand, increasing collaboration can be expected when the countries of the Union want to flex their muscles as an economic unity in relation to other powers such as the United States or China as well as when they feel it necessary to collaborate on security matters and to set limits to irregular immigration. On the other hand, where states see the requirements of integration as challenging features of their sovereignty or identity,[27] they are likely to be particularly reluctant to change. Timing can be all important – as is shown by the failure of the proposed European constitution immediately after the considerable enlargement of the Union. But when countries are trying to be accepted as new members it is obvious that they are more open to the requirements of 'conditionality'. Sometimes symbolic change will be accepted as long as daily life is allowed to continue much as before. At other times it is exactly symbols which are rejected – and this may again explain why the proposed European constitution was rejected whereas the European treaty is perhaps more acceptable, (though few countries are willing to put this to the test via a referendum).

In studying outcomes the running has been made mainly by lawyers, political scientists and economists. But there is also some interesting work by comparative lawyers and social scientists. As against the mainstream scholarship that seeks to harmonize legal rules or at least codify 'best practice', there are also authors who focus on the difficulties of changing legal cultures. Legrand, for example, tells us that despite the best efforts of those involved, private law in Europe 'has not converged, is not converging now, and will not do so'.[28] Some sociologists who adopt the language of systems theory have also emphasized the difficulty law has in communicating with (rather than just about) practices which belong to other sub-systems of society such as politics or economics. While it may be

---

26 Nelken, D. (2001), 'The Meaning of Success in Transnational Legal Transfers', *Windsor Yearbook of Access to Justice* 19, 349–66.

27 Some politicians in Turkey, for example, which is presently being considered for membership in the European Union, would rather risk rejection than accept what they view as dishonour. Journalists Ibrahim Kabogklu and Baskin Oran are currently on trial (under article 301) for having brought Turkey into disrepute by providing information for an international report on human rights in Turkey. After the European Union again recently warned Turkey that this law represented a bar to accession, a statement has been issued expressing willingness to amend the law.

28 Legrand, P. (1996), 'European Legal Systems are not Converging', *International & Comparative Law Quarterly* 45:1, 52–81.

going too far to say that this means that we can never predict outcomes, we should also anticipate that many results will indeed be unexpected. At best, it is claimed, law may 'irritate' these other subsystems into unpredictable changes.[29] On the other hand it has been persuasively argued that differences in historically shaped 'cultural' conditions should not be reified into irremovable obstacles.[30]

Lawrence Friedman continues to insist that as global trends bring about social economic and cultural similarities, this will bring pressure on law to follow suit.[31] And it is certainly true that attempts to produce European integration are part of, and are traversed by, larger processes. Some of these developments may be parts of efforts to provide the basis for political, economic and financial stability in Europe as elsewhere, they may parallel what is going on in Europe itself on these fronts, or they may even run against them. As with globalization, so with Europeanization, it makes less and less sense to think of 'domestic' norms as forming part of distinct national jurisdictions that interact with transnational norms. Legal fields are increasingly internationalized, even if this process does not affect all fields to the same extent and varies by different areas of legal and social regulation. A contrast is often made between, on the one hand, those areas of law that are relatively internationalized, such as international business contracts, antitrust and competition policy, internet and new technology, labour law, social law, and environment law, and, on the other, family law and property law. But experts in the latter fields also often find much evidence of international and cross-cultural influences.

Attempts to revise our ideas about integration may also take inspiration from the interesting line of work in international law that studies transnational legal processes. Harold Koh, one of the pioneers of this field of international law, is particularly interested in the way transnational norms modify behaviour – the theory and practice of how public and private actors – nation-states, international organizations, multinational enterprises, non-governmental organizations and private individuals – internalize rules of transnational law.[32] Likewise, Friedman describes transnational law as the 'norms and institutions which span, are valid

29 Teubner, 'Legal Irritants', 11.

30 Krygier, M. (1997), 'Is there Constitutionalism after Communism? Institutional Optimism, Cultural Pessimism, and the Rule of Law', *International Journal of Sociology* 26:4, 17–47.

31 Friedman, L.M (2007), 'Preface', in Clarke, D. (ed.) *Encyclopedia of Law and Society Vol. 1* (London: Sage).

32 Koh, H.H. (1996), 'Transnational Legal Process', *Nebraska Law Review* 75, 181; Koh, H.H. (1997), 'Why Do Nations Obey International Law?', *Yale Law Journal* 106, 2599; Koh, H.H. (1999), 'How is International Human Rights Law Enforced?', *Indiana Journal of Law* 74, 1397, and Koh, H.H. (2005), 'Internalization through Socialization', *Duke Law Journal* 54, 975. For a good collection of empirical studies see Likosky, M. (ed.) (2002), *Transnational Legal Processes: Globalisation and Power Disparities* (Cambridge: Cambridge University Press).

in, or apply to more than one country or jurisdiction'. He distinguishes imposed norms, planned voluntary norms and unplanned evolutionary norms.[33]

These writers all agree that the increasing interchange of commerce, populations, and information makes it less and less appropriate to think of 'domestic' norms as forming part of distinct national jurisdictions that then interact with transnational norms. With the reduction in national sovereignty, legal fields are increasingly internationalized. Instead of governments, the talk now is increasingly of 'governance' – power exercised at a series of other levels and by other institutions, in collaboration, or otherwise, with state bodies.

The 'denationalization' of rulemaking[34] means that transnational public and semi-public networks substitute, to an increasing extent, for national fora. Rule-formulation and settlement increasingly takes place within new agencies of transnational governance, such as NAFTA, the OECD and the WTO, but also in many lesser-known public–private forums. Lawyers and accountants also play an increasing role as entrepreneurs of new forms of dispute prevention and settlement,[35] mainly, if not entirely, so as to service the increasingly important international business community. In turn, the opportunities for such activity transform the legal profession(s).

The language of legal transplants from one jurisdiction to another, as hitherto used by comparative lawyers, is less suited to studying the new forms of norm-making, dispute-channelling and regulation which thrive in the neo-liberal trading environment. Given the way the relationship between the global and the local is changing, scholars now investigate what some have called the making and acceptance of 'global prescriptions'.[36] Increasing interdependence means that the most pressing questions do not just concern how transplants or prescriptions move from place to place but also the way 'place' itself is constructed and deconstructed. As Sally Merry has argued,[37] a world characterized by 'the space of flows' puts the very idea of 'place' in doubt. Writing about human rights, she points to three such flows: transnational consensus building, the way international discourse shapes transnational programme transplants, and the localization of transnational knowledge by national and local actors who participate in transnational events and bring their experiences home.

---

33 Friedman, L.M. (1996), 'Borders: On the Emerging Sociology of Transnational Law', *Stanford Journal of International Law* 32, 65.

34 Sassen, S. (2002), 'Opening Remarks: Producing the Transnational Inside the National' in Likosky, *Transnational Legal Processes*, 189–95.

35 Dezalay, Y. and Garth, B. (1995), *Dealing in Virtue* (Chicago, IL: University of Chicago Press).

36 Dezalay, Y. and Garth, B. (eds) (2002), *Global Prescriptions: The Production, Exportation and Importation of a New Legal Orthodoxy* (Ann Arbor, MI: University of Michigan Press).

37 Merry, S.E. (2005), *Human Rights and Gender Violence: Translating International Law into Local Justice* (Chicago, IL: University of Chicago Press).

We are now living in what Manuel Castells has called the 'network society',[38] where power is diffused in global networks of wealth, power, information and images that circulate and transmute in a system of variable geometry. For him, flows of capital, information, technology, organizational interaction, images, sounds and symbols go from one disjointed position to another and gradually replace a space of locales. Power now increasingly lies in codes of information and in images of representation produced by people's minds and constructed in identities. We also should bear in mind, however, as Merry reminds us, that crucial decisions regarding legal change take place in specific places. To keep track of these transnational flows we need to find ways to study 'placeless phenomena in a place'.[39] The specificity of time, it may be added, is also coming to be reconfigured through the same larger processes, and, as we shall see later, there are also deliberate attempts to reduce existing differences in legal time.

It is not always sufficiently emphasized that, as with globalization in general, it can be important to distinguish the objective and subjective sides of integration. Such processes have an objective aspect when they have to do with places or individuals being drawn into large–scale interdependencies, and include unplanned as well as intended moves towards greater convergence. But there is also an all important subjective aspect, which has to do with how local patterns or standards are thought about when contrasted with those deemed to be superior. Under these conditions legal culture tends ever more to become what we could call subjectively 'relational' rather than objectively 'embedded' in environing contexts.[40] With increasing contact between societies there are ever more opportunities to define one's own legal culture in terms of relationships of attraction to but also repulsion from others. For example, when comparative European prison rates first began to be published in the 1980s, policy makers in Finland, which came high in the list, decided to cut back on prison building, whereas the Netherlands felt entitled to build more.

To make further progress in describing and explaining interaction between legal cultures, more attention therefore needs to be given to identifying the subjective processes involved. What can be described as the imposition and signalling of conformity[41] is one such process that seems to play an increasing

---

38 Castells, M. (1996), *The Rise of the Network Society* (Oxford: Blackwell); Castells, M. (1998), *The Information Society* (Oxford: Blackwell).

39 Merry, *Human Rights and Gender Violence*, 44.

40 Nelken, D. (2006), 'Il radicamento della penalità', in Febbrajo, A., La Spina, A. and Raiteri, M. (eds), *Cultura Giuridica e Politiche Pubbliche* (Milano: Giuffré), 200–235, and Nelken, D. (2008), 'Theorising the Embeddedness of Punishment', in Melossi, D., Sozzo, M. and Sparks, R. (eds), *Travels of the Criminal Question: Cultural Embeddedness and Diffusion* (Oxford: Hart).

41 Nelken, D. (2006), 'Signalling Conformity: Changing Norms in Japan and China', *Michigan Journal of International Law* 27, 933–972. For two good (but contrasting) studies of this phenomenon see Whitehead, C.K. (2006), 'What's Your Sign? – International Norms, Signals and Compliance', *Michigan Journal of International Law* 27, 695, and Feldman, E.

role alongside, and often connected to, more familiar mechanisms of imposition, borrowing and imitation. The imposing and signalling of conformity, for example, plays a role in all three of the 'flows' that are identified by Merry – those oriented toward building consensus, copying programmes, or localizing innovation. What interests us in this chapter is the way pressures to conformity are different from the insistence on compliance with particular orders because they relate more to the necessity and willingness to appear 'normal' in terms of international standards and patterns of behaviour. The relationship between the normative and the normal, so often forgotten or repressed, here comes to the surface. In the case study of court delay in Italy that follows we will see that such delays do undermine individual rights, but that they also show that Italy's legal institutions are embarrassingly out of line with others with which it wants to be compared. It thus provides an instructive example of how legal culture, as 'the cement that binds normality and normativity',[42] shapes change and is shaped by it.

Pressures to conformity may make less noise than dramatizations of political, religious or cultural differences, but their significance should not be underestimated, (and demonstrations of dissent are often justified by the experience of increasing similarities or the fear that foreign models will be imitated). Many countries in Latin America and Eastern Europe are making gestures towards doing what is required so as to take their place in the globalizing economy. Inge Markovits, for example, argues that states in Eastern Europe have abolished the death penalty (whatever their populations may actually think or want), as a way of signalling their desire for acceptance into the European Union.[43] On the other hand, for any specific issue, it is possible to point to countries and places that are not (yet) coming into line. Rather than seeing dissent and conformity as opposites we should note that there may be various indirect connections between these phenomena. Emphasizing points of disagreement is often a way of concealing more profound conformities. Conformity to common standards may be promoted by and through law but the homogeneity of norms is not an inevitable consequence of processes that involve the imposing and signalling conformity. Globalization involves processes of both homogenization and integration, and economic integration in particular often presupposes and accentuates difference.[44] Likewise, even common standards are often encouraged so as to allow more, not less, competition. Globalization can, and often does, have quite different or sometimes opposite consequences, even in the same state. Similar laws, in different places, may produce or presuppose

(2006), 'The Culture of Legal Change: A Case-Study of Tobacco Control in Twenty-First Century Japan', *Michigan Journal of International Law* 27, 743.

42 See footnote 1.

43 Markovits, I. (2004), 'Exporting Law Reform: But Will it Travel?', *Cornell International Law Journal* 95, 98.

44 Nelken, D. (1997), 'The Globalization of Crime and Criminal Justice: Prospects and Problems', in Freeman, M. (ed.), *Law and Opinion at the End of the 20th Century* (Oxford: Oxford University Press), 251.

different social conditions. And the use of similar technologies may become an instrument for creating antagonistic differences.[45]

The imposition and signalling of conformity is bound up with processes of economic and political inclusion and exclusion. Often it is directed by stronger states, which take their own standards as norms and act either directly or indirectly to impose them through their dominance of international organizations. The attempts of the WTO to impose the introduction of GMO seeds and produce provides a good example of this dynamic, with much of the struggle depending on who should be made to carry the burden of proof of the possible risks involved. We also need to explore who gains and loses through the proposed introduction of common standards. So we will need to distinguish, for example, between local and cosmopolitan bureaucrats and between those legal actors with an interest in promoting change and those with an interest in resisting it. The interests of the elites and the population at large will often not coincide.

A variety of public and private agencies and rating institutes seek to shape international standards and prevent international risks, whether the issue is dumping products under cost price, food safety, shared computer and telecommunication codes. Such standards typically emerge in the process of seeking agreement rather than being pre-standing. Some – like the definition of corruption used by Transparency International – depend on endorsing the judgments of foreign and local observers. Learning of the failures of conformity may also be important (though ignorance has its uses too); hence, the agencies that set and vet standards play a crucial role, although the growth of domestic civil society is another and often better route to increasing information. But the problem of who guards the guardians can never be fully resolved. All this makes it especially important to distinguish between different types of common standards, some which lead to 'a race to the top' and others a 'race to the bottom'. Another set of issues concerns how new conformist standards are spread – and resisted. Who are the actors involved? Who actually formulates and judges what conformity requires? How is any index for measuring compliance actually constructed and popularized? How are such indexes used or misused, understood or misunderstood? What does conformity require in any given case? Is it about reaching a certain standard or about not being out of line or both? Not least, how easy is it to fake commitment to common standards and when and why is such lip service acceptable?[46]

It is against this background that we can return to the question of European integration. Are European developments just reflections of these wider changes or are they, in any way, examples of resistance to them? A key question now emerging (or re-emerging) is what is really at stake in the European slogan of 'Unity in

45 Roversi, A. (2008), *Hate on the Net* (Aldershot: Ashgate).

46 An issue discussed extensively in the literature on norms is how to recognize those who use signalling to mimic the commitments of good future collaborators without actually being committed to cooperation. See Nelken, 'Signalling Conformity'.

diversity'?[47] The problem is probably being posed at this stage of the European project because of the rapid rate in which the Union has been expanding, and the alleged 'clash of civilizations' between the Christian and Muslim worlds. What makes greater integration worth pursuing? When should differences in cultures – and legal cultures – be seen as problems that need to be overcome and when as something to be protected? The answer of course depends on what we are talking about and what we are trying to achieve. From an economic point of view it is self-evidently valuable (because efficient) to reduce 'transaction costs'.[48] On the other hand, Cotterell[49] has recently suggested that comparative law should shift focus from seeking legal similarity (via harmonization or unification) towards appreciating the virtues of legal diversity. For him,

> law is faced with representing or managing difference in legal aspirations no less than with promoting similarity in legal experience. Questions about national sentiment and diversity of cultural allegiances are also becoming legally significant, (as matters bearing on law's practical claims to authority) in a far more obvious way than in past decades. In a culturally complex world, allegiances (to law as to most other embodiments of authority), become complex and multiple.[50]

He goes on to suggest that the process of unifying law between different legal systems could be compared to the process of assimilation between different cultural groups in the same society.

As a matter of principle we could probably agree with Cotterell that 'productive integration requires not assimilation, but mutual acceptance and mutual learning about the other, in a framework of universal respect for human dignity and autonomy'.[51] But deciding what this principle requires in practice is a little more complicated. There may be more than one way of interpreting it, as seen in the different approaches to integration of immigrants for example as between the UK and France,[52] or the different attitudes to permitting the wearing of the veil and other religious symbols in school in France as compared to the Netherlands.[53] It can also border on the paradoxical that one of the key conditions imposed on candidate

47 Although enormous attention is given in official publications to the need to integrate diversity, the reference is almost always to the need to accommodate the needs and claims of minorities or immigrants.

48 Ogus, A. (2007), 'The Economic Approach: Competition between Legal Systems', in Orucu and Nelken, *Comparative Law*, 155–68.

49 Cotterell, R. (2007), 'Is it so bad to be different? Comparative Law and the Appreciation of Diversity', in Orucu and Nelken, *Comparative Law*, 133–54.

50 Cotterell, 'Is it so bad to be different?', 147.

51 Cotterell, 'Is it so bad to be different?', 137.

52 Favell, A. (1998), *Philosophies of Integration* (Basingstoke: Macmillan).

53 De Blois, M. and Bruinsma, F. (2007), 'Pluralism in the Netherlands and Laicité in France: The Case of the Islamic Headscarf', in Bruinsma and Nelken, *Explorations in Legal Culture*.

nations in the name of mutual acceptance is that they show more willingness to tolerate diversity.

There is also the further difficult question of what sort of diversity we wish to protect. We need to distinguish carefully what we (and/or the members of the culture in question) want to preserve from that which we – or they – want to change. We then need to face the problem that there may be different ideas about this (and interests involved). We may not be willing to defend all those practices that a given country, group or institution concerned knows of, is proud of, and itself wishes to preserve. But, conversely, could unknown, unacknowledged – even disowned – cultural patterns ever be worth preserving? What if valued parts of one's culture – or legal culture – are linked to less acceptable ones? If there is anything valid in the idea of culture then we must expect legal and other cultural practices sometimes to come in packages that it can be difficult to break up into parts that are more or less valuable. The following case study of the effort involved in trying to change court delays in Italy illustrates a (perhaps not uncommon) situation where a pattern of behaviour is in fact disowned even by those whose actions maintain it in being.

## Italian Court Delays and Normalization Processes

Comparative studies of how nation-states comply with European directives usually place Italy in the category of those who are slowest to conform.[54] But speed of compliance is not as unambiguous an indicator of willingness to comply as it is sometimes made to seem. It does not correlate for example to degree of commitment to the European Union. Italy is one of the most enthusiastic supporters of European Union integration, whereas England and Denmark for example, despite being the quickest to comply, are those most likely to object to directives for infringing their sovereignty. One explanation for this is the cynical one that it is easy to be enthusiastic about rules if you can easily find ways round applying them in practice. But this is reasoning as if types of legal culture were all the same. Much the same attitude in Italy is taken to their own national laws. Unlike some Northern European countries, law in Italy is treated as something that may take some time to become fully institutionalized, especially where the 'culture of legality' has not fully taken root. To emphasize the way Italy is sometimes slow to comply would also miss the crucial role of the European Union in the integration of Italy itself. European Union provisions, from the Maastricht limits on expenditure to the adoption of the common currency Euro are what have allowed Italy to overcome

54 Already Wilhemson, T. (1995), 'Legal Integration as Disintegration of National Law', in Petersen and Zahle, *Legal Polycentricity*, 127, told us that Denmark had a 96 per cent implementation rate of European Union directives whereas Italy is 'the tardiest'. But this is just measuring the speed of bringing law 'into force'. The actual 'enforcement' of law is a further and much more difficult stage of 'implementation'.

its previous history of periodic runaway inflation. It has proven very convenient to explain that such rigorous requirements come from 'elsewhere'.[55]

But the need for patience to allow Italy to come into line seems to be wearing thin when it comes to court delays. At the beginning of the new millennium as many as 3,500,000 civil cases and 5,400,000 penal cases were awaiting trial. Civil cases in Italy in 1999 took on average five years to go through the first trial stage, and over nine years[56] to go through the first and appeal stage (which is essentially a re-trial of the facts). There is then a further final appeal stage on legal points which can be taken to the numerous sections of the Supreme Court. Penal cases can take only a little less time. The overall length taken by court processes does not correspond to the time actually devoted to the cases but results from the 'dead times' (the expression used in Italian) which have to pass between each hearing because the judge's calendar is full. By contrast, in some other European countries time of trials from start to finish is measured in months rather than years.

Although trial delays are a national problem, there is, as might be expected, also considerable variation around the country, as well as from tribunal to tribunal. The time courts took to dispose of civil cases from their case-loads ranged from around six to eleven years, and waiting was usually longer in the courts in the South.[57] Nonetheless, as compared to larger cultural differences in what is a relatively young state, legal culture may be seen as having more in common across the country. These similarities derive from the sharing of common rules, procedures and nationally-appointed judges as well as aspects of institutional practice and law in action, such as the way lawyers are paid. Indeed, legal culture is often deliberately used as a nationalizing and integrating force to correct for the 'backwardness' of outlying areas.

---

55 But, of course, this is now beginning to taint the positive image of the Union. I still remember waking one day to discover that the government had helped itself to a contribution from my current account in the bank so as to help it meet its Maastricht target.

56 These official figures need considerable interpretation. For some purposes they overestimate the time required, for others they underestimate it! This figure is the *average* time taken by all cases and includes those that finish by agreement between the parties or for other reasons before a sentence is delivered. Further time is required for 'depositing' the sentence of the judge and even more for actually carrying out the court's judgment and getting your money and property back. For a series of reasons which have to do with the lack of court bailiff resources (and the competition from private and even illegal actors), the actual 'recovery' of the debt is the most problematic stage of the legal process.

57 According to the Ministry of Justice statistics for the Civil courts in 1999, the shortest period was found in the small town of Bolzano in the (Austrian influenced) far north of the country, where first stage trials took on average around four and a half years and the process of appeal court hearing took around a further year and a half (making a total 6.2 years). The court with the record for the longest trials was Caltanisetta, a small town in Sicily where, on average, cases took seven and half years for the first trial stage, and a further five and a half for the appeal stage (total time 13.15 years).

The main challenge to Italy's trial delays comes from the Strasbourg Court of Human Rights. The court – though not an agency of the European Union – makes crucial decisions affecting Europe and beyond. Representing 'European ideals', its decisions, as in Merry's examples, though taken in one place, are thus meant to represent 'universal' standards. The right to a trial within a reasonable period is one of the fundamental rights of the Convention of Human Rights (Article 6) which this Court seeks to protect. In 1999 there were over 40 signatories to this convention but 36 per cent of all sentences handed down were findings holding Italy responsible for unreasonable delay in its trial processes.[58] The cases which reach Strasbourg are not necessarily representative of Italian court cases in general, but it is by no means only the extreme cases that arrive there.[59] At a conservative estimate a good 20 per cent of court cases take longer than the time Strasbourg considers reasonable; so, absent particular reasons of legal complexity, a good part of the Italian system could automatically just be transferred to Strasbourg after a certain period of normal waiting time! The Strasbourg Court itself got into difficulty in handling all these appeals within a reasonable period and set up Committees to overhaul its machinery in an attempt to catch up with its backlog.

In the course of policing the extent to which states abide by the convention on human rights, the Strasbourg Court of Human Rights and the Council (now Committee) of Ministers draw on all three sources of legal suasion identified by Henrik Zahle: external power, tradition and underlying natural justice.[60] Thus the role of the Strasbourg court well illustrates the complexities of charting the relationship between the local and super-national influences on legal culture. Because Italy was a willing signatory to the convention we could consider the European Court as no more than a higher level court of appeal of the same legal culture. But it is a higher court with a difference. According to one Italian 'human rights' lawyer who specializes in taking cases to Strasbourg, '... the European Court, the Court is almost a "Court of Miracles" because it seems to be an organisation which is outside time and space. You can go there to punish the powerful. Because that is what it is all about we could say that what it offers is revolutionary, even

58 In 1999 a total of 6,885 complaints from Italy, almost all concerning legal delay, were waiting before the court. This represented over 20 per cent of the total from all countries for breaches of all the various provisions of the Convention. The Italian state was condemned to pay moral damages to almost all the successful applicants.

59 I carried out research on a sample of 50 court sentences handed down by the court in the late 1990s. This revealed that delays ranged from four to 18 years. Most cases were on the civil side (penal cases tend to end by prescription and the accused person often tends to leave it there); interestingly, no more than a seventh involved anything like commercial disputes. The Italian state usually tried to defend the cases at Strasbourg on the grounds of court overload but this defence was always rejected.

60 Zahle, H. (1995), 'The Polycentricity of Law or the Importance of Polycentricity for Legal Dogmatics', in Petersen and Zahle, *Legal Polycentricity*, 185.

anarchic justice.'[61] To make things more complicated, however, we should add, that, even if not as such an *institution* of the Italian legal system, this idea of law as an antidote to power is part of the *belief system* of many judges, lawyers and jurists within the Italian legal system itself.

The Italian government has taken a variety of measures to try to deal with the problem. There have been 'managerial' type reforms aimed at combining different levels of criminal court and reducing the number of hearings in civil cases. Judges who are found responsible for breaching bureaucratic time limits in writing their judgements now risk having to pay damages and not, as previously, only criticism, as a result of internal disciplinary hearings by the Supreme Judicial Council. Some gains in speed in civil cases resulted, at least at first, from the re-routing of pre-1995 cases to be dealt with by honorary judges. But the most relevant, if controversial, measure taken to stave off criticism from Strasbourg involves the so-called Legge Pinto (Pinto's Law) which was passed in 1999. After the introduction of this law, cases of alleged delay had to be submitted to the court of appeal of the nearest district, where decisions were then supposed to be provided within four months. This initially held back recourse to Strasbourg and thus succeeded in its aim of preventing parties from placing Italy in a bad light internationally. But this new trial stage of course itself easily adds to delay. In addition, unlike actions before the Strasbourg court, here it was necessary to prove that delay had led to material damage, and the expenses of bringing the action were not reimbursed. So cases still go to Strasbourg.[62]

More recently, a new constitutional principle (art. 111; 1999) emphasizing the need for trial lengths to be reasonable was included in the framework of the so called 'just process' legislation. Significantly, however, this does not give private individuals any rights. No thought was given to how to make this right effective,[63] nor ensure its priority in relation to the other rights and protections being introduced simultaneously and their tendency actually to lengthen court processes. Judges have told me that they have begun to use this new principle as a means of closing cases where, formally speaking, this would otherwise have been problematic. Clement Mastella, the last Minister of Justice, announced that he wanted all civil and penal cases of medium difficulty to be completed in the space of five years. But I am not aware of any worked out managerial action-plan, or,

61 In this interview with a human rights lawyer, carried out in 2000, the lawyer went on to add that the actual damages that the Strasbourg court awards to someone 'crushed by the national legal system' were far too low to compensate for what can have been lost.

62 At the recent Padua Conference on 'The reasonableness in the length of trials' (30–31 May 2003), which I attended, the Legge Pinto was described as 'diabolic'.

63 Italian legal (and political) culture is one where rights are often not related to effective resources. For example, female judges (an ever increasing proportion of the magistracy) are guaranteed excellent paid maternity leave but no substitute is supplied for them at this time and the cases they are responsible for are usually just put on hold.

still less, any offer of more resources, as a means of realizing this aim. Italy is not yet near to coming into line with the European norm.

On the criminal side especially the real commitment of the political and legal elites to the aim of 'speedy trials' must be suspect in the light of the continuing and even increasing emphasis on multiplying points and methods of procedural rights and controls. In any event, for most of the ordinary trial lawyers I have interviewed, the average time taken for court cases in Italy is something they have adapted to; exceptional cases are the ones which *overrun the Italian norm*, either because of legal complexities, more than normal problems in the availability of judges, administrative errors by the court administration (the *cancelleria*), the number of parties involved, the need for complicated expert evidence, difficulties in obtaining the collaboration of parties or witnesses, or unfair tactics used by the other side, and so on.

So far we have been discussing court delay as if it was an objective problem whose definition was self-evident. But this is far from true and different definitions suggest different 'remedies'. The Strasbourg court does not have a hard and fast definition of what constitutes unreasonable delay, but it offers relief if trials take much longer than is normal for other signatories to the convention. No allowance is made for differences in institutional structures. Italy's own 'administrative- bureaucratic' definition, the one used most extensively both in media and policy discussions of the problem has little to do with the time taken in other countries but concerns whether the courts are getting through more new cases each year than those still waiting to be dealt with. The problem of 'delay' is a question of *backlogs*. It is measured simply by subtracting cases dealt with from those still outstanding. There is no acknowledgement of the possibility that this could reflect the increasing demand for legal services, greater claims-consciousness and the creation of new rights. Nor is consideration given to the risk that speeding up throughput might only lead to a further increase in demand for legal services.

The administrative-bureaucratic definition encourages drastic remedies such as those in which legislative reforms re-start the clock with new rules and hence cancel or relegate to a bureaucratic limbo those antecedent cases in the waiting list. Cases which began before the 1995 revision of the civil process, for example, are left to be dealt with in the so called '*sezione stralcio*' by poorly paid lawyers deputizing as judges. Increasingly, in much public commentary, the Strasbourg definition is coming to assume the same significance as the 'administrative-bureaucratic' definition. As dramatized by the regular holdings of the Strasbourg Court in favour of those who appeal to it, Italy's record on trial times is seen as bad for attracting investment but, more generally, as bad for its image as a fully functioning European state. Lengthy trial times are shameful because of what they signal about the distance Italy has still to cover to become fully 'modern'. Delay is bad because of what others will say.

Unlike the bureaucratic-administrative definition, however, it is difficult for the Strasbourg criterion to feed back in to the record keeping of the court system.

Delay is also something that is constructed differently by internal and external legal culture. The Italian legal system *itself* defines what it will consider acceptable and unacceptable delay, both through its jurisprudence and everyday practice. This is true both for the so called 'prescription' periods, within which criminal cases must be finished, or the priority given to different types of civil cases or for given procedures. Interestingly, in the New York courts where court delays were first studied by sociologists of law, priority was given to business cases, and it was this which allegedly led to relatively more delay in other kinds of cases.[64] In Italy, by contrast, the legislator has given priority to cases where workers risk losing their jobs. For legal remedies for delay to take effect they have to engage such internal 'autopoietic' definitions of the system, both in doctrine and the law in action, for it is these which determine how it allocates its scarce resources.

The most obvious external definition of delay is that oriented to users' needs and expectations. Insofar as Italian court times may have come to be experienced and/or labelled as slow, this is likely to have been exacerbated by the contrast between court times and the time taken to do other things in business or personal life. In particular the increased use of information technology and the internet may also have made court processes seem even slower. Media portrayals of trials give the impression that it is possible to do things more expeditiously. For many years now Channel Five (owned by Premier Berlusconi), has hosted a highly popular television show called *Forum* in which a series of civil disputes, no matter how complicated and painful, each get heard and resolved live in less than 15 minutes by a studio judge, applying the Italian civil code![65]

There is obviously no time for careful investigation of the facts; typically the judge just decides who he or she believes. The 'plot' of the show is one in which both parties usually think they are in the right, but the law is introduced at the end as a higher unquestionable wisdom as far as the parties are concerned. Some time is also provided before this for the studio audience to express their opinions and vote their verdict, which may not always coincide with the law. Interestingly, there is nothing adversarial about the format, and there are of course no lawyers. As significant perhaps, the Italian public, like most of those who watch television in Europe, has been exposed for a generation to a diet of films and shows in which American criminal proceedings are taken as the norm. The trials in these films, framed to finish within the space of the transmission, for a long time had little in common with the Italian system.[66] But some in Italy, as elsewhere, may have

64 Kalven, H. and Zeisel, H. (1959), *Delay in the Courts* (New York: Little, Brown).

65 In his appearances in trials for corruption in Milan, Silvio Berlusconi turned his trial into (even more of) a media event by offering 'spontaneous declarations', which could not be tested by the court, but which were aimed at the television watching public.

66 A public television channel used to regularly transmit material from the real Italian courts called 'a day in the courts'. This was especially important during the Tangentopoli trials. The series was later suspended. Perhaps 'a day' in the courts provided too little material!

thought the American system a better model (reference was regularly made to the exploits of Perry Mason), or even assumed that it has already been adopted.

Nonetheless, we should not exaggerate the point about the disappointed expectations of public users of courts. From a comparative perspective, many aspects of social life also move more slowly in Italy than in some other societies. Relationships often depend on family or family-like group allegiances. People are slow to leave home; they like to live near where they grew up and to keep very close contact with their families. Ties are slow to build and difficult to end. For the groups which occupy key roles in social, economic and political life, co-option of others is the norm, seniority is of considerable importance, and merit is gained to a large extent by *waiting* ones turn. In many matters which involve government or public agencies, queuing is inevitable and there is an overriding need, especially in some parts of the country, to follow the case file through all its stages, and to be ready to intervene, personally or preferably through an important intermediary, to secure a successful outcome.

It is likely that many members of the Italian public see the time taken by the courts as more or less comparable to that taken by public bureaucracies in general. There is much in common between the inefficient justice system and the cumbersome and deliberately unresponsive bureaucratic machine which takes refuge in legal formalities and is uninterested in outcomes. Many of the delays attributed to inefficient courts – so-called '*malgiustizia*' – in fact represent efforts by the courts to deal with cases of poor administration – or '*maladministrazione*'. The two sorts of inefficiency overlap and interrelate in various ways. When one looks at the data, few of the long, drawn-out civil cases have to do with disputes between businessmen. Especially, but not only in the South of the country the courts are engulfed with cases regarding employment and pension rights, to some extent a legacy of political promises which are not calibrated to resources. So there is a good dose of 'fatalism' in the public continuing to turn to institutions which are slow to produce results.

What is 'too slow' from one point of view can be 'too fast' from another. To understand court times it is essential to investigate differences in the 'rhythms' of time of the organizations, professionals, court personnel and those of the parties themselves. What one side sees as delay others may see as necessary time for preparation for trial – or simply as one of the procedural possibilities that any system of trial offers. If courts, like other bureaucratic institutions in Italy, are allowed to take their time in dealing with case files, this may be described as 'default time' available to ordinary citizens. Where there are influential individuals or authorities involved, they are normally able to accelerate or (as often) deliberately delay things. But the same can even apply to less powerful individuals. Because everyday social and economic life is so little governed by legal norms that purport to be in play, social actors are able to use the law as a reserve weapon whose effect is often precisely to block or at least delay decisions which would otherwise take place according to the ruling bureaucratic or relevant patron–client logics.

More generally, drawing on the sociology of time as developed by George Gurvitch,[67] it is easy to show that there is nothing constant about the relationship between law and time. He describes, for example, what he calls 'effervescent time', which may be seen in the way time seemed to be 'speeded up' during the Tangentopoli anti-corruption investigations which drove all the established parties from power in the early 1990s.[68] In that period, 'media time', where yesterday's news is already forgotten, was made to coincide, amazingly, with the usually much more drawn out legal time. By contrast, we could note the importance of what Gurvitch called 'reverse time' as in the way prescriptions, amnesties and so on succeed, in different ways, in re-writing the past. The problem of 'overlapping time', and its consequences, can be seen, as already noted, in the operation of the 1995 civil justice and similar reforms. The increased speed required of new cases led to less attention and time being given to the backlog of cases accumulated up until the date of the reform, which were therefore dealt with more slowly than before.

Why is such a situation of enormous trial delay allowed to persist despite the shame of the condemnations from Strasbourg? This question is easier to ask than to answer. A variety of factors are cited as explanations for the rise in delay: the shortage of judges in relation to the rise in litigation, the explosion in the number of lawyers, the way lawyers are paid for each piece of trial-related work they do, and so on. Some, but by no means all of these cannot be easily remedied. Although, inevitably, some in Italy do claim that this situation is in the interests of the powerful, it is highly unlikely that anyone planned the current levels of legal delay. It is plausible to say that politicians may fear that a more efficient and speedy criminal justice system could be turned against them with even more success than during the Tangentopoli anti-corruption investigations. And they may be unwilling or unable to restructure trial times in the civil justice system without this leading to an improved criminal system. In addition, as we have already shown, 'the problem' is not the same problem for all, or a problem for everyone. Those working within, or alongside (as alternatives to) the current inefficient system, do find many ways to benefit from it[69] although this does not account for why others let them get away with it.

On the civil side the largest businesses can and do have recourse to arbitration, using judges and/or distinguished jurists, as a way of resolving their disputes. But this is a costly solution as a percentage of the value of the case has to be paid in return for quick justice. The large majority of Italy's economy, however, relies on small business, which would surely benefit from a more expeditious and

67 Gurvitch, G. (1964), *The Spectrum of Social Time* (La multiplicité des temps sociaux) (Dordrecht: Reidel).

68 Nelken, D. (1996), 'Judicial Politics and Corruption in Italy', in Nelken, D. and Levi, M. (eds), *The Corruption of Politics and the Politics of Corruption*, special issue, *Journal of Law and Society* 23, 95–113.

69 Nelken, 'Using the Concept of Legal Culture.

responsive court system. Delay mainly helps those in the wrong who can postpone payment (or prison), especially, as has happened, when the interest on funds that can be obtained in the market place is higher than the legal interest which has to be paid when the case is eventually settled. Therefore there is no reason to assume that those who gain most in any given delay will always be the more powerful party. The widely read and authoritative financial daily, *il Sole 24 ore*, which is owned by the *Confindustri* employers association, certainly treats delay as a serious problem. The courts are described as yet another aspect of the poor infrastructure that they have to tolerate. It regularly denounces their inefficiency; indeed this newspaper is the main disseminator of information about court delay.

On the criminal side, there are certainly tragic stories of both powerful and ordinary innocent people suffering whilst waiting for their cases to be heard – what Feeley describes as 'the Process is the Punishment'.[70] But, in many of the cases involving Italians, because of the possibility of prescription if cases overrun their set time-limits, court delays are in some ways less of a problem here than on the civil side. In fact, those who can afford to do so (and who do not find themselves in prison in the meantime), employ defence lawyers who adopt as one of their main strategies the *deliberate delaying of matters* so as to benefit from the possibility of such overrun. Often, therefore, in Italy, 'the Process is the *Non*-Punishment'. It is for this reason that relatively few of the cases that take an unconscionable time on the criminal side actually end up before the Strasbourg court.[71]

## Conclusion

It remains to underline some of the ways our case study relates to our earlier overview of the theoretical issues involved in studying the integration of legal cultures. We can say immediately that traditional comparative law categories of 'families of law' are of little help to us here. The distinction between common and civil law countries in Europe does not correlate well with speed of trials. Amongst civil law countries Germany and the Netherlands, and even Portugal, have relatively short trial periods, Italy and Greece very slow ones.[72] More, as we have tried to show, can be expected from the concept of legal culture. But the concept has to be employed in ways that recognize its complexities and the current

70 Feeley, M. (1979), *The Process is the Punishment* (New York: Russell Sage).

71 In my analysis of a sample of 50 cases I found a proportion of 9:1 in favour of civil cases.

72 Much cited quantitative research has examined more than a hundred countries worldwide whose legal systems follow one or other of these two families of law. This shows that common law countries are much more geared to economic requirements than are civil law ones. See La Porta, R., Lopez-de-Silanes, F., Shleifer, A. and Vishny, R.W. (1997), 'Law and Finance', *Development discussion papers*, Harvard institute for international development, Issue 576.

fluidities of culture. When speaking of internal legal culture, for example, we have shown the need to understand the influence of the Strasbourg court as both internal and external to Italy's national legal culture. In terms of external legal culture we have noted the way public expectations of what should be normal trial times are affected by increasing awareness of how long trials actually take elsewhere, as well as by fictitious media representations of trials that finish within the time-bounds of a television programme. In general we have shown the need to relate changes in legal culture to larger processes of imposing and signalling conformity.

But to begin to fathom the persistence of trial delay in Italy we needed to make sense of the specificities of how internal and external legal cultures go together. We might suggest that those who are obliged to rely on legal remedies are forced to submit to the considerable time these take to bear fruit because they can in some senses be held 'to blame' for not being in sufficiently good standing in wider social hierarchies or groupings. If they were they would be able to use more privileged routes or alternatives to vindicate their claims. A frequent explanation for failure to get on in Italy (even though sometimes of course this is only an alibi) is the lack of the right supporters or '*appoggi*'. An important consequence (even if not necessarily a cause) of court delay is the way it reinforces such dependence on relevant groups and hierarchies, and underlines the importance of such allegiances as compared to the individualistic assertion of rights. For clientelistic ways of organizing power relations and rewarding loyalty law represents more of a threat than a promise. More effective court dispute-mechanisms might replace or at least attenuate such bonds.

If this is all that is at stake in preserving Italy's diversity, it is difficult to find much to object to in the Strasbourg court's attempt to normalize Italian trial delays. Not only is it offering remedies to the individual applicants whose rights to trial in a reasonable period have been infringed. Given the Italian state's failure to improve its record (and in some cases even to pay the imposed damages), it is also insisting on the need for more structural changes. The aim is to make Italian society one where legal remedies will have more everyday purchase. But there may also be a price to be paid if these aims were to be realized. So things could be lost as well as gained. Strasbourg rightly does not accept the excuse regularly put forward by the Italian state that delays happen because the current trial times are all that the courts can manage with their current resources. The judges reply bluntly that it is the state's task to provide more resources. But it should be noted that, in the absence of any prison-building programme, if Strasbourg's strictures were taken to heart, and trials were speeded up, this would quickly increase prison numbers and probably lead to riots. And building more prisons to increase capacity (as the Netherlands did when reacting in its own way to the discovery of not having a 'normal' level of prison population), would hardly be an unmixed blessing.

Moreover, on the criminal side, the wider issue raised by court delays has to do with what 'due process', or what the Italians call *garanzie*, actually requires. How many stages of appeal should there be? How much need is there for separate scrutiny at each stage by different judges, and how appropriate is it to restrict all such decisions to legally trained people? Why is it not enough to trust to the systems' own internal legal definition of when cases that overrun fall into prescription?

The exceptional court delays of the Italian legal system also reflect the high level of independence from political control enjoyed by its judges and prosecutors. Courts in this type of polity (and the legal culture which goes with it) can, in exceptional circumstances, take action against the most powerful in the land, as seen in the corruption investigations of the 1990s. Admittedly, this level of activism cannot be sustained on an everyday basis without upsetting those social norms which are geared to the reproduction of social hierarchies. The Tangentopoli investigations themselves demonstrate both the exception and the rule as far as the place of legal delay within legal culture is concerned. In the special political circumstances of the early 1990s (in particular the changed geo-political situation after the collapse of the Iron curtain), ruling politicians lost legitimacy as soon as the newspapers released the information that they had been sent 'advice' that legal proceedings were being taken against them for corruption. But most of these cases then took a large number of years actually to run their course, and virtually no one went to jail. Once the Tangentopoli cycle of corruption scandals had run its course, politicians on Berlusconi's side (and not only) found that there was much to gain from exploiting and increasing the possibilities of postponing cases where their legitimacy and interests are at stake; at the same time, however, they often loudly accused the judges of being the direct cause of such disgraceful delays.

It is controversial how far the specificities of internal Italian legal culture in these respects could serve as a model for other societies. Certainly, the anti-corruption investigations excited admiration in many countries with criminal justice systems that are more efficient – provided they are not trying to deal with leading politicians. When teaching on judicial training courses in Rome, the judge whose thankless task it is to defend the Italian state at Strasbourg always emphasizes what he sees as the relative lack of procedural protections for the accused in countries like Sweden or England and Wales. Speed is not everything.[73] We should not forget, on the other hand, that trials can also be over *too* soon. Even in Italy, the trials of immigrants caught in the act (*in flagrante*) are dealt with speedily, with no chance of appeal.[74] It is worth asking why the

73 Efficiency in penal systems can sometimes be counter-productive. Recently, for example, Rod Morgan, Head of the Youth Justice Board in England and Wales (and, before that, an academic criminologist) resigned from his post because the English government's stress on dealing with caseloads more expeditiously had led to a 26 per cent rise in youth custody, in contradiction to its general commitment to reduce the number of young people sent to prison. This problem, at least, is unlikely to arise in Italy.

74 Cottino, A (1998), 'The Big Thieves Hang the Little Thieves: Equality before the Criminal Law in an Unequal Society', in Ruggiero, V., South, N. and Taylor, R. (eds),

Strasbourg court gives so little attention to this as a breach of human rights, as compared to over-lengthy trials. On the civil side some countries, like England and Wales, have much higher costs for using the courts than in Italy. Again, even if this serves as a deterrent to going to court it is not qualified as a breach of rights.

In a broader perspective it may be that slowness is given more value in Italy than in many other societies. For example, at a conference in Padua on the topic of legal delay in which I participated it was suggested that delayed trials give victims time to get over their upset so as not to be so emotional. This may seem less strange a suggestion if we see criminal justice, as one leading Italian theorist does, as primarily a means to restrain vendetta in the interest of the offender.[75] But this is certainly a very different perspective from the current trend to make the victim and her feelings play a more central role in the trial. At its most positive, Italy has also been called the spiritual home of the slowness movement – the call to all of us to slow down so as to get more out of life.[76] Perhaps slow food and fast trials are incompatible?

Nonetheless, the fact that Italy is so far from complying with Article 6 of the convention should not be seen as representing 'resistance' to the principle at stake. The Italian government and Italian citizens in general are very much in favour of the human rights being defended by the Strasbourg court (including Article 6) especially if they are the ones who lose out through delay. As one small illustration of public discourse on the question, President Ciampi, on leaving office in 2005, said that he considered his greatest disappointment to have been unable to bring about a reduction in trial times (and this despite being titular president also of the judges self-governing council). But the behaviour of those involved – the politicians, lawyers, judges and the parties involved – by failing to introduce measures which make it possible to reach such standards, or by their everyday trampling on them, certainly does send mixed signals.

This conflict between word and deed is far from unknown in governance regimes based on the imposing and signalling of conformity, especially where regulation by means of soft law is involved.[77] But this case study of the normalization of

*The New European Criminology: Crime and Social Order in Europe* (London: Routledge), 136.

75 Ferrajoli, L. (1989), *Diritto e Ragione* (Rome: Laterza) and Nelken, D. (1993), 'Le giustificazioni della pena ed i diritti dell'imputato', in Gianformaggio, L. (ed.), *Le Ragioni del Garantismo* (Turin: Giappicheli), 275–307.

76 Honorè, C. (2004), *In Praise of Slow: How a Worldwide Movement is Challenging the Cult of Speed* (Toronto: Vintage Canada).

77 See Whitehead, 'What's Your Sign?', on how the regulators of the Basle agreement on minimal bank deposits accepted the fact that for long periods, during its economic difficulties, Japan was knowingly not complying with the agreement but only pretending to be complying.

standards has not concerned the use by regulators of 'soft law'. We are dealing with a court which relies on individual complainants to come forward to claim redress. As we have seen, there seems to be much less room for negotiation and constructive hypocrisy about such standards when normalization is pursued by a court as part of the project of protecting human rights. Here there are no half measures. The court has defined the Italian state as a persistent offender, placing it under surveillance and threatening to exclude it from the Council of Europe. The only other signatory treated in this way is Turkey, for its refusal to collaborate over Cyprus and for its continuing maltreatment of the Kurds. Justice delayed is very often justice denied. But it is at least questionable whether excessive court delay represents the same gravity of breach of human rights as torture and is sufficient to justify excluding Italy from the Council of Europe. The problem of course is the apparent persistence in defying the Committee of Ministers. But as we have suggested, seeing this as 'defiance' may be to ignore a variety of factors which help explain, even if not necessarily justify, the distinctiveness of legal times in Italy.

# Chapter 19
# Henrik Zahle (1943–2006)

Ditlev Tamm

Henrik Zahle was born in November 1943. He died in July 2006. His father was an art historian and director of the Danish Museum of Art and Design. His mother was also an art historian and, in an advanced age, still active as a writer within her field. His paternal grandfather was by education a lawyer and a well-known prime minister,[1] and the family also includes a well-known founder of a private educational institution (Nathalie Zahl (1827–1913), founder of N. Zahles Skole) as well as a diplomat, a barrister of the Supreme Court, a headmaster, and other pillars of society. The name Zahle is no burden, even though it can be said to impose a slight sense of duty on one who is able to fulfil it. And Henrik Zahle was. If he were to choose a family-related career, he had several options: art, politics, education or law, and in a way, Henrik Zahle united all of them in his professional life, ultimately choosing law. A serious choice, as always, when Henrik Zahle made a decision.

Henrik Zahle received his law degree from the University of Copenhagen, Faculty of Law, in 1968, and immediately thereafter, he worked as a trainee lawyer in a law firm of Supreme Court barristers. But the university seemed more appealing to him than a profession as a lawyer, and in 1969 he joined the University of Copenhagen in order to write a thesis on one of the fundamental issues of law, the production of legal evidence. The subject is 'quite hardcore' with ample opportunities to demonstrate analytical skills, but it is at the same time a legal hornet's nest where, at that time, notably a number of Swedish lawyers had developed theories they were not ready to give up without any further ado, just because a new post-graduate researcher entered the stage.

To the description of Henrik Zahle should be added that, throughout his life, he remained a socialist: 'Marxism became, to us who joined it, a particular sort of culture that separated us from many others, who did not chose as we did', he critically wrote as late as in 2005. During those years, barriers were created among colleagues.that took time to tear down again. As a young legal candidate he participated in the reunions of the socialist lawyers, and he was an early member of the radical left wing party Venstresocialisterne.[2] Until the end of his life he remained faithful to basic socialist ideals – ideals he had not seen realized in any socialist state, but which concerned a fundamental view upon the relations between people, where the consideration for the weak in society was crucial. But

1 Carl Th. Zahle, Prime Minister 1909–10 and 1913–20.

2 Founded in 1967.

to a person with the integrity of Zahle, it was at the same time crucial that his political engagement and his work as a scientist were kept strictly apart.

Likewise, it is important for the understanding of Henrik Zahle's person to mention the disputes of ideological and sometimes more personal nature amongst lawyers during these years – disputes that turned the Faculty of Law at The University of Copenhagen into an extremely unpleasant and uninspiring working environment, at the time when Henrik Zahle and the author of these lines were striving to become legal scholars. Practically everyone who lived through it suffered from it. Some broke down, others left the faculty, and others actually lived through it and thus – some more than others – were inflicted damaging mental scars. Those of us who were more or less able to adjust to the conditions and made an effort to maintain a mental isolation, succeeded probably better than the rest. To Zahle, things were apparently more complicated. He was by conviction 'red', but was not able to identify himself fully with an environment that in many ways was more open and progressive than the freezing climate within the part of the faculty, to which those of us who in the eyes of others were 'black', belonged. By referring to 'red' and 'black', I employ terms used by Henrik Zahle – terms the implications of which I cannot fully accept. For in reality, the 'blacks' were not particularly black, nor did they form a united front. They were rather a number of individuals who neither expressed any sort of mutual solidarity, nor felt a natural, reciprocal sympathy towards one another. They were a group of persons who rarely spoke an appreciative word about anyone, and who in reality only could be considered as forming a unity to the extent that they were opposed to the 'reds', defining themselves with terms such as 'critical', inspired by 'Marxism' or 'materialist philosophy', but who, according to Zahle's critical description, at the same time were organized thus: 'The professors of the red faculty did not in any way – neither in words nor in action – encourage scientific work ...'

Therefore, Henrik Zahle did not really belong to any of the factions. He was not the only one, but it was probably more difficult for him than for others to act as if it did not affect him. Zahle has to me always represented the incarnation of a university professor; he was wise, thoughtful, learned and possessed just the degree of detachment from the world that, united with the necessary intelligence, makes a university career an obvious choice. From the time when I was still pursuing my studies, I can recall him as one of the older students – one of those whose future opportunities as a lawyer were a common subject of discussion amongst other students – and later as a colleague at the Faculty of Law during many years. As far as Zahle was concerned, he left and re-entered the faculty's teaching staff, but in my opinion, he was predisposed to be appointed to a professorship of law – a professorship he, as we know, finally received. But it was actually only when I got the opportunity to read his last essay, published after his death, that I realized that things had not been so easy for Henrik, who may not have been critical enough after all – or rather, sufficiently critical to be critical towards both factions

– to be able to fit in anywhere.[3] As already noted, Henrik was probably not the only one to occupy such a position, but it was a sign of his upright behaviour that he did not simply accept the conditions and adjust to them, but that he tried to change things. For attempting this, one does not always receive appreciation. It was not the last time Zahle had to realize that the choices he had made forced him to reconsider them during the course of time. The old cliché about life that is lived forwards, but understood backwards, became, in Henrik's case, a reality. In the brilliant essay to which I have just referred, he writes about his early years at the university, his professional and human disappointments, as well as how he experienced the creation of factions within the faculty which followed the events of 1968.

His thesis on legal evidence, published in 1976,[4] did not claim the success it was anticipated receiving. On the contrary, it was strongly criticized and did not clear the path for providing him a professorship of law. After a short period working as an assistant judge in Roskilde, Henrik Zahle returned to the university as an assistant professor teaching legal procedure. Then in 1979 he was assigned a temporary professorship of public law, and in 1983 he was appointed professor of constitutional law, a position that, I believe one can state without hesitation, he fulfilled completely.

Confiscation of mopeds and judgements by default – that is, judgements in law-suits where the defendant does not show up in court – were two subjects about which Zahle wrote an article and a book.[5] It came as a surprise that such subjects of somewhat minor importance were of interest to him, and I have only realized recently that they were part of a larger project that dealt with issues concerning the underprivileged in society. Both these works were based on his experiences as a trainee lawyer and later as an assistant judge, and they show that even though Henrik Zahle shared the view of those who realized that Marxism as such did not have anything to offer the practice of the law, it was possible to find neglected issues – issues that were part of a plan, aimed at making lawyers aware of the effects of the law on others than on people who were well-off.

But it was his book in three volumes on Danish constitutional law, published in the 1990s, that was to become his most comprehensive book and probably also his main work.[6] Constitutional law deals with the Danish constitution and the highest state institutions, as well as human rights and civic rights. Zahle's book follows a long tradition of textbooks on constitutional law by famous predecessors such as Poul Andersen and Alf Ross. His book is not easy to read, and the language is not as simple as that of Ross's book – the one he and I were exposed to during our

---

3 Zahle, H. (2007), '1968 og derefter. Et tilbageblik med spejl', in Zahle, H. (2007), *At forske ret. Essays om juridisk forskningspraksis* (Copenhagen: Gyldendal).

4 Zahle, H. (1976), *Om det juridiske bevis* (Copenhagen: Juristforbundet).

5 Zahle, H. (1983), *Udeblivelsesdomme* (Copenhagen: Jurist- og Økonomiforbundet).

6 Zahle, H. (2001–2004), *Dansk forfatningsret Vols 1–3* (Copenhagen: Christian Ejlers Forlag).

studies. The book is argumentative and open in dealing with the numerous issues concerning constitutional law in a way that clearly distinguishes it from former books on the subject, and it is at the same time clearly influenced by Zahle's thoroughness. It is not an easy task to write a new book on Danish constitutional law after his. Everything is already there, so to speak. It could have been briefer, maybe better adapted to educational needs, but all aspects are covered. While one can agree or disagree with the conclusions, anyone who has read Zahle's description of constitutional law knows what it is.

To me, it seems clear that Henrik always dealt with large and important issues. Within procedural law, he examined the role of evidence; within constitutional law, of course, the constitution. When he dealt with philosophy of law, it had to be nothing less than Justice itself or the question of the *sources of law*. Stressing the role of the lawyer as that of making legal decisions, he simultaneously aimed high in his own works and attacked even the most difficult questions of legal matters. Maybe that was in reality a dilemma as well.

But before looking closer at that aspect of his life, there is one episode that cannot be overlooked in a description such as this. In 1999 Henrik Zahle applied for a position as judge at the Danish Supreme Court and was appointed the same year. He was – which was understandable – tired of the university and wanted new challenges where he felt he could contribute more profoundly. To be appointed judge in the highest court of the country is normally considered the final occupation before retirement for a lawyer. Henrik Zahle was probably not the first person to doubt whether this was the right way to end his career, but he was the first person to take the consequences and return to his former employment. He was not happy working at the Supreme Court and did not like the working conditions. As he said himself, he lacked openness towards other opinions, and he was scandalized by the amount of work that was given to younger judges, while older judges presumably had ample time to deal with things that were not directly related to their work in the Court. I suppose he felt that the work of the court to some extent was led by other things than the care for justice which he had expected to find. This led, in 2002, after a few years, to his decision to leave the court and accept a proposal to return to the university and to the professorship of legal theory he had shifted to in 1996. His return to the university where he was again to be in charge of the overall subject of law, dealing with the fundamental questions about what justice is, caused great satisfaction at the faculty.

Legal theory had been a preoccupation of Zahle's from his early years. In his case – as in the case of others – it began with a criticism, already during the 1970s, of the dominating legal philosophy of law of Alf Ross. Some of Zahle's later important contributions to legal theory considered the legal sources and the so-called pluralism of law. In 1986, he introduced the term 'legal polycentricity',[7] an important criticism of the idea of the unity of the legal sources and the triangular

7 Petersen, H. and Zahle, H. (eds) (1995), *Legal Polycentricity: Consequences of Pluralism in Law* (London: Dartmouth/Ashgate).

structure of law, as well as a demonstration of the fact that several conceptions of legal sources can exist side by side. The inspiration came to him from the theory of legal evidence and from his reluctance to accept that legal method and estimation of legal evidence could be formalized. Things were more complicated than that, he thought. And he was right.

Henrik Zahle's works within legal theory appear to someone who in many ways holds and held different views, such as myself, as very personal contributions, in a positive sense of the word. His years at the Supreme Court sharpened his attention to the situation of the legal practitioner, and the title of his book in legal theory therefore became 'Legal Philosophy in Practice'.[8]

The word Justice had since Ross's days appeared to be an empty term amongst Danish lawyers, but now it once again entered the language of lawyers. As a professor of legal theory, he did not create a complete theoretical framework, but especially described the relations between the practice of law and theoretical law. A paragraph of a short essay in one of his last books is entitled 'Oprør eller tilpasning' ('Rebellion or Assimilation').[9] The paragraph describes the dilemma of the practitioner: is the aim 'that things go exactly as I wish', and must I, if things do not 'avoid the dilemma by leaving the institution'? I suspect that this book is a key to understanding Henrik as a person – especially the phrase: 'Boredom can thus be the mental state where one is open to new influences and one is receptive. But it is necessary that one listens and feels – has one's eyes open.' Henrik Zahle did all this, but he also expected that people listened to him.

Henrik Zahle did not belong to those people who make things too easy for themselves or for others. He made no intellectual short-cuts, no flourish remarks and no simplistic statements. Instead he was constantly developing his own thinking, and his work and importance are not summed up by only referring to his legal engagement, even though it is impressive, being centred around legal evidence, constitution and Justice. Henrik was a highly cultivated person who maybe also personally fought with the dilemma that he was aware of the fact that not everyone was as privileged due to his or her background as he was, or for that matter as brilliant or knowing as himself. In high-school Henrik Zahle studied Latin and Greek language and literature, which were at the time obvious components of an ideal in education that embraced the classic humanistic heritage. He was in all respects the opposite of the lawyer Tangle in Dickens's novel *Bleak House* that he mentions in the book 'Care for Justice'[10], and of whom it is said, that he knew the case, *Jarndyce v. Jarndyce*, the main motive of the book, thoroughly: 'He is famous for it – supposed never to have read anything else since he left school.'

Today, this is considered somewhat old-fashioned as it is only obtained by extensive reading and a joy of general culture.

8 Zahle, H. (2005), *Praktisk retsfiloso* (Copenhagen: Christian Ejlers).

9 Zahle, H. (2003), *Omsorg for retfærdighed – essays om retlig praksis* (Copenhagen: Gyldendal).

10 Zahle, *Praktisk retsfiloso* .

One could agree or disagree with Henrik's opinions. His awareness of dilemmas and his great respect for others perhaps had the effect that he preferred to avoid confrontations. However, he spoke his mind – luckily – and one never doubted his seriousness or that he knew what he was talking about. Henrik Zahle's person was a combination of general education, a certain detachment from the foolishness of life, the joy of working and, from time to time, maybe even a self-effacing sense of responsibility due to which his work became highly esteemed in Denmark as well as amongst foreign colleagues. He who in his youth had felt highly out of place in a divided faculty became himself, by the end of his career, one of its unifying figures.

It was a privilege to work within a field close to his and to meet him in scientific contexts. It is a bitter condition of life when people pass away in the midst of their work. Henrik's scientific work was from his early years driven by a clear involvement that is probably best characterized by his own term, 'care' – meaning both care towards the weak in society and care towards the way we attend to the duty each one of us has received in life. Henrik Zahle did not only perform a task that had been given to him. He defined it himself, and completed it in a deeply personal way that distinguishes most of what he has written from others' writings on law. Henrik Zahle embraced originality and general education in a way that made him unique. He achieved many things and could have achieved even more, but what he did ensures him a place in the memory of colleagues and students as well as in the memory of a scholarly branch that does not necessarily attract personalities such as his – and that is not always being fair to them.

He, on the other hand, was steadfast till the end. In the spring of 2006, an incurable pancreas cancer was finally diagnosed. After that, it was only a question of months, and he spent the time collecting earlier works and adding new articles, so that the book they were to be part of[11] could be published after his death. In this book is an essay called 'Lacking Appreciation: The Academic's Struggle for Recognition'. Within the universities, he writes, exists 'a fertile soil for not appreciating others' and a neglect of 'the negative effect this has on people's self esteem and respect for others'. If Zahle during his younger years had experienced these feelings, he would today at least be pleased with finally receiving the general acclaim offered to him from so many.

11 Zahle, H. (2006), *At forske ret. Essays om juridisk forskningspraksis* (Copenhagen: Gyldendal).

# Index

For Product Safety Concerns and Information please contact our EU
representative GPSR@taylorandfrancis.com
Taylor & Francis Verlag GmbH, Kaufingerstraße 24, 80331 München, Germany

www.ingramcontent.com/pod-product-compliance
Ingram Content Group UK Ltd.
Pitfield, Milton Keynes, MK11 3LW, UK
UKHW020021200926
475702UK00014B/1992

* 9 7 8 1 1 3 8 2 5 4 1 7 6 *